THE CONSTRUCTION OF GUILT IN CHINA

Drawing on insights from the author's own empirical data obtained from systematic observation of the daily routines within Chinese criminal justice institutions, this ground-breaking book examines the functional deficiency of the criminal justice system in preventing innocent individuals from being wrongly accused and convicted. Set within a broad socio-legal context, it outlines the strategic interrelationships between key legal actors, the deep-seated legal culture embedded in practice, the deficiency of integrity of the system and the structural injustices that follow. The author traces criminal case files in the criminal process – how they are constructed, scrutinised and used to dispose of cases and convict defendants in lieu of witnesses' oral testimony. This book illustrates that the Chinese criminal justice system as a state apparatus of social control has been framed through performance indicators, bureaucratic management and the central value of collectivism in such a way as to maintain the stability of the authoritarian power.

The Construction of Guilt in China will appeal to academics, researchers, policy advisers and practitioners working in the areas of criminal law, comparative criminal justice, criminology and Chinese studies.

Volume 17 in the series Studies in International and Comparative Criminal Law

Studies in International and Comparative Criminal Law

General Editor: Michael Bohlander

Criminal law had long been regarded as the preserve of national legal systems, and comparative research in criminal law for a long time had something of an academic ivory tower quality. However, in the past 15 years it has been transformed into an increasingly, and moreover practically, relevant subject of study for international and comparative lawyers. This can be attributed to numerous factors, such as the establishment of ad hoc international criminal tribunals and the International Criminal Court, as well as to developments within the EU, the UN and other international organisations. There is a myriad of initiatives related to tackling terrorism, money laundering, organised crime, people trafficking and the drugs trade, and the international 'war' on terror. Criminal law is being used to address global or regional problems, often across the borders of fundamentally different legal systems, only one of which is the traditional divide between common and civil law approaches. It is therefore no longer solely a matter for domestic lawyers. The need exists for a global approach which encompasses comparative and international law.

Responding to this development, this new series will include books on a wide range of topics, including studies of international law, EU law, the work of specific international tribunals and comparative studies of national systems of criminal law. Given that the different systems to a large extent operate based on the idiosyncrasies of the peoples and states that have created them, the series will also welcome pertinent historical, criminological and socio-legal research into these issues.

Recent titles in this series:

Genocide and Crimes against Humanity: Misconceptions and Confusion in French Law and Practice
Caroline Fournet

The Emergence of EU Criminal Law: Cyber Crime and the Regulation of the Information Society
Sarah Summers, Christian Schwarzenegger, Gian Ege and Finlay Young

Transitional Justice and the Prosecution of Political Leaders in the Arab Region: A Comparative Study of Egypt, Libya, Tunisia and Yemen
Noha Aboueldahab

Caribbean Anti-Trafficking Law and Practice:
Jason Haynes

The Construction of Guilt in China: An Empirical Account of Routine Chinese Injustice
Yu Mou

The Construction of Guilt in China

An Empirical Account of Routine Chinese Injustice

Yu Mou

•HART•

OXFORD • LONDON • NEW YORK • NEW DELHI • SYDNEY

HART PUBLISHING

Bloomsbury Publishing Plc

Kemp House, Chawley Park, Cumnor Hill, Oxford, OX2 9PH, UK

1385 Broadway, New York, NY 10018, USA

HART PUBLISHING, the Hart/Stag logo, BLOOMSBURY and the Diana logo are trademarks of Bloomsbury Publishing Plc

First published in Great Britain 2020

A catalogue record for this book is available from the British Library.

Library of Congress Cataloging-in-Publication data

Names: Mou, Yu (Law teacher), author.

Title: The construction of guilt in China : an empirical account of routine Chinese injustice / Yu Mou.

Description: Oxford ; New York : Hart, 2020. | Series: Studies in international and comparative criminal law ; vol 17 | Based on author's thesis (doctoral - University of Warwick, 2015) issued under title: Written evidence and the absence of witnesses : the inevitability of conviction in Chinese criminal justice. | Includes bibliographical references and index.

Identifiers: LCCN 2019051002 (print) | LCCN 2019051003 (ebook) | ISBN 9781509913022 (hardcover) | ISBN 9781509913039 (Epub)

Subjects: LCSH: Criminal procedure—China. | Judicial error—China. | Evidence, Criminal—China. | Fair trial—China.

Classification: LCC KNQ4610 .M68 2020 (print) | LCC KNQ4610 (ebook) | DDC 345.51/05—dc23

LC record available at https://lccn.loc.gov/2019051002

LC ebook record available at https://lccn.loc.gov/2019051003

ISBN: HB: 978-1-50991-302-2
ePDF: 978-1-50991-304-6
ePub: 978-1-50991-303-9

Typeset by Compuscript Ltd, Shannon

ACKNOWLEDGEMENTS

At one point, I thought that I would never finish writing this book. Luckily, this premonition did not materialise, thanks to all the encouragement that I have received from the remarkable people who kept me going.

My special thanks go to Professor Jackie Hodgson, an excellent scholar and an encouraging mentor. Words fail to convey my gratitude for the special role she has played in my academic life. I must express my deep gratitude to Professor Mike McConville. His guidance to prompt me to think critically, his insightful comments on the entirety of my PhD thesis have been an important part of this book. Heartfelt thanks also go to Professor Fu Hualing, one of the finest scholars that I have met, who persistently gave me helpful advice on how to improve this research, as well as providing insightful comments on my book. I would like further to thank Professor Sun Changyong. Without his encouragement, this project could never have been able to start. At the University of Warwick, where this book began, Professor Alan Norrie, Professor Roger Leng and Dr Bill O'Brian gave me helpful academic advice and taught me practical skills that have benefited me tremendously. At SOAS, Professor Carol Tan has regularly motivated me to finish this overdue work. I also would like to thank Michel Massih QC for his great support.

I owe a lot of thanks to those people who kindly offered me enthusiasm in the field site. My guarantees of anonymity prevent me from identifying those to whom I am deeply grateful. Given the challenging research environment in China, their openness and helpful assistance made this research less difficult than it would otherwise have been, and was quite often undertaken in a joyful mood. I would also like to express my sincere thanks to my good friends and best neighbours Nigel and Barbara Double. Their 'prodding' and affectionate support have helped me in crossing the finishing line.

Finally, this book is dedicated to my husband John, who has been a brilliant reservoir of inspiration. His unfailing assistance with proofreading and unreserved enthusiasm made this book possible. His affection and humour have been the motivation for me to move forward and to better myself.

CONTENTS

1

Introduction

In a compact courtroom, a prosecutor arduously reads out loud a witness statement against the defendant standing in the dock. The defendant, who is charged with selling drugs, denies the charged facts. After hearing the accounts against him, he looks bewildered; yet he appears to have reconciled himself with what has been reported. Three witnesses have given evidence against him, but they are nowhere to be seen in the court – all the prosecution evidence, including the witness statements and interrogation records, has been typed up and neatly bound, forming a criminal investigative dossier (*zhencha juanzong*). The case dossier, now in the hands of the prosecutor, will be passed on to the judge to be studied more closely later on. Based on what he reads, the guilt or innocence of the defendant shall be determined.

This is one of the most common scenes in Chinese basic courts, where tens of thousands of people are adjudicated in a similar fashion. It is the norm that witnesses do not testify in contested criminal trials. Criminal cases are routinely disposed of and resolved on the basis of case dossiers. A sense of unfairness may be quickly detected from such procedural arrangements – it seems to be fundamentally wrong that defendants are given no chance to confront people who provide accounts incriminating them in situations where the alleged facts are disputed. More intriguingly, if the evidence in the form of written transcripts at trial is determinative, what is the point of having a public trial? The credibility of case dossiers is also a subject of concern. Is the evidence gathered in the course of the investigation truly reliable? Are judgments that rely on the written evidence safe? Are there any effective safeguards in place to prevent wrongful convictions of potentially innocent people? These questions are important, because, as Ronald Dworkin notes, 'people have a profound right not to be convicted of crimes of which they are innocent'.[1] Amongst the damage that can be enumerated, the moral harm caused by the conviction of an innocent person to society is the most far-reaching and hard to repair.[2]

[1] R Dworkin, *A Matter of Principle* (Oxford University Press, 1986) 72.

[2] ibid 83. ALT Choo, *Hearsay and Confrontation in Criminal Trials* (Oxford University Press, 1996) 12.

My enquiries into these questions carry me through three key stages of the criminal justice process, beginning with the police investigation, on through the review of the prosecution, and ending with the trial and resolution of cases. In this book, as the main title alludes, I will be investigating the way in which criminality is constructed and presented in the form of the case dossier, and the implications this has for a better understanding of justice and injustice in China's authoritarian regime. The centrality of case dossiers (*juanzong*) to investigations and trials is an established ideology that envisages writing as a means to ensure accountability across time, space and bureaucratic hierarchies.[3] As a pivotal technology for bureaucratic activities,[4] the case dossier is not merely a passive instrument of agents of legal institutions, but is active in the creation and maintenance of those agents.[5] In this context, criminal justice is understood as a process and a system. As a process, the movement of the case dossier between different phases constitutes and marks a chain of events which develop linearly to reach an outcome of the case. As a system, the case dossier is a golden thread around which legal actors, their activities and interactions are woven and their relationships intertwined. The case dossier is a chronicle of its own making, bearing signs of its own development as well as the people referred to within it.[6] It precipitates the formation of operations of the criminal justice institutions, which are tightly coupled and linked to the social control goals.[7]

Chinese criminal justice can, therefore, be observed through the lens of the case dossier: its mobility, from one stage to another, between different offices and different hands, documents the inner workings of the system and the history of the case as it progresses. The case dossier, in turn, functions as the official channel to convey information in multistage hierarchical proceedings. The system is embedded in the sociopolitical culture, and criminal justice in China should be understood against the backdrop of pertinent themes and a framework of ideology that shape the structure of law and law in action. Such knowledge is a prerequisite to grasping the richness and complexity of the system as a whole. Therefore, the remainder of this introductory chapter outlines criminal justice and injustice in China, the ideology of truth and the idiosyncrasies of the criminal justice institutions, all of which are essential to the analysis of this book.

[3] MS Hull, 'The File: Agency, Authority, and Autography in an Islamabad Bureaucracy' (2003) 23 *Law and Communication* 287; M Suresh, 'The "Paper Case": Evidence and Narrative of a Terrorism Trial in Delhi' (2019) 53 *Law and Society Review* 173.

[4] M Weber, *Economy and Society: An Outline of Interpretive Sociology*, vol 1 (University of California Press, 1978); J Goody, *Logic of Writing and the Organisation of Society* (Cambridge University Press, 1986).

[5] B Latour, *The Making of Law: An Ethnography of the Conseil D'Etat* (Polity, 2010); Hull (n 3) 290.

[6] Hull (n 3) 296.

[7] J Hagan, 'Why Is There So Little Criminal Justice Theory? Neglected Macro and Micro-level Links between Organisation and Power' in ER Maguire and DE Duffee (eds), *Criminal Justice Theory*, 2nd end (Routledge, 2015) 57; S Biddulph et al, 'Criminal Justice Reform in the Xi Jinping Era' (2017) 2 *China Law and Society Review* 63.

I. Criminal Injustice in China

Miscarriages of justice are nothing new to China. Chinese legal history is fraught with wrongful convictions (*cuo'an*, or *yuan jia cuo an*), many of which are widely known.[8] However, the sheer scale of wrongful convictions that have been revealed and quashed in the last two decades still comes as a surprise to many, which is not only unprecedented in Chinese history, but ranks high worldwide. Over 180 cases in which innocent people were falsely convicted of serious crimes have been reported by the media in recent years.[9] A high proportion of these were death penalty cases.[10] According to the Supreme People's Court, 94 convictions of serious crimes (involving 46 cases) were quashed between 2013 and February 2019.[11] While these figures demonstrate laudable courage of the courts to correct fundamental wrongs of its own making, they send a strong signal that the system is deeply flawed. Worryingly, a good number of these wrongful convictions came to light due to coincidences, that is, the supposedly deceased murder victim transpired to be alive, or the real perpetrator was apprehended and confessed to the misjudged crime.[12] No effective mechanism is in place to systematically and

[8] Yan Xinpei, 'Lishishang yuanjia cuoan shi zenyang liangcheng de (How Did the Miscarriages of Justice Come into Being in Chinese Legal History?)' (2014) 6 *The Legendary Life of Procuratorates* 10–11; Wu Haihang, 'Zhongguo gudai ruhe fangzhi yuanjia cuoan de fasheng (How Did Ancient China Prevent Miscarriages of Justice)' (2016) 7 *The People's Forum* 136; Wang Yishan, 'Zhongguo gudai yuanyu fangfan zhidu de fali fenxi (Legal Analysis of the Prevention of Miscarriages of Justice)' (2018) Master's dissertation, Zhejiang Financial University.

[9] However, there are no official statistics about how many wrongful convictions have occurred in recent decades. By 15 April 2019, 185 quashed wrongful convictions had been compiled by Henan Weizhe Law Firm, which is available on their website. See China Wrongful Conviction Network, www.zgyjca.com/lm.asp?id=3&page=1 (accessed 15 April 2019).

[10] There were 122 miscarriages of justice involving the death penalty between 1983 and 2012. See M Xiong and M Miao, 'Miscarriages of Justice in Chinese Capital Cases' (2018) 41 *Hastings International and Comparative Law Review* 273, 338.

[11] Pengpai, 'The Supreme People's Court: 46 Cases of Major Wrongful Convictions were Corrected since 2013', *Pengpai News* (27 February 2019) www.sohu.com/a/297965505_260616 (accessed 15 April 2019).

[12] For example, in Liu Bin and Duan Yanli's study of 40 sample cases of wrongful convictions, 10% (4 cases) qualified as wrongful convictions because the allegedly deceased victims were found out to be alive and 62.5% of the cases (25 cases) were identified as wrongful convictions based on the real perpetrator confessing the crime wrongfully attributed to another person. The rest of the cases were acquitted based on the defendant's appeals. Liu Bin and Duan Yanli, 'Xingshi zaisheng chengxu cuoan jiuzuo gongneng zhi chongsu: yi shenpan jieduan cuoan he jiuzheng wei shijiao (Reshaping the Correcting Function of Wrongful Convictions in Criminal Justice: Based on the Perspective of Identifying and Correcting Wrongful Convictions)' (2014) 6 *China Criminal Law Magazine* 91. Similarly, in Li Yonghang's study of 34 wrongful conviction cases, 21 out of 34 were initiated by the real perpetrator's confession and 3 cases were corrected by 'victims back from the death', with the remaining cases reopened by the convicted's perseverance in appealing. Li Yonghang, 'Xingshi cuoan jiuzhengnan wenti yanjiu: jiyu 34 qi xingshi cuoan jiuzheng lichen de sikao (Research on the Difficulty in Correcting Wrongful Convictions: Based on 34 Corrected Miscarriages of Justice)' (2015) 30 *Journal of Shanghai University of Political Science and Law* 19. It should be noted that confessions alone should not be readily accepted as exculpatory evidence to disprove the guilt of the convicted person. According to Gudjonsson's research, even 'special knowledge' cannot be guaranteed to validate the truthfulness of the confession because the relevant information can be gleaned from the media, or through informal

rigorously review cases that are potentially wrongly decided.[13] These cases are uncovered partly because of their newsworthiness and sensationalism.[14] Cases in which the judgments were based on precarious information (such as relying on unreliable evidence), but are devoid of serendipitous circumstances, are not deemed serious enough or the media has no interest in reporting them, are less likely to be reopened and quashed. It may well be that the wrongful convictions that have been revealed are the tip of the iceberg – more injustice is yet to be seen, but most may never come to light.

A society's understanding of justice and injustice is grounded on 'a complex mixture of sentiment, belief and reason that is in turn conditioned by ethical principles and moral values embedded in custom and culture'.[15] In the Chinese tradition, justice (*yi*) is a morally and politically charged expression that judges the value system of the ruling class and the way in which the governed individuals are treated.[16] Injustice (*buyi*, *bugong*, *yuan* and *qu*), in this discourse, questions the moral supremacy and legitimacy of the ruler. The term is also used to condemn the creation of miscarriages of justice in a different sense.[17] In this cultural and political context, the concept of a miscarriage of justice implies public denunciation of the degraded morals and professional ethics of those responsible for running the legal system who fail to fulfil their duties.[18]

Although miscarriage of justice, as a concept, is not unfamiliar to most people in China, the way the notion is understood and used is somewhat different from its Western counterpart.[19] Miscarriages of justice within the Chinese context refer exclusively to wrongful convictions, that is, a factually innocent individual

interactions with the police. There are a host of reasons why innocent people sometimes voluntarily confess, such as interrogative suggestibility, the vulnerability of the suspect, the suspect's false belief or other motivations (such as protecting the real perpetrator or gaining 'fame') pursued by the suspect. See GH Gudjonsson, *The Psychology of Interrogations and Confessions: A Handbook* (Wiley, 1992). See also RA Nash and KA Wade, 'Innocent but Proven Guilty: Eliciting Internalised False Confessions Using Doctored Video Evidence' (2009) 23 *Applied Cognitive Psychology* 624.

[13] The recovery of wrongful convictions in China relies on the retrial procedure (*zaishen chengxu*). However, this procedure is deeply flawed and fails to address the issue effectively. See Liu Bin and Duan Yanli (ibid). Since 2012, expectations have been raised in various official announcements, demanding criminal justice institutions to tackle this problem. In particular, an overly optimistic target of 'zero error' was set to eradicate false convictions. However, like a lot of vices built up over time, it is hard to correct all the wrongs by simply resorting to the top-down resolution.

[14] Notably, many victims of these miscarriages of justice are eligible for the death penalty.

[15] J Rosenzweig, 'State, Society and the Justice Debate in Contemporary China' in F Sapio et al (eds), *Justice: The China Experience* (Cambridge University Press, 2017) 28.

[16] According to Delia Lin, the two levels of justice do not affect each other automatically: D Lin, 'High Justice versus Low Justice: The Legacy of Confucian and Legalist Notion of Justice' in Sapio et al (n 15) 67–69.

[17] ibid.

[18] Despite the dissonance between the two levels of justice, justice today is clearly a mixture of moral and legal concept. This can be drawn from the context of the dual emphasis on rule of law and rule by morality in recent years. Lin (n 16) 88–89.

[19] Cui Min and Wang Lelong, 'Xingshi cuoan gainian de shencengci fenxi (Deep Analysis of the Concept of Cuo'an)' (2009) 1 *Rule of Law Research* 10, 14.

is convicted of a crime that she has never committed in the first place.[20] This narrow approach to miscarriages of justice is in contrast to the prevailing perception in Western jurisdictions, where due process principles are placed at the core.[21] For example, Gudjonsson summarises four situations in which justice has miscarried:[22] (i) the defendant may be factually guilty, but is deprived of a fair trial; (ii) a defendant who was marginally involved in a case is disproportionately convicted of a more serious crime; (iii) the person is convicted of an offence that she has never committed; and (iv) the *actus reus* of the alleged crime for which the defendant was convicted has not been established properly.[23] Likewise, Belloni and Hodgson suggest that the concept of miscarriage of justice ought to be linked to the condemnation of convictions produced by malpractice that undermines the 'rationale of the criminal process'.[24] To be blunt, what would constitute a miscarriage of justice in this perspective does not correlate with conviction of the factually innocent or the acquittal of the factually guilty.[25]

These two understandings of miscarriage of justice diverge in the way the courts and the other criminal justice institutions respond to cases that may constitute miscarriages of justice. Take as an example the Criminal Case Review Commission (CCRC) and the Court of Appeal, which are the statutory bodies dealing with alleged miscarriages of justice in England, Wales and Northern Ireland.[26] As part

[20] Na Jiang, *Wrongful Convictions in China* (Springer, 2016) 16; Dong Bangjun and Qiu Jiaji, 'Xingshi cuoan yufang yu jiucuo jizhi yanjiu: jiyu Zhejiang zhangshi shuzhi qiangjianan de qishi (The Mechanism of Prevention and Identification of Miscarriage of Justice: An Inspiration of Uncle–Nephew Zhang Case in Zhejiang)' (2013) 5 *Journal of Shandong Police College* 11. Cui Min and Wang Lelong (ibid).

[21] R Nobles and D Schiff, *Understanding Miscarriages of Justice: Law, the Media and the Inevitability of a Crisis* (Oxford University Press, 2012) 14. See also S Seppanen, 'Rawls Rejected, Ignored and Radicalised: Debating Procedural Justice in China' in Sapio et al (n 15) 92–100.

[22] For example, the American case *Blair v Armontrout* 916 F2d 1310 (1990) is a typical example of the first category. In that case, the deceased black defendant Walter Blair was convicted by an all-white jury in Missouri of murdering a white female victim. *Bolender v Singletary* 898 F Supp 876 (1995) is an example of the second category. Bernard Bolender was involved in a drug deal, but was convicted of murdering four men during the drug transaction. Post-conviction evidence suggests that Bolender was innocent. In the case *In re Troy Farris* clemency petition (1999), the murder for which Troy Farris was convicted could in fact never have been committed. There are a significant number of wrongful convictions that belong to the third category. This includes high-profile cases such as Stefan Kiszko, the Birmingham Six, the Maguire Seven and the Cardiff Three in the UK. For more details of these cases, see Ronald Huff and Martin Killias, *Wrongful Conviction: International Perspectives on Miscarriages of Justice* (Temple University Press, 2008) ch 6. An example of the fourth type would be that the deceased committed suicide but a person is mistakenly convicted as the murderer of the deceased.

[23] Gudjonsson (n 12) 206.

[24] F Belloni and J Hodgson, *Criminal Injustice: An Evaluation of the Criminal Justice Process in Britain* (Macmillan Press, 1999) 2.

[25] M Naughton, 'The Criminal Cases Review Commission: Innocence versus Safety and the Integrity of the Criminal Justice System' (2012) 58 *Criminal Law Quarterly* 207, 213.

[26] CCRC is the statutory body responsible for investigating alleged miscarriages of justice in England, Wales and Northern Ireland. It was established by s 8 of the Criminal Appeal Act of 1995 and came into effect on 31 March 1997. The Court of Appeal decides whether or not a conviction can be quashed. See the Criminal Appeal Act 1995.

of a system characterised as one which emphasises due process safeguards, the test that is applied by the two institutions in deciding whether an alleged conviction is allowed to be challenged is that the conviction is legally unsafe.[27] This may not be 'the solution to the wrongful conviction of the factually innocent that it was widely thought to be'.[28] However, it is a demanding test for the system that does help the factually innocent in overturning their convictions. This test is adopted to uphold the integrity of procedural justice.[29] This means that even if a conviction is factually reliable, it may still be quashed if the Court of Appeal finds that the criminal process fails to conform to the rule of law principle.[30]

The approach to a miscarriage of justice in China could not be more different. Rehearing a convicted criminal case is extremely difficult. Despite the fact that the law allows a case to be retried on grounds of malpractice of the state officials or procedural irregularities,[31] the parameters under which the courts may consider reopening a convicted case are extraordinarily narrow. Under many circumstances, rehearing a convicted case seems to be limited to the situation where fresh evidence has emerged to prove that the convict was factually innocent.[32] When miscarriages of justice are understood in such a narrow scope, the emphasis is placed on the end result or substantive justice. Procedural values, such as fairness or integrity of the process, are pertinent only to the extent that they contribute to the pursuit of the 'correct outcome'.[33] Procedural justice must be balanced if it contradicts the ultimate purpose of finding factual truth. Failures of the system are often treated as technical errors in certain parts of the process.[34] Minimising wrongful convictions in this sense entails piecemeal tinkering of law and practices,[35] rather than a holistic evaluation of the system in its entirety or critical reflections of the principles and legal culture that underpin the operation. Compared with the due

[27] See CCRC, 'Applicant Guidance: Questions and Answers', https://s3-eu-west-2.amazonaws.com/ccrc-prod-storage-1jdn5d1f6iq1l/uploads/2018/12/QandA-reset-final.pdf (accessed 27 June 2019).

[28] Naughton (n 25) 210.

[29] ibid 241.

[30] *R v Mullen* [1999] 2 Cr App Rep 143. It should be noted that there is criticism against the Court of Appeal in using the criminal control principle to interpret the test. See K Malleson, 'Appeals against Conviction and the Principle of Finality' (1994) 21 *Journal of Law & Society* 151.

[31] Criminal Procedure Law 2018 (CPL 2018), Arts 252–55.

[32] Hu Yangyi, 'Xingshi cuoan jiuji jizhi yanjiu: Zhongguo ban wuguzhe jihua tanwei (The Mechanism of Redressing Miscarriages of Justice in China: Exploring the Chinese Version of Innocent Project)' (2016) 24 *Journal of Chengdu University of Technology* 28.

[33] Seppanen (n 21) 95.

[34] See, eg Li Xia, 'Yuanjia cuoan de chengyin fenxi ji fangfan: Chongti tupeiwu an (The Analysis and Prevention of the Causes of Miscarriages of Justice)' (2014) 10 *Journal of Hubei Police College* 25.

[35] A good example of this includes statements on preventing and correcting wrongful convictions that have been issued by the Chinese central legal institutions. See Central Politics and Law Commission, *Guidance on the Effective Prevention of Miscarriages of Justice* (August 2013); Supreme People's Court, *On the Establishment of a Sound Working Mechanism to Prevent Miscarriages of Justice in Criminal Opinions* (2013).

process approach, the prevention of miscarriages of justice in China is guided by factual truth.[36] Yet what constitutes factual truth in specific cases has never been clarified. This makes it hard to implement in criminal justice practices.[37]

This sense of injustice corresponds with the domination of outcome-oriented perception and prevailing demands for substantive justice under the authoritarian regime of China. Johnson has noted that legitimacy in authoritarian regimes is outcome-based, and is drawn on substantive instead of procedural justice.[38] So long as justice meets the substantive interests of the majority population in authoritarian states, its legitimacy and the support and voluntary cooperation of the citizens are sustained, despite deficiencies in procedural justice.[39] Thus, in China, what counts as fairness among the majority population is heavily informed by the sense of substantive justice. It does not necessarily correlate with the notion that it is based on a shared commitment to the procedural principle that people should be perceived as free, equal and self-respecting human beings in exercising their rights.[40] The achievement of correct outcomes is treated as the primary aim of criminal procedure. Although academic debate on substantive and procedural justice has brought a wider awareness of the value of due process,[41] it has had a limited impact on criminal justice practices. Procedural justice is instrumental in terms of identifying who is guilty and should be punished. This is well illustrated in most of the miscarriages of justice that have been reported in recent decades. Among the most prominent wrongful convictions are those of *She Xianglin*,[42] *Teng Xingshan*,[43]

[36] Just as with any other criminal justice policy, factual truth is always regarded as the basis (*yi shishi wei jichu*) of preventing miscarriages of justice. See Supreme People's Court (ibid).

[37] The ideology of factual truth will be discussed later in this chapter.

[38] EA Johnson, 'Criminal Justice, Coercion and Consent in "Totalitarian Society": The Case of National Socialist Germany' (2011) 51 *British Journal of Criminology* 599.

[39] S Karstedt, 'Trusting Authorities: Legitimacy, Trust and Collaboration in Non-democratic Regimes' in J Tankebe and A Liebling (eds), *Legitimacy and Criminal Justice: An International Exploration* (Oxford University Press, 2013) 135.

[40] J Rawls, *A Theory of Justice* (Harvard University Press, 2009) 348.

[41] See Ji Weidong, 'Chengxu bijiaolun (Comparative Proceduralism)' (1993) 1 *Comparative Law* 1; Ji Weidong, *Falv chengxu de yiyi: dui zhongguo faxhi jianshe de lingyizhong sikao (The Meaning of Legal Procedure: Alternative Thoughts on Chinese Legal Construction)* (China Legal Publication, 2004).

[42] The *She Xianglin* case is one of the most notorious miscarriages of justice in China. She Xianglin was sentenced to death with a two-year reprieve (later commuted to life imprisonment) after having been convicted of the murder of his wife Zhang Zaiyu in 1994. His wife was believed to have been killed and thrown into a river nearby. However, 10 years later, in 2005, Zhang Zaiyu was found to still be alive and had returned to her village. Subsequently, She Xianglin was released, following the discovery that the confession had been made under torture. For more case details, see Yang Zhengwan, *Sixing anjian de chengxu xianzhi (Procedural Constraints on Capital Punishment)* (China People's Public Security University Press, 2008) 157–59.

[43] Teng Xingshan was convicted and executed in 1989, on the evidence of confessions, of murdering and mutilating a victim, Shi Xiaorong. Similar to the *She Xianglin* case, the innocence of Teng Xingshan came to light when Shi Xiaorong was found alive four years later, after Teng's execution. For a full case description, see Na Jiang (n 20) 44–46.

Zhao Zuohai[44] and *Uncle and Nephew Zhang*.[45] The revelation of these cases evoked long-lasting repercussions in society and unleashed widespread condemnation of brutality and incompetence among state officials, all of which undermine the legitimacy of the criminal justice system. In order to examine how the flawed facts came into being, I will look at some of the most highly visible cases in greater detail.

Of all the miscarriage of justice cases, instances in which the innocence of the convicted is revealed by the reappearance of the 'murdered victim' gain the most notoriety. The cases of *Teng Xinshan*, *She Xianglin* and *Zhao Zuohai* are in this category. Teng Xinshan was executed on 28 January 1989, a victim of China's severe and swift justice – the 'Strike Hard anti-crime campaigns' (*Yanda*) in which the evidential standard for conviction was substantially relaxed.[46] He was exonerated 18 years later, when the alleged murder victim returned to her home village. Similarly convicted of murder, She Xianglin and Zhao Zuohai escaped capital punishment due to the lack of sufficient evidence – the main inculpatory evidence of their cases was their confessions. She Xianglin was sentenced to a 15-year term of imprisonment after having been convicted of the murder of his wife, Zhang Zaiyu, in 1994. The sentence decision was an application of the implicit criminal law policy 'extenuation for reasonable doubt' (*zui yi cong qin*), indicating that the evidence in the case was inadequate to convict the defendant in the first place.[47] Rather than acquitting She Xianglin following the doubt of his guilt, the court had decided to compromise on his sentence and commute it to a jail term.[48] The same approach was applied to *Zhao Zuohai*. The lack of inculpatory evidence qualified

[44] This case bears some similarities with *She Xianglin* and *Teng Xingshan*. Zhao Zuohai was convicted in 2002 of murdering a fellow villager, with whom he had previously fought. The evidence consisted of an incorrect identification of the dead body and of coerce-compliant confessions. However, having been in prison for eight years, in 2010, the Henan High People's Court quashed the conviction of Zhao Zuohai when the alleged 'victim' returned alive. ibid 46–48.

[45] Zhang Gaoping and Zhang Hui, uncle and nephew lorry drivers, were convicted in 2004 for raping and murdering a girl from their home village, to whom they gave a lift en route to Shanghai. By the tremendous efforts of a prosecutor stationed in the prison where Zhang Gaoping and Zhang Hui were imprisoned, who was sympathetic to the two men, a leave to appeal was accepted. Their case was reopened, and subsequently quashed in 2011, following the discovery that there were a number of procedural improprieties. These included the use of an informant (a cell inmate) to coerce the uncle and nephew to make false confessions and police-directed brutality in the detention centre. There was also critical DNA evidence suggesting that the real perpetrator could be someone else, but this had deliberately been ignored by the investigators. The real perpetrator, Gou Haifeng, who was executed in 2005 for separate offences, was discovered by matching DNA traces found under the victim's fingernail. ibid 49–51.

[46] For more discussion of the Strike Hard campaign, see S Trevaskes, 'Severe and Swift Justice in China' (2007) 47 *British Journal of Criminology* 23.

[47] For more discussion, see Duan Hongyan, 'Dui woguo sixing anjian zhengmin biaozhun de fansi (Rethink about the Standard of Proof of the Death Penalty Cases)' (2007) 2 *Journal of LvLiang Education Institute* 24; Niao Zhaowei, 'Woguo sixing anjian zhengmin biaozhun de chongxin xuanze (Re-think about the Standard of Proof in Capital Cases)' (2008) 8 *Rule of Law Research* 28.

[48] See Congressional-Executive Commission on China 'Hubei Man Convicted of Wife's Murder Ten Years Ago Exonerated' (8 April 2005) www.cecc.gov/publications/commission-analysis/hubei-man-convicted-of-wifes-murder-ten-years-ago-exonerated (accessed 28 September 2017).

him to a reprieve from immediate execution, and he was subsequently sentenced to a 29-year prison term.[49]

In all three examples, the conviction was almost entirely pivoted on confessions.[50] The probative value of confessions is highly rated for the obvious reason that no one would confess unless she were guilty. The strong belief that confessions amount to factual guilt led to the convictions, albeit intrinsically unreliable ones. A judge of appeal in Hubei High Court recalled that the evidence in *She Xianglin* was inadequate to form a coherent explanation: She Xianglin confessed to four or five different ways of murdering his wife, all of which were self-contradictory and were duly recanted by the defendant at trial. Nevertheless, these inconsistencies were disregarded and one of the confession accounts was selected to incriminate him.[51] Likewise, the main inculpatory evidence in *Zhao Zuohai* was his guilty plea. Other evidence in the case (such as the identification of the body of the deceased, which later turned out to be erroneous) could not provide any link between the accused and the alleged murder. From 1999 to 2001, Zhao Zuohai pleaded guilty to murder on nine occasions, all of which resulted from oppressive questioning tactics. Zhao Zuohai recalled that the police taught him how to plead guilty: 'they told me to repeat what they said, and I had to, or I would be beaten up. They wrote down what I repeated and said it was my confession.'[52] In both *Zhao Zuohai* and *She Xianglin*, torture was employed to extract confessions. She Xianglin suffered from broken fingers and other bodily injuries after the brutal treatment of the Jinshan police.[53] Zhao Zuohai was violently beaten with sticks, forced to drink chilli water and had firecrackers set off over his head. During the police interrogation, they were deprived of meals and sleep.[54]

A common issue that surfaced in these instances is the underinvestment of scientific investigative skills in Chinese criminal justice. In all three cases, errors could have been easily avoided had a DNA analysis been conducted at an early investigative stage.[55] The mortuary identifications of the decomposed and dismembered bodies in *She Xianglin* and *Zhao Zuohai* were based on unconfident identifications of the presumed victim's families, rather than a more reliable DNA comparison. In *She Xianglin*, when facing uncertainty from the family of the alleged victim Zhang Zaiyu, the police made it clear that they could not afford

[49] Kong Pu, 'Zhao Zuohai bei xingxunbigong 33 tian, jingcha 24 xiaoshi shenxun na qiang za tou (Zhao Zuohai Was Tortured for 33 Days, Police Conducted 24-Hour Interrogations and Used Guns to Beat His Head)', *New Beijing Post* (25 August 2012) http://news.china.com/domestic/945/20120825/17393711_1.html (accessed 13 August 2017).

[50] Na Jiang (n 20) 44.

[51] 'Hubei Shexiang Murder Case: How did Wrongful Convictions Come into Being?', *Xinhua Net* (7 April 2005) http://news.sohu.com/20050407/n225078501.shtml (accessed 9 September 2007).

[52] See C Coonan, 'Zhao Zuohai: Beaten, Framed and Jailed for a Murder that Never Happened', *The Independent* (13 May 2010) www.independent.co.uk/news/world/asia/zhao-zuohai-beaten-framed-and-jailed-for-a-murder-that-never-happened-1973042.html (accessed 30 September 2017).

[53] Na Jiang (n 20) 44.

[54] Kong Pu (n 49).

[55] ibid.

the expense of a DNA test. As a result, no such test was carried out until the error came to light.[56] In *Zhao Zuohai*, the police did commission a forensic department to conduct DNA matches of the headless corpse found in the well. However, due to the limitations of the technical equipment, the forensic department was unable to confirm the result.[57] Problematically, in *Teng Xinshan*, the police used the highly inclusive blood type test to identify the perpetrator. Since Teng Xinshan's blood type happened to be the same as that of the perpetrator found at the crime scene, his blood type match was used as inculpatory evidence.

Similar issues are reflected to various extents in other wrongfully convicted cases in China. In the *Uncle and Nephew Zhang* case, torture was not directly conducted by the police, but by their agent – the 'cell boss (*laotou*)' in the detention centre. In 2004, the truck driver Zhang Gaoping and his nephew Zhang Hui were arrested on the suspicion of rape and murder of a village girl, whom they gave a free ride to when transporting freight to Shanghai. When they were detained, torture was carried out by their cellmates, as instructed by and on behalf of the police. The cell boss, Yuan Lianfang, who controlled the inmates in Zhang Hui's cell, was responsible for securing his confessions throughout his time at the detention centre.[58] Physical violence was carried out in combination with continuous sleep deprivation, deprivation of food and drink, threats and intimidation, all of which were synchronised with intensive police interrogations. Eventually, the uncle and nephew gave in and signed confession statements prepared by Yuan Lianfang. In this case, the suspect confessed to throwing the body of the victim into a place where he could hear the flow of water. To corroborate this piece of information, the chief investigating officer gathered local hydrological records, which proved that there was heavy rain around the time of the offence and the ditch was indeed flooded. The account provided by Yuan Lianfang, detailing Zhang Hui's cell confession, was also accepted as a witness statement to corroborate its veracity. A piece of DNA evidence found under the deceased victim's fingernails, which did not match that of either of the suspects, suggested that the real perpetrator might be someone else. However, this piece of evidence was suppressed, as the police were certain that both suspects were guilty and the case was strong and flawless. Despite these efforts of the police, the case eventually took a turn and the uncle and nephew were exonerated 9 years later.[59]

[56] see Na Jiang (n 20) 66–67.

[57] Na Jiang (n 20) 47.

[58] A similar strategy has been used elsewhere in China. It is recalled that in the case of Li Qiaoming, the accused, arrested for unlawful lumbering, was violently beaten to death by his cellmates in Yunnan Yuxi Detention Centre. The police authority published the cause of his death as '"playing hide and seek" with other inmates in the cell when accidentally knocked his head on the wall'. See Dai Yan, '"Hide and Seek" Case is Tried Today, Two Prison Jailors Were on the Trial', *China Court* (2009) http://old.chinacourt.org/public/detail.php?id=368374 (accessed 5 October 2017).

[59] The details of this case can be found in Na Jiang (n 20) 49–51. Bao Zhiheng, 'From the Beginning to the End: the Report of Zhang Hui and Zhang Gaoping Case (Zhang Hui Zhang Gaoping yuanan baodao shimo)', *NFmedia* (8 July 2016) www.nfmedia.com/cmzj/cmyj/cxb/201305/t20130524_360364.htm

It is true that every wrongful conviction deserves a detailed analysis of how it came about, and the few cases of miscarriage of justice presented here are far from enough to represent all the cases of false conviction that have occurred in the last few decades. However, the cases here are illustrative of common features of the tragedies and types of malpractice associated with wrongful convictions: the fabrication of evidence, especially confession evidence; police brutality and torture;[60] the limited and problematic use of scientific evidence; and the lack of a fair trial. Interestingly, the defence lawyer's role was entirely absent in all the reports of these cases, although some of them played a robust part in the subsequent reopening and quashing of the convictions.[61] Apparently, in making these wrongful convictions, these flawed prosecution cases were not vigorously challenged initially for unknown reasons,[62] nor were the defence views adopted by the court in determining the ultimate issue of guilt or innocence in these capital cases.

While detailed research on these high-profile miscarriages of justice is certainly needed, another source of injustice, which is experienced by people implicated in the criminal justice system on a daily basis in China, has received scant attention. This type of injustice may not involve sensational crimes, major offences that carry heavy penalties (including death penalties) or crimes that have a big impact on society. These cases are not interesting enough to attract the public attention, and therefore may never be reported by the media. They are sometimes considered less important because the suspect is not of significant social standing, or the offence does not carry a long-term imprisonment.[63] However, the accused people in these cases have experienced a kind of injustice that has been so deeply engrained and integrated into the system that it, to a certain extent, defines the idiosyncrasy of Chinese criminal justice. Here I am referring to the malpractices that any suspect may have routinely undergone in the criminal process. This includes invisible injustice, demonstrated in the way in which a suspect is treated by the police; how the police build a case against her; her experience with the prosecutor; the way in which the prosecution case is prepared and a decision to prosecute is made; her experience at trial. The routine injustice may be concerned with seemingly 'minor' matters, such as the suspect being given no time to read the transcript of her confession statement before she is asked to sign; the prosecutor's disinterest

(accessed 5 October 2017); 'Uncle and Nephew Zhang's Ten Year False Imprisonment: 7 Opportunities Missed to Correct the Wrong (Zhang shi shuzhi shinian yuanyu beihou: Cengyou 7 ci jiuzheng jihui)', *East Morning Post* (27 March 2013).

[60] For more discussion on torture and miscarriages of justice in China, see E Nesossi, 'The Politics of Torture and Miscarriages of Justice in Contemporary China' (2016) 11 *Journal of Comparative Law* 166.

[61] For example, the defence lawyer, Zhu Mingyong, played a significant role in reopening and quashing the *Zhang Gaoping and Zhang Hui* case. Zhao Jiayue, 'The Defence Lawyer Zhu Mingyong for the Uncle–Nephew Zhang Case: Criminal Defence is Like Playing Cube Games', *News.ifeng* (8 June 2013) http://news.ifeng.com/shendu/nfrwzk/detail_2013_06/08/26225795_0.shtml (accessed 18 April 2019).

[62] The case dossiers of these wrongful convictions are not open to the public. The details of these cases are primarily based on news reports.

[63] It is worth noting that in China, offences that carry penalties of imprisonment for less than three years are often regarded as 'minor'. This is very different from many Western countries.

in hearing the suspect's story other than confirming her guilty pleas; or the close relationship between judges and prosecutors; or the fact that a standard ordinary trial in a basic court lasts less than 20 minutes.

This level of injustice is related to the aforementioned miscarriages of justice in China. The failings identified in wrongful convictions are part and parcel of the criminal justice system's routine processing of suspects and defendants towards conviction. Conversely, the routine injustice experienced by the accused is a normalised miscarriage of justice. Despite the 'trivial' issues that it deals with, this source of injustice affects a vast number of people involved in the system on a daily basis. It fundamentally shapes their way, as citizens and subjects of law, of perceiving criminal justice from within, and of understanding how state power is exercised against them. In every sense, this level of injustice has a great impact on their life, determining how they are treated as suspects pending trial, whether their cases are appropriately handled, whether they are to bear the stigma of being a criminal for the rest of their life and the punishment that is going to be imposed on them. As the subtitle of this book suggests, this routine injustice, which happens to ordinary suspects at the most basic level, is the very focus of this study. Routine injustice occurs, amongst other reasons, because the state officials, who adhere to the crime control principle, believe that they pursue the factual truth of the cases. Seeking the factual truth is known as the primary aim of criminal procedure and the laws of evidence. However, truth – factual truth – may not be the objective concept that some hope it to be.

II. Truth as Objectivity, Constructions and Rhetoric

With regard to ascertaining the facts of a case, two divergent approaches provided by the inquisitorial and adversarial systems are notably influential: the account of the crime can be established either by (i) entrusting an impartial judicial officer with the power to collect relevant evidence to prove the facts or (ii) relying on opposing parties presenting competing versions, challenging each other's accuracy, thereby ultimately bringing about a picture of the truth.[64] Differing from both systems, Chinese criminal justice does not have a clear theory as to the truth-finding process. Nevertheless, the discovery of objective truth is regarded as the ultimate purpose[65] of the administration of criminal justice, guiding official practices.

The concept of objective truth and its pivotal status in Chinese criminal justice stemmed from Marxist–Leninist philosophical fundamentals. As a socialist

[64] See T Weigend, 'Is the Criminal Process about Truth? A German Perspective' (2003) 26 *Harvard Journal of Law & Public Policy*, 157, 158.

[65] A Shytov and P Duff, 'Truth and Procedural Fairness in Chinese Criminal Procedure Law' (2019) 23 *International Journal of Evidence and Proof* 299, 300.

country, key legal notions, such as truth and wrongful convictions, are heavily influenced by and attuned to Marxist materialist dialectics. According to the rationale of the Marxist materialist dialectics, the material world exists external to and independent of human consciousness, which, in turn, is capable of reflecting and engaging rationally with the material environment. Central to this philosophical system lies the proposition that the substance of thought is determined by its physical milieu. Therefore, a person's consciousness, ideas and knowledge are entirely acquired from her material surroundings and are wholly conditioned by her human and social being. Human beings, conversely, are able to comprehend and explore the material world, which is believed to be fully knowable. Even though there are things that are currently unknown, they will nevertheless be discovered and resolved with the efforts of practice, science and technology.[66] In this optimistic philosophy, truth is an intellectual reflection, which mirrors the external reality accurately and faithfully.[67] According to the Marxist frame of reference (which was later developed by Lenin), truth is

> the corollary of a special moment in the incessant process of interaction of being and thought, an attribute of various stages of brief equilibrium in the interplay between matter and consciousness in the course of the ascendant progression of history's dialectical chain.[68]

The connotation that objective truth is cognisable and human beings are capable of grasping material reality by their consciousness has been transposed into the laws of social life.[69] In criminal justice, this means that official activities must be 'loyal to the truth'.[70] State officials are expected to bring their knowledge to bear in reaching the unique factual truth of every case. This belief is unequivocally expounded in Chen Guanzhong et al's argument:

> If we admit the guidance of the dialectical materialism epistemology of our evidence system, we must acknowledge that a case fact, as an objective reality, is independent of police officers. Police officers can understand and ascertain case facts, but they cannot change it. The so-called finding the truth is a process in which investigators' subjective knowledge is dovetailed with the objective reality. Their understanding will be transformed from perceptual knowledge to rational insight. We should also mention that

[66] HT Wilson, *Marx's Critical Dialectical Procedure* (Routledge, 1991) 88–89.

[67] M Cornforth, *Dialectical Materialism: An Introduction* (Lawrence and Wishart, 1976) 11–12.

[68] G Ginsburgs, 'Objective Truth and the Judicial Process in Post-Stalinist Soviet Jurisprudence' (1961) 10 *American Journal of Comparative Law* 53, 55.

[69] Like other dialectic conceptions, the objective truth comprises 'opposite tendencies' at work and follows the laws of dialectical development, viz a 'struggle' from the two opposites that accomplishes the critical transformation through a gradual quantitative change. The two opposed forces are absolute truth and relative truth. Therefore, human beings are believed to be capable of reflecting reality by their consciousness, either at a particular historical stage or infinitely. Cornforth (n 67) 90; Chen Guangzhong, Chen Haiguang and Wei Xiaona 'Xingshi zhengju zhidu yu renshi lun – jianyu wuqulun, faliu zhenshilun, xiangdui zhenshilun shangque (Criminal Evidence and Epistemology: A Discussion with Confusion, Legal Realism and Truth Realism)' (2001) 1 *China Law Studies* 37. See also ibid 59.

[70] See Art 51 of Criminal Procedure Law 2012.

> practice is the test of truth. It not only forms the basis which should be relied upon in gathering evidence to ascertain case facts, but also the only criterion to check whether the facts are correct.[71]

This idea that the truth in any case can be 'ascertained by gathering and analysing evidence correctly' has been a prevailing legal tenet in China.[72] In criminal procedure law, this perception of truth is imported into the standard of proof, according to which the defendant should be convicted on the basis of 'objective truth'. Thus, pursuant to Article 162 of Criminal Procedure Law 1996 (CPL 1996), judges must be satisfied that there exists 'concrete and sufficient evidence (*zhengju queshi chongfen*)' in the prosecution case in order to convict the defendant. This concrete and sufficient evidence is categorically interpreted by judicial practices and academics as objective truth.[73] According to the mainstream scholars, the truth can be, and ought to be, employed as the yardstick to measure the adequacy of evidence and the guilt or innocence of the defendant due to its uniqueness and absoluteness.[74] From the standpoint of believers of objective truth, its uniqueness can be identified and reached even 'at the outset of the investigation'.[75]

In Western literature, this viewpoint of objective truth has been challenged by sociological theories about reality. Most predominantly, social constructivism argues that reality is socially constructed and knowledge is observer-relevant.[76] In this view, truth is not the end product of the criminal process, but rather a

[71] Chen Guangzhong et al (n 69).

[72] Pei Cangling, *Zhengju faxue xinlun (New Studies on Evidence)* (China Law Publishing, 1989) 183; Zhang Zipei, *Xingshi susongfa jiaocheng (Criminal Procedure Law Textbook)* (Masses Publishing, 1987) 192.

[73] However, judicial interpretations have not explicitly referred to 'sufficient and concrete evidence' as objective truth. For example, according to s 9, Art 104 of the Judicial Interpretation issued by the People's Supreme Court on 20 December 2012, concrete and sufficient evidence means 'the truthfulness of a piece of evidence shall be examined by taking into consideration the overall evidence of a case. The strength of a piece of evidence to prove a fact shall be examined and judged based on actual circumstances from the perspective of the degree of relevance between the evidence and the fact to be proved, and the linkage between different pieces of evidence. A piece of evidence shall be admitted as the basis for deciding a case only if: it is inherently related to other pieces of evidence; it and other pieces of evidence all point to the same fact to be proved; and there is neither any irremovable contradiction nor any inexplicable doubt.' It is worth noting that a number of academics do not agree that objective truth should be used as the standard of proof in convicting defendants; however, this does not deny the fact that there has been a consensus that the facts established by sufficient and concrete evidence are labelled as 'objective truth'. See Fan Chongyi, *Xingshi susong faxue yanjiu zongshu yu pingjia (Criminal Procedure Law Research Review and Comments)* (China Political Science and Law University Press, 1991) 222; Liu Shanchun et al, *Susong zhengju guize yanjiu (A Study on Evidence in Litigations)* (China Legal Press, 2000) 307. For more discussion, see Long Zongzhi, '"Queding weuyi" – woguo xingshi susong de zhenming biaozhun ("Absolute Certainty": The Standard of Proof in Chinese Criminal Justice)' (2001) 11 *Studies of Law* 29.

[74] Chen Guangzhong, 'Xingshi zhenju zhidu gaige ruogan lilun yu shijian wenti zhi tantao: yi liangyuan sanbu «liangge zhengju guiding» zhi gongbu wei shijiao' (On A Number of Theories and Practical Issues of Criminal Evidence Reform: From the Perspective of the publication of 'Two Regulations on Evidence') (2010) 6 *China Law Studies* 5.

[75] ibid.

[76] P Berger and T Luckmann, *The Social Construction of Reality: A Treatise* (Penguin, 1979).

properly structured inquiry.[77] Profound scepticism is hence cast against the very existence of objectivity of truth in criminal justice. The specific agglomerations of truth, as an institutional reality, pertain to specific legal agents and participants, whose perspectives, motivation and interpersonal relationships determine truth in the realist sense.[78] Criminal evidence, facts and cases are no longer seen as outer entities that are discovered by legal actors; instead, they are created by legal actors. Mike McConville et al observed that:

> It must be emphasized that at each point of the criminal justice process 'what happened' is the subject of interpretation, addition, subtraction, selection and reformulation. The process is a *continuous* process so that the meaning and status of 'a case' are to be understood in terms of the particular time and context in which it is viewed, meaning and status that it may not have possessed earlier or continue to possess thereafter. The construction of a case is not confined to one aspect of the process, such as the creation of an internal record or the compilation of evidence, but infuses every action and activity of official actors from the initial selection of the suspect to final case disposition.[79]

Rather than focusing on the ambiguous notion of objective truth in criminal cases, legal constructivists are concerned about the *process* of creating facts and justification. In criminal investigations, this means understanding that the police have, at a fundamental level, an autonomy to evaluate, select, edit and reject information in order to generate a version of the facts that fit that context.[80] In terms of adjudication, the construction of truth entails participation of the parties who tell their stories. Truth, in this sense, emerges from the structured discussion – 'the more you let them argue, freely ask questions and justify their positions, the more you can be confident in the accuracy of outcomes'.[81] The shift of emphasis, however, by no means suggests that constructions of the facts are entirely subjective or arbitrary. Legal constructions are embedded in specific social contexts that define the perspectives of legal actors.[82] The existing social context, such as occupational culture, established practice and institutional background, is unique and time-relevant. Only under particular social circumstances can the legal actors make a choice and decision in relation to the legal construction.

[77] Ibid; J Searle, *The Construction of Social Reality* (Penguin, 1995). M Damaška, 'Truth in Adjudication' (1998) *49 Hastings Law Journal* 289, 294; M McConville, Andrew Sanders and Roger Leng, *The Case for the Prosecution* (Routledge, 1991) 11–13.

[78] Kersten Reich, 'Constructivism: Diversity of Approaches and Connections with Pragmatism' in Larry A. Hickman et al (eds), *John Dewey between Pragmatism and Constructivism* (Fordham University Press, 2009) 41; McConville et al (ibid) 11–13. Richard Galvin, 'Rounding Up the Usual Suspects: Varieties of Kantian Constructivism in Ethics' (2011) 61 *The Philosophical Quarterly* 16, 17.

[79] McConville et al (ibid) 12. The italic is from the original text.

[80] ibid 56.

[81] Damaška (n 77) 294.

[82] K Reich, 'Constructivism: Diversity of Approaches and Connections with Pragmatism' in LA Hickman et al (eds), *John Dewey between Pragmatism and Constructivism* (Fordham University Press, 2009) 40–41.

Social constructivism has spread to China, where it is known as the 'legal truth (*falv zhenshi*)', and has gradually gained momentum in criminal justice.[83] However, objective truth remains the orthodox school, dominating the theories of criminal justice. The jurisprudence argument aside, objective truth has served as a form of rhetoric for the shortage of procedural accountability in the Chinese judicial system. In democratic countries, an important function of the criminal process is to provide a ritual of recognition and acknowledgement through which a citizen (the defendant) is called to answer to her fellow citizens. In order to hold the defendant to account, the criminal process itself must have legitimacy. This means that in order to call the accused to account, procedural accountability is required from the legal institutions to seek the condemnation of the alleged crime. The judiciary, in particular, is responsible for providing a forum for dialogues that justify the 'criminal' label of the accused. This procedural accountability entails different roles and divisions of power between the legal actors. Thus, adversarial systems can be interpreted as a model of power-sharing in which the prosecution and the defence both engage in fact-finding. The facts presented by the two parties before a neutral court in public constitute the source upon which the outcome of the case is based. At the other end of the spectrum, enquiries of the case facts are controlled by judicial officers in inquisitorial systems. The procedural accountability relies heavily on judicial reviews where the view of the defence is taken into account. When an inquisitorial system is practised in authoritarian China, the party-state has monopolised fact-finding through a series of bureaucratic procedures where effective checks and remedies are lacking. For example, there are numerous hidden procedures that constitute the internal judicial deliberation process in which issues of a case are discussed and resolved, requests are approved, paperwork is produced and executed, and decisions are made. In these internal procedures, independent inquiry of the case is reduced to an irrelevance. According to the official discourse, these are procedures to pursue objective truth.[84] Such a truth-finding process is certainly not underpinned by a mechanism that enables the judge(s) to be answerable to the defendant. Rather, these procedures are in place to assist the relevant judicial leaders and state officials to reach a consensus, thereby controlling the outcomes of criminal cases.

The lack of procedural accountability echoes the legitimacy framework in the form of the combination of 'low accountability' and 'high coercion' operated by non-democratic regimes. Karstedt observes that there is a deficiency in governing bodies to respond to the demands of the ruled in non-democratic states ('low accountability').[85] Meanwhile, authoritarian states also employ unfettered use of

[83] See, eg Fan Chongyi (n 73) 222; Liu Shanchun et al (n 73) 307. For more discussion, see Long Zongzhi (n 73) 29–33.

[84] Yang Jicheng and Yang Zonghui, 'Dui "falv zhenshi"zhenming biaozhun de zhiyi (Questioning the Standard of Proof Based on Legal Truth)' (2002) 4 *Legal Studies* 8.

[85] Karstedt (n 39) 135.

state power and oppression by the government and state institutions to maintain stability and achieve compliance and cooperation of its citizens. This 'high coercion' attribute is also prevalently manifested in China. Article 2 of the Criminal Law 1997 states that the tasks of the law are to use criminal punishments to fight against all criminal acts in order to defend the security of the state and the political power of the people's dictatorship. The people's dictatorship, according to socialist ideology, means that the Communist Party, representing the mass of the people, has no interests of itself other than the interests of the people.[86] This declared conflation of interests creates a carte blanche for the Party. Public power is exercised in the name of the people,[87] leaving little room for the discussion of accountability. Thus, when expressions of discontent and grievances occur, coercion is often imposed to silence debate on 'alternative visions of justice that could compete with the interests of the Party',[88] rather than branching out dialogic routes to redress the arbitrary exercise of power. While a high degree of coercion may temporarily subjugate victims of power abuse and suppress diverse values, the system's constant conflictions of the basic sense of fairness and justice of the public might eventually lead to a crisis of legitimacy for the political regime.[89]

In this political context, accountability mechanisms, albeit only to a limited extent, are still necessary to initiate effective rectification and to open up dialogues on human rights protection and fair procedures.[90] In the Supreme People's Court's (SPC) official notice on building a working mechanism to prevent miscarriages of justice, objective truth has taken on a salvage function to re-establish the legitimacy of criminal justice institutions and public support.[91] Here, factual truth is regarded as 'the principal requirement of activities of criminal proceedings (*xingshi susong huodong de jiben yaoqiu*)', and is construed as safeguarding the innocent from being wrongfully convicted.[92] Specifically, the prevention of miscarriages of justice is linked to five principles in relation to due process values: human rights protection; the independent exercise of judicial power; procedural justice; judicial transparency; and the evidential adjudication rule.[93] In the official discourse, although a dual (and paradoxical) approach of crime control and due process is adopted in implementing criminal procedure law, the due process principle had

[86] Wang Weiguang, 'Continuing with People's Dictatorship Is Not Short of Reasoning (Jianchi renmin minzhu zhuanzheng bingbu shuli)' (2014) 18 *Red Flag* 14.

[87] In China, the police, procuratorate and the court are all titled as of the people. The police are named the People's police, the procuratorate is named the People's procuratorate and the court is called the People's court.

[88] E Nesossi and S Trevaskes, *Procedural Justice and the Fair Trial in Contemporary Chinese Criminal Justice* (Brill, 2017) 7.

[89] ibid.

[90] R Mulgan, *Holding Power to Account: Accountability in Modern Democracies* (Palgrave, 2003) 9.

[91] See Supreme People's Court of China, 'Opinions on Establishing and Strengthening Working Mechanisms for Preventing Miscarriages of Justice in Criminal Cases' (31 July 2014) www.court.gov.cn/shenpan-xiangqing-6620.html (accessed 5 April 2019).

[92] ibid.

[93] ibid.

always been referred to as complementary to crime control.[94] Judicial authorities now appear to be willing to expand the ambit of due process within the criminal justice sphere at a rhetorical level. Hence, to redeem the trust of criminal justice institutions amidst the crisis of miscarriages of justice, objective truth – the concept that bears an ideological birthmark of Marxist dialectics – is malleable enough to encompass due process values in this day and age.

This due process rhetoric promoted by the SPC, however, does not adequately capture the true characteristics of the reality, or the rules, of the criminal justice system. Currently, there is a schism between the rhetoric of the system and the rules (which display mixed values of due process and crime control), and the reality (which is predominantly crime control). What counts as objective truth changes over time and is subject to the context and circumstances. This book will reveal that the theory of objective truth, as a dogmatised principle in criminal procedure, is profoundly problematic in directing criminal justice practices, especially evidence acquisition. Accepting the constructionist perspective, it tells the story that crimes, facts and evidence, as social constructs, are often fused with institutional interests, practices and values, and take on the image of authority and rationality through a discourse of objective officialdom. It can be constructed by the state as well as actors outside of the state. The so-called objective truth is often involved with legal actors engaging with and manipulating rules. As a key theme, the construction of cases runs through the main chapters of this book. Chapter three proffers a detailed empirical account of the way in which the official version of a case is constructed by the police in practice. Chapter four illustrates how the facts presented by the police are reviewed, moderated and approved by the prosecutor. Following that, chapter five explains the prosecutor's decision-making process based on the version of truth built by the police. Finally, chapter six turns to the marshalling arena between the prosecution and the defence where the judicial construction takes place. The case dossier constructed by the police (and sometimes the prosecutor) plays a critical role throughout the process, tipping the scale of justice heavily towards the interests of the prosecution.

III. Bureaucracy, Ideology and Performance Indicators in Chinese Criminal Justice

In this final section of the opening chapter, I shall introduce some of the idiosyncrasies of the Chinese criminal justice system, or, more specifically, features of the core criminal justice institutions, which is a prerequisite to making sense of their functioning within the sociolegal context. The Chinese criminal justice system

[94] Guo Zhiyuan, 'The First Step of the Long March: Implementing the Exclusionary Rule in China' (2017) 25 *Asia-Pacific Law Review* 48.

draws heavily on a civil law tradition. Although China claimed to have reformed in the direction of adversarial systems,[95] the general feature of adversariness is very weak or non-existent in its procedures. Adversariness necessitates independence. However, the idea of an independent fact-finding process before a neutral court has been lacking in this context. The criminal process in China is dominated by the activities and decisions of the police, the procuratorate and the courts. The concept of the Iron Triangle – the coalition of the three core criminal justice institutions – defines the system as a whole, leaving the defence with little standing, status and influence.[96] While the most recent law reform in 2018 has strengthened the rights of the accused by expanding the legal aid coverage, especially allowing duty lawyers to provide custodial legal advice at detention centres,[97] crucial defence services in the pretrial phase, such as being present and offering legal advice during the police or prosecutorial interrogations, are not permitted. In later chapters (chapters three, five and six), I shall explain the constraints which bind defence lawyers in proactively constructing defence cases and the impact this has in effecting their later input at trial. Being a marginalised group, defence lawyers, in general, are treated as outsiders of the system by state officials.

Damaška has divided criminal justice systems into two main categories based on their structures of authority, namely the hierarchical and coordinate officialdoms. In this typology, the hierarchical structures of authority seek to maximise the certainty and uniformity of decision-making; state officials are given limited opportunity to exercise discretion to achieve standardised decisions. In contrast, the coordinated approach is featured in a wide distribution of authority where decision makers have a weak sense of institutional loyalty, but enjoy a broad spectrum of discretionary powers.[98] The authority structure of the Chinese criminal justice system is reminiscent of the hierarchical model. The authority is explicitly salient in its legal institutions, with power originating from the top echelon, trickling down through the layers. This model of an organisation represents a remarkable concentration of power at the higher end of the authority pyramid. The power holders at the top are responsible for the supervision of detailed handling of matters for the lower ranks. Criminal justice policies, political agendas, reform measures and so on are schematised and implemented within the hierarchical disposition. In this arrangement, there is a strong sense of order for uniformity and distrust of

[95] Perhaps the most notable reform in the direction of an adversarial system is the criminal justice reform in 1996. For more extensive discussion see M McConville et al, *Criminal Justice in China: An Empirical Enquiry* (Edward Elgar, 2011) 8–16.

[96] This term has often been used by scholars who study the Chinese criminal justice system, see Li Enshen, 'The Li Zhuang Case: Examining the Challenges Facing Criminal Defense Lawyers in China' (2010) 24 *Columbia Journal of Asian Law* 129, 161.

[97] See CPL 2018, Art 36. The legal services are limited to legal consultation, suggestions on procedural selection, applications for modification of compulsory measures and submitting opinions on the case handling.

[98] M Damaška, *The Faces of Justice and State Authority: A Comparative Approach to the Legal Process* (Yale University Press, 1986) 19.

individual judgements in lower echelons. The exercise of official discretion is kept to a minimum in order to 'satisfy the strong demands in the hierarchical model for the ordering, systematisation and simplification of the normative universe'.[99]

However, differing from a pure hierarchal ideal, the institutional power was divided to various extents at the local level in China. The criminal justice institutions are simultaneously accountable to their local congress at the same level. This dual subordination has resulted in the fact that the local government largely controls its personnel and the operational budget.[100] Local influences are also able to interfere with individual cases via higher ranked officials. Meanwhile, the criminal justice institutions' loyalty to the Party allows certain Party institutions to intervene in their decision-making. Most predominantly, the Political-Legal Committee, a Party institution responsible for coordinating the relationship between different legal institutions, has, historically, created a tension between the independence of the procuratorate and the courts, and the requirement that the procuratorate and the courts follow the Party's leadership.[101] This has been demonstrated in the exercise of the Political-Legal Committee's power to issue directions to prosecutors in influential cases that have resulted in miscarriages of justice. After a negative social response in recent years, the Political-Legal Committee has gradually suspended its power to issue instructions in individual cases. However, Party institutions still have an overriding authority over the institutions in practice, albeit in a subtle and less formal way.[102]

This multiplicity of bureaucratic authority in criminal justice has a social and cultural foundation. Lying behind the edifices of authority structure and actions of the state is a collective value underpinning a stratified society in which people are traditionally ranked by their familial and social status. Differing from the Western liberal concept that individual rights are deemed as a potent shield to protect citizens from the long arm of the state,[103] there is no such thing as individual rights that are possessed by people in the Chinese collectivism tradition.[104] According to the classical legal theory of *Li* in ancient China, a core doctrine of which was absorbed and demonstrated in Confucianism, people are born naturally unequal

[99] See JS Hodgson, 'Hierarchy, Bureaucracy, and Ideology in French Criminal Justice: Some Empirical Observations' (2002) 29 *Journal of Law and Society* 227, 232.

[100] Y Du and J Zhang, 'Research on the Personnel Management of the Procuracy', the 13th Annual Conference Paper of Shanghai Social Science 2015. C Yuan, 'The Financial Safeguards of the Procuracy' (2014) 4 *Law and Society* 229.

[101] See Yu Mou, 'Beyond Legitimate Grounds: External Influences and the Discretionary Power Not to Prosecute in the People's Republic of China' in M Caianiello and J Hodgson (eds), *Discretionary Criminal Justice in a Comparative Context* (Carolina Academic Press, 2015) 121.

[102] 'Self-Reform of the Central Political-Legal Committee: No Interference with Individual Cases', *News.ifeng* (14 July 2013) http://news.ifeng.com/mainland/detail_2013_07/14/27479910_0.shtml (accessed 3 September 2014).

[103] See T Paine, *Rights of Man, Common Sense and Other Political Writings* (Oxford University Press, 1995) 64.

[104] R Weatherly, *The Discourse of Human Rights in China: Historical and Ideological Perspectives* (Palgrave, 1999) 98.

and bound to fulfil their duties based on their social and familial roles to maintain the collective harmony of the society.[105] The welfare of the individual is believed to be in line with the interest of the state. People have no rights, but do have a duty to keep social order. It is also unnecessary for people to hold rights against the state because the benevolent government works purely for the interests of the individual. Such collectivism in Chinese culture coincides with the ideology of Marxism, which advocates that each individual's self-realisation is ultimately dependent upon society.[106] Thus, to achieve the emancipation of the world, each individual, as a member of society, should first and foremost fulfil the duties that are owed to that society in pursuit of the greater good.[107]

This collectivism, which emphasises authority and hierarchical order, has therefore been an important source of legitimacy of the state.[108] In this discourse, the criminal justice system is only a subordinate state apparatus, with its legitimacy deriving from the party-state policy.[109] A chief and effective way to ensure diligent performance of the law enforcement agents, especially low-level officials, is through the employment of managerial tools, such as performance indicators. Thus, over four decades, the police force, or the Public Security Bureau (PSB), the procuratorate and the courts had all been subjected to a regimented Appraisal System (*jixiao kaohe zhidu*). For every legal strand, a set of audit systems has been employed to evaluate the core institutions' achievements in terms of arresting and prosecuting criminals.[110] Take the PSB, for example. In many parts of China, a targeted number of suspects to be kept in custody and successfully prosecuted used to be assigned to the local police stations every year.[111] Within each police station, the assigned quota would be apportioned to its individual police officers to fulfil the overall target. Whereas accomplishing a task would put the police officers in an advantageous position for bonuses, promotions and other career opportunities, failure to achieve the task would result in a reduction in salary and other related

[105] See G MacCormack, *The Spirit of Traditional Chinese Law* (University of Georgia Press, 1996) 108–17; Weatherly (ibid) 46.

[106] Weatherly (ibid) 93.

[107] ibid 99.

[108] M McConville, 'Criminal Justice in China and the West' in M McConville and E Pils (eds), *Comparative Perspectives on Criminal Justice in China* (Edward Elgar, 2013) 50.

[109] ibid 51–52.

[110] ibid.

[111] Li Enshen (n 96)163; Zhu Tonghui, 'Jixiao kaohe yu xingshi sifa huanjing zhi bian: G sheng X xian jianchayuan, sifaju guilai suosi (Analysis of the Appraisal System and the Criminal Justice Environment: Thoughts on the Visit of the Procuratorate and Justice Bureau in X Town, G Province)' (2007) 2 *Criminal Law Review* 253; Bao Xianrong, 'Xingshi sifa jixiao kaohe de kunjin yu chulu (The Dilemma and Solution of the Appraisal System of Criminal Justice)' (2015) 4 *Social Scientist* 91. I also found this in my own empirical research. There are two criteria that measure whether the task has been fulfilled according to police working in the field site. They are: (i) for minor offences, such as dangerous driving cases, the suspect does not need to be remanded in custody and the police must make sure the case is prosecuted; and (ii) for more serious crimes, the suspect should be remanded in custody and the suspect must be authorised to be locked up. Failing in either condition means the police have not fulfilled this given task: Field notes APU-6, APU-26; Interviews EPO-1, FPO-1.

sanctions. The sharp end of this performance indicator was that an uncompleted task would affect everyone working in the particular police unit, given the task was allocated to the overall police station. This could result in a tarnished reputation for the police station, which, like the individual police officer, would be financially penalised and would become disadvantaged in the overall ranking of the police stations in the region. The ranking of the police station was not only related to the funding opportunity of the PSB's operation, but was also linked to the political achievement of the local government, which, in turn, directly determined the careers of individual police officers. Those negative consequences aside, perhaps the most direct and effective result of a 'poor' performance record was concerned with the career prospects of the chief police officer in charge of the station. In order to disprove his incapability of managing the police force and to change the force's fortunes around, a drastic measure was likely to be initiated in the following years, ensuring that a good number of criminals were apprehended and punished.[112]

A similar Appraisal System was also applicable to the procuratorate and the courts. For prosecutors, their bonuses and promotion opportunities were connected to the conviction rate of prosecuted cases.[113] Prosecutors who had a high percentage of conviction rates were more likely to be rewarded internally in the next round of tenures, whereas those whose cases had been acquitted by the court would have been marked with minus points and subsequently lost their advantageous position in competing for upcoming bonuses and promotions in the next round.[114] As far as the courts were concerned, the judgment correction rate (*gaipan lv*), which indicated the proportion of cases being overruled at a higher level, was the assessment point. If the judgment in the first instance was overruled or overturned by the court of the second instance (quite often the case was required to be retried by the trial court),[115] the trial judges who had made the initial decision[116] and the respondent court leader who had approved the judgment would be financially sanctioned and became disadvantaged in their judicial career.[117]

This particular Appraisal System was officially abolished in 2015 due to widespread criticism of the unreasonable quota in legal practice and its negative impact

[112] Interview BPO-1.

[113] Li Enshen (n 96) 163.

[114] See Zhu Tonghui, 'Xingshi susong zhong de jijian kaohe (The Appraisal System in the Criminal Justice System)' (2009) 1 *Law and Social Science* 5.

[115] According to Art 225 of CPL 2012, the appellant court can overrule the judgment made by the trial court in two ways: (i) if the case facts are correct but the application of the law is wrong, the appellant court should change the judgment directly; or (ii) if the facts are unclear and the evidence is insufficient, the appellant court can either return the case back to the trial court for retrial or the appellant court can try the case itself. However, if the case is retried by the trial court and appealed by the defendant or counter appealed by the procuratorate, the appellant court should make a final decision. In legal practice, if the appellant court overrules the decisions of the trial court, the case would normally be returned to the trial court for retrial.

[116] If there were dissenting opinions by other judges, these judges could be immune from the sanction.

[117] Li Enshen (n 96) 164.

on major cases that resulted in miscarriages of justice.[118] Albeit being ultimately abolished, the Appraisal System, as a typical format of evaluation, displayed features of cultural collectivism and exemplary society that have had a long-lasting influence on the operation of the justice system. It was effective in terms of strengthening control and representing a highly visible authority. In comparison with the normative counterpart described by Foucault,[119] Bakken observed that the exemplary norm applied to the Chinese context is prescriptive and visible.[120] This prescriptive exemplary norm was evident in the former Appraisal System, which was subsumed under the logic of bureaucracy in the process of evaluating outputs of individual state officers, with the purpose of enhancing their conformity and performance control. Different from normal techniques applied in other social settings, such as moral evaluation, the disciplinary mechanism manifested in the Appraisal System was crafted in such a way as to fortify the collegiality of the criminal justice institutions: it bound everyone's fate with that of the organisation.[121] At the micro-penal level, the plus points (*jiafen*) and minus points (*jianfen*) contributed by each officer were not merely about the merits or demerits of one individual, but were crucial and meaningful components of the group being examined.[122] Every state official was forced to be accountable for his results, constantly (and anxiously) comparing his achievements with others. It was through this intricate rewards and sanctions exercise that institutional solidarity was moulded and the highly efficient criminal justice institutions were built to carry out the social control tenet.

Although the Appraisal System regime was ended, the era of evaluation or the evaluation culture embedded in the criminal justice system did not stop there. Bakken has noted that 'evaluation is an integrated part of collective life' – it is a 'way of being' that connects individuals to the greater society.[123] Evaluation is omnipresent in every establishment of China, and it is impossible to imagine the

[118] Zhang Baosheng and Zhang Huangrong, 'Jiancha yewu kaoping yu cuoan zeren zhuijiu jizhi de wanshan (The Appraisal System for the Procuratorate and the Perfection of Mechanisms to Prevent Miscarriages of Justice)' (2014) 4 *China Criminal Law Magazine* 94.

[119] M Foucault, *Discipline and Punishment: The Birth of the Prison* (Vintage, 1979).

[120] B Bakken, *The Exemplary Society: Human Improvement, Social Control and the Dangers of Modernity in China* (Oxford University Press, 2000) 250.

[121] This type of disciplinary mechanism is not new as far as Chinese officials are concerned. The ancient penal system of 'punishment by association', or 'joint liability' (*lianzuo zhi*), was well known by policy makers in modern times. For example, in the Qin dynasty, a system of units of five and joint responsibility is prevalently seen in military management. According to the Qin regulations within the army, 'five men constitute a unit of five; [the members of] a unit of five stand surely for each other … When there is somebody in the unit who disobeys orders, or violates prohibitions, [and someone from his unit] exposes him, [the other members] will be exempted from punishment. When [the other members] know about it but do not expose [the offender], the entire unit will be punished'. U Lau and T Staack, *Legal Practice in the Formative Stages of the Chinese Empire: An Annotated Translation of the Exemplary Qin Criminal Cases from the Yuelu Academy Collection* (Brill, 2016) 298.

[122] Bao Xianrong (n 111); Zhang Baosheng and Zhang Huangrong (n 118).

[123] B Bakken, *The Exemplary Society: Human Improvement, Social Control and the Dangers of Modernity in China* (Oxford University Press, 2000) 243.

Chinese criminal justice system operating without an audit mechanism of any sort. In fact, within each strand of the criminal justice profession, new but similar performance indicators have either been introduced or proposed to meet new organisational targets. For example, the vast majority of basic courts have adopted the case closure rate (*jie'an lv*) to quicken the disposition of large volumes of criminal cases.[124] Some local courts still rely on the correction rate to evaluate the judges' performance, although the way in which the correction rate is calculated has been modified.[125] Similar measures are proposed by the police and the procuratorate.[126] The techniques utilised in the Appraisal System might be useful in effectuating the performance of the state officials, delivering objectives set out by the system and maintaining the stability of the political regime. Yet, in the following chapters, I shall show that they may also have undermined these purposes in the long run.

In the following short chapter, I present the research setting in which this study was carried out. It is a useful chapter to further elaborate on some of the characteristics of the criminal justice institutions, particularly at the micro-operational level. With that done, we are in a position to embark on the journey of enquiry with regard to how criminal cases are constructed in China.

[124] Wang Lingfang, 'Jixiao kaoping mang, sikan jieanlv (Busy Appraisal Evaluation, Four Points on the Closure Rate)', *China Court* (21 January 2019) www.chinacourt.org/article/detail/2019/01/id/3710203.shtml (accessed 10 April 2019).

[125] See 'The Evaluation Methods and Criteria in Binhai New Strict, Tianjin city' (BHXQFY- Chinacourt, 25 January 2019) www.bhxqfy.chinacourt.gov.cn/article/detail/2019/01/id/3715173.shtml (accessed 10 September 2019).

[126] 'Jianchaguan jixiaokaohe jizhi zhuanti zhengwen qishi (A Call for Papers for the New Appraisal System for the Procuratorate)', *The Procuratorate Daily* (31 July 2017) www.xinhuanet.com/legal/2017-07/31/c_129668382.htm (accessed 10 April 2019).

2

Researching the Chinese Criminal Justice System

I. Outline of Fieldwork

Conducting empirical data in China has never been an easy task. Donald Clarke once lamented that for researchers studying the Chinese legal system, 'useful data is generally not available, and the available data is not very useful'.[1] A lot of data that would be of interest to those seeking to understand the Chinese criminal process are regarded as secret by the authorities. This poses significant obstacles for research into a prolonged pretrial process, specifically from the initial criminal case building to the preparation of prosecution cases. To generate any meaningful knowledge of the way criminal justice operates in a natural setting, direct observation is best suited to the study of complex processes, where important and relevant issues can be identified and data yielded in multidimensional ways on social interaction in the context as it occurs (such as text analysis and verbal responses to informal interviews).[2] Hence, my initial research plan was to observe the acquisition of evidence by the police, experiencing the interactive situations that happened there. This plan, however, soon ended in disappointment. Every aspect of police practice was treated as sensitive, and police stations were closed to external researchers. It also proved that gaining access via official channels was entirely hopeless, so my research plan needed to be modified.

As an alternative, I approached a local procuratorate in site A. Thanks to the help of informal contacts, I was fortunate enough to be permitted to observe inside a prosecutor's office. I was allowed to have unmediated access to the investigative dossiers pending trial and had the opportunity to follow around the prosecutors working there, observing their daily activities and speaking to other legal actors involved in the process. In total, I spent 182 days observing prosecutors at work. This intense immersion at the procuratorate was a productive research experience. I observed a substantial number (46) of prosecutorial interrogations and

[1] D Clarke, 'Empirical Research into the Chinese Judicial System' in E Jensen, C Thomas and T Heller (eds), *Beyond Common Knowledge: Empirical Approaches to the Rule of Law* (Stanford University Press, 2003) 164.

[2] J Manson, *Qualitative Researching*, 2nd edn (Sage Publications, 2002) 85.

accompanied prosecutors to trials. I spoke to the police officers who sent new cases to the office, and had both formal and informal conversations with prosecutors. I was able to scrutinise legal documents and case dossiers, and had casual conversations with a range of other legal actors (such as defence lawyers, judges, victims and witnesses) who had interactions with the prosecutors. This observational experience offered me a rich reservoir of information, giving me an insight into the inner workings of Chinese criminal justice institutions. Although most of my observation was directly related to issues regarding prosecutions, the fact that pretrial preparation of the prosecution is a transitional procedure connecting both the police investigation and the trial enabled my observational data to cover the main stages of the criminal process.

Direct observation was not the only approach I employed in gathering data. At the end of the observational period, 42 semi-structured interviews with different legal actors (10 police officers, 9 judges, 10 prosecutors and 13 defence lawyers) were conducted in 10 geographical areas (sites A–J).[3] The purpose of this secondary qualitative method was threefold. First, it allowed me to excavate relevant topics in a thorough and informed way while leaving both my respondents and myself the ability to explore new leads. Secondly, I was able to explore the perspectives of the legal actors that I had little opportunity to observe, such as judges and defence lawyers, whose roles and understanding of the related issues were nevertheless critical to, and in need of being integrated into, the study. Thirdly, since the participant observations were confined to a single local procuratorate, the validity of the observational data had to be tested by data from alternative sources and geographical sites. Thus, juxtaposing the two different types of data confirmed that my knowledge generated by direct observation was valid, as it was corroborated by interview conversations. The interviewees comprised four different strands of the legal profession in different regions. The observational data could, therefore, be cross-checked. In light of this comparison, I discovered that criminal justice practices in site A were certainly not restricted to the particular institutional culture in the area where the observation took place. Nevertheless, on a cautious note, it remains the case that this research may not represent the overall practice across China, given its vast landscape and cultural diversity. In this regard, further studies on a more comprehensive scale are required.

During my observation in site A, I availed myself of other data-gathering opportunities. I attended several training sessions of the prosecutors and assisted prosecutors in organising prosecution dossiers in their archives. Most importantly, I reviewed a total of 240 evidence dossiers[4] in site A, where drug

[3] This includes 28 interviews conducted immediately after the two-staged observation, in 2012 and 2013 respectively, in China and 14 Skype follow-up interviews from May 2015 to June 2017. As with the participant observation, the interviewees were promised to be anonymised to protect their identities.

[4] At least one volume of the evidence dossier is dedicated to one suspect according to the dossier system. Depending on the amount of evidence, one suspect may have an evidence dossier that runs to multiple volumes.

trafficking, dangerous driving, the sale of (illicit) receipts and theft constituted about 80 per cent of cases. Among these dossiers, 64 criminal cases (eight of which involved co-defendants in the case) were recorded and monitored from the point that the case was transferred to the prosecution to the outcome of the trial. All case dossiers used by the legal institutions for decision-making were paper-based files. These dossiers contain documents that were entirely created by state officials (mostly, the police), including (but not limited to) the registration form of the criminal case (*bao'an cailiao*), the process of apprehending the suspect (*zhuabu jingguo*), interrogation records (*xunwen bilu*), the victim's statement(s) (*beihairen bilu*), witnesses' statements (*zhengren zhengyan*), crime scene inspection (*xianchang kanyan bilu*), a list of seized items (*kouya wuping qingdan*), expert conclusion forms (*jianding jielun*) and the record of identification (*bianren bilu*). In reviewing these dossiers, content analysis was carried out to scrutinise the pattern and the frequency of keywords, narrative styles, the sequence of listing items, the use of ambiguous and unambiguous words, and the repetition of language format within and between the case dossiers.[5] These text data analyses allowed new insights to emerge, which proved to be particularly useful in illustrating the way police cases are constructed.

II. The Social Makeup of the Suspects

My field research consisted of two separate stages. The first phase of fieldwork, from June to September 2012, focusing on the observation in the procuratorate in site A. This was followed by a revisit to the same site and interviews with a range of legal actors from September to November 2013.[6] At both stages, participant observation[7] undertaken in site A was at the heart of my fieldwork. By way of a backdrop to the analysis of the central themes in the chapters that follow, it is useful to describe the environment of the field and the key individuals upon whom this research relied in shedding light on the way the criminal justice system operates.

The basic procuratorate in site A is located at the centre of a big city in Western China, covering a large metropolitan area, with over 630,000 residents in its jurisdiction. Fuelled by a fast-growing economy in the last two decades, the urban area of the city has been a prosperous hotspot of business investment and an affluent

[5] Since evidence case dossiers are the most important assets in Chinese criminal justice, they were handled with great care and were not allowed to be taken outside of the prosecutor's office. As a result, all the content analysis was conducted manually, without the aid of any computer software.

[6] When the second phase of the fieldwork took place, the amended Criminal Procedure Law 2012 came into force.

[7] In this book, participant observation and direct observation are used interchangeably, that is, it uses the process of collecting descriptive data by immersing oneself inside a legal institution and a legal culture.

area of the megalopolis. Economic development accentuates social stratification. About one-third of the local population could be labelled as a low socioeconomic status group, comprising unskilled and semiskilled migrant workers drawn from the surrounding countryside and unemployed, unskilled local labourers. The class–crime relationship remains under debate.[8] Nonetheless, recent studies, including Webster and Kingston's longitudinal research, strongly indicate that there is a correlation between economic inequality and criminality between and within countries, and across time.[9] Such a connection between poverty and crime is partly reflected in the pooled suspect profiles in site A. Out of the 240 case dossiers that I reviewed, 91.3 per cent of drug offences, 97 per cent of prostitution-related offences, 98.4 per cent of violent offences and 96.5 per cent of property offences (predominantly thefts) were committed by people from a relatively low social class. A typical suspect's profile (apart from those involved in corruption offences or motor offences) contains information of an unemployed male (or occasionally a male without a stable occupation) migrating from the surrounding countryside, who lived in a decaying inner city area, with an average education level of primary school or middle school.[10] The overrepresentation of lower social classes is much in line with Liu Xiaomei's survey of the suspect population in Tianjin, where migrant workers account for over 40 per cent of the population. She found that over 90 per cent of the suspects were migrant male peasants or unemployed adults under the age of 35, who had missed out on the educational system. The main cause of crime, according to her analysis, was poverty: 34 per cent of crimes were driven by intolerable hardship in life; 36 per cent were caused by unemployment pressures; and 17 per cent of the offences were committed because of idleness.[11] In Western welfare systems, a main cause of crime is known as relative deprivation – 'the excess of expectations over opportunities for fulfilling them'.[12] What Liu Xiaomei outlined in China was that sheer poverty led to destitution and desperation. The commission of crimes was often economically motivated and violent in nature.[13]

[8] See RG Dunaway et al, 'The Myth of Social Class and Crime Revisited: An Examination of Class and Adult Criminality' (2000) 38 *Criminology* 589, 621; P-O Wikstrom and D Butterworth, *Adolescent Crime. Individual Differences and Lifestyle* (Devon Willan, 2006); DRE Wright, 'Reconsidering the Relationship between SES and Delinquency: Causation but not Correlation' (1999) *37 Criminology* 175. The class–crime relationship literature has also noted that there is a social bias in some of the research. See, eg J Braithwaite, 'The Myth of Social Class and Criminality Reconsidered' (1981) 46 *American Sociological Review* 36, 56.

[9] C Webster and S Kingston, *Anti-poverty Strategies for the UK: Poverty and Crime Review* (Joseph Rowntree Foundation, 2014) 6.

[10] A similar social makeup of the suspects is found in McConville et al's 2011 study, where most of the defendants observed in summary trials were 'unemployed males whose education did not go beyond primary school'. See M McConville et al, *Criminal Justice in China: An Empirical Enquiry* (Edward Elgar, 2011) 267.

[11] Liu Xiaomei, 'Liudong renkou fanzui wenti shizheng fenxi: yi tianjinshi weili (Empirical Study of the Crime on Floating Population: A Case of Tianjin)' (2010) 5 *City Problems* 75.

[12] J Lea and J Young, 'Relative Deprivation' in E McLaughlin, J Muncie and G Hughes (eds), *Criminological Perspectives: Essential Readings* (Sage Publications, 2003) 147.

[13] For example, a large number of migrants kept in the prison were absolutely penniless, according to her account. Liu Xiaomei (n 11) 76.

The crime rates, especially crimes committed by migrants, are believed to grow in number commensurate with the vastly divided income distribution in China.[14] Between 2006 and 2016, the inequality of income distribution, reflected in the Gini coefficient, reached alarming scores ranging between 0.47 and 0.49, suggesting that social unrest is likely to ensue from polarised wealth distribution.[15] As of 2008, the top echelon of society earned 55 times more than those from the lower working class, and the average salary in the most opulent sector was 16-fold that of the least fortunate industries.[16] Zheng Yonghong's research from 2004 indicates that the variation of the Gini coefficient correlates with the increase in some of the most morally condemned offence rates in society, including homicide, robbery, theft, fraud and prostitution.[17] By the same token, Shi Jinchuan and Wu Xingjie's research in 2010 found that China's overall crime rates are principally affected by regional income inequality:[18] the greater the disparity among regional income, the higher the crime rate at the state level.[19] Given the marked discrepancy in the distribution of material means and opportunities, there is no surprise that offending has become a natural choice for the lower working class, who are socially and economically marginalised.

Crime is a sensitive indicator of the degree of social deprivation (including material assets, social capital, social integration and health), which mirrors the constrained relationships of a community.[20] In this regard, the current social environment in China fails to provide any effective cohesive measure to integrate various segments of society. Inadequate social benefit offers little relief to the financially disadvantaged; the lack of civil organisations or informal networks diminishes opportunities for labour force participation and educational attainment; widespread discrimination between regions and industries further produces injustice, discontent and alienation; and the low level of trust within society exacerbates the sense of resentment, frustration and hopelessness.[21]

[14] See Zheng Yonghong, 'Jini xishu yu liudong renkou fanzui (Gini Coefficient and Crimes Committed by Floating Populations)' (2004) 76 *Journal of Hubei Police College* 47; Wang Zhiqiang, 'Dui jinnianlai liudong renkou fanzui wenti de shizheng fenxi (Empirical Study of Crimes Committed by Migrants in Recent Years)' (2006) 2 *Journal of Chinese People's Public Security University* 44.

[15] From 2006 and 2016, China's Gini coefficient points were 0.487, 0.484, 0.491, 0.49, 0.481, 0.477, 0.474, 0.473, 0.469, 0.462 and 0.465, respectively. See 'Gini Coefficient in China: Inequality of Income Distribution in China from 2005 to 2016' (Statista) www.statista.com/statistics/250400/inequality-of-income-distribution-in-china-based-on-the-gini-index/ (accessed 4 April 2018).

[16] M McConville, 'Comparative Perspectives on Criminal Justice in China' in M McConville and E Pils (eds), *Comparative Perspectives on Criminal Justice in China* (Edward Elgar, 2013) 65.

[17] Zheng Yonghong (n 14).

[18] Shi Jinchuan and Wu Xingjie, 'Woguo diqu shouru chaju, liudong renkou yu xingshi fanzuilv de shizheng yanjiu (An Empirical Study on China's Regional Income Inequality, Floating Population and Criminal Offence Rate)' (2010) 40 *Journal of Zhejiang University* 74.

[19] This finding is consistent with Kennedy et al's research: BP Kennedy et al, 'Social Capital, Income Inequality, and Firearm Violent Crime' (1998) 47 *Social Science & Medicine* 7.

[20] I Kawachi et al, 'Crime: Social Disorganisation and Relative Deprivation' (1999) 48 *Social Science and Medicine* 719.

[21] Liu Yiqiang, 'Shehui fencing zhong de bianyuan qunti jiqi liuminghua wenti (Social Stratification, the Marginalised Group and Being Vagrant)' (2000) 3 *Legal System and Society* 18; Yu Haisheng, 'Fanzui yuanyin de xinweidu – jieceng fenhua (A New Dimension of Crime: Social Stratification)'

Socioeconomically disadvantaged areas short of communal cohesion (such as visibly high inequality, distrust and social stratification) are susceptible to high delinquency rates.[22] This problem has been exacerbated by the rapid urbanisation in China. The emergence of a large number of ill-schooled 'left-behind' children (*liushou ertong*) who received inadequate parental supervision has contributed a great deal to juvenile delinquencies[23] and violent crimes.[24] Social bond theory suggests that young people's weak attachment to parents is less likely to develop a commitment to conventional social order, thereby making them more likely to commit a crime.[25] Charles Murray found that high crime rates should largely be imputed to the lack of the fatherly role in single-parent families in nurturing upright young men and teaching them how to integrate into the social world of work.[26] If this diagnosis is correct, a whole generation of 'left-behind' adolescents, most living in China's countryside, whose upbringing is devoid of the parenting roles, conveys a bleak message for the future.[27]

Aside from the deprived lower class and fragmented society, it should be noted that the constitution of the suspect population (or the 'selection' of the suspect profile) is also a product of conscious policing. A long line of criminal justice research into Western societies has established that individuals drawn from less privileged social milieux are more likely to be the subject of policing intervention.[28] In particular, people who are convicted or suspected of offences in the past and who are known to the police are likely to be subjected to stringent criteria of law enforcement, such as stop and search, as well as the criminal procedures

(2017) 8 *Social Science Review* 86; Song Jian, 'Lun shehui fenhua yu fanzui: jianping shehui jiegou zhuanxing lilun he erzhong fanzui chenyin shuo (Social Stratification and Crime: On Social Restructure Theory and Two Causes of Crime)' (2000) 14 *Review of Jiangsu Police College* 19.

[22] Kawachi et al (n 20). See also Ching-Chi Hsieh and MD Pugh, 'Poverty, Income Inequality and Violent Crime: A Meta-analysis of Recent Aggregate Data' (1993) 2 *Criminal Justice Review* 182.

[23] Tan Shiyun and Li Mei, 'Nongcun liushou ertong jianhu wenti yu fanzui shizheng yanjiu (Empirical Research of the Custody of "Left-Behind Children" and Crimes in Rural China)' (2010) 3 *Journal of Chinese People's Public Security University* 133; Huang Xin, 'Nongcun liushou ertong fanzui wenti yanjiu (Research on Crimes Committed by "Left-Behind Children")' (2008) 12 *Legal System and Society* 286; Liu Chongfeng, 'Dangqian nongcun liushou ertong fanzui wenti yanjiu (Research on Current Crimes Committed by "Left-Behind Children")' (2014) 6 *Legal System and Society* 285.

[24] Xiao Yimao, 'Diyuxing zhiye fanzui qunti zhili tanjiu: yi fujiansheng sanmingshi weili (Research on Local Criminal Communities: An Example of Sanming City, Fujian Province)' (2016) 6 *Journal of Yunnan Police College* 79, 80.

[25] MR Gotfredson and T Hirschi, *A General Theory of Crime* (Stanford University Press, 1990).

[26] C Murray, 'The Underclass' in McLaughlin et al (n 12) 133–34.

[27] According to official statistics released in November 2016, there are 9,020,000 'left-behind' children in China's countryside. For the first time, 'left-behind' children (*liushou er'tong*) are officially defined as minors under the age of 16 with both parents who work afield or with one parent who leaves home to work and the other does not have the capacity to be the guardian. See '902 wan nongcun liushou ertong zongshu ruhe chansheng? ("How Does the Total Sum of 9,020,000 'Left-Behind' Children Come into Being?")', *China News* (9 November 2016) http://www.chinanews.com/gn/2016/11-09/8057969.shtml (accessed 29 March 2018).

[28] See S Choongh, 'Policing the Dross: A Social Disciplinary Model of Policing' (1998) 58 *British Journal of Criminology* 623.

that follow.[29] Thus, selecting targets and labelling those who are dangerous are often informed by police working rules and stereotypes.[30] Such observations are equally applicable to China. It is clear that the lowest rank of society has certainly been harassed much more frequently than the middle and upper echelons. Between 2011 and 2013, prostitution-related offences constituted about 18 per cent of the total crimes in site A. Drawing from the domiciles of suspects involved in organising and sheltering other persons to engage in prostitution, it is evident that certain groups of people were specifically targeted.[31] People who were residents of the notorious 'red-light district' or clients of a chain of cheap hotels were subjects of police operations.[32] These seedy areas were on the police's radar and were often selected as the target of crackdowns. Some suspects reported that they attracted police attention purely because of where they lived:

> Suspect: The street where I live was known for its prostituting business. It is the 'red light district'. After we rented the place, from time to time, there was someone knocking our door and asking for 'misses'.[33] It used to be a lot. But now the number of customers has become much smaller because the police check our places so frequently. During those crackdown periods, the police visited every household almost every other day. Our neighbours were arrested, detained and released. We are on the checklist of the police.[34]
>
> Suspect: I was arrested because the police knew me and where I live. I have told them (the police) that I no longer rent rooms to 'the misses', but still they wanted to arrest me because they knew where I live.[35]

Different types of people commit different types of crimes. Dangerous driving and corruption-related crimes, which comprised 23 per cent of the total crime rate in site A, were commonly committed by middle classes, including governmental officials. Property offences and offences against the person were normally perpetrated by lower social classes. By gleaning from suspects' profiles in the case

[29] See D Smith, *Police and People in London. Vol. 1. A Survey of Londoners* (Policy Studies Institute, 1983); D Dixon et al, 'Realty and Rules in the Construction and Regulation of Police Suspicion' (1989) 17 *International Journal of the Society of Law* 185; MA Walker and T Jefferson, 'Ethnic Minorities in the Criminal Justice System' [1992] *Crim LR* 83; W Skogan, *The Police and the Public in England and Wales: A British Crime Survey Report* (HMSO, 1990); W Skogan, *Contacts between Police and Public: Findings from the 1992 British Crime Survey* (HMSO, 1994); B Bowling and C Phillips, 'Disproportionate and Discriminatory: Reviewing the Evidence on Police Stop and Search' (2007) 70 *MLR* 936; L Lustgarten, 'The Future of Stop and Search' (2002) 8 *Crim LR* 603.

[30] S Choongh, *Policing as Social Discipline* (Oxford University Press, 1997) 60.

[31] According to Art 358 of the Criminal Law, 'whoever arranges for or forces another person to engage in prostitution shall be sentenced to a fixed-term imprisonment of not less than five years but not more than 10 years and shall also be fined … whoever assists in arranging for another person to engage in prostitution shall be sentenced to a fixed-term imprisonment of not more than five years and shall also be fined; if the circumstances are serious, he shall be sentenced to a fixed-term imprisonment of not less than five years but not more than 10 years and shall also be fined'.

[32] *CASEA*: A13–42, A63–90, A92–110, A112–64, A170–228, A230–310.

[33] The Chinese way of saying prostitutes.

[34] Field note APU-60.

[35] Field note APU-32.

dossiers, it shows that a good proportion of suspects (28 per cent) drawn from the less privileged background were recidivists. It seems to be the rule that those with a case record (*an'di*) – those who have been convicted, subjected to other forms of coercive measures (such as administrative penalties) or fallen under suspicion of criminal conduct – are arrested more frequently than others. During a prosecutorial interrogation, a suspect complained that the reason why he was arrested was primarily that 'the police officer knew his history and fixed an eye on him'.[36] In another robbery case, the suspect protested that his case was unfairly processed, as it was founded on the bias of his previous conviction for theft. His allegation seemed to be supported by the (lack of) evidence: he was accused of mugging a woman for a gold necklace, and was immediately constrained by some passersby and sent to the police station. However, no witness confirmed that it was the suspect who robbed the woman, and the necklace was nowhere to be found.[37] It would be difficult to justify the charge laid against the suspect, with no substantiated evidence other than the fact that he had a criminal record. This case was nevertheless prosecuted and the suspect was convicted on the flimsy evidence. The continued scrutiny of certain categories of people is confirmed by some police officers, who suggested that they were dealing with habitual criminals:

> An experienced police officer is capable of figuring out what bad guys are doing, especially those you have dealt with for years. For example, we are familiar with the pickpockets in our area and I can guarantee you that when you come across those people, they are stealing other people's property. Those people are on the loose. They don't have proper jobs. What else do you think they are doing?[38]

Such a remark has a strong resonance with Satnam Choongh's finding of 'the permanently suspect' in Britain: it is about whom the police have known, rather than what they did.[39] This population is known as 'police property', over whom the police's authority is to be exerted, often in an aggressive manner. Just like many other places in the world, the population in site A is divided into the camps of the law-abiding and those who are subjected to police control.[40] The section of the public who are the common targets of police operations largely overlaps with the lower social classes. For some of them, their disadvantaged backgrounds render them no meaningful assistance when they are implicated in the criminal justice system. For all these reasons, their contribution to crime statistics seems to be magnified.

[36] Field note APU-32.
[37] Field note APU-9.
[38] Interview BPO-2.
[39] Choongh (n 30) 44.
[40] This does not take into account the large number of dangerous driving cases or corruption cases, which were investigated exclusively by the procuratorate.

3

The Construction of the Police Cases

> Justice is the first virtue of social institutions, as truth is of systems of thought. A theory however elegant and economical must be rejected or revised if it is untrue; likewise, laws and institutions no matter how efficient and well-arranged must be reformed or abolished if they are unjust … Being first virtues of human activities, truth and justice are uncompromising.
>
> John Rawls, *A Theory of Justice*

With almost no reliance on the live testimonies other than that of the defendant, criminal investigative dossiers encompassing all the evidence gathered and decisions made in the course of the investigation are often the single most important source of information for the adjudication in China. Investigative dossiers built by the police are at the core of the criminal justice system and determine the ultimate issue of guilt or innocence of the accused.[1] How are these dossiers created? Are they truly reliable? In this chapter, I will examine the activities of the police surrounding the building of the case dossier and reveal the way written evidence is constructed at this crucial stage. Studies in Western jurisdictions repeatedly show that once suspicion against a particular person takes shape, so does the investigator's belief that the person is guilty.[2] I shall show in this chapter that the same principle also applies in the Chinese instance; what the investigator believes certainly goes a long way towards structuring the perceptions of other official actors later in the process. As this book unfolds, it will become clear that the time when the 'seeds' of miscarriages of justice are sown can be traced back to the outset, when the police carry out their functions.

I. The Context: The Chinese Police and their Role in the Criminal Justice System

The police are arguably the most powerful institution within the Chinese criminal justice system. They have extensive powers in detecting crime, apprehending

[1] Zuo Weimin, 'Zhongguo xingshi juanzong zhidu yanjiu: yi zhengju juanzong wei hexin (Chinese Criminal Case Dossiers: On the Basis of Evidence Dossiers)' (2007) 6 *Legal Studies* 94, 101.

[2] A Ashworth, *The Criminal Process: An Evaluative Study* (Oxford University Press, 1998) 93. See also F Belloni and J Hodgson, *Criminal Injustice: An Evaluation of the Criminal Justice Process in Britain* (Palgrave, 2000) 22.

the perpetrators and gathering evidence. They control criminal investigations and are entrusted to make decisions on intrusive issues, such as temporarily detaining a suspect for up to 37 days,[3] imposing residential surveillance for as long as 6 months,[4] granting bail,[5] searching persons or premises, seizing material evidence, and freezing properties and financial accounts whenever they deem necessary. All these measures are conducted with little external scrutiny.[6] Aside from remand in custody (*daibu*), for which the police must seek approbation from the procuratorate,[7] the decision to impose other coercive measures during investigations

[3] According to Art 91 of CPL 2018 (Art 89 of CPL 2012), the police can detain a suspect for up to 30 days before they submit a request for formal custody where that suspect is involved in committing major crimes in various locations, repeatedly or in a gang. The procuratorate then has a further 7 days to approve or reject the request. In practice, the police tend to use the maximum time (37 days) for ordinary cases.

[4] Compared to bail, residential surveillance (*jianshi juzhu*) restricts the liberty of suspects to a greater extent in that the suspects are not allowed to leave their domicile, meet or communicate with other people without the permission of the police. Migrant suspects who have no fixed abode or suspects who are under investigation for committing crimes involving national security, terrorism and serious corruption have to be removed to a designated place to implement the residential surveillance.

[5] For suspects of alleged minor offences that may not be sentenced with imprisonment, less dangerous suspects who may not endanger society, suspects who have a serious illness or female suspects who are pregnant or nursing, the police may allow bail (*qubao houshen*) not exceeding 12 months and attached with legal conditions. The bail is similar in a way to the police bail (before and after charge) in England and Wales. To be granted bail, the suspect would be asked to provide a certain amount of money or provide a guarantor who has no involvement in the current case, a fixed domicile and a steady income.

[6] See CPL 2018, Arts 136–40 (CPL 2012, Arts 134–43). As Art 138 of CPL 2018 (Art 136 of CPL 2012) stipulates, when a search is to be conducted, a search warrant must be shown to the person to be searched. If an emergency occurs when an arrest or detention is being made, a search may be conducted without a search warrant. Unlike many Western jurisdictions, where the authority to approve the request to conduct searches and seizures normally rests with an external independent judicial officer (such as a magistrate or a prosecutor), the decision to issue such warrants in China is decided entirely by the police, and search warrants can be granted by any officer with a rank of county chief or higher. This convenient procedural arrangement makes the safeguards in protecting the right of the accused ineffective. Li Chaofeng and Xing Yongjie's 2014 study illustrates that a search warrant can be so easily facilitated that search warrants were found in less than 10% of criminal cases in Beijing, even though evidence indicates that over 75% of the cases were involved with searches and seizures. They concluded that searches without warrants have become such a standardised process that many frontline officers did not even take the trouble to request a warrant. See Li Chaofeng and Xing Yongjie, 'Woguo soucha zhidu de yunxing xianzhuang, wenti ji wanshan (The Status Quo, Problem and Perfection of the Operation of Search in China)' (2014) 2 *Jiangxi Social Science* 158, 159. In line with this finding, Zuo Weimin's empirical research also found that search warrants were scarce in real practice, although searches and seizures were commonly used: Zuo Weimin, 'Guibi yu tidai: Soucha yunxing zhidu de shizheng kaocha (Avoidance and Substitute: Empirical Study of the Operation of Searches)' (2007) 3 *China Law Studies* 114, 116.

[7] Many scholars use 'arrest' rather than 'remand in custody' as an English translation term of the compulsory measure *daibu*, eg M McConville et al, *Criminal Justice in China: An Empirical Enquiry* (Edward Elgar, 2011). The literal translation of the Chinese term *daibu* is arrest. However, the compulsory measure itself is closer to the remand in custody in common law, ie to commit an accused person to custody according to a remand order, rather than arrest. To avoid confusion, this book uses the term of 'remand in custody'. When the police have detained a suspect, the suspect will be interrogated within 24 hours, after which the police will decide whether to submit a request to the procuratorate for custody of up to 30 days, release the suspect unconditionally or make the suspect subject to either bail or residential surveillance during an adjournment. The procuratorate has 7 days to approve or reject

is entirely within the police remit. Their authority also extends to a wide range of administrative sanctions, which enables them to dispose of minor offences directly or bypass the law when collecting criminal evidence.

Chinese criminal justice deals with what are often labelled as serious crimes in many Western countries. The vast majority of transgressions in public disorder and deviant conducts are regulated by administrative law.[8] For those minor offences governed by administrative law, penalties are unilaterally meted out by the police without judicial review or affording legal advice to the offender.[9] These powers are exercised at the police's own discretion. There is no clear-cut distinction between administrative punishment at the police's disposal and criminal coercive measures.[10] As a result, the two types of power tend to be alternated by the police in the course of the criminal process as a matter of convenience to maximise the extent of police authority[11] and to avoid procedural requirements stipulated by law.[12] This issue has become more prominent since the law allowed the evidence gathered during the administrative law enforcement to be admitted in criminal proceedings.[13] As a consequence, the police tend to routinely channel criminal

the request according to Art 81 of CPL 2018. Under the following circumstances, the suspect should be remanded in custody if there is evidence to prove the facts of a crime and the suspect may be sentenced to fixed-term imprisonment or a heavier punishment: (i) the suspect is likely to commit further crimes; (ii) the suspect poses a realistic danger of harming the national security, public safety or public order; (iii) the suspect is likely to destroy or falsify evidence, interfere with witnesses or falsify statements; (iv) the suspect is likely to take revenge on the victim, case reporter or complainant; (v) the suspect is likely to commit suicide or abscond; or (vi) the suspect is likely to be sentenced to a punishment of a minimum of 10 years' imprisonment, or there is evidence to prove the fact in issue, the subject is likely to be sentenced to a punishment minimum of imprisonment, the subject has a criminal record or his or her identity is unknown.

[8] The reason for the development of the administrative justice system can be found in S Lubman, *Bird in a Cage: Legal Reform in China after Mao* (Stanford University Press, 1999) 138–73; Shao-Chuan Leng and Hungdah Chui, *Criminal Justice in Post-Mao China* (State University of New York Press, Albany, 1985) 150–55.

[9] It is worth noting that some of the administrative punishments, such as public order custody for up to 20 days and custody and education for between 6 months and 2 years, are notoriously draconian and involve deprivation of an individual's liberty with little effective redress. According to Art 16 of the PRC Security Administrative Punishment Law, the maximum detention period for minor offenders in breach of public orders (such as being drunk and threatening other people or properties in public places) is 20 days for a combined penalty. Detention and education is a compulsory administrative detention targeting prostitutes and their clients. It is established by legislative decisions and administrative regulations, including Measures on the Custody and Education of Prostitutes and their Clients (promulgated by the State Council, issued on 4 September 1993) and Notice on Implementing the National People's Congress Standing Committee's Decision on Strictly Prohibiting Prostitution and Whoring (promulgated by the Ministry of Public Security, issued on 23 November 1991).

[10] These compulsory measures are retained with minor revises in CPL 2012 and CPL 2018.

[11] Zuo Weiming (n 6).

[12] For example, the police can use an administrative search (*jiancha*) rather than research (*soucha*) in the criminal procedure to avoid applying for a search warrant. The two types of search can reach the same outcome except the administrative search does not require a search warrant. Zuo Weiming (ibid).

[13] CPL 2018, Art 54(2) states that 'the physical evidence, documentary evidence, audio-visual materials, electronic data and other evidence gathered by administrative organs during administrative law enforcement and case investigation and handling may be used as evidence in criminal cases'. See Lian Yuqiang, 'Xingzheng zhifa yu xingshi sifa xianjie zhong zhengju zhuanhua yanjiu (Research on the

cases through the administrative avenue, collecting evidence that can be used later in any criminal proceedings.[14] It is widely recognised that administrative offenders rarely challenge the decisions against them in practice.[15] This has become a subject of concern, given that such practice can easily undermine the safeguards of the suspect in the criminal process, essentially supplanting the formal criminal investigation procedures.[16]

In legal rhetoric, police are often portrayed as impartial investigators, responding to the existing evidence and arresting only the perpetrators with a goal to restore factual truth.[17] Thus, pursuant to Article 52 of the Criminal Procedure Law 2018 (CPL 2018), the police have the legal duty to obtain both exculpatory and inculpatory evidence to prove the case and to be loyal to the facts.[18] In this view, their task is to gather evidence objectively and put defendants against whom there is sufficient evidence of guilt before the courts. Despite the rhetoric in law, it is difficult for the police to behave in a quasi-judicial manner in practice.[19] As a vital part of the state apparatus, their chief functions are to curb rising crime rates and to maintain social order and the stability of the political regime. Police in China are responsible for 'everyday forms of social management', preventing and suppressing various scales of protests and revolts.[20] This, in many ways, is linked to the Marxist ideology and the history of the Chinese police, which is in close proximity to the centrality of the Chinese Communist Party. According to the Marxist–Leninist political theory, the police force represents the 'bodies of

Admissibility of Criminal Evidence Obtained in the Course of the Administrative Process Which Later Used in Criminal Proceedings)' (2017) 4 *Exploration and Free Views* 97.

[14] Chen Gang and Jiang Yong, 'Gongan jiguan "liangfa xianjie" zhong de zhengju zhuanhua yingyou: yi jingcha xingzhengquan wei shijiao (A Concern Over the Use of Evidence in Connection with Two Powers of the Police: From the Perspective of Administrative Powers of the Police)' (2014) 3 *Journal of Chinese People's Public Security University* 28.

[15] In theory, offenders may apply for a reconsideration (*fuyi*) of their case from the PSB at a higher level in the first place. If the applicant is not satisfied by the decision, she can bring administrative actions, according to Art 6 of the Administrative Reconsideration Law. In reality, the two channels are largely hopeless for the applicant. On most occasions, the offender's reconsideration applications are rejected because the rules are often to the applicant's disadvantage. For more detailed discussion, see Li Enshen, 'Prisonization or Socialisation? Social Factors Associated with Chinese Administrative Offences' (2010) 27 *UCLA Pacific Basin Law Journal* 213.

[16] ibid. For instance, the police are vested with more coercive administrative power in relation to properties and persons. These measures to control a suspect include taking protective compulsory methods; conducting interrogation, compulsory summons, compulsory examination, detention and reviewing; and controlling the suspect's activities. See Art 42 of the Regulation on Procedures of Handling Administrative Cases by the Public Security Bureau (No 125 of the Ministry of the Public Security, issued on 25 December 2012).

[17] Xu Jingcun (ed), *Criminal Procedure Law*, vol I (China Law Press, 1999) 218.

[18] It should be noted here that this Article (Art 52 of CPL 2018) is applicable not only to the police, but also to the prosecutor and judges. Although the judge should not be an investigator according to the adversarial model of trial, her power to gather evidence remains in this Article, even though, in reality, the judge today rarely gathers any evidence to prove the case facts.

[19] Mengyan Dai, 'Policing in the People's Republic of China: A Review of Recent Literature' (2008) 50 *Crime, Law and Social Change* 211.

[20] Yuhua Wang, 'Empowering the Police: How the Chinese Communist Party Manages its Coercive Leaders' (2014) 219 *The China Quarterly* 625, 627.

armed men and women' that defend and implement the will of the ruling class by means of violence, coercion and other military-like repressions to safeguard the national security and social order.[21] This violent, coercive and military image of police was embedded in the development of the Chinese police force, namely the Public Security Bureau (PSB).

The predecessor of the PSB was the State Police Security Bureau (*guojia zhengzhi baowei ju*). It was a secret military agency loyal to the leadership of the Party in the 1930s, replicating the KGB of the Soviet Union.[22] In the early era of the People's Republic of China, crime was always tagged with a class character and had political implications.[23] In the combat with counterrevolution, the PSB undertook the task of 'eliminating the enemies and antagonistic elements in the class struggle'[24] to defend the fledgling socialist regime. Throughout the period of political upheaval, the police served as coercive agents and eyes for public security. They were responsible for executing the Party's mass line policy[25] and had taken on campaign-style operations. The police function adapted to the changing context of the 1980s, when the Party subdued the ideology of class repression and entered an era of economic reform. Nonetheless, the Party continued to require the police to adhere to its directives and policies.[26] To maintain state security and social order, the Chinese Communist Party has strategically elevated the police's bureaucratic rank and has appointed police chiefs to core Party roles, placing bigger shares of fiscal funding and greater political power within their hands.[27]

Despite the changing function, the political ethos and campaign-style policing from the 1950s had long-lasting implications in the 'Strike Hard (*yan'da*)' crackdowns, which have been a 'mainstay of criminal justice operations against serious crime' in the last few decades.[28] Politically motivated, Strike Hard is a movement to swiftly and harshly combat crime waves or worrying crime trends for a specified period of time.[29] These anti-crime campaigns have been launched since the

[21] Chen Weidong, *Xingshi shengqian chengxu yanjiu (Research on Criminal Pre-trial Procedure)* (China Rnemin University Press, 2004) 101.

[22] Zhang Zhaorui, ' Jincha Lishi Yanjiu Lunyao (The Synopsis of the Research on the History of the PSB)' (1999) 1 *Journal of Jiangxi PSB Training School* 91. Yuhua Wang (n 20) 626.

[23] K Mühlhahn, *Criminal Justice in China* (Harvard University Press, 2009) 192.

[24] Tao Lung-sheng, 'The Criminal Law of Communist China' (1966) 52 *Cornell Law Review* 43, 44.

[25] The mass line (*qunzhong luxian*) is a political ideology and organisational tactics employed by the Chinese Communist Party to consolidate its power. Mühlhahn (n 23) 193.

[26] Mengyan Dai (n 19) 213.

[27] Yuhua Wang (n 20) 626–48. See also Fu Hualing, 'Zhou Yongkang and the Recent Police Reform in China' (2005) 38 *The Australian and New Zealand Journal of Criminology* 241–53.

[28] M Dutton, *Policing Chinese Politics: A History* (Duke University Press, 2005) 137–42; SE Scoggins, 'Policing Modern China' (2018) 3 *China Law and Society Review* 79, 84.

[29] S Trevaskes, *Policing Serious Crime in China: From 'Strike Hard' to 'Kill Fewer'* (Routledge, 2010) 24–78; M Dutton and L Tianfu, 'Missing the Target? Policing Strategies in the Period of Economic Reform' (1993) 39 *Crime and Delinquency* 316; MS Tanner, 'Campaign-Style Policing in China and Its Critics' in B Bakken (ed), *Crime, Punishment and Policing in China* (Rowman and Littlefield Publisher, 2005) 171–88; HM Tanner, *Strike Hard! Anti-crime Campaigns and Chinese Criminal Justice 1979–1985* (Cornell University East Asia Program, 1999).

mid-1980s, with ongoing sequences through to the current time.[30] During Hard Strike periods, suspects and convicted criminals alike are treated as enemies of the state and are targeted for 'severe and stern blows'.[31] The PSB usually concentrates on particular categories of crime, involving vast amounts of frenetic police activity, with suspects being publicly arrested *en masse*.[32] During the campaigns, the cases are processed in a hasty manner. The majority of the cases are adjudicated to a relaxed standard of the law in order to meet the requirements of the special task.[33]

Although it has been asserted that Strike Hard campaigns are based on the rationale of the 'deterrent' theory of crime and social order management,[34] official crime statistics and research analysis reveal that such campaign-style policing is, in fact, incapable of staunching the long-term upward spiral in the crime rate.[35] Trevaskes suggests that the vast scale of crackdowns is a political statement to reinforce the legitimacy of the Party authority.[36] It is also an ideological tool of propaganda that is motivated to show the Party has absolute control of the criminal justice system.[37] On this note, the Strike Hard campaigns should certainly be credited as more than crime control operations.

The campaign-style policing has often worked hand in hand with the Appraisal System to ensure that the police officers, especially those on the bottom rung, are focused on carrying out the given tasks. As discussed in the introductory chapter, the Appraisal System is devised to incentivise legal institutions to engineer the success of criminal prosecution.[38] For a long period of time, the performance of the police was measured and ranked by quantified statistics, such as clear-up rates (*po'anlv*),[39] rejection rates of custodial applications

[30] There are three major Hard Strike periods, in 1983, 1996 and 2001–2003, respectively. The most recent nationwide Strike Hard movement was initiated in January 2018 following publication of the Chinese Communist Party Central Committee and State Council's official document, 'Zhonggong zhongyang guowuyuan fachu "guanyu kaizhan saohei chue zhuanxiang douzheng de tongzhi" (Notification on Carrying Out a Special Struggle to Clean Up Gang Crime and Eliminate Evil)', *Xinhua Net* (24 January 2018) www.xinhuanet.com/2018-01/24/c_1122309773.htm (accessed 18 March 2018).

[31] S Trevaskes, 'Severe and Swift Justice in China' (2007) 47 *British Journal of Criminology* 23, 41; Tanner (n 29) 171–88.

[32] Tanner (n 29) 171.

[33] He Yongjun, *Duanlie yu yuanxu: Renmin fayuan jianshan (1978–2005) (Construction of the People's Court: 1978–2005)* (China Social Science Press, 2008).

[34] Trevaskes (n 31) 33.

[35] Tanner (n 29) 180–83.

[36] Ibid; Trevaskes (n 29) 118–20.

[37] Trevaskes (n 31) 39.

[38] Li Enshen, 'The Li Zhuang Case: Examining the Challenges Facing Criminal Defense Lawyers in China' (2010) 24 *Columbia Journal of Asian Law* 129, 163; Zhu Tonghui, 'Jixiao kaohe yu xingshi sifa huanjing zhi bian: G sheng X xian jianchayuan, sifaju guilai suosi (Analysis of the Appraisal System and the Criminal Justice Environment: Thoughts on the Visit of the Procuratorate and Justice Bureau in X Town, G Province)' (2007) 2 *Criminal Law Review* 253; Bao Xianrong, 'Xingshi sifa jixiao kaohe de kunjin yu chulu (The Dilemma and Solution of the Appraisal System of Criminal Justice)' (2015) 4 *Social Scientist* 91.

[39] In China, clear-up rates are measured by whether suspects are arrested and key evidence is secured. In the past, the police's clear-up rates were ranked by comparing them with the same police

(*bubulv*),[40] prosecution totals (*qisushu*) and the proportion of police cases that are later decided not to prosecute (*busulv*).[41] By linking the ranking of these targets with sanctions and bonuses, the Appraisal System has fundamentally shaped the mindset of the police, whose actions are driven by the success of prosecutions.[42] This is predominantly illustrated in evidence gathering. For many police, securing convictions is their ultimate guidance of criminal investigations. This quote from one police officer is particularly revealing:

> We don't put the wrong version into the dossier – it only causes confusion. We just include the one which we believe is true. At the end of the day, we have to try our best to make all evidence look consistent so that the prosecution decision or final conviction can be secured.[43]

This was confirmed by a prosecutor, who was familiar with the practice of police investigations. He suggested that contradictory facts were often processed by screening statements that were in the accused's favour.

> The police will not let witnesses say something different from the suspect's guilty confession! If some witnesses' statements were far away from the facts they [the police] believe to be true, they will just throw them away.[44]

This remark has a statutory basis. Article 200 of CPL 2018 states that, in order to convict the defendant, the *corpus delicti* must be clear and the incriminating evidence should be reliable and sufficient (*zhengju queshi chongfen*). According to the interpretation of the Supreme People's Court, this means that conviction must be established by a chain of inculpatory evidence, all of which points to the same facts without reasonable doubt.[45] This is known as the corroboration rule

station's average clear-up rates in the previous three years. Thus, if the clear-up rate of a given year was lower than the average of clear-up rates before, the police station would be sanctioned. See Wu Meilai and Sui Ouli, 'Xingshi susong zhineng de yihua yu zhili: yi gongjianfa xingshi susong guanlian jixiao kaohe wei zhongxin (The Alienation of Solution of the Function of Criminal Justice: Based on the Correlation of the Appraisal System in Criminal Justice Institutions)' in He R (ed.), *Gongzheng Sifa yu Xingzhengfa Shishi Wenti Yanjiu (Shang Ce) (Judicial Justice and the Implementation of the Administrative Law (Part 1))* (People's Courts Press, 2014) 349.

[40] This rate is ascertained by the procuratorate. If the rejection rate of the police was higher than average in the region, the police station would be penalised. ibid.

[41] Similar to the rejection rate of the custodial application. If the police station had a higher rate in the cases that are decided not to prosecute, the police station would be penalised. ibid.

[42] Lu Shaofeng and Liu Yang, 'Jixia kaohe, guojia peichang yu xingshi cuoan: yi jianchajiguan wei shijiao (Appraisal System, State Compensation and Miscarriages of Justice: From the Perspective of the Procuratorate)' (2016) 7 *Legal System and Society* 30; Guo Song, 'Zuzhi lixing, chengxu lixing yu xingshi sifa jixiao kaoping zhidu (Organisational Rationale, Procedural Theory and the Appraisal System in Criminal Justice)' (2013) 31 *Political Science and Law Forum* 69; Hang Kang, 'Woguo zhongda xingshi yuanan chengyin fenxi jiyingdui celv: yi gongan sifa jiguan de jixiao kaohe jizhi wei shijiao (The Analysis of Major Miscarriages of Justice in China and the Solutions: From the Perspective of the Appraisal System of the PSB)' (2013) 10 *Journal of Zhengzhou institute of Aeronautical Industry Management* 125.

[43] Interview EPO-1.

[44] Field note APU-1.

[45] See Art 104 of Interpretation of the Supreme People's Court on the Application of the Criminal Procedure Law of the PRC 2012: the truthfulness of a piece of evidence shall be examined by taking into consideration the overall evidence of a case. The strength of a piece of evidence to prove a fact

(*yinzheng zhengming yuanze*), and is employed by the courts to decide the admissibility and probative value of evidence.[46] This rule demands that, in order to secure a conviction, facts of the prosecution case must be supported by corroborating evidence. The aim of this rule is to restrict the courts' discretionary power and to place a legal bar to the conviction of a defendant on the basis of a single piece of uncorroborated evidence, especially a confession.[47] This rule is often perceived as a safeguard for the defendant by asking for more pieces of evidence to minimise the falsity of evidence.[48] Despite good intentions, what is meant by corroboration and whether it has the assumed effect in supporting the safety of conviction are far from straightforward. For one thing, the concept of corroboration has a technical and sometimes disputed meaning.[49] It is not clear to what extent a piece of evidence can be deemed as adequately supported. Must every element of the confession be sufficiently supported? What would happen if, say, only 50 per cent of the confessed facts are enhanced by other evidence? What about 30 per cent or 80 per cent? Should the court differentiate the material facts from the peripheral? Is there any requirement of the supporting evidence? Does the supporting evidence only need to show that the confession is likely to be true? If a piece of evidence (X) is obtained through information gained from another piece of evidence (Y) (say, a piece of DNA evidence is found according to a confession), can evidence X be used to support evidence Y? Is the video recording conducted by the police during the interrogation eligible as a piece of supporting evidence? It is uncertain how the adequacy of corroboration can be assessed in real terms. Besides that, the law fails to clarify the level to which the facts need to be corroborated. While the law clearly requires sufficient evidence to prove that a crime has occurred, there is no corroboration requirement to indicate that it is the defendant who committed the crime, nor does it demand any proof of the requisite mental state of the defendant

shall be examined and judged based on actual circumstances from the perspectives of the degree of relevance between the evidence and the fact to be proved, and the linkage between different pieces of evidence. A piece of evidence shall be admitted as the basis for deciding a case only if: it is inherently related to other pieces of evidence; it and other pieces of evidence all point to the same fact to be proved; and there is neither any irremovable contradiction nor any inexplicable question.

[46] See Wang Haiyan, 'Yinzheng: Jingyanfaze, zhengju guize yu zhengming moshi (Corroboration: Rule of Experience, Evidence Rule and Model of Proof)' (2018) 3 *Contemporary Law* 4.

[47] See Art 55 of CPL 2018.

[48] Long Zongzhi, 'Xingshi yinzheng zhengmin xintan (Exploration of the Corroboration Rule)' (2017) 2 (*Legal Studies* 149; Luo Weipeng, 'Yinzheng yu zuijia jieshi tuili: Xingshi zhengming moshi de duoyuan fazhan (Corroboration and IBE: The Pluralistic Development of Criminal Proof)' (2017) 5 *Jurist* 117.

[49] For example, in England and Wales, the corroborative evidence must be independent, which confirms the guilty fact in some material particulars. According to the New Jersey test in the USA, the corroboration would be provided by 'independent proof of facts and circumstances which strengthen or bolster the confession and tend to generate a belief in its trustworthiness, plus independent proof of loss or injury'. The different meanings of corroboration in jurisdictions in the USA and the UK can be seen in M McConville, *The Royal Commission on Criminal Justice: Corroboration and Confessions, the Impact of a Rule Requiring that no Conviction Can Be Sustained on the Basis of Confession Evidence Alone* (HMSO, 1993) 51–65.

or other specific elements of the crime.[50] None of these questions and doubts have been answered or explained with clarity in practice.[51]

In spite of the ambiguity, the police have exercised their discretion to gather and construct evidence in a way that conforms with the rule based on their own interpretation. The corroboration rule is sometimes found to have been construed in a narrow sense. Thus, confession evidence, for example, can be corroborated by facts mentioned by the defendant in the course of the confession itself.[52] In particular, if certain facts could have been known only to the perpetrator of the crime, the procured facts are permitted to buttress confessions or other inculpatory evidence. Examples of this include some of the most notorious wrongful convictions. In the case of *Nie Shubin*, the conviction was based on the defendant's confessions, which dovetailed with the statements of the key witnesses. The first instance judgment shows that Nie Shubin had 'guided' the police to the crime scene, describing in great detail the victim's clothes, which was in perfect consistency with the accounts of the victim's husband and another witness.[53] Nie Shubin's confessions were considered reliable, as they contained facts which it was believed only the perpetrator of the crime was privy to.[54] The key issue here is *how* the defendant acquired the special knowledge. Did the information emanate directly from the confessor or from other sources, such as the police? Likewise, in the uncle–nephew Zhang case, Zhang Gaoping confessed that 'he disposed of the body at a location where he could not see because of the darkness, but he could hear the sound of water'.[55] This fact was admitted by the court to connect Zhang Gaoping with the commission of the crime and was supported by the crime scene

[50] M McConville et al, *Criminal Justice in China: An Empirical Inquiry* (Edward Elgar, 2011) 362.

[51] Wang Haiyan (n 46).

[52] See Cai Yuanpei, 'Lun Yinzheng yu xinzheng zhi ronghe: Yinzheng moshi de loudong jiqi mibu (The Merging between Corroboration and Ascertainment: The Loophole of the Corroboration Rule and Its Solution)' (2016) 3 *Legal Science* 171; Zuo Weimin, 'Yinzheng zhengmin moshi fansi yu chongsu: Jiyu zhongguo xingshi cuoan de fansi (Rethink and Recast of the Corroboration Rule: Rethink about the Miscarriages of Justice)' (2016) 1 *Legal Studies* 162; Yang Jiwen, 'Yinzheng zhengming de lixing jiangou: Cong xingshi cuoan zhili lunzheng chufa (Construction of Corroboration Rule: From the Argument of Miscarriages of Justice)' (2016) 6 *Legal System and Social Development* 173; Zhou Hongbo, 'Zhongguo xingsh yinzheng lilun pipan (Criticism over the Corroboration Rule)' (2015) 6 *Legal Studies* 136; Long Zongzhi (n 48); Luo Weipeng (n 48); Mou Lvye, 'Lun feifazhengju paichu guize he yinzheng zhengming moshi de chongtu ji mihe lujing (The Conflict between Exclusionary Rule of Inappropriately Obtained Evidence and Corroboration Rule and Its Solution)' (2017) 29 *Peking University Law Review* 1068.

[53] Nie Shubin was convicted for the rape and murder of a woman called Kang Juhua in 1994. He was executed in 1995. His conviction was eventually quashed in 2005 by the Supreme People's Court, after a man named Wang Shujin confessed to the killing. The judgment of Nie Shubin (first trial), The People's Intermediate Court, Hebei province (1995) No 53, http://infzm.com/content/91773 (accessed 9 September 2012).

[54] In this regard, the Chinese corroboration rule is similar to the *corpus deliciti* rule stipulated by the Supreme Court of New Jersey in a modified test in *State v Lucas* 152 A 2d 50 (1959), as well as the Scottish rule. McConville (n 49) 52–54.

[55] 'Zhejiang Zhangshi shuzhi yuanan' (The Wrongful Conviction of Uncle–Nephew Zhang in Zhejiang Province)', *Ifeng News* (April 2014) http://news.ifeng.com/mainland/special/zhangshiyuanan/content-3/list_0/0.shtml (accessed 19 September 2015).

evidence that the deceased body was found in a wet ditch. This information also appeared to be confirmed by the local weather records produced by the police, proving that the ditch was indeed filled with water after the rain on that particular day. Thus, Zhang's confession was deemed to be reliable. The confession encompassed material particulars in relation to the crime that occurred as well as the defendant who actually committed it. Unfortunately, the corroboration rules failed to afford real protection in both instances. A fundamental flaw of the rule is that the required corroboration is largely *constructive* in nature. It informs the police how to build a case, but it does not tell how the established facts should be scrutinised. It is, therefore, relatively easy to establish seemingly objective facts to secure conviction given the low threshold required by the rule. For the defence, however, it is difficult to deconstruct the case unless they are given access to examine how the evidence was obtained and whether it is truly reliable. As these two wrongfully convicted cases reveal, the confessions were solicited by police who had knowledge of the crime. Likewise, the supporting evidence turned out to be irrelevant or was discredited. It was sought purely to fulfil the requirement of corroboration.[56] For the police, the law concerned here is clear and informative: the corroboration rule that guides judges to convict a case is equally applicable in the investigation that builds the case. The malpractices of the police that have been identified in high-profile cases can also be found in criminal cases in general.

II. The Official Version of Truth

Finding the truth is a difficult task under any given circumstance.[57] I have shown in chapter one that Chinese criminal justice does not have a clear theory with regard to the truth-finding process; yet, the Chinese criminal procedure law appears specifically designed to ensure the factual truth of cases. Truthfulness has been used as a rule to test the admissibility of evidence,[58] and state officials 'are obliged to be loyal to factual truth'.[59] To ensure that 'all citizens who know the case facts can provide the evidence objectively and sufficiently', criminal procedure law expressly prohibits extorting confessions by torture and collecting evidence by threat, enticement, deceit or other unlawful means.[60] This has been further strengthened by the introduction of video/audio recording in criminal procedure law.[61] According to CPL

[56] See the Zhao Xinjian rape and murder case. Zhao was forced to confess how he cut the electric wire in order to align his confession with other pieces of evidence in the case. Zuo Weimin (n 52) 166.

[57] T Weigend, 'Is the Criminal Process about Truth? A German Perspective' (2003) 26 *Harvard Journal of Law & Public Policy*, 157, 158.

[58] See Art 50 of CPL 2018 (Art 48 of CPL 2012), which provides 'all facts that prove the true circumstances of a case shall be evidence'. See also McConville et al (n 7) 70.

[59] See Art 53 of CPL 2018.

[60] The rule regarding the exclusion of illegally obtained evidence in criminal cases will be discussed in later chapters. See Art 52 of CPL 2018.

[61] According to Art 121 of CPL 2012 (Art 123 of CPL 2018), video/audio recordings must be used in police interrogations concerning cases in which the accused might be sentenced with the death penalty,

2018, the accused is entitled to the privilege against self-incrimination, despite law stipulating that the accused must 'answer truthfully during police questioning'.[62] These rules have been laid out to convey the belief that objective truth is there to be discovered or excavated: by piecing together the evidence, the truth will be restored and presented. This legal assumption, however, has no real foundation in criminal justice practices. I shall show that criminal cases are in fact constructed. Legal actors may create different accounts of the case. However, only the version of facts that is constructed by the police and the prosecutor is recognised as 'the official version of truth' and given credence in criminal proceedings.

McConville's 2011 empirical study of Chinese criminal justice found that the police in China play a subsidiary role in the discovery of crime in that the vast majority of the criminal cases were reported by the general public.[63] This finding is confirmed in this research. Out of that 240 investigative dossiers that I reviewed, I found that only 24 per cent of the cases were discovered by the police. Public reporting was not only important in contributing to the total number of cases, it often formed the cornerstone in building up the police cases, playing a significant role in formulating the case facts or setting the tone for investigations. Reports from victims or other witnesses had often been the earliest recorded accounts in the case dossiers. In many instances, the keywords used by the victim and the way that the crime was depicted repeatedly reappeared in other documentary evidence, most specifically confessions. Aside from cases in which suspects were arrested red-handed, in other crime types (such as assault, robbery, theft or rape) the pattern of the language used in the suspect's confessions was overwhelmingly similar to the testimonies of the witnesses who reported the crime. In a closely scrutinised sample of 64 cases, the keywords used by the witnesses often matched those in the suspect's confessions. Sometimes the details recorded in the confessions were so starkly similar to the victim's statements that the patterns of usage in sentence construction, grammar, word choice and narrative structure overlapped. Compare, for example, the following statements extracted directly from the evidence dossier:

> *CASEA* 32
>
> The victim's statement:
>
> The victim: Our neighbour who was selling pears called at him (the suspect), 'give me two bowls of noodles'. Then the young man came to me and accused me of having told everyone that he sold dumplings for 4 yuan (under the market price). I did not say

life imprisonment or other serious sentences. For other cases, video/audio recorded interrogation is optional.

[62] CPL 2018, Art 120. See interview with the Vice Director of the Committee of Law of the National People's Congress, Lang Sheng. Interview with Lang Sheng, '"No One Shall Be Compelled to Self-Incriminate Himself" Does Not Contradict "Answer Truthfully"', official public conference addressed to international journalists in regard to the revision of the Criminal Procedure Law 2012 on15 March 2012, http://lianghui.people.com.cn/2012npc/GB/239293/17332481.html (accessed 16 March 2015).

[63] McConville et al (n 50) 27.

> things like that. Then the man said it was my neighbour told him about it. I asked him which neighbour said. The young man threw a bowl at me. The dirty sauce in the bowl was splashed on my clothes. Then we started to cuss at each other. The young man came over and pulled me out. We were fighting together. Soon my husband came out of the shop to protect me. Then the young man came over and punched my husband three times on his face. He injured his eyes, nose and mouth.
>
> Interrogation record (second account):
>
> The suspect: The woman's (victim's) neighbour who was selling pears called me, 'give me two bowls of noodles'. Then I asked the woman (the victim) whether she told people that my dumplings were sold at 4 yuan. She said that she did not say things like that. Then I said it was the man (the woman's neighbour) told me about it. She asked me which neighbour said. I threw a bowl at her. The dirty sauce in the bowl was splashed on her clothes. Then we started to cuss at each other. We were fighting together. Very soon, her husband came out of the shop to protect her (the victim). I was so mad that I punched him three times on his face. His eyes, nose and mouth were injured.
>
> *CASEA* 35
>
> The witness statement:
>
> The witness: I ran to K (the suspect) and told him that they were fighting. Then K grabbed a metal tube and ran to the place where the fight took place to help his brother … I saw K beating at a fat man. The man retraced to his shop. K struck him several times in vain, so he started to beat other people around.
>
> Interrogation record (second account):
>
> The suspect: L ran to me and informed me that they were fighting. I took a metal tube and joined the fight to help my brother… I remember there was a fat man. I beat him and he retraced to his shop. I struck him several times in vain, so I started to hit other people around me.
>
> *CASEA* 36
>
> The victim's statement:
>
> The victim: Y (the suspect) and his wife led a dozen people to enter my shop through the back door and the other camp of people from the front door. Y grabbed the cash box. My husband tried to stop him and he slashed at my husband … I was about 2 metres away, so I couldn't hear clearly what they were talking. I only heard he said something like 'what are you going to deal with me'. Then these men (about 24 or 25 of them) rushed up and started to beat my husband, my two brothers, and my brother in law.
>
> Interrogation record (second account):
>
> The suspect: My wife and I took about 12 people to the shop from the back door; another 12 people from the front door. I saw the cash box and tried to grab it. Then S wanted to stop me. So, I slashed at him … Then I shouted, 'what are you going to deal with me'. After that my people rushed up and started to beat the man and the man's brothers.

These precisely overlapping contents only occurred in a relatively small number of cases (six). In most instances, the dovetailed details were exhibited in the choice of words, the narrative styles and the level of language command. Nonetheless, it is still extraordinary that suspects and victims, many of whom were from very different social and educational backgrounds, chose to use identical language to recount what happened.[64] Hence, on one occasion, I asked a police officer about the curious similarity in the description of incidences.

> Researcher: Why are the languages in those different statements so similar?
>
> Police: We have to determine the investigative direction in the beginning. The initial account reported by the victim and informant sometimes is the cornerstone of the investigation … later evidence must reflect on the victim's account.[65]

It appeared that the police had been using the information that reached them first, either from the source of the victim or other witnesses, as the compass for their investigations. This was subsequently confirmed by an experienced prosecutor, who explained the widespread practice in police investigations:

> Prosecutor: In practice, police officers always tailor the suspect's statement to the victim's account. They force the suspect to say the same thing as the victim said to them. They will ask the victim first and then interrogate the suspect in such a way that the suspect's statements can dovetail with the victim's statement.[66]

This comment seemed to be true. On one occasion, a prosecutor had to admonish two police officers since the details of the fact and narrative styles in some statements could have aroused suspicion in relation to the reliability of the evidence in question:

> I have to warn you that if you keep making all the details of different accounts exactly the same, the truthfulness of these statements will be doubted. In many circumstances, witnesses cannot remember the exact time … So, if you just keep the details roughly the same and leave some reasonable discrepancies, the evidence is more convincing. If you try to match everything in the dossier, the effect may be contrary.[67]

The early version of the fact could be adjusted if other witness testimonies were available. It is true that these accounts may have faithfully reflected what happened from the witness's perspective in light of her fresh memory. However, there are a host of reasons why credibility should not be attached lightly to these statements provided by the victim or other witnesses. Empirical research has shown that there are a number of factors that influence the accuracy of witnesses. For example, a witness (including the victim) may not perceive an event accurately; she may have been exposed to the event for a limited length of time or frequency,

[64] The linguistic analysis in this aspect, see RA Leonard et al, 'Forensic Linguistics: Applying the Science of Linguistics to Issues of the Law' (2017) 45 *Hofstra Law Review* 881; BS Howard, 'Comparative and Non-comparative Forensic Linguistic Analysis Techniques: Methodologies for Negotiating the Interface of Linguistics and Evidential Jurisprudence in the American Judiciary' (2006) 83 *University of Detroit Mercy Law Review* 285. For criticism of forensic linguistics, see EK Cheng, 'Being Pragmatic about Forensic Linguistics' (2013) 21 *Journal of Law & Policy* 541.

[65] Field note APU-13.

[66] Interview BPS-1.

[67] Field note APU-55.

or she may be affected by a visual handicap.[68] Loftus's research points out that in the three-stage process of information – acquisition, retention and retrieval – a witness's memory might be affected, distorted or contaminated by various stimuli, such as former experiences, beliefs, and mental and physical state.[69] It has been reported that thousands of erroneous witness statements were caused by post-event memory contamination alone throughout Western countries.[70] Although there are no empirical data to reveal the number of statements that have proved to be unreliable, there is no evidence to suggest that China is an exception to the general rule. Using witnesses' accounts as the yardstick to formulate the facts could be straightforward if they are accurate and genuinely reliable. However, since these early recounts are not subject to further close scrutiny, especially via the mechanism of cross-examination, human errors are likely to be compounded if they are readily utilised to mould the facts.

On the other hand, witnesses' accounts are not always available. In cases like murder, theft and fraud, the early evidence may not be adequate to present a full picture of what has happened. Under those circumstances, the police's formulation of facts will often rely on other factors, such as the probability of conviction. Therefore, if a defendant can be charged with different crimes based on the way in which the facts are assembled, the facts eventually submitted by the police are usually selected for evidence considerations. The chosen crime may not always be the most serious, but it must be the most winnable. For example, in a case which involved an assault inflicting serious bodily harm with intent (*guyi shanghai*) as well as sexual assault, the victim was in an unconscious state and could not provide any valuable testimony of what occurred. The suspect reported to the prosecutor that he was encouraged by the police to confess the intention of rape rather than physical assault and sexual assault. Given that the criminal law provides an assumption to establish the *mens rea* of rape when the victim is unconscious, proving a rape case here has a better prospect of standing up in court.[71]

> The police officer tried to persuade me to confess that I wanted to have sex with the girl. I said no. I would rather confess to a crime carrying a heavier penalty than an offence with a light one that I never committed.[72]

The prosecutor who handled this case confirmed that the lack of evidence for an assault charge had led the police to reconsider the direction of the investigation.

[68] ALT Choo, *Hearsay and Confrontation in Criminal Trials* (Oxford University Press, 1996) 22–23.

[69] Generally speaking, these factors can be categorised as 'event factors' and 'witness factors'. See EF Loftus, *Eyewitness Testimony* (Harvard University Press, 1979) ch 3. As is noted, the biggest memory impairment is post-event information, which occurs after the memory of the original event has been formed. GH Gudjonsson, *The Psychology of Interrogations, Confessions and Testimony* (Wiley, 1992) 90–91.

[70] EF Loftus and HG Hoffman, 'Misinformation and Memory: The Creation of New Memories' (1989) 118 *Journal of Experimental Psychology* 100.

[71] See the judicial interpretation issued by the Supreme People's Court, the Supreme People's Procuratorate and the Ministry of Public Security on 'Several Explanations of Concrete Application of Current Dealing with Rape Cases'(26 April 1984, No 7 of [84] Law Research).

[72] Field note APU-30.

Applying the same principle, the police in site A had chosen to investigate cases as drug possession rather than drug trafficking (*CASEA*s 25, 37 and 38) and sheltering prostitution rather than fraud (*CASEA*s 15, 17, 38 and 41) after balancing the strength of the evidence at hand. The version of truth is selected not because it is loyal to the facts, but it is based upon the chances of conviction.

Reported miscarriages of justice have also indicated that the version of truth presented by the police may be concerned with factors of stereotyping, intuition or even imagination.[73] The facts contemplated provide some sort of link to explain the real evidence associated with the crime in question. The suspects' statements were known to be malleable, and had been shaped to fit to the premeditated version of facts. Again, the case of uncle–nephew Zhang is a telling example. After Zhang Gaoping and Zhao Hui were arrested, the forensic expert identified a piece of male DNA evidence in the victim's eight fingernails which was unrelated to the suspects, implying that the real perpetrator might be someone else. However, the police decided to focus on extracting confessions from the two innocent suspects and dismissed the forensic evidence. They interpreted the DNA evidence as from someone the victim had random contact with prior to her death and thereby nullified this crucial piece of evidence.[74] In another murder case, which happened in Yibin, Sichuan province in 2002, the suspect, Li Jie, gave a strong alibi that he was visiting a patient in a hospital with two friends when the murder occurred. However, the police firmly believed that he was lying, and this alibi was quickly rejected, resulting in the wrongful conviction of the accused.[75]

It should be noted that the blind-sided logic of the police is not limited to China. Andrew Sanders has commented on a similar mindset of the police after the notorious *Confait* case was reported in England in the 1980s:[76]

> If the suspect were guilty and the alibi could not be disproved then the alibi had to be inapplicable. Unfortunately for the police, logic is double-edged and worked in the reverse direction in this instance: the alibi was applicable and the suspects were eventually exonerated.[77]

[73] In the publicly acknowledged wrongful conviction case, Nie Shubin was suspected of murdering the victim because of a rumour that a certain youngster riding a blue bicycle followed women in the village. Yuan Tong, 'Nie Shubin an danfu huanyuan lishi zhenxiang de zhongren (Heavy Responsibility of Restoring Historical Fact in Nie Shubin Case)', *Renminbao* (16 February 2015) www.renminbao.com/rmb/Arts/2015/2/16/60934.html (accessed 9 September 2016). Similarly, in the *Teng Xinshan* case, the police officer was certain that Teng was the murderer based purely on the fact that the police had overheard that Teng 'had a casual lifestyle' and was disliked by the locals. See He Jiahong, *Wangzhe guilai: xingshi sifa shida wuqu (Resurrection: Ten Pitfalls of Criminal Justice)* (Peking University Press, 2014) 39–43.

[74] Huang Shiyan, 'The Psychological Reason of Wrongful Convictions' (2014) 3 *Legal Studies* 26, 38.

[75] Liu Zhiming, 'Investigation of the Wrongful Conviction of 11/28 Yibin Sichuan Murder Case' (2005) 9 *Phoenix Weekly* 27.

[76] In the *Confait* case, the police were faced with a strong alibi given by the suspects at the time the victim was estimated to have died. Instead of realigning the investigation's direction, the police creatively stretched the possible period in which the victim could have died and invalidated the alibi. There is a similarity in the police mentality between the *Confait* case and those wrongfully convicted cases already mentioned.

[77] A Sanders, 'Constructing the Case for the Prosecution' (1987) 14 *Journal of Law and Society* 229, 231.

Clearly, the police are not as independent as they are portrayed in legal rhetoric. Despite the bureaucratic restrictions, the police have a great deal of discretion in selecting, rejecting and creating the fact, determining whether an incident should be treated as a crime, whether a certain suspect should be prosecuted and, if so, under what offence. To some extent, they have become involved in a determination of guilt or innocence at the outset of the investigation.[78]

III. Aligning Confession Evidence with the Official Version of the Truth

A. Background of Interrogations

Once the official version of facts has been formulated, the next step is to confirm the pre-established facts by procuring confessions in writing. As noted, there is no voluntary requirement of confession within Chinese law. Instead, suspects have a duty to answer police questioning truthfully according to the law.[79] In essence, this is an 'accused speaks' model – a process strikingly similar to the ancient Western criminal process, which pressurises the accused to speak and restricts her access to counsel and defence witnesses.[80] That said, CPL 2012 declares in contradiction that no one 'shall be forced to provide evidence proving his/her own guilt'.[81] Whether this is a symbolic gesture in passing or a sincere introduction of the privilege against self-incrimination is puzzling and has yet to be seen.[82] This paradoxical position of law was certainly not clarified after the official explanation of the legislative spokesman, whose diplomatic interpretation seemed more interested in disengaging from the debate than in clearing up the confusion.[83]

[78] Interview with a defence lawyer, JDL-1.

[79] See Art 120 of CPL 2018 (Art 118 of CPL 2012), which states that when interrogating a criminal suspect, the investigators shall first ask the criminal suspect whether or not he has committed any criminal act, and let him state the circumstances of his guilt or explain his innocence; then they may ask him questions. The criminal suspect shall answer the investigators' questions truthfully, but he shall have the right to refuse to answer any questions that are irrelevant to the case.

[80] JH Langbein, 'The Historical Origins of the Privilege against Self-Incrimination at Common Law' (1994) 92 *Michigan Law Review* 1047, 1048; JH Langbein, *Torture and the Law of Proof: Europe and England in the Ancien Regime* (University of Chicago Press, 1976) 5–8.

[81] CPL 2018, Art 52. This Article was initially introduced in the 2012 law reform (Art 50 of CPL 2012).

[82] Wan Yi, 'Lun "buqiangpo zizhengqizui" tiaokun de jieshi yu shiyong: xingshi susongfa jieshi de celv yu jishu (The Interpretation and Application of "No One Shall Be Forced to Provide Evidence against Herself": Strategy and Technique of the Construction of CPL)' (2012) 3 *Legal Forum* 31.

[83] The spokesman of the National People's Congress Legal Committee, Lang Sheng, stated that 'it is a consistent spirit of criminal justice that no one shall be compelled to prove his guilt, which is provided in criminal procedure law. To further curtail and prevent torture, CPL 2012/18 provides that no one shall be forced to prove his guilt. This is a rigid and hard requirement. With regard to the duty to answer truthfully, this is a different perspective. Criminal law provides that suspects should answer

This unsettling issue was completely ignored when the Criminal Procedure Law was amended in 2018. A good number of Chinese academics are willing to interpret this proclamation as the establishment of the right to silence[84] in the Chinese criminal process, celebrating the 'landmark for safeguarding the rights of the accused and human rights protection'.[85] The interpretation itself might be well-intended. However, it is hard to see how the right to silence can be truly exercised by the accused in criminal justice practice, where no supporting legal measures are in place and where there is an entrenched obligation for her to answer honestly during police questioning.

Police interrogation takes place in either detention centres[86] or police stations.[87] In both circumstances, the police have unmediated access to suspects and can question them at any stage of an investigation.[88] Police interrogations are understood as private situations, where the police have absolute 'ownership'. No third party is present. Suspects are not able to communicate or consult privately with solicitors. This enables the police to utilise a range of physical and psychological tactics in order to influence the decision-making of suspects. Following the interrogation venue layout regulation, interrogation rooms have officially become 'prohibited areas', under full command of interrogating officers.[89] All the interrogation rooms within police stations are required to be refurbished to be 'injury-proofed' and insulated from other parts of the station.[90] Video recording devices are installed in the interrogation room, although the efficacy of such recording should not

questions faithfully and he can be treated leniently. There are two very different angles and are not in conflict.' See Lang Sheng, 'It Is Not Contradictory between "no one shall be forced to prove his guilt" and "a duty to answer honestly"', *Renmin net* (8 March 2012) http://lianghui.people.com.cn/2012npc/GB/239293/17332481.html (accessed 16 March 2015).

[84] It should be noted that there is a nuanced difference between the right to silence and the privilege against self-incrimination. According to Lan H Dennis, the difference between the two concepts is that 'the privilege against self-incrimination deals with the questions of direct compulsion of an accused to provide evidence against himself, whereas the right to silence covers certain situations of indirect compulsion'. LH Dennis, *The Law of Evidence* (Sweet & Maxwell 2013) 151.

[85] See, eg Yang Yugui, 'Xingshisusongfa xiugai aoxian renquan baozhang: lun bude qiangpo zizheng youzui he feifa zhengju paichu tiaokuan (Human Rights Protection of CPL: The Provision of Illegally Obtained Evidence and the Privilege against Self-Discrimination)' (2012) 5 *Law Magazine* 19; Guo Jiancheng, 'Dui xinxiuding xingshi susongfa zhong chengmoquan wenti de yanjiu (Research on the Newly Added Issue of Right to Silence in CPL)' (2015)1 *Journal of Wuhan Public Security Cadre's College* 69; Wang Qi, 'Xinxingsufa xia guanyu chengmoquan zhidu de sikao (Thoughts about the Right to Silence in CPL 2012)' (2017) 6 *Legality Version* 224; Liu Boxian, 'Lun chenmoquan linian: jianlun dui woguo xingshisusongfa xiugai de qishi (On Right to Silence: Revelation to the Revision of Criminal Procedure Law in China)' (2013) 12 *Legal System and Society* 66.

[86] See Art 117 of CPL 2012 and Arts 122 and 124 of the Regulation on the Procedures of Handling Criminal Cases by the Public Security Bureau (No 127 of the Ministry of Public Security).

[87] CPL 2012, Arts 84 and 92.

[88] Wei Wu and TV Beken, 'Police Torture in China and its Causes: A Review of Literature' (2010) 43 *Australian & New Zealand Journal of Criminology* 557, 564.

[89] Ministry of Public Security, 'Regulation on the Law Enforcement Venue Layout by the Public Security Bureau' (2010) Reg No 56.

[90] For a discussion of this, see He Xiaojun, 'Xunwen changsuo jianshe ruogan wenti yanjiu (Research on Interrogation Venues)' (2015) 25 *Journal of Railway Police College* 22.

be overstated.[91] While the police have been used to working under surveillance ever since CPL 2012 introduced the devices, it by no means suggests that unlawful interrogation tactics have been effectively curbed. In practice, few video recordings have been conducted for the entirety of an interrogation since the law came into force.[92] Video recordings adduced as evidence have constantly been found to have been 'sanitised': tapes are tampered with and recorded interrogations are rehearsed and reproduced.[93] Such practices seem to have a limited contribution to prohibiting misconduct in police interrogations. Certain academics have suggested that, as long as the personnel in charge of video recording are recruited by the investigating authorities, at best the video recording drives illicit interrogation methods underground, making them less visible, and at worst, validates the confession-eliciting process, making illegally obtained evidence more difficult to exclude.[94] Thus, after a few years of implementation, unlawful interrogation methods were still found to be prevalent.[95] In order to tackle this problem, the Ministry of Public Security issued the Regulation Concerning the Public Security Authorities using Audio-Video Methods to Record Their Work in 2016, specifically requiring that recordings should be conducted from the very beginning to the very end of the criminal procedures.[96] It states that relevant organisations and individuals will be liable for clipping, editing, damaging or losing recordings, that the recording must be properly stored for a minimum of six months, and, if it constitutes criminal evidence, it should be stored indefinitely.[97] This regulation may have provided a promising solution to manage video recording practices. But whether it is implemented faithfully in policing or not is another matter, and is yet to be seen.

[91] CPL 2012, Art 121 (CPL 2018, Art 123). Currently, the synchronised video recording mainly applies to serious crimes, including crimes in which defendants might be sentenced to the death penalty or life imprisonment. According to the police reform agenda, the video recording during the police interrogation will gradually be applied to all criminal cases in China. See 'The Responsible Chief of the Ministry of Public Security of the People's Republic of China Answering the Journalist Interview', *Xinhua net* (15 February 2015) http://news.xinhuanet.com/legal/2015-02/15/c_1114379163.htm (accessed 10 February 2016). On the limited effect of video recording during police investigations, see Ma Jinghua and Zhang Liaohan, 'Xunwen Lunying lunxiang yu feifa zhengju paichu: yige shizheng de kaocha (Video-Recording and Exclusion of Illegally Obtained Evidence: An Empirical Research)' (2016) 7 *Southwest People University Review* 87.

[92] Ma Jinghua and Zhang Liaohan (ibid); Han Dongcheng and Gu Juan, 'Caipan wenshu zhong de tongbu lunying luxiang zhi gongneng yanjiu (Research on the Functions of the Video Recordings in the Judgments)' (2015) 30 *Journal of Shanghai University of Political Science and Law* 126, 128.

[93] Ma Jinghua, 'Feifa xunwen yu jiankongshi xunwen jizhi: yi gongan jiguan zhengcha xunwen wei zhongxin de kaocha (Unlawful Interrogation and Monitored Interrogation Mechanism: On the Basis of Police Interrogation)' (2015) 6 *Jurist* 116, 126. Ma Jinghua and Zhang Liaohan (ibid).

[94] Zhu Kuibin and DM Siegel, 'Electronic Recording of Custodial Interrogations with Chinese Characteristics: Tool for Transparency or Torture' (2015) 45 *Hong Kong Law Journal* 795. See also Chen Ruihua, 'Lun beigaoren kougong guize (On Defendants' Confessions)' (2012) 33 *Law Magazine* 46.

[95] Ma Jinghua (n 93) 117.

[96] Regulation Concerning the Public Security Authorities using Audio-Video Methods to Record their Work (gongan jiguan xianchang zhifa shiyin ping jilu gongzuo guiding), Gongtongzi No 14 (2016) Art 8(2).

[97] Ibid, Arts 13 and 19(2).

B. The Interrogation Record

Confession evidence in the form of the interrogation record is by far the most important evidence in the investigative case dossier. As the central piece of the dossier, its evidential and procedural purposes are not confined to solving a crime and securing a conviction. Police interrogations serve multifaceted objectives. The police may glean useful information during the interrogation to amplify what they already know, to clarify their suspicions or to gather information about matters on which they are ignorant.[98] Interrogations may produce information that leads to the finding of other evidence that incriminates a suspect, such as the discovery of a weapon. The traced evidence may buttress, in return, the veracity of the confession made.[99] Since the accused is seen as the repository of information, interrogations are also useful in updating police files and records, building the intelligence network, tracing stolen goods, etc.[100]

Amongst the 240 evidence dossiers (of 240 suspects) that I have reviewed, denials at the police station contribute to only 6.7 per cent (16) of the overall cases. This figure is roughly in line with the research undertaken by Liu Fangquan, subsequently by Mike McConville et al and Mou Jun, who have reported confession rates in the range from 88.4 per cent to 100 per cent.[101] The high confession rates are directly related to the final conviction of the accused. For many police officers, the police case is secured as soon as the suspect confesses.[102] Alongside that, there are two salient functions that confessions have in the Chinese criminal process. First, suspects' confessions, no matter whether they are a full or a partial admission of the alleged guilt, signal that the accused is prepared to give up the contested trial procedure and the case can be fast-tracked to court.[103] Secondly, confessions usually provide an overarching narrative from the perspective of the accused to explain other evidence in the dossier. Through a relatively detailed account guided by the investigator's questions, readers of the dossier can formulate a scenario of what happened and piece other scattered evidence together. The second function of confession works hand in hand with the corroboration rule, which lends confession evidence considerable weight. The confession evidence in the case dossier comprises multiple interrogation records in chronological order.[104] When a case

[98] M McConville and J Baldwin, *Courts, Prosecution and Conviction* (Clarendon Press, 1981) 142.
[99] GH Gudjonsson(n 69) 79.
[100] McConville and Baldwin (n 98) ch 8.
[101] Liu Fangquan, *Zhencha Chengxu Shizheng Yanjiu (Empirical Research on Investigations)* (China Procuratorate Press, 2007) 3–5. Mou Jun, 'Jiekai zhengcha xunwen gongneng de miansha: jiyu shizheng jiaodu de fenxi (Unveal the Function of Investigatory Interrogation: An Analysis from an Empirical Perspective)' (2013) 1 *Nanjing University Law Review* 200. See also McConville et al (n 7) 72–75.
[102] Field notes APU-14 and 18.
[103] They can be disposed of via the simplified procedure (*jianyi chengxu*) or the expedited process (*sucai chengxu*). This will be discussed in chs 5 and 6.
[104] Suspects' confessions are immediately placed following the report of how the suspect was arrested (*zuahuo jingguo*) and a notice of the rights and duties of the suspect (*quanli yiwu gaozhishu*), before other types of substantive evidence, such as witness statements and identification evidence.

dossier is assembled, the interrogation records are always placed at the forefront, potentially generating a guilty impression for those who read the dossier. Such prior belief, once established, will have a lasting effect in influencing the final decision-making,[105] and a person (such as a judge) who reads the case dossier may need less diagnostic evidence to decide the guilt of the accused.[106]

Adjudication as a decision-making process is explanation-based.[107] Both Bennett and Feldman and Pennington and Hastie, who studied jury trials in the USA have shown that the jurors tend to organise the evidence by building stories about what might have happened in the case.[108] In their view, stories are 'essentially networks of events which are causally linked and explain the observations in the case through abductive inference to the best explanation'.[109] Storytelling offers a structure that can accommodate the agent, the scene, and the acts involved in a particular setting that are introduced by evidence adduced at trial. In assessing consistency, completeness and plausibility of the connections drawn in the competing accounts, jurors make their verdict of the case based on which narrative best describes what happened.[110] In the context of China, where witnesses rarely testify at trial and judges rely on case dossiers to make decisions, the storytelling role is undertaken by interrogation records, which provide the most detailed accounts of the case. In this sense, interrogation records are not merely a type of evidence constituting the facts; they are constructed narratives in the voice of the accused, the content of which can be considerably malleable.[111]

As a type of standardised official document, interrogation records follow a set format. Interrogating officers are required to fill in some of the basic details at the beginning of the record, such as the duration and the location of the interrogation, and their names (including the name of the interrogators and the transcriber).

[105] B Schünemann, 'Experimentelle untersuchungen zur Reform der Hauptverhandlung in Strafsachen' in J Kerner et al (eds), *Deutsche Forschungen zur Kriminalitätsentstehung und Kriminalitätskontrolle* (Köln Heymanns, 1983) 1109–52.

[106] WA Wagenaar et al, *Anchored Narratives: The Psychology of Criminal Evidence* (St Martin's Press, 1993) 27.

[107] N Pennington and R Hastie, 'Explaining the Evidence: Tests of the Story Model for Juror Decision Making' (1992) 62 *Journal of Personality and Social Psychology* 189.

[108] WL Bennett and M S Feldman, Reconstructing Reality in the Courtroom (Quid Pro Books, 2014); Pennington and Hastie (ibid) 190; N Pennington and R Hastie, 'A Cognitive Theory of Juror Decision Making: The Story Model' (1991) 13 *Cardozo Law Review* 519. N Pennington and R Hastie, 'Reasoning in Explanation-Based Decision Making' (1993) 49 *Cognition* 123, 124; N Pennington and R Hastie, 'Juror Decision Making Models: The Generalisation Gap' (1981) 89 *Psychological Bulletin* 246; N Pennington and R Hastie, 'Evidence Evaluation in Complex Decision Making' (1986) 51 *Journal of Personality and Social Psychology* 242; N Pennington and R Hastie, 'Explanation-Based Decision Making: The Effects of Memory Structure on Judgement' (1988) 14 *Journal of Experimental Psychology: Learning, Memory and Cognition* 521.

[109] FJ Bex and B Verheij, 'Story Schemes for Argumentation about the Facts of a Crime' in *Computational Models of Narrative: Papers from the AAAI Fall Symposium* (2010) 6; Wagenaar et al (n 106); MS Pardo and RJ Allen, 'Judicial Proof and the Best Explanation' (2008) 27 *Law and Philosophy* 223; FJ Bex and D Walton, 'Burdens and Standards of Proof for Inference to the Best Explanation: Three Case Studies' (2012) 11 *Law, Probability and Risk* 113.

[110] A Amsterdam and J Bruner, *Minding the Law* (Harvard University Press, 2000) 111.

[111] On some occasions, the accused may confess in writing, but this is very rare in practice.

At the beginning of the police questioning, the suspect's rights during the interrogation are provided in a printed format. The layout of interrogation records appears to mirror the way the interrogation proceeds in the format of dialogue. But a closer examination suggests that these contemporaneous records kept during police interrogations do not always faithfully reflect the way the interrogations were carried out. One clear indication is that the majority of the recorded interrogations in site A claimed to have lasted for hours (usually between 45 minutes and 3 hours),[112] yet the interrogation records were usually in the range of 3–10 A4 pages (with the typed letter size of 14 pt). Reading out these written accounts slowly would take less than 15 minutes on average.[113] With no other source available to shed light on how the interrogation was conducted,[114] it is hard to explain the disparity between the length of these records and the extended duration time. If the duration time is accurate, these records – or at least some of them – were not taken verbatim, and certain exchanges between the interrogators and the suspect were apparently omitted. This suspicion was confirmed by a senior police officer who had worked for a number of police stations and criminal investigation squads. He divulged that the interrogation records were rarely noted down verbatim.

> We don't record the interrogation verbatim – we only write down the basic information, such as name, address, family relations and substantive stuff … In terms of substantive content, we will selectively write down the important factors, including who, when, where, what happened and what consequences have been caused, and anything that has legal implications, including statements with evidential value, or things that we can further look into to corroborate the confession.[115]

Meanwhile, the period of time that an interrogation has been claimed to have lasted might not always be accurate. On one occasion, a prosecutor returned a case dossier back to the police in site A as the interrogation record had a duration time lasting more than 12 hours, which is forbidden by law. When the case was resubmitted to the procuratorate, the content of the document remained intact but the time had been modified.[116] In another case (*CASEA* 30), the prosecutor discerned

[112] Art 119 of CPL 2018 stipulates that 'summons or compelled appearance in court shall not last longer than 12 hours. For complicated cases of grave circumstances where detention or arrest is necessary, summons or compelled appearance in court shall not last longer than 24 hours. A criminal suspect shall not be detained under the disguise of successive summons or compelled appearance. A criminal suspect shall be guaranteed with necessary food and rest when he/she is summonsed or compelled to appear before investigators.'

[113] This is consistent with the 2016 study of Zuo Weimin, who pointed out that many interrogation records were unusually brief while a normal police interrogation normally lasts over many hours. Zuo Weimin, 'Yizheng zhengming moshi de fansi yu chongsu: jiyu zhongguo xingshi cuoan de fansi (Rethink About and Reshape the Corroboration Rule: Based on the Rethink of Chinese Criminal Justice)' (2016) 1 *Legal Studies* 162, 167.

[114] Unfortunately, there was no video recording for most of the cases that I have viewed; of those cases for which there was a video recording, I was not given the opportunity to view the video recordings at site A.

[115] Interview HPO-1.

[116] Field note APU-13.

a discrepancy between the date on an interrogation record and the date declared by other suspects, who indicated the date of the interrogation in their confessions but who were supposed to have been arrested and interrogated on the same day. When asked why the dates did not match, the police officer explained:

> the main problem is if we write the time that we took them [the suspects] back to the police station, we would have violated the law. According to the law, we have to interrogate the suspects within 24 hours after they are detained. However, the first time I interrogated the other three suspects was three days after they were taken back to the police station. Therefore, if I use the time we took them back to the police station and confirmed their status, we have falsely imprisoned them for three days. So, I have to put the right date in the statement.[117]

Prosecutors and police were subject to the Appraisal System, and one of their mutual tasks was to maintain a high conviction rate.[118] This common interest has bound the two legal actors, who are allied to strengthen the persuasiveness of the evidence in the dossier and enhance the chances of conviction. From a researcher's perspective, such a police–prosecutor relationship provides an excellent opportunity to gain insight into the police work. In particular, police officers in site A frequently consulted prosecutors for legal advice, 'seeking to rectify some of the procedural issues which may run the risk of appearing unlawful'.[119] Hence, an experienced police officer informed me that critical elements in the statements, such as the duration of the interrogations, were usually left blank until the end of the investigation process to ensure that the details in the official record conformed to legal requirements.[120] This is consistent with other empirical evidence, revealing the tactics utilised by the police,[121] suggesting that the police are at liberty to select the information that is compatible with the requirements of law.

Pursuant to Article 122 of CPL 2018, the suspect is entitled to check the written records of interrogation before she signs. In an insulated interrogation environment with unequal powers, this right seems to be unguaranteed.[122] In fact, there is no authentication process to ascertain the reliability of official records; no rules or regulations are in place to ensure the credence of police recording; nor does any other validating mechanism exist to scrutinise the credibility of the official records. The absence of an authentication process is surprising, given that confession evidence plays such a decisive role in determining the fate of the suspect, yet no practical mechanism is available to safeguard the reliability of these critical statements.

[117] Field note APU-18.
[118] Li Enshen (n 38) 163; Zhu Tonghui (n 38); Bao Xianrong (n 38).
[119] Field notes APU-17, 18, 19 and 45.
[120] Field note APU-15.
[121] Liu Fangquan (n 101) 8 found that the time duration in the police's interrogation records might be falsified.
[122] It is a common phenomenon in Chinese criminal procedure law for there to be a lot of legal principles without corresponding legal sanctions or legal remedies, and this provision is one of them. There is no specific sanction provided by law to enforce its implementation.

Falsified information in the interrogation record is not restricted to the duration time. The credibility of the interrogation record is also compromised by the fact that some of its contents were collaborations between the police and the accused. In theory, the interrogation record should mirror the conversation between the police and the suspects. This appears to be reflected in the format of the record, which alternated between questions and answers. Reading the response of the accused gave an impression that the record was faithfully transcribed, as the statements were straightforward narratives. However, further scrutiny suggests that some of them were so implausible that they were clearly constructed in a joint effort between the police and the suspect. In a fraud case concerning multiple victims, for example, the suspect provided the names of 18 victims and their telephone and bank account numbers, and the names of 20 hotels where the fraud took place. The fraud activities occurred over a five-year period, with the record giving precise times and dates when the fraudulent transactions occurred.[123] It is doubtful that the suspect could have memorised all the details perfectly, especially the eighteen 16-digit bank card numbers and 11-digit telephone numbers. In a like manner, a suspect confessed to stealing 209 items from a shop. Surprisingly, he recalled all the reference numbers of the goods without a single mistake during the police interrogation.

An Excerpt of the Record of Interrogation (first time) for a Theft Case:

Police: What did you steal from the shop?

Suspect: I stole 49 items of clothing; their serial numbers are: KVI-34-P90, JRV-54-V20,

RKI-89-99 V, RSK-39K-90 K, REK-49-PE3, KVQ-90S-VI3, ISIP-39L-GIS, EKSE30-SLK, KO0-LD-3L8 … I also stole 59 pieces of jewellery; their serial numbers are: KOS-39S-SKJ, K39-SKI-SKP, QID-JI3-VIP, SIS-39K-SI3, DI9-3KS-S9 S, ISI-SI9-3SI, DI0-D83-SKI, LA9-S9D-3KD, IDK-3K9-S39 … I also stole 101 bags; their serial numbers are: IP0-SKI-SKE, KI3-ISS-90 S, SI9-SE9-SIV, SIS-DI8-S83 …

Police: Did you confess the truth?

Suspect: Yes, I did.[124]

In this case, when the suspect was interrogated for a second time, these large chunks of serial numbers appeared again in the exact sequence. It is hard to be convinced that these records truly reflect what actually happened in the interrogation. Apparently, interrogations like this were planned in advance, with the cooperation of the suspect. Sometimes, the accounts were constructed in such a way that they drew upon details of other evidence, such as identification of crime scenes and witness statements. When these interrogation records were assembled in the dossier and submitted to the court, they were treated as the accused's own unaided words objectively noted down by police officers.

[123] Field note APU-6.
[124] Field note APU-6.

My finding of the interrogation record is consistent with Yang Shiping's content analysis, in which she scrutinised the files of three bribery cases and found that the interrogation records followed the same model. The guilty facts in those cases were summarised at the very beginning of the confessions; there was a use of the same 'modular words', but no meaningful discussion between the interrogators and the suspects.[125] Unfortunately, the sample pool of only three cases was too small to make any valid generalisation.[126] Nevertheless, it strongly suggests that the interrogation records were purposely constructed, rather than being transcribed in a natural manner.

One strategy that was prevalently employed by the police to secure a case was repeating and emphasising the guilty facts. The prohibited act (the *actus reus*) and the forbidden state of mind (the *mens rea*) are basic building blocks of criminal cases. Therefore, once these elements were confessed, the police would make sure that they were duly consolidated by reproducing the suspect's narrative a number of times.[127] The case dossiers showed that a suspect was normally interrogated between 3 and 11 times, depending on the case.[128] In most instances, her later accounts were mainly repetitions of the statements she had made previously. There seems to be two purposes for repeating some of the statements. The first purpose is that, by repeating the facts, the *corpus delicti* is self-corroborated. Each and every interrogation record would be regarded as a separate confession that mutually supports the others. This logic leads to the second purpose of reinforcement, according to which a story is more likely to be true if it is repeated consistently a number of times. As a result, it makes it very difficult for the suspect to retract his confessions. Whilst it might be possible to prove that one or two pieces of confession evidence are obtained through unlawful means, it is much harder to prove that all of them have been done in the same way. Unfortunately, this may well be the case in reality. A potentially innocent individual who was coerced or manipulated to make a false confession may gradually accept the situation that an error has been made and it is useless to resist. Her assessment of the circumstances may lead her to yield and surrender to the reality that she is trapped and confessing repeatedly and consistently is the only logical choice for her.[129] The 'phenomenology of innocence' may also be a factor on occasions. This suggests that innocent individuals may be prone to confess as a gesture of compliance stemming from

[125] Yang Shiping, 'Xingshi xunwen bilu de yupian fenxi fangfa yanjiu (Research Methods of the Content Analysis of Criminal Interrogation Record)' (2013) 3 *Law and Economy* 110, 112.

[126] Yang's article (ibid) aims to use the three cases as an example to introduce content analysis.

[127] Interviews BDL-1 and CDL-1 and 3.

[128] Field note APU-34.

[129] RA Leo and RJ Ofshe, 'The Social Psychology of Police Interrogation: The Theory and Classification of True and False Confessions' (1997) 16 *Studies in Law, Politics and Society* 9; SM Kassin et al, 'Police-Induced Confession: Risk Factors and Recommendation' (2010) 34 *Law and Human Behavior* 3.

a belief in a just world, and with the expectation that they would eventually be exonerated.[130] This naivety could prompt them to make a false confession when under pressure. Although it might be true that the interrogations were actually conducted repeatedly without yielding any new information, some defence lawyers pointed out that the later interrogation records were simply fabricated by copying and pasting the suspect's previous statements. They noted that many such interrogation records contained the same errors and spelling mistakes that occurred in the earlier accounts:

> Defence lawyers: Many interrogation records are pre-typed before the interrogation. Since computers are widely used today, interrogation statements are worse than they used to be .... Now we see the same spelling mistakes and the same paragraph styles being repeated in different statements – they just use copy and paste! I read many of the suspect's statements in the dossier. In the final four statements, the spelling mistakes and paragraphs were exactly the same![131]

This is also reflected in my own observations. From all the prosecutorial interrogations that I witnessed, 17 suspects reported that some of the interrogations on the record did not take place.[132] Seven of them averred that some of the later statements in the dossier were regurgitations of their earlier interrogations, with certain details amended.[133] Such a practice seems to be widespread throughout China. Hao Yinzhong and Shi Da found that copying and pasting of suspects' early confession statements was one of the most frequently used reasons to apply for exclusion of illegally obtained evidence.[134] However, there is no generally agreed principle governing the exclusion of confession evidence that bears a high level of similarity. Courts have been left to interpret the law and regulations as they see fit. Over the years, the courts have come to divergent conclusions in terms of whether or not the confession evidence in question should be deemed as admissible. For example, Baoji Weibin District Court and Cangnan District Court declared that all the identical confession statements must be excluded on the grounds that they contravene the principle of the CPL and contain a risk of false confessions.[135] A judgment of Dingyuan District Court decided to exclude the interrogation record, which was 'clearly a product of copying and pasting', because it did not match the

[130] JT Perillo and SM Kassin, 'Inside Interrogation: The Lie, the Bluff and False Confessions' (2011) 35 *Law and Human Behavior* 327, 332; SM Kassin, 'On the Psychology of Confessions: Does Innocence Put Innocents at Risk?' (2005) 60 *American Psychologist* 215.

[131] Interview BDL-1.

[132] Field notes APU-30, 32 and 40.

[133] Field notes APU-40 and 41.

[134] Hao Yinzhong and Shi Da, 'Fayuan shiyong feifa zhengju paichu guize shizheng yanjiu: jiyu 587 feng caipan wenshu de fenxi (Empirical Research on the Application of Illegally Obtained Evidence: Analysis of 587 Judgments)' (2017) 1 *Guizhou Minzu University Review* 136, 140–41.

[135] Baoji weibin district People's Court Judgment (2014) Weibin xingchuzi No 00148; Cangnan District People's Court (2014) Cangwen xinchuzi No 650, http://wenshu.court.gov.cn/Index.

video recording of the interrogation.[136] Xuzhou Yunlong District Court decided that the exclusionary rule should only apply to the later interrogation records that have a high level of resemblance with the previous ones.[137] Fuzhou Intermediate Court questioned the reliability of these confession statements.[138] Despite these decisions to exclude (some of) the interrogation records, a greater number of courts have decided that identical statements or interrogation records that are likely to be manufactured by cutting and pasting should be accepted as lawful prosecution evidence, on the basis that these confessions were 'genuine presentations of the suspect's own will', fulfilling the requirements of law; their reliability 'cannot be denied', or there was no evidence to prove that 'cutting and pasting was actually employed'.[139]

Allegations of evidence fabrication were not limited to similar confession statements. In some instances, suspects reported that the police completely falsified confessions that had not been made by them.

> Suspect: I did not hide anything from the police but I know the police fabricated my statement. They told me 'don't worry, it is the same. Just sign your name on this paperwork and you can leave.' I glanced at the statement. It was not what I said. Then they told me to thumbprint it. They told me to admit that I had taken the bag with me. I did not. I couldn't admit to something I never did. Why on earth did they do that to me?[140]

In a case concerned with possession of drugs, the suspect alleged that she was forced to sign a statement which was entirely manufactured:

> The police officer said that they were going to have lunch and they wanted to finish it off. I expected to read the statement, but they told me that it was what I said and were reluctant to allow me to read. I read two pages and found the details were very different. They put a lot of new things in. They were anxious and just pressurised me to sign. Officer, the document is not what I said![141]

I was in no position to investigate the credibility of these allegations, but the number of complaints (17) and the similarity across these cases certainly cast doubt on the integrity of confession evidence. The confession statements assembled in the case dossier were not always consistent. There were a number of cases in which suspects gradually changed their mind and confessed to offences that were more serious, or they decided to make full admissions of guilt as time elapsed. However, despite the shift in position, the statements within the case dossier remained largely coherent.

[136] Dingyuan District People's Court (2017) Wan 1125 xinchu No. 138, http://wenshu.court.gov.cn/Index.

[137] Xuzhou yunlong district People's Court (2017) Su 0303 chu No 5, http://wenshu.court.gov.cn/Index.

[138] Fuzhou Intermediate People's Court (2014) Ronghang Zhongzi No 467, http://wenshu.court.gov.cn/Index.

[139] See Liu Jingkun, *Zhengju shencha guize yu fenxi fangfa: yuanli, guifan, shili* (*Criminal Evidence Examination and Analysis Rules: Norms, Regulations and Examples*) (China Law Press, 2018) ch 3. See also Hao Yinzhong and Shi Da (n 134) 140–41.

[140] Field note APU-30.

[141] Field note APU-14.

It was clear that efforts had been made to smooth out discrepancies between the different accounts. When addressing the changed statements, the police routinely asked the question: 'Why did you not confess this earlier?' The answer was invariably concerned with the suspect's reformed thoughts, such as 'I have now been reformed and decided to face my guilt' or 'I am now moved by my consciousness and have decided to repent'.[142] Such explanations flagged up that the suspect decided to disown her 'inaccurate confessions', emphasising the 'factual truth' that was confessed. Since the suspect's later confessions constituted the fruits of the police's labour, there was no surprise that they were relied upon to construct the police case.

> Police officer: Most of them (suspects) do not tell the truth initially. What they say during the course of the interrogation can be inconsistent.
>
> Researcher: For those suspects who have changed their account, which one would you rely on?
>
> Police officer: The last one. I would ask him why he did not tell the truth in the beginning. Then he would say that he had not given the matter his full consideration … If the suspect is put in the detention centre, he will feel dramatically different from when he is in the community. It is very stressful inside.[143]

According to the CPL, suspects are entitled to check the record of interrogation before they sign.[144] As a matter of practice, they had always been asked to sign their names and impose their thumbprints on every signature on each page. In addition, they were required to make a further declaration in writing at the end of the document, stating that they had read the entire content and agreed that it was a true reflection of what they said in the interrogation. These measures may have given the statements a trustworthy image, thereby enhancing their probative value. However, of those 64 cases that I closely monitored, nearly one-third of suspects (21) had complained to the prosecutors that some of their accounts had not been taken down verbatim. Twenty-seven of them (42 per cent) claimed that they were not given sufficient time to read the records before they signed; and 15 suspects (23 per cent) openly protested that their statements were distorted, exaggerated, manipulated, misinterpreted or completely falsified. These disputes over signatures resonate with the empirical research of McConville et al, who also found that suspects were 'invited' to sign confessions they disagreed with.[145] The following quotes from prosecutorial interrogations illustrated the controversy.

> *CASEA* 13: Possession of drugs
>
> Prosecutor: During police questioning, you said that you wanted to keep them [the drugs] for yourself because you had a quarrel with your ex-boyfriend who had these drugs.

[142] Field note APU-36.
[143] Interview EPO-1.
[144] CPL 2018, Art 122 (CPL 2012, Art 120).
[145] McConville et al (n 50) 340–42.

Suspect: No, it is not true. I did not say anything like that. It was made up by the policeman … I was only asked to sign.[146]

CASEA 6: Drug trafficking

Prosecutor: Did you sign the record?

Suspect: They did not let me read what they wrote. They forced me to sign my name.[147]

CASEA 9: Sheltering and introducing women to engage in prostitution

Suspect: I signed the statement, but I did not have a chance to read.

CASEA 10: Theft

Prosecutor: So you denied what you said in the police station?

Suspect: I did not. I never said anything like that before. I did not know what the police had written down. They only asked me to sign.

CASEA 12: Illegal trading of receipts

Prosecutor: You have changed what you said in front of the police.

Suspect: I had told the police but they did not put it down in the record.

Article 52 of CPL 2018 explicitly prohibits extraction of confessions through torture, threat, enticement, deceit or other unlawful means and compelling the accused to incriminate themselves. In line with this, Article 22 (4) of the Police Law states that the police are not allowed to torture suspects under any circumstances. In addition, a complicated corpus of legislative documents at different levels of authority has been arranged to combat torture,[148] especially after official notices on miscarriages of justice.[149] Despite these prohibitive measures and criminal consequences,[150] empirical research indicates that interrogational torture still prevails, and occurs regularly as an 'unwritten rule in law enforcement'.[151] Wu and Beken found that inflicting torture was a 'very common' practice in criminal interrogations, being witnessed by 95 per cent of students participating in internship programmes in the PSB and admitted by a majority of police officers (51.6 per cent).[152] Likewise, Wang Zheng's 2015 analysis of 145 police questionnaires[153] and Zheng Yun's 2016 analysis of 72 police questionnaires in a

[146] Field note APU-21.

[147] ibid.

[148] E Nesossi and S Trevaskes, *Procedural Justice and the Fair Trial in Contemporary Chinese Criminal Justice* (Brill, 2018) 46–67.

[149] See 'Establishment of a Sound Working Mechanism to Prevent Miscarriages of Justice in Criminal Opinions by the Supreme People's Court' in 2013.

[150] These sanctions include Art 247 of the Criminal Law, which provides that any judicial officer who extorts a confession from a criminal suspect or defendant by torture, or extorts testimony from a witness by violence, shall be sentenced to a fixed-term imprisonment of not more than three years or criminal detentions (a type of short-term imprisonment). CPL 2012, Art 54 provides that the illegally obtained evidence in criminal cases should be excluded. This will be discussed at length in ch 6.

[151] Zhou Fengting, 'Xingxunbigong de fansi yu duice (Reconsideration on Interrogational Torture and Countermeasures') (2006) 2 *Gansu Political and Law School Review* 116, 117.

[152] Wei Wu and Beken (n 88) 560.

[153] Wang Zheng's 2015 questionnaire survey of 145 police officers in criminal detective squads and police stations indicates that 44% of the police officers have conducted interrogation unlawfully since

Western region of China both indicate that almost half of police officers believe that torture is an effective investigative method 'to punish criminals', provided 'no serious consequence is caused'.[154] The fact that the practice of torture is still widespread marks the weakness of the law, which is declaratory in nature. In Nesossi's periodisation of contemporary China's battle against torture, she highlights the link between the official approaches in different eras and their relevance to the official discourse. Thus, under Jiang Zemin's leadership, torture was construed as antithetical to the 'Governing the Nation through the Law' agenda and should be banned; in Hu Jintao's time, torture and miscarriages of justice were unfitting to the harmonious society slogan. When it comes to Xi Jinping's leadership, 'the occurrence of torture could not be tolerated and the central Party should regain its strong hold on work of the courts'.[155] Of all these official narratives towards torture, a 'stable and ordered society controlled by the Communist Party' are the main focus, whereas the violation of the basic human rights of the accused has been absent.[156]

The police officers who were interviewed in this study talked optimistically that interrogational torture had diminished substantially in recent years. However, the notion of interrogational torture for extracting confession (*xingxun bigong*), as referred to by the police, may be narrowly interpreted. My encounter with suspects showed that although physical violence directly employed by the police was relatively limited (I found only four examples), psychological compulsion and various forms of coercion were quite often used when suspects were asked to sign the interrogation records. For example, 13 suspects stated that their signatures on the interrogation records were extorted by threatening the safety of their families.[157] As with other instances, these suspects reported that they were compelled to give certain answers desired by the police:

> Suspect: They [the police] threatened me and asked me to sign the statement. If I did not sign, my family would be in danger. I did this to protect my family.[158]

In light of the significant role that confession evidence plays in the Chinese criminal justice process, there is a strong incentive for a defendant to exclude the

2013, mostly due to workload pressures. See Wang Zheng, 'Zhengcha xunwen shishi zhuangkuang shizheng yanjiu (Empirical Study of the Implementation of Investigative Interrogation)' (2015) 24 *Journal of Henan Police College* 115, 120.

[154] In 2016, Zheng Yun analysed 72 questionnaires carried out in Maizhi district, Gansu province, and found that 14% of officers fully endorsed the use of torture as an effective interrogative method; 36.1% believed that torture is 'a feasible method, as it can punish crimes'; and 43.1% of them were in favour of using torture 'as long as no serious consequence occurred'. See Zheng Yun, 'Xin xingsufa beijingxia zhengcha xunwei shizheng yanjiu: yi gansusheng tianshuishi maizhequ wei zhongdian (Empirical Study of Interrogation Against the Background of the New Criminal Procedure Law: Focused on Maizhe District, Tianshui city, Gansu province)' (2016) 16 *Journal of Hebei Vocational College of Public Security Police* 27, 29.

[155] E Nesossi, 'The Politics of Torture and Miscarriages of Justice in Contemporary China' (2016) 11 *Journal of Comparative Law* 166, 183.

[156] ibid 184.

[157] Field note APU-22.

[158] Field note APU-47.

evidence in question if it is obtained by oppressive means. Unfortunately, the existing exclusionary rule on illegally obtained evidence is extremely vague, making its implementation difficult in practice.[159] For example, Article 56 of CPL 2018 (Article 54 of CPL 2012) states that 'confessions by a suspect extorted through torture and other illegal means should be excluded'. However, what amounts to 'torture and other illegal means' is far from clear. In practice, there have been disputes over whether 'slapping the suspect's face' or denying suspects access to medication, a toilet or clothing was sufficient to qualify as torture.[160] For cases in which torture was acknowledged, the law requires the defence to provide details on the alleged abuse before the matter can be investigated and the confession evidence in question considered. Given that the interrogation process is shielded from external scrutiny, gathering evidence to prove the unlawfulness of interrogational techniques is fraught with difficulties. During my observation in site A, no case was moved for exclusion of illegally obtained evidence, largely due to the lack of prima facie evidence to open an enquiry.[161]

Empirical research shows that there is an exceedingly high evidential threshold for triggering and surviving the exclusionary procedure in practice. As a result, cases in which the exclusionary rule was employed are few and far between.[162] These cases often featured 'solid evidence' (most importantly, a strong medical report) proving the link between the infliction of corporal punishment and the serious bodily harm suffered by the defendant. Currently, the burden to prove the source of illegally obtained evidence is on the prosecution. However, this burden of proof has often unwittingly been shifted to the defence, who was invariably expected to provide critical information on the names of the interrogators, when, where and how the torture took place, the disputed intended content, etc.[163] Empirical research has also suggested that even if a court held that the police had breached the exclusionary rule, there was no guarantee of an outcome in favour of the defendant. Take Ye and Wu's study of the criminal cases in S province, for example. Thirty-nine cases between January 2013 and July 2015 were

[159] Guo Zhiyuan, 'The First Step of the Long March: Implementing the Exclusionary Rule in China' (2017) 25 *Asia-Pacific Law Review* 48, 54.

[160] Guo Zhiyuan, 'Feifa zhengju paichu fanwei jieding de kunjing yu chulu (Plight and Way Out for Exclusionary Rule of Illegal Obtained Confessions and a Probe into Reform of Criminal Interrogation)' (2015) 6 *Evidential Science* 645, 648.

[161] The exclusionary procedure is similar to the *voir dire* hearing in adversarial systems, a trial process that takes place prior to the formal adjudication, where the judge will hear representations from prosecutors and defence lawyers on the admissibility of such evidence.

[162] Zhang Jian, 'Shenpai zhongxin gaige beijing xia feifa zhengju paichu guize de luoshi yu wanshan: jiyu 2013 nian lai 486 feng xingshi panjueshu de shizheng kaocha (Implementation and Perfection of Exclusionary Rule of Illegally Obtained Evidence against the Background of Trial Focused Reform: Empirical Research on 486 Judgments since 2013)' (2016) 5 *Journal of Xi'an Electronic and Technology University* 40, 41.

[163] Zhang Jian, 'Feifa zhengu paichu guize shishi Beijing xia de tingshen fangong wenti yanjiu: dui 2011 dao 2013 nian 655 qi anjian de shizheng kaocha (Research on Retracting Confessions in the Context of the Implementation of Exclusionary Rules)' (2015) 4 *Jinan Journal* 108, 110.

qualified to be heard by the court for the exclusion of illegally obtained evidence. Of those cases in which the confession evidence was excluded, none of them led to an acquittal.[164] This finding was confirmed by Xu and Fang's study and that of Zhang Jian.[165] Thus, on the one hand, the courts were overly cautious in applying the exclusionary rule. Confessions containing copying and pasting of the suspect's early statements, for instance, were often deemed insufficient to render the confessions inadmissible.[166] On the other hand, few judges were genuinely interested in holding an enquiry into alleged torture claims. Some cases in relation to interrogational torture were deliberately prolonged with no progress, creating undue stress for the defendant.[167] Trials involving illegally obtained evidence were constantly dealt with in a perfunctory manner.[168]

In 2017, the SPC, the Supreme People's Procuratorate, the Ministry of Public Security, the Ministry of State Security and the Ministry of Justice jointly issued a judicial interpretation, emphasising that illegally obtained evidence, especially confessions extracted through torture or threat, should be excluded.[169] Significantly, it has seemingly adopted voluntariness as the criterion to decide whether or not the evidence in question was lawfully obtained. Therefore, 'evidence that is against the person's will' is now to be regarded as gathered in an unlawful way and should be excluded. It also clarified that multiple consistent confessions are not admissible if one of them has been ascertained to have been gathered unlawfully.[170] Despite the salient progress in law, recent empirical research on the implementation of the exclusionary rules found that defence lawyers have little access to look into the way in which the disputed evidence was elicited and to collect evidence to prove their contention. The power to conduct the 'satellite investigation' is absolutely monopolised by the state officials.[171] Taking into account the intricate relationships between the criminal justice agencies, there is no surprise that the

[164] Ye Rui and Wu Qingguo, 'Feifa zhengju paichu guize shiyong wenti shizheng yanjiu: yi S sheng C shi wei yangban (Empirical Research on Exclusionary Rule of Illegally Obtained Evidence: Based on the Sample of S province and C city)' (2015) 6 *Journal of Railway Police College* 78, 79.

[165] According to their finding, in 2014, only 28 out of 17,526 cases were invoked with an exclusionary procedure, with just four of them being successful; in 2015, only 20 out of 17,518 cases were involved with an exclusionary procedure, five of which were successful; between January and June 2016, only 10 out of 9214 cases applied the exclusionary rule, and none of them were successful. See Xu Jianxing and Fang Binwei, 'Woguo xingshi feifa zhengju paichu guize sifa shijian shizheng yanjiu: yi W shi xingshi shengpan shiwu wei shijiao (Empirical Study of Judicial Practice in the Use of the Exclusionary Rule of Illegally Obtained Evidence)' (2016) 24 *Evidence Science* 682, 684. Zhang Jian (n 162) 41.

[166] Hao Yinzhong and Shi Da (n 134).

[167] Zhang Jian (n 162) 41.

[168] Guo Zhiyuan (n 159) 55.

[169] 'Provisions on Several Issues Regarding the Strict Exclusion of Illegal Evidence in Handling Criminal Cases', jointly issued by the Supreme People's Court, the Supreme People's Procuratorate, the Ministry of Public Security, the Ministry of State Security and the Ministry of Justice on 27 June 2017 www.spp.gov.cn/zdgz/201706/t20170627_194051.shtml (accessed 12 September 2019).

[170] ibid.

[171] Guo Zhiyuan, 'Torture and Exclusion of Evidence in China' (2019)1 *China Perspective* 45.

rules remain inadequate in terms of offering safeguards to the accused and having little impact on the outcome of a case.[172]

IV. Interviewing Witnesses

Surprisingly little is known about how witnesses are interviewed by the police during investigations. Chinese literature on witness interviews has almost exclusively focused upon 'good interview practices' drawn from Western experience, detailing what interviewers are supposed to do in order to extract useful information.[173] Occasionally, issues about police investigations have referred to generic matters, such as inappropriate attitudes towards witnesses and the poor selection of language during witness interviews.[174] But none of the studies provide valuable data to shed light on the way in which interviews have been conducted in day-to-day practice.

It should be noted that the law concerned with witnesses is rather ambivalent. Article 62 of CPL 2018 (Article 60 of CPL 2012) stipulates that all those who have information about a case have a duty to give testimony. Paradoxically, there seems to be no legal consequence if a witness breaches this obligation, and state officials (including the police, prosecutors and judges) are not allowed to compel a witness to testify if he or she refuses. The lack of compellability, however, does not mean coercive methods do not exist in the course of evidence acquisition. Quite the opposite, extracting testimony from witnesses by force (*baoli quzheng*) exists widely, and has been known as a perennial problem in investigations.[175]

[172] Guo Zhiyuan (n 159) 62; Human Rights Watch, 'Tiger Chairs and Cell Bosses: Police Torture of Criminal Suspects in China', *Human Rights Watch* (13 May 2015) www.hrw.org/report/2015/05/13/tiger-chairs-and-cell-bosses/police-torture-criminal-suspects-china (accessed 16 May 2016).

[173] See, eg Cai Guoqin, 'Zhencha Xuwen Zhengren de Jiben Celue (Basic Strategies of Interviewing Witnesses during Police Investigation)' (2007) 3 *Journal of Shandong Police College* 80; Yang Jiangang, 'Yifa xuwen zhenren, renzheng zhizuo bilu (Interviewing Witnesses According to the Law and Making Statements Carefully)' (2001) 2 *Journal of Liaoning Police Academy* 37; He Ting, 'Zhencha quzheng-zhong qiangzhi xunwen zhengren tanxi (Exploration of Compulsory Witness Interviews during the Investigation)' (2011) 3 *China Criminal Law Magazine* 77; Fang Bin, 'Lun zhencha xunwenzhong de jiaoliu jiqiao: yi zhengren he beihairen wei (Communicative Skills in Investigative Interviews: A Focus of Witnesses and Victims)' (2013) 1 *China Criminal Law Magazine* 75.

[174] See, eg Zhang Yaobing, 'Xunwen zhengren zhong de budang fangfa jiqi fangzhi (Inappropriate Ways to Interview Witnesses and Its Prevention (Inappropriate Ways to Interview Witnesses and Its Prevention)' (2006) 4 *Journal of Shanxi Police Academy* 75; Chen Guozhong, 'Shixi xunwen zhengren shibai de yuanyin (An Analysis of the Reason of the Failure Occurred during the Interview of Witnesses)' (2008) 1 *Compiled Documents of Science and Teaching* (*Kejiaowenhui*) 106; Un Mingtao and Tian Guoxing, 'Xunwen zhengren guifanhua zhi tanjiu (Exploration of the Way to Interview Witnesses)' (2007) 22 *Journal of Jiangsu Police Officer College* 53, 55.

[175] According to the Supreme People's Procuratorate, between 2015 and 2017 over 15,162 cases were dealt with in relation to extraction of confessions through torture and extracting testimony by force in 8,370 police stations in 10 provinces. The Supreme People's Procuratorate, 'Zhongdian jiandu gongan paichusuo xingxunbigong, baoli quzheng deng anjian (Focus on Cases in Relation to Extraction of Confessions Through Torture and Extracting Testimony By Force Occurred in Police Stations)',

Although Article 247(2) of the Criminal Law prohibits extracting testimony by force, as with interrogational torture, this offence is difficult to detect, given that investigations are insulated processes and the collegiality of the police would quite often thwart proper investigations into crimes that are committed by the police officers themselves.[176]

The public perception of the police has changed significantly in the course of societal transition. The long-term trust in police authority by the general public has gradually diminished and crumbled.[177] When asked about the obstacles in investigations, some police officers responded that it has become increasingly difficult to get witnesses to cooperate in recent years. Acknowledging the fact that witnesses were not compellable, most of them emphasised the importance of 'persuasion and education (*shuofu jiaoyu*)' in witness interviews:[178]

> Police: The problems of witnesses are more about social changes. It is different from the 1980s … (In the 1980s) when a policeman asked people for help, they would offer all the information they knew. In recent years, as the social problems in the underclass arise, people hate the rich and the state officials. They would naturally drive state officers into opposition. Under such circumstances, they do not cooperate with the police.[179]

Neither does the limited protection of witnesses make the investigating officer's job easier. Despite the safety measures and anonymity safeguards of witnesses,[180] fear of revenge is listed as the top concern that holds witnesses back from giving evidence to the police.[181] In practice, police sometimes assure witnesses of their safety when gathering evidence. However, their promises are not always honoured. One police officer recalled an event that exemplified the breach of trust:

> Police: A couple of years ago, one of our leaders went to review the testimony of an eyewitness. I went there with him. We found this witness and he said he would like to identify the suspect in person, but with the condition that his (the witness's) face would be covered. The leader then made a promise to him and said 'don't worry, we have the safeguard. You can see the suspect from the mirrored glass'. When it came to the time that the witness identified the suspect, the leader let them face to face directly without anything to obscure the witness's face. The leader asked the witness 'is he the right man'?

The Procuratorate Daily (30 March 2017) www.xinhuanet.com//legal/2017-03/30/c_1120727717.htm (accessed 22 May 2019).

[176] He Ting observes that the lack of regulation has led to the infringement of the basic right of witnesses as a form of police brutality: He Ting (n 173) 82.

[177] This is widely identified in the literature: Wu Yuning and IY Sun, 'Citizen Trust in Police: The Case of China' (2009) 12 *Police Quarterly* 170, 191; KC Wong, 'The Police Legitimacy Crisis and Police Law Reform in China: Part I' (2004) 6 *International Journal of Police Science & Management* 199, 218; KC Wong, 'The Police Legitimacy Crisis and Police Law Reform in China: Part II' (2005) 7 *International Journal of Police Science & Management* 1, 14; IY Sun et al, 'Social Capital, Political Participation, and Trust in the Police in Urban China' (2012) 45 *Australian & New Zealand Journal of Criminology* 87, 105; IY Sun et al, 'Procedural Justice, Legitimacy, and Public Cooperation with Police: Does Western Wisdom Hold in China?' (2017) 54 *Journal of Research in Crime and Delinquency* 454, 478.

[178] Field notes BPO-1, 2 and 3, DPO-1, EPO-1, FPO-1 and HPO-1.

[179] Interview DPO-1.

[180] CPL 2018, Arts 63 and 64 (CPL 2012, Arts 61 and 62).

[181] Field notes BPO-2 and 3, DPO-1, EPO-1, FPO-1 and HPO-1.

> The witness was under extreme stress. I thought he said 'yes' … I cannot remember what happened after that. I think this was really inappropriate. The witnesses' protection is highly problematic in China.[182]

With regard to witness protection, most police officers indicated that there were not enough police resources to carry out the task. Police officers who were interviewed complained that police stations were understaffed and they were constantly requested to perform a large amount of non-police work delegated by the local government.[183] In terms of providing witness protection, the only advice they offered was a verbal warning to the suspect – 'if the suspect dares to take revenge on the witness, he will be punished severely'.[184]

As noted previously, the victim's initial account plays a crucial role in constructing the official version. But the concept of the victim itself is a construction, and the labels of 'victim', 'witness' and 'perpetrator' are fluid and interpretable.[185] In reality, this usually hinges on who reported the offence to the police first. For example, *CASEA* 4 was concerned with a breach of public disorder (*xunxin zishi*). In that case, a drunk man who teased a girl in a night club had a fight with, and was wounded by, the girl's boyfriend. The drunk man was identified as the victim because his friend called the police. The girl's boyfriend, who was also injured, albeit less seriously, was arrested as a suspect. Here, the police's ascription of 'danger to society' was based on the simple judgement of who had requested support from the police in the first place:

> Police: We received the report from the man's friend. He was the complainant. He asked us to intervene. The (girl's) boyfriend should not attack the man. He could choose to leave. But he decided to fight. That's why everything went wrong.
>
> Researcher: But the man teased the girl and the boyfriend's protection was justifiable under that circumstance?
>
> Police: I understand. It is problematic that the drunk man was wrong at the very beginning. It would be different if the girl called us first … This might be different, even though the drunk man's injury was more serious.[186]

Despite the importance of the victim's or other witness's account in formulating the official version of truth, when a statement offered by a witness is inconsistent with the contemplated truth, especially without the corroboration of other evidence, the police have to engage in evidence evaluation, selecting and rejecting facts that were not in line with the official version:

> Police: This happens occasionally … If it is just minor discrepancies, it will be fine and we will keep it. But if the discrepancies are quite big, the statement will not be accepted.[187]

[182] Interview BPO-3.
[183] Interview BPO-2; see also Fu Hualing (n 27) 246; Mengyan Dai (n 19).
[184] Interview BPO-3.
[185] Similar findings can be found in police practices in England: M McConville, A Sanders and R Leng, *The Case for the Prosecution* (Routledge, 1991) 31–35.
[186] Field note APU -12.
[187] Interview BPO-1.

Such a mindset is in compliance with the corroboration rule, which requires the evidence in the case dossier to be consistent with one another. Therefore, when a witness's testimony is at odds with the aligned facts, the testimony might be automatically filtered out or adapted. This selection or modification is entirely at the discretion of the police. The notions of eligibility of witnesses, permissibility of evidence and probative value were mixed and applied in an arbitrary manner. For instance, when asked under what circumstances witnesses' statements would be likely to be disregarded, a police officer answered: 'Some witnesses may be biased. For example, the witness may be related to the suspect and if they give evidence in favour of the suspect, we would dismiss it.'[188]

As my conversation with the police officer went on, it became clear that testimonies that could potentially exculpate the suspect tended to be treated with suspicion. The police officer emphasised that when a witness's statement turned out to be in the suspect's favour, a line of enquiry in relation to the witness might be initiated to explore whether the witness in question was related to the suspect or had other interests involved in the given case. Such investigation was deemed necessary: 'if we don't know their relationship, we may treat the testimony as an objective statement, which could be disastrous', the officer explained. This remark conveyed the message that exculpatory testimony given by a witness was treated with extra caution. However, such suspicion did not seem to have extended to testimonies that might incriminate suspects. Some police officers implied that inculpatory testimony was likely to be 'neutral' and was credible. In order to obtain evidence that could prove the guilt of the accused, the police might sometimes even go the extra mile to encourage witnesses to place themselves in the victim's shoes:

> Police: There are several ways to persuade witnesses to give their testimonies. For example, we will try to seek the witnesses' sympathy by saying that 'the innocent victim has been robbed' or we can lecture him by saying 'it is a citizen's duty to give an objective testimony. If you were the victim, would you want the offender to escape punishment?'[189]

Clearly, prejudice against certain categories of witnesses, especially those who have given strong evidence in favour of the suspect, could easily be detected.[190] The suppression of exculpatory evidence has far-reaching consequences. Given that few witnesses are cross-examined at trial and defence lawyers are constrained to provide additional witnesses' testimony to challenge the prosecution case,[191] critical evidence that may shed light on what happened might never be traced again. With no effective mechanism in place to bring to the fore the pivotal evidence, the 'biased constructs' could very well lead to miscarriages of justice.

Some of the wrongfully convicted cases have unfortunately confirmed this concern. The quashed case of *Yang Yunzhong* is an example. In 1994, a fur worker,

[188] Interview BPO-3.
[189] Interview BPO-1.
[190] Interview HPO-1.
[191] This will be discussed in further detail later in this chapter.

Yang Wennai, was brutally murdered in a public toilet. Since Yang Wennai's wallet and valuable items were left intact, the investigation direction was aimed at 'romantic revenge'. After an enquiry about Yang Wennai's social life, Yang Yunzhong was quickly identified as the suspect because of his romantic relationship with Yan Wennai's potential girlfriend. Coincidentally, a blood stain was found on Yang Yunzhong's shoes. While Yang Wennai's friend, Zhang Jinjiang, explained to the police that the blood stain was caused by an affray that Yang Yunzhong had been involved in on a previous night, this testimony was dismissed by the police. To discredit this exculpatory evidence, the witness, Zhang Jinjiang, was later prosecuted and convicted for 'giving falsified evidence requested by Yang Yunzhong's parents for the purpose of concealing the guilt of the suspect' and was sentenced to 3 years' imprisonment.[192] Similar to many other wrongfully convicted cases, Yang Yunzhong's innocence only came to light when the real perpetrator confessed the murder in another unrelated criminal case.

In this case, when the police decided that Zhang Jinjiang's exculpatory evidence was unreliable and falsified, they did not challenge the testimony directly. They attacked the credibility of the witness by questioning the relationship between Zhang Jinjiang and Yang Yunzhong's parents instead. The testimony was disputed not because a positive relationship was found between the witness and the suspect's parents, but because it was believed to be the incentive of the making of a falsified testimony. The credibility of Zhang Jinjiang's testimony was questioned mainly because the testimony was exculpatory. The logic of the police, in this case, was simple: Yang Yunzhong was guilty, so Zhang Jinjiang's testimony, which contravened that belief, must be false. Such a mindset of the police is best captured in Lord Devlin's comment on miscarriages of justice in the UK, despite the different social context: 'the tendency of the police, once their mind is made up, [is] to treat as mistaken any evidence that contradicts the proof of guilt'.[193] In this sense, witness testimony, just like other evidence, is subject to evaluation and selection by the police.

V. Crime Scene Identification

The crime scene evidence contained in the case dossier is a piece of evidence that carries significant weight in China. It is a type of evidence of great controversy. Crime scene investigations may yield different types of evidence. As a general practice in Western countries, the initial responding officer may identify potential victims, witnesses and the suspect when they first arrive at the scene. In the USA and the UK, for example, investigating officers at the scene are under a duty to

[192] For the case details of *Yang Yunzhong*, see Liu Zhaofu, 'The Truth of the Murder in the Public Toilet', *People.com* (21 January 2002) www.people.com.cn/GB/shehui/44/20020121/652466.html (accessed 22 September 2016).

[193] P Devlin, *The Judge* (Oxford University Press, 1979) 73.

document the scene, identify the evidence, properly process and collect evidence, and prepare written reports and additional supporting materials. Collecting physical evidence (such as forensic searches and seizures) is an important part of the crime scene investigation. Other investigating activities, such as note-taking, sketching, taking photographs and writing reports, are also important in processing the scene. The cardinal principle to eliminate mistakes and minimise omissions in this investigation process is that the investigating officers must remain neutral. Crime scene investigators must deal with the evidence as what it is. They may have developed a disposition when entering the scene, especially if the crime that occurred provokes moral outrage, but professional investigators are expected to keep their emotions and biases under check and focus on the task at hand. This neutral principle of crime scene investigation is summarised well by MSgt Larry Spruill, who was a training officer in the USA: 'We do not work for the victim. We don't work for the suspect. We don't work for the chief of police. We don't work for the defence. We don't work for the prosecution. We work for the truth.'[194]

In China, crime scene investigations involve similar activities as those in Western countries, such as protecting the scene from contamination, and processing and securing physical evidence.[195] However, the actual physical evidence is rarely enclosed in the case dossier. The most frequently seen crime scene evidence assembled by the police in the dossier is a less sophisticated graphic document, known as the crime scene identification (*xianchang zhiren*). This is a type of evidence that indicates the location of the crime scene and the features therein.[196]

Although it is recognised as a type of real evidence by law,[197] the evidence format is unregulated, and how this evidence is produced seems to lack in guidance.[198] In site A, the crime scene identification evidence often comprised two photographs, in which the suspect was pointing to a location or an object (such as a building or a vehicle). At the bottom of the photographs was a brief note, indicating

[194] E Baxter, *Complete Crime Scene Investigation* (CRC Press, 2015) 8.

[195] Interview HPO-1. See also Ma Jianping, 'Xianchang kanyan jiancha guize chonggou: yi xingshi susongfa xiugai zhi guiding wei qierudian (Reconstruction of Crime Scene Inspection and Examination: From the Perspective of the Revision of Criminal Procedure Law)' (2012) 5 *Journal of Chinese People's Public Security University* 60; Pi Jianhua et al, 'Fanzui xianchang kanyan DNA wuzheng wuran de fangkong (Crime Scene Inspection and Prevention of DNA Contamination)' (2012) 3 *Journal of Chinese People's Public Security University* 21; Chen Gang, 'Jicheng gongan jiguan shixing "zhengkan heyi" gaige de lixing sikao (Rational Rethink of the Reform of Conflation of Investigation and Crime Scene Inspection in Basic Police Organ)' (2006) 6 *Journal of Chinese People's Public Security University* 94.

[196] Xiang Rong, 'Shilun xianchang zhireng yu "bude qiangpo zizhengqizui (On Crime Scene Identification and the Privilege against Self-Incrimination)' (2015) 24 *Journal of Guangxi Administrative Cadre Institute of Politics and Law* 95, 96; Cai Qiuming, 'Xiangchang zhiren gai hequhecong (The Future of Crime Scene Identification)' (2015) 5 *Legality Exhibition* 213.

[197] The most frequently seen crime scene evidence in the dossier is the crime scene identification record, which belongs to the evidential category of 'written records, inquests and examination, identification and investigative experiments'. See Art 48 of CPL 2012.

[198] Ma Lianlong, 'Xingshi xianchang zhiren bilu de zhengju shuxing jiqi guifan (The Nature of Crime Scene Identification and Its Legal Regulation)' (2017) 24 *The People's Procuratorate* 49; Li Ying, 'Xianchang zhiren bilu de zhengju shuxing ji shengcha panduan (The Nature and Examination of Crime Scene Identification)' (2017) 9 *Chuanbo yu banquan* (*Broadcast and Copy Right*) 180.

that the suspect was pointing at the crime scene. This was complemented by the name of the crime scene investigators and the date of making.[199] Ironically, the evidence itself contained very little information as to the actual crime scene in question. Although the photographs claimed to demonstrate the crime scene, quite often they bore little information as to where the place that was shot actually was or why the photographs were relevant to the material facts at issue. It was also unknown whether the photograph was free from distortion. Invariably, the photographs show that the suspect was pointing at a location, in close range, showing absolutely no concern of the crime scene contamination. But what does that mean? Does it suggest that the suspect assaulted the victim at that spot, or that the victim who was injured was later found there, for example? With very limited information in this cursorily made document, it seems that the so-called crime scene evidence is incapable of conveying unequivocal information. Unfortunately, the poor quality of this type of inculpatory evidence is regarded as essential for the prosecution case, which corroborates the confessions of the accused.[200]

As one of the standardised evidence documents in the dossier, the crime scene identification was routinely accepted by the court in site A. It also carried a significant weight that was almost impossible to challenge at trial.[201] For such a compelling piece of evidence, its formation was highly problematic. The way the evidence was produced appears to be artificial and arbitrary. It was usually a by-product of the confessions deriving from the police interrogation.[202] Chen Hongbin and Zhao Wei observed that capturing the suspect's gesture of identifying a specific direction is a staged official confession.[203] This was confirmed by a defence lawyer who was a former police officer. He revealed that the way the crime scene evidence was constructed should be a subject of serious concern:

> The policeman who has made the record of the crime scene identification or the policeman who maintained the suspects' identification record rarely goes to the court to testify. For the crime scene identification, it is a bit … [worrisome]. A police officer would take the suspect to a nominated place and take a photograph of him. That is the so-called identification evidence. Actually, the suspect has not identified anything at all. The suspect might not even know where the crime scene was and then the police told him where it was. For some migratory offenders, they are not familiar with a place as big as [site C]. They had no idea where the crime scene in the dossier was.[204]

[199] Field note APU-14.

[200] Yang Wenge, 'Minan zhengcha zhong de "xianqi poan" yu "xianchang zhiren" (The Deadline of Cracking Criminal Cases and the Crime Scene Identification in Murder Investigations) (2018) 26 *Journal of Shanxi Police College* 12, 16; Wu Changqing, 'Xianchang zhiren jiqi lifa guizhi (The Crime Scene Identification and Its Statutory Regulation)' (2011) 1 *Theoretical Exploration* 128.

[201] Guo Taiping, 'Xingshi xianchang zhiren bilu de bianhu celv (Defence Strategy of the Crime Scene Identification)' (2010) 10 *Chinese Lawyers* 54; Xiang Rong (n 196).

[202] See Art 48 of CPL 2012.

[203] In order to strengthen its probative value, the suspect was sometimes 'dressed up', with handcuffs and scars on her face and body. Chen Hongbin and Zhao Wei, 'Xianchang zhiren zhaoxiang hefaxing zhiyi (Questioning the Legitimacy of the Photography of the Crime Scene Identification)' (2003) 4 *Journal of Guangxi Public Security Management Cadres Institute* 13.

[204] Interview CDL-1.

As a type of photographed confession evidence, the identification of the crime scene also lacks some of the crucial information in relation to the evidence construction, such as whether the suspect was present voluntarily, under what circumstances the photograph was taken and whether the photographs contain prejudice against the defendant. The opacity of the photograph-making process clearly allows the occurrence of malpractice, which can potentially lead to miscarriages of justice. An example of this is the crime scene evidence in *She Xianglin*. In that case, She Xianglin was led, under the instruction of the police, to a location that the officers told She Xianglin was where the murder had taken place.[205] The crime scene identification evidence was then manufactured against the victim of the miscarriage of justice. Likewise, the crime scene identification in *Wang Shuhong* was found to be directed by the investigator in the same fashion.[206] In another quashed murder convictions of Qin Junhu and Lan Yongkun, the investigator refused to record the crime scene pointed out by Qin Junhu, as the investigating officer found that the identification was inconsistent with other evidence in the dossier.[207] Cai Qiuming noted that there has been a collaboration between the police and the accused in the creation of crime scene identifications in general. In such a cooperation, the accused is an actor who is instructed by the play script provided by the police.[208]

Apart from the crime scene identification, other types of 'objective evidence' are seldom seen in the investigative dossier. Tangible evidence that carries considerable weight in proving the facts at issue is not compiled in the dossier or adduced in court. The common practice is to capture the real evidence as a photograph and attach that to the evidence dossier (with a short note stating when and where the photo was taken). Once all the evidence of the investigation has been reduced into a processed written form, the original real evidence is no longer needed, so is permanently left in a vault within the police office building.[209]

VI. The Defence Predicament in the Investigative Phase

What defence lawyers can do at the investigation stage is limited.[210] Pursuant to Articles 38 and 39 of CPL 2018, the defence lawyer is allowed to have meetings

[205] Guo Taiping (n 201).

[206] Wang Shuhong was investigated for and confessed to the murder of a sex worker, Zhu Yongqiong, in 2002. It was decided not to prosecute the case because of inconsistency of evidence. It was also reported that torture and misleading questions had been used during the interrogations. See 'Yunnan nongmin xingxun bigong yuanan zhaoxue zuigaojian biaozhang zhuananzu (The Torture of Yunnan Peasant Came to Light, the Supreme People's Procuratorate Praised the Special Investigative Team for Hardwork)', *Sina* (27 August 2008) http://news.sina.com.cn/s/p/2005-08-27/00087605015.shtml (accessed 4 July 2018).

[207] Cai Qiuming (n 196).

[208] ibid.

[209] Interviews FPO-1 and BPO-1.

[210] CPL 2012, Art 33 provides that a suspect is entitled to entrust a defender after she is interrogated for the first time or as of the date on which compulsive measures are taken.

and correspondence with suspects who are under detention; she can provide the suspect with legal advice, file petitions and complaints on the suspect's behalf, apply for alteration of the compulsory measures, find out from the investigating institution the offence of which the criminal suspect is accused and offer her opinions; she may also collect information from witnesses and request the court to inform the witnesses to appear in court and give testimony. Despite these services, the law makes it abundantly clear that legal advice prior to and at the interrogation stage from the defence lawyer is not permissible, even though this is the phase in which suspects are at their most vulnerable.[211] It is true that the police–suspect interaction in interrogations could very well be encumbered by the presence of any third party, particularly a defence lawyer. This nevertheless suggests that the interests of the accused, who may be inarticulate, illiterate, suffering from a mental disease or in a particular disadvantaged position, and therefore unable to comprehend the full implications of the investigative activities, are secondary to the grand objective of seeking the truth. The police have absolute control over the accused at this critical stage. Given the secrecy of interrogation and the structural features of power associated with it, this process without participation of defence lawyers remains a matter of concern.

A highlight of CPL 2018 is the introduction of the duty lawyer scheme, which enables suspects to access legal services pro bono. The permitted legal services include legal consultation, offering advice on procedural options or assisting the suspect to apply for alternative compulsory measures.[212] It should be acknowledged that writing the scheme into the law itself can be celebrated as a major breakthrough and the first step of building up a more effective defence mechanism in the pretrial phase. Nevertheless, the role of duty lawyers and the scope of legal services provided by the scheme at this time cannot be overstated. Problematically, it remains unclear whether a duty lawyer can act as defence counsel to suspects at a later stage of the criminal proceedings.[213] This issue largely lies in the wording of CPL 2018, which has not clarified the role of duty lawyers. In particular, the scope of legal services enumerated in Article 36, deliberately or inadvertently, does not entirely encompass the legally recognised defence rights. As a result, it is debatable whether the duty lawyer has the right to access case dossiers or the right to visit suspects in the detention centre.[214]

[211] M McConville et al, *Standing Accused: The Organisation and Practices of Criminal Defence Lawyers in Britain* (Oxford University Press, 2003) ch 4.

[212] To facilitate the services, the duty lawyers are based in detention centres and procuratorate buildings. See Art 36 of CPL 2018.

[213] Han Xue, '2018 nian xingsufa zhong renzui renfa congkuan zhidu (The Guilty Plea Procedure in CPL 2018)' (2019) 1 *Rule of Law Research* 35; Lian Yizhi, 'Xinxingshi susongfa xia dui zhiban lvshi zhidu de tanxi (Exploring the Duty Lawyer Scheme under the New Criminal Procedure Law)' (2019) 3 *Legal Exhibition* 194.

[214] Bian Jianlin, 'xingshisusongfa zaixiugai mianmian guan (All Perspectives of the Revision of Criminal Procedure Law)' (2019) 1 *Rule of Law Research* 3; Song Lihong, 'Zhiban lvshi zhidu yunxing de fumian xingtai ji duice (The Negativity and Solution to the Operation of the Duty Lawyer Scheme)' (2019) 4 *Legal Exhibition* 5.

On another negative note, empirical research based on the pilot scheme project has criticised the scheme as being more of a symbolic gesture than meaningful safeguards for suspects. Lu Xu and Xu Rui, for example, found that the limited operational funding in the duty lawyer scheme did not attract experienced defence lawyers.[215] Many of the lawyers who joined the scheme were young and not specialised in criminal defence law.[216] As a result, the quality of service that was provided was far from satisfactory.[217] Han Xue also noted that duty lawyers may be susceptible to role confusion. Considering that duty lawyers are based in detention centres and procuratorate buildings, their long-term relationships with the state officials causes their position to shift and they become an ally of the police and the prosecution, rather than the legal actor who challenges their case robustly.[218] To some extent, these issues identified in the empirical studies appear to be similar to the problems found in the duty solicitor scheme in England and Wales.[219] Since the duty lawyer scheme itself is a legal transplant, this is not surprising. Despite the inadequacies and concerns, it is worth noting that the scheme is still in its infancy and may yet develop over time. In this regard, its operation and the impact it may have on the criminal justice system as a whole remain to be seen.

It has almost become a consensus that defence lawyers have little room to manoeuvre in effectively advising their clients and constructing a defence case parallel to the police investigation.[220] Whereas the defence rights (such as meeting with suspects and collecting defence evidence) are prescribed in law, exercising these rights is a completely different story – one which is fraught with obstacles and hazards. Defence lawyers face marginalisation and discrimination generated by the criminal justice institutions in general.[221] The institutional bias against defence lawyers may not, however, be unique to the Chinese criminal justice system. Notably, French defence lawyers have been known as outsiders of their criminal justice system, distanced by the key figures of *magistrats* (ie judges

[215] Lu Xu and Xu Rui, 'Renzui renfa congkuan shiyu xia zhiban lvshi zhidu de wanshan (Perfection of the Duty Lawyer Scheme in the Context of Guilty Plea Procedures)' (2019) 36 *Journal of Political Science and Law* 92.

[216] Sheng Haojie, 'Xingshi susongfa zhong zhiban lvshi zhidu eryuan jiazhi fenxi (Binary Analysis of the Duty Lawyer Scheme in the Criminal Procedure Law)' (2019) 31 *Journal of Hunan Police Academy* 66.

[217] See also Zhu Yuling and Li Ning, 'Xingshi falv yanzhu zhiban lvshi gongzuo zhize tanxi (Exploring the Role of Criminal Law Duty Lawyer Scheme)' (2019) 32 *Journal of Shanxi Politics and Law Institute for Administrators* 62; Wang Yichao and Tu Longke, 'Zhiban lvshi tigong youxiao falv bangzhi de fali dingwei yu zhidu goujian (Jurisprudence and Institution Construction of Duty Lawyer Scheme That Can Provide Effective Legal Service)' (2009) 2 *Rule of Law Society* 40.

[218] Han Xue (n 213).

[219] M McConville et al, *Standing Accused* (Clarendon Press, 1994); D Newman, *Legal Aid Lawyers and the Quest for Justice* (Bloomsbury Publishing, 2013).

[220] E Nesossi and S Trevaskes, 'Procedural Justice and the Fair Trial in Contemporary Chinese Criminal Justice' (2017) 2 *Brill Research Perspectives in Governance and Public Policy in China* 56.

[221] Hou Shumei and R Keith, 'The Defence Lawyer in the Scales of Chinese Criminal Justice' (2011) 20(70) *Journal of Contemporary China* 379.

and *procureurs*).[222] But the consequences that defence lawyers in China might face in just fulfilling their role of defending their clients are beyond the comprehension of their peers in other jurisdictions. Sida Liu and Terence Halliday describe the defence activities undertaken by defence lawyers as working 'in a minefield filled with trenches and bombs, sometimes with their hands cuffed'.[223] The antagonistic relationship between the police and defence lawyers has cost the career and liberty of many defence lawyers, making criminal defence a high-risk profession.

Grave misgivings about defence lawyers' safety have emanated from Article 306 (perjury offence committed by the defence counsel) of the Criminal Law 1997,[224] which have been frequently utilised by police and prosecutors alike to silence and subjugate active defence lawyers. Known as 'the big stick 306' or a 'sword of Damocles' within the defence community, this article has often been referenced in the intimidation, detention and prosecution of defence lawyers for allegedly committing this crime in relation to their defence preparation.[225] It puts defence lawyers in severe professional jeopardy when they are merely engaged in good defence preparation, such as verifying witness testimonies or proactively gathering

[222] For example, the role of defence lawyer is often depicted as being associated with corruption in France, undermining the integrity of the criminal process. In Jacqueline Hodgson's 2009 study, when responding to the proposal that lawyers gain access to their clients at the start of police detention, a police officer stated 'a lawyer lives from his clients and in the past, we often observed that the deontology of the lawyer comes after his own interests and those of his client. [There would be a] risk of accomplices fleeing of searches rendered unless after friends had been informed.' This quote does not make sense: see J Hodgson, 'Human rights and French Criminal Justice: opening the door to the pre-trial defence rights' (2009) Warwick SSRN Working Paper No 20. Similarly, suspicion and mistrust of defence lawyers still linger with the police force in the Netherlands: see T Spronken, *An EU-Wide Letter of Rights* (Intersentia, 2010) 136. In adversarial systems, such as that of England and Wales, it has taken a long period of time to establish trust between the police and the defence lawyers. Suspicion of defence lawyers in the police force had lingered in England and Wales for a long time, and the trust was only established over the last two decades. For example, in the 1970s, the Commissioner of the Metropolitan police said: 'A reputation for success, achieved by persistent lack of scruple in the defence of the most disreputable, soon attracts other clients who see little hope of acquittal in any other way. Experienced and respected metropolitan detectives can identify lawyers in criminal practice who are more harmful to society than the clients they represent.' See M McConville and J Hodgson, *The Royal Commission on Criminal Justice: Custodial Legal Advice and the Right to Silence* (HMSO, 1993) 155.

[223] Sida Liu and T Halliday, *Criminal Defence in China: The Politics of Lawyers at Work* (Cambridge University Press, 2016) 64; Sida Liu and T Halliday, 'Dancing Handcuffed in the Minefield: Survival Strategies of Defence Lawyers in China's Criminal Justice System' (2008) May *SSRN Electronic Journal* 34, http://ssrn.com/abstract=1269536.

[224] The Criminal Law 1997, Art 306 stipulates, 'if in criminal proceedings, a defender or agent *ad litem* destroys or forges evidence, helps any of the parties destroy or forge evidence, or coerces the witness or entices him into changing his testimony in defiance of the facts or give false testimony, he shall be sentenced to fixed-term imprisonment of not more than three years or criminal detention; if the circumstances are serious, he shall be sentenced to fixed-term imprisonment of not less than three years but not more than seven years.'

[225] FL Cooke et al, 'Who Are "Managing" the Lawyers in China? Control and Commitment in an Evolving Institutional and Cultural Context and Gendered Implications' (2013) 24 *The International Journal of Human Resource Management* 3418, 3423. See also Sida Liu and Halliday, *Criminal Defence in China* (n 223) 44–45; McConville et al (n 7) 181–84; Sida Liu and Halliday, 'Dancing Handcuffed' (n 223). Hou Shumei and Keith (n 221).

evidence at the investigation stage.[226] It is suspected that more than 500 defence lawyers were incriminated due to the (abusive use) abuse of Article 306 in practice between 1997 and 2005, the majority of whom were found innocent.[227] The estimation suggests that 80 per cent of the application of the law involved retaliatory investigation, as the PSB and the procuratorate that dealt with the perjury offence relating to the defence lawyer were the same ones that were responsible for investigating and prosecuting the case that the defence lawyer was defending.[228] This retaliatory persecution clearly has a chilling effect on prospective legal professionals who are enthusiastic about defending the rights of the accused. According to the survey of defence lawyers conducted by the Beijing Shangquan Law Firm in 2013 (hereinafter referred to as the Shangquan survey), only 11.9 per cent of junior lawyers (who had practised law less than 2 years) chose to practise criminal law due to the danger they would face.[229]

In order to conciliate the antagonism between the defence lawyer and the criminal justice institutions, particularly after the high-profile *Li Zhuang* case in 2009,[230] the revised CPL 2012 provided that the PSB who investigates the offence that the defence lawyer who is suspected of committing perjury is defending should not work in the perjury case of that defence lawyer.[231] In this aspect, the tooth of 'the big stick 306' has been blunted in tackling professional retribution.[232] However,

[226] See Ping Yu, 'Glittery Promise vs. Dismal Reality: The Role of a Criminal Lawyer in the People's Republic of China after the 1996 Revision of the Criminal Procedure Law' (2002) 35 *Vanderbilt Journal of Transnational Law* 827, 852.

[227] The All China Lawyers Association reported 18, 30 and 31 cases in 1999, 2000 and 2001, respectively, and 22 between 2002 and 2004. Individual lawyers, however, have given a much higher estimate. For example, leading lawyers such as Tian Wenchang and Mo Shaoping have indicated that as many as 500 lawyers may have been punished for doing their work between 1997 and 2005, while others have reported as many as 100 cases per year. Although lawyers are prosecuted for a variety of criminal offences, falsification of evidence under Art 306 had the highest percentage of prosecutions from 1999 to 2001 (14/29, 48%). The trend continued. Of the 22 cases from 2002 to 2004, 10 were falsification of evidence charges. It is commonly asserted that about 80% of the cases related to Art 306 offences. See Fu Hualing, 'When Lawyers Are Prosecuted: The Struggle of a Profession in Transition' (2007) Social Science Research Network, http://papers.ssrn.com/sol13/papers.cfm?abstract_id=956500, 3–4.

[228] ibid.

[229] See Beijing Shangquan Law Firm, 'The Annual Report of the Implementation Effect of the New Criminal Procedure Law 2013' (2014) www.sqxb.cn/content/details16_1644.html (accessed 9 March 2014).

[230] Li Zhuang is a Beijing lawyer who acted as a defence lawyer for one of the alleged leaders of organised crime in Chongqing, Gong Gangmo. Gong Gangmo faced serious accusations of murder, illegal weapons trade, drug dealing and heading a criminal organisation, and his prosecution was one of the key cases in Chongqing's anti-crime campaign. Having attempted to prepare a defence case based upon the torture that Gong Gangmo had suffered during police detention, Li Zhuang was subsequently prosecuted. During the trial, it was believed that Gong Gangmo was forced to allege that Li Zhuang had advised him to withdraw prosecution evidence, which eventually led to the charging and conviction of Li Zhuang for fabricating evidence and obstructing defence evidence. Li Zhuang was sentenced to 18 months' imprisonment. The *Li Zhuang* case is believed to be the direct reason for adding Art 42 to CPL 2012. See Sida Liu et al, 'The Trial of Li Zhuang: Chinese Lawyers' Collective Action against Populism' (2014) 1 *Asian Journal of Law and Society* 79. Sida Liu and Halliday, *Criminal Defence in China* (n 223) ch 6. Li Enshen (n 38) 134–38.

[231] See Art 42 of CPL 2012 (Art 44 of CPL 2018).

[232] See also Sida Liu and Halliday, *Criminal Defence in China* (n 223) 60.

the majority of defence lawyers remain sceptical and are not convinced that such a solution could effectively address the problem.[233] They believe that the PSB from another district would still take the retaliatory action against them, due to the influence of the procuratorate and the highly bureaucratic police system, by which the leader of the PSB determines the direction of the investigation.[234] Indeed, such a premonition was later confirmed in a number of Article 306 cases after CPL 2012 came into force. According to the Shangquan survey, defence lawyers continued to be targeted by employing 'the big stick 306' regardless of the law.[235]

Many defence lawyers therefore remain deeply concerned about the risk and difficulties they have to face as far as Article 306 is concerned. Perhaps even worse is that those enhanced defence rights in CPL 2012 and CPL 2018 could become latent pitfalls, luring defence lawyers into an ambush. This problem is particularly salient as the law is gradually expanding the scope of defence lawyers' interventions at various stages of the process. This has increased the frictions between defence lawyers and the legal institutions. One instance concerns the monitoring of meetings between the suspect and their defence lawyers. Although the law states that defence lawyers' meetings with their clients should not be monitored,[236] many defence lawyers are advised not to divulge any defence strategies during the meetings, as the confidentiality of the meeting might not be guaranteed.

> Defence Lawyer 1: There is another risk with meeting the suspect. When we meet the suspect, the conversation could be bugged. Even though it is said that the meeting should not be heard or recorded, as an experienced lawyer, I deeply doubt that this is the case. I believe that the police would record the conversation.
>
> Defence Lawyer 2: In the detention centre in the rural site, video was installed in every room, including the meeting room.
>
> Defence Lawyer 1: What really concerns us is when the conversation is recorded and the police have heard me asking the suspect to change his statement; then we will be in big trouble. Even if they would not produce the recording as evidence, they could force the suspect to confess to what we have talked about in the meeting room. Once the defendant has told the police what we discussed in the meeting room, his statement will become evidence against us. Another concern of the recorded conversation might be if any detailed information is involved in our conversation which is not yet known by the police during the course of the investigation. The police could then follow up this

[233] According to the defence lawyers' annual survey, 24.5% of defence lawyers (78 defence lawyers) believed that the new law could ease the professional retaliation; however, 240 defence lawyers believed that the retaliatory prosecution was still unresolved because of the bureaucratic police system. Beijing Shangquan Law Firm (n 229).

[234] ibid.

[235] For example, in 2013, defence lawyer Zhang Mengshi was suspected of committing perjury for his client in Zhuzhou city, Hunan province. The PSB, which investigated the case represented by Zhang Mengshi, was also the police force in charge of Zhang Mengshi's perjury case. In court, Zhang Mengshi launched a move to challenge the qualification of the police. However, the court dismissed Zhang Mengshi's challenge, disregarding the law. See Beijing Shangquan Law Firm (n 229).

[236] CPL 2018, Art 39.

> information and find out more evidence that may be detrimental to our client. That's why I always advise young lawyers not to discuss much the details of the case even if we are given enough time to meet with the suspect, otherwise, the suspect could be in greater trouble.[237]

These concerns expressed by the defence lawyers are certainly not unfounded. The degree of law compliance varies from region to region, and is often contingent on the sensitivity of the case in question. In site A, an officer would routinely be seen during defence lawyer–suspect meetings in the year of 2013.[238] Although openly violating the law has become less frequent, flouting the law is common if the cases involved are influential, serious or sensitive.

> Defence lawyer: There have not been many cases in which the policeman has asked to be present in our meeting nowadays. Since the Lawyers' Law has been promulgated, the police have been starting to adjust their practice to the new law … For some sensitive and serious crimes, the police will still ask someone to be present in our meeting. So far, I haven't dealt with such cases. My colleagues have told me that the police sent someone to listen to the conversation for serious drug trafficking cases and serious bribery cases.[239]

The relationship between the legal institutions and the defence lawyer since 2013 are observed to be more intensified than ever.[240] A number of defence lawyers reported that criminal justice institutions (particularly the PSB and the procuratorate) had pressured the suspect or her family into revoking the defence contract, thus ensuring that certain devoted defence lawyers are excluded from criminal practice.[241] A good proportion of suspects and their families were also compelled not to retain any defence lawyers if their cases were sensitive, thereby depriving them of the right to representation.[242] With these malpractices sabotaging the defence rights, it is worrying that the defence sector might slowly shrink.

As far as the police are concerned, the new law has brought challenges to their work. For many of them, their attitude towards defence lawyers has solidified around the view that it is the job of the defence lawyer to set the bad guy free. They have complained about the greater 'freedom' defence lawyers now have in exonerating the guilt, which defies the purpose of police interrogations. For example,

[237] Interview DBL-1.
[238] See Field note APU-21.
[239] Interview CDL-2.
[240] Beijing Shangquan Law Firm (n 229).
[241] For instance, in Chengdu, Sichuan province, as the defence lawyer filed a complaint against the PSB, which refused to arrange a meeting between the defence lawyer and the suspect, the family of the suspect was asked to dissolve the defence contract with his defence counsel. Similarly, in Jiexi, Guangdong province, the local PSB pressurised the close relative of the suspect to terminate the contract with his defence lawyer, who disclosed and complained of the illegal conduct of the investigating officers. Certain PSBs were reported to very often grant bail on the condition that the suspect dissolved the contractual relationship with his defence lawyer. Such hostility from the police is apparently a gross infringement of the defence right of suspects. See Beijing Shangquan Law Firm (n 229).
[242] ibid.

a police officer expressed the animosity towards defence lawyers that had been amplified with the implementation of CPL 2012:

> Researcher: What do you think of the safeguards in the CPL 2012, such as the defence lawyer meeting the suspect during the investigation?
>
> Police officer: It affects justice. A lawyer can provide legal aid to the suspect. But how does a lawyer offer his service? The lawyer knows the law. As their private conversation is not even monitored, the defence lawyer can collude in the crimes … It not only affects our work, it also has an effect on the procuratorate and the court's work. The impact is massive.[243]

Meeting suspects under detention used to be the biggest hurdle that defence lawyers faced in criminal justice.[244] The situation has improved since CPL 2012 came into effect. The Shangquan survey indicates that over 50 per cent of defence lawyers were able to meet their clients more than twice during the investigation period; only in 4.1 per cent of the cases did detention centres fail to arrange the consultation meetings within 48 hours after the requests.[245] Despite the amelioration, the insulated investigative model and the institutional hostility against defence lawyers remain largely unchanged. When dealing with defence lawyers, state officials deliberately create obstacles. Of all the difficulties reported by defence lawyers during investigations, the physical facilities in the detention centre were one of the main concerns.[246]

The detention centre is controlled by the Ministry of Public Security and administered by the police at the local level.[247] Given that defence lawyers were rarely able to see their clients during the period of custody prior to CPL 2012, many detention centres are short of rooms to accommodate meetings' needs. For example, only one meeting room was available in the central detention centre in Zaozhuang city, Shandong province, where defence lawyers had to queue from the very early hours in the morning.[248] For detention centres where meeting rooms are provided, many of them are designed in such a poor fashion that the meetings proceed only with great difficulty. For instance, the meeting rooms in one of the detention centres in site A were segregated by a wall in which small glass panels were inset. The suspect and the defence lawyer had to shout to each other in order to be heard. In another detention centre in site A, the suspect and the defence lawyer had to communicate by telephone, which could be cut off by the detention

[243] Interview FPO-1.

[244] The remaining difficulties include persuading judges and accessing case files. Sida Liu and Halliday, *Criminal Defence in China* (n 223) 50–51.

[245] ibid.

[246] In total, 65.4% of defence lawyers reported that practical difficulties, particularly the arrangement of meeting facilities, were the critical issues when interviewing the suspect. ibid.

[247] For a discussion of China's pretrial detention centres reform, see Lei Cheng and E Nesossi, 'China's Pre-trial Detention Centres: Challenges and Opportunities for Reform' in E Nesossi et al (eds), *Legal Reforms and Deprivation of Liberty in Contemporary China* (Routledge, 2016) 95–109.

[248] ibid.

centre at any time. It is suggested that these meeting rooms are designed in such ways as to control the communication between the defence lawyer and the suspect.

Other constraints imposed by detention centres have also created significant hurdles for defence lawyers.[249] One common complaint is related to 'three-type cases' (*sanlei anjian*). According to CPL 2012, the defence lawyer must seek permission from the PSB to meet their client if the case is categorised as endangering national security, or involving terrorism or serious bribery.[250] This provision has been so broadly interpreted by the detention centres that defence lawyers have felt that they have been constantly denied access.[251] Thus, although only bribery cases involving more than 500,000 yuan can be technically labelled as serious, almost all the bribery-related cases were classified as serious cases in order to prevent defence lawyers from seeing their clients.[252] A vast array of other innovative methods were also reported, including (but not limited to) the PSB disguising the identity of the suspect, detention centres falsely claiming construction work and the manipulation of register records.[253]

The precarious situation that defence lawyers experience in exercising defence rights has not damped their enthusiasm for advocating more defence rights in criminal justice. As with academics who cry out for effective participation of the defence in police interrogations,[254] this right has been championed by all the

[249] For example, defence lawyers are required to provide extra documents, such as the suspect's marriage certificate and additional files permitted by the Department of Justice, to Fengtai detention centre in Beijing in order to meet the suspect; in Haidian detention centre, Beijing, different defence lawyers who represent co-defendants in the same case are not allowed to interview their client on the same day; in Chaoyang detention centre, Beijing, defence lawyers must make an appointment one week before they are allowed to meet the suspect. See Beijing Shangquan Law Firm (n 229).

[250] See Art 37 of CPL 2012. It should be noted that CPL 2018 has removed the category of serious bribery. See Art 39 of CPL 2018.

[251] Beijing Shangquan Law Firm (n 229).

[252] Other examples include that the detention centre randomly categorises the 'three type cases'. Shangquan Law Firm's report tells a common story that when a defence lawyer asked the detention centre to provide the legal grounds on which his case was regarded as serious, and therefore his application to meet his client was rejected. The detention centre did not reply. ibid.

[253] ibid.

[254] There is a large body of literature on this topic. See, eg Qu Xin, 'Lun bianhu lvshi zaichangquan de queli (On the Establishment of the Defence Lawyer's Right of Access to Police Interrogations)' (2011) 1 *China Criminal Law Magazine* 44; Zhu Kuibing, 'Bijiao yu shizheng: Lvshi zaichangquan toushi (Comparison and Empiricism: Perspectives on the Defence Lawyer's Right of Access to Police Interrogations)' (2008) 3 *Journal of Sichuan University Review* 125; Qu Xin and Lyu Yunchuan, 'Cong youxiao dao zhengyi: Lvshi zaichangquan zai woguo de shiyong kongjian (From Effectiveness to Justice: The Scope of Application of Defence Lawyer's Right of Access to Interrogations)' (2017) 6 *People's Rule of Law* 10; Zhang Jihao, 'Lun Lvshi zaichangquan zai wo guo de zhidu goujian (On the Establishment of the Defence Lawyer's Right of Access to Police Interrogations in China)' (2016) 8 *Theoretic Observation* 94; Fang Boxing, 'Lvshi zaichangquan bentuhua de lilun fansi (Reconsideration of the Defence Lawyer's Right of Access to Interrogations within the Context of China)' (2015) 6 *Journal of Chengdu University of Technology* 1; M Tudi and D Niyazi, 'Cong Luoji dao shijian: Dui Lvshi zaichangquan ji gongneng de zai renshi (From Logics to Practice: Rethink about the Defence Lawyer's Right of Access to Interrogations)' (2016) 3 *Journal of Yili Perfecture Communist Party Insitute* 74.

defence lawyers whom I interviewed.[255] They acknowledged that their presence in interrogations will have a positive impact on combating torture and other police malpractice, thereby reducing the system's reliance on confessions.[256] Their desire to protect and advance the legal rights of their clients was expressed by some defence lawyers, who were seriously concerned about the way in which confession evidence is constructed.

> Defence lawyer 1: The most important stage we really care about is the investigation. The evidence has been consolidated in this stage and we don't even know how it is formed ... If the investigation is properly designed and we are allowed to be present, a lot of defence work would be solved subsequently. For example, there should be a rule that all the suspect's words should be recorded honestly, including his negations and defence. If such work has been done properly, there is little work that we would need to do in the later stages.[257]
>
> Defence lawyer 2: As a defence lawyer myself, I would be thrilled if I were allowed to see how my client has come to the stage of making a confession. This is so important, as we do not know what actually happened.[258]

In spite of the zeal for future reforms, some doubt has been cast upon the practicality and financial burdens with which the accused might be encumbered were the defence lawyer to be allowed to attend the police interrogation.

> Defence lawyer: If the defence lawyer participated in the interrogation, it would be very good. However, I am quite concerned about my clients. They may have to pay quite a large amount of money for the lawyer's fee. Most clients cannot afford this. Just think about it; the police have to interrogate the suspect within 24 hours after he is arrested.

[255] The role of the defence lawyer in interrogations is enshrined in many Western jurisdictions. For example, in England and Wales, the role of the defence lawyer in interrogations is set out in guidance contained in the Police and Criminal Evidence Act 1984, Code of Practice C, which states that 'the solicitor's only role in the police station is to protect and advance the legal rights of their client'. In the Netherlands, an instruction issued by the Public Prosecutor's Office (Aanwijzing rechtsbijstand politieverhoor 2010) has also recognised that the lawyer's role is to ensure that no excessive pressure is used by police in respect of a suspect, to ensure that the interrogation is correctly recorded. Similarly, in France, Art 63-4-3 of the Code de procédure pénale provides that the lawyer is permitted to attend an interrogation, put questions to the suspect and make observations.

[256] See, eg Pan Chunwei, 'Zhongmei susongfa bijiao shiye zhong de lvshi zaichangquan yanjiu (Comparative Study of the Defence Lawyer's Right of Access to Interrogations between the USA and China)' (2013) 5 *Journal of Guangxi Administrative Cadre Institute of Politics and Law* 30; Zhu Kuibing, 'Xingxunbigong zhili yu lvshi xunwei zaichangquan de gongneng dingwei (Regulation of Torture and the Lawyers' Role in Interrogations)' (2011) 11 *Journal of Southwest University for Nationalities* 94; Chen Shaolin, 'Lun bianhu lvshi de zaichangquan (On Defence Lawyers' Right of Access to Interrogations)' (2000) 5 *Law Review* 67; Yuan Lihong, 'Lun xunwenzhong de lvshi zaichangquan zhidu (On Defence Lawyers' Right of Access to Interrogations)' (2007) 2 *Sun Yatsen University Forum* 187; Lin Lin, 'Zhengcha chengxu lvshi zaichangquan bianxi (Defence Lawyers' Right of Access to Police Interrogations)' (2004) 12 *Legal Application* 33; Chen Tao, 'Lun lvshi de zaichangquan (On Defence Lawyers' Right of Access to Interrogations)' (2006) 11 *Procedural Law Review* 107; Yu Cheng, 'Lun woguo lvshi zaichangquan zhidu de goujian (On the Establishment of the Defence Lawyer's Right of Access to Police Interrogations)' (2015) 3 *The Chinese Procurator* 36.

[257] Interview BDL-1.

[258] Interview CDL-1.

> What happens if the police do not question my client when I was there or interrogate him after I have left? OK, even though they may interrogate the suspect when we are there, we cannot sit there like a suspect ourselves for a long time. Unless the client is extremely rich and he can hire several lawyers, so that we can sit during the interrogation taking our turn, it is not very practical. It may work if a provision is made that only when defence lawyers are present is the interrogation valid. I think this is very difficult to put into practice. But we have to charge him a lot of money in such circumstances because we have to confront the police directly. If the police were to ask some misleading questions, are we allowed to intervene?[259]

From a comparative perspective, the EU Directive on the right of access to a lawyer in criminal proceedings has enumerated the lawyer's role in interrogations, which entails:

> advising clients on their legal position; seeking to ensure that their client's decisions, especially as to whether to exercise their right to silence, are respected; providing 'moral' support to their client; challenging unfair or unlawful questioning; ensuring, where appropriate, that the client's version of events is articulated; and ensuring that the record of the interrogation is sufficient and accurate.[260]

Compared to this standard, the operation of the defence rights at police interrogations in China seems to have a long way to go. However, some pilot research suggests that the outcome may not be as ominous as predicted by certain scholars if the defence lawyer is allowed to attend interrogations.[261] Fan Chongyi's study in three provincial regions of China shows that interrogating police officers displayed strong dissatisfaction and hostility against the defence lawyer at the very beginning of the project. As the research progressed, their relationship improved significantly, and both the police and the defence lawyer had gradually developed professional respect and a greater understanding of each other.[262] This research indicates that the police's antagonism against the defence lawyer is caused by bias and a lack of understanding of the legal profession. In this respect, defence lawyers' attendance at interrogations offers an opportunity to dispel misconceptions and to reorientate the police's attitude towards other legal professions in a more rational manner.

[259] Interview CDL-2.

[260] J Blackstock et al, *Inside Police Custody: An Empirical Account of Suspects' Right in Four Jurisdictions* (Intersentia, 2014) 394–95.

[261] See, eg Ma Xiaoqing, 'Xinxingshi susongfa shiye xia lvshi xunwen zaichangquan zhi zaipanduan (Rejudging the Defence Lawyer's Right of Access to Interrogations within the Context of New Criminal Procedure Law) (2014) 32 *Jiamusi University Social Science Review* 39.

[262] Fan Chongyi, *Xingshi shenqian chengxu gaige shizheng yanjiu: xingshi zhengcha chengxu zhong de lvshi zaichang (Empirical Research on Pre-trial Reform: Defence Lawyers' Attendance at Interrogations)* (People's Public Security University Press, 2006) Part 3. This finding is echoed by Sukumar et al's 2016 study, where researchers in England also found that a suspect's interview experience may depend on the working relations between lawyers and police: D Sukumar et al, 'Strategic Disclosure of Evidence: Perspectives from Psychology and Law' (2016) 22 *Psychology Public Poicy and Law* 306.

VII. Conclusion

Investigative dossiers, which have been used to determine the guilt or innocence of defendants in lieu of witnesses' oral testimony, are virtually unchallengeable in a court in China. In this chapter, I have examined the way in which the police case is constructed and the credibility of the official statements contained in the investigative dossier. What has been seen from the construction process is that the *integrity* of the investigations is seriously flawed. As a manifestation of state power and the values held by the authority, the integrity of the criminal justice system should be an important objective, setting good examples in upholding the law and maintaining a moral standing when dealing with the accused as a fellow citizen.[263] However, from what we have seen from the assembly process, the integrity of criminal justice has been compromised in every single aspect. The written documents compiled in the dossier, which will be relied upon by the court to make a decision, do not faithfully reproduce the way an investigation is actually carried out. Confession evidence, which lies at the heart of the case dossier and could be used to dispose of the case at a later stage, is not recorded verbatim. Confession statements may be the product of a collaborative effort between the police and the suspect, and subject to distortion, manipulation or even fabrication. The evidence construction principles also apply to other types of evidence, such as witness statements and crime scene identifications, where a written statement is always preferred to an oral testimony for its official presentation which is deemed as reliable and carries more probative force. The end product of the police case is a conscious construction under the guidance of the corroboration rules in presenting facts approved by the state officials, regardless of the concession of moral legitimacy.

The integrity of the criminal justice system is also compromised when courts act on evidence that has been illegally obtained and defence lawyers are inappropriately treated by the criminal justice authority (such as the police and the detention centres).[264] When a court admits improperly obtained evidence, it brings the administration of justice into disrepute.[265] Research has shown that the vast majority of cases in which the defendant has sought to exclude illegally obtained evidence were handled unfairly, in an unprofessional manner against the accused. In so doing, the courts were condemning the harm to society caused by the crime while vindicating the wrongdoing of the police. In the same vein, the fact that obstacles were deliberately placed before the defence lawyer in meeting their clients, and that the defence lawyers had to run tremendous risks in order to gather evidence to defend their clients, reflects the bad faith of the criminal justice institutions. The way in which the investigation is operationalised profoundly

[263] A Ashworth and M Redmayne, *The Criminal Process* (Oxford University Press, 2010) 346.
[264] M McConville and L Bridges, *Criminal Justice in Crisis* (Edward Elgar, 1994) 14.
[265] Ashworth and Redmayne (n 263) 346.

undermines the moral authority of the institutions, sapping public confidence in the criminal legal system.

The police's case construction process illustrates that the Chinese criminal justice system is not specifically designed in a way that enables scientific evidence to be meticulously relied upon or witnesses' testimonies to be skilfully cross-examined in order to discover the truth. The dominant role played by the police in shaping evidence means that there is a lack of the functional equivalence of defence construction required to formulate a competing version of facts during this critical stage. There has been a dramatic power imbalance between the two parties, with defence lawyers being systematically marginalised and discriminated against for doing their work. A number of active defence lawyers have been persecuted when they merely engaged in good defence practices. Even with the reform of the law, they still face significant obstacles in meeting with their clients, gathering evidence or providing legal advice to their clients, who are controlled by the police.

With the same legal culture and ideology continuing to underpin investigations and dictate the conduct of the police, the practices introduced to safeguard the legality of the process (such as video recordings, exclusion of illegally obtained evidence and the duty lawyer scheme) may merely be another device to gloss over the unregulated malpractices occurring in the process. The validity of the evidence dossier is legitimised and justified by the status of the investigator: as the most powerful authority in the criminal justice system, the police have been given unconditional trust and shielded from external scrutiny. It is known that the bulk of injustices can be traced to the initial actions of the police in carrying out their functions.[266] The seeds of injustice are sown from the inception of the investigation and thrive as the following phases unfold.

[266] Belloni and Hodgson (n 2) 22.

4

Reviewing the Police Case

As soon as the case dossier (including the chief police officer's recommendation to initiate a formal prosecution) is sent to and registered by the procuratorate, the 'ownership' of the case is temporarily transferred to a prosecutor, who is responsible for evaluating the strength and persuasiveness of the police case and taking any actions she sees as necessary. The prosecutor in charge of the case will then engage in a series of activities, which entails a thorough examination of the case dossier, interrogating the suspect, interviewing the victim, if needed, and drafting a case report on her decisions. The review process is designed to facilitate prosecutors to make a rational decision on whether the case should proceed to trial. As we shall see, extra-legal considerations, criminal justice policy and institutional culture may be factored in and play a role in shaping this important decision-making. The relevant issues which have occurred at this scrutiny and prosecution stage (*shencha qisu jieduan*) are discussed in two separate chapters, chapter four and chapter five. In this chapter, I follow the storyline of case dossiers and focus on the prosecutor's role in reviewing police cases; the next chapter deals with prosecutors' discretionary power in making various decisions, which have significant effects on the forthcoming criminal proceedings and the accused's fate. By way of a backdrop to the following analysis, I start with the nature of power that the procuratorate embodies and the role that prosecutors play within the context of Chinese criminal justice.

I. The Soviet Legacy and the Intricacy of the Supervisory Power of the Procuratorate

The Chinese prosecution service, the People's procuratorate, is modelled on the procuracy system in the Soviet Union, which is not limited to a prosecution service but is broadly defined as a legal supervisory body.[1] This supervisory role allows the procuratorate to engage with all critical stages of the criminal process and to ensure the legality of the performance of the criminal justice institutions. Up until March 2018, when the National Supervisory Commission (NSC) was

[1] Shi Shaoxia and Guo Lixin, 'Lilin de falv jiandu sixiang yu zhongguo jiancha zhidu (Lenin's Supervisory Theory of Law and Chinese Procuratorate)' (2003) 6 *Law and Social Development* 3, 5.

established, the supervisory function of the procuratorate had encompassed criminal case registration, anti-corruption investigations, trials, enforcement of criminal penalties, reviews of death penalty cases, enforcement of coercive measures and compensation of victims.[2] The power of anti-corruption investigations was important to the procuratorate: it was the 'sharp teeth' that enabled it to investigate various kinds of corruption and malfeasance of public servants (including judicial staff).[3] A major structural reform took place and the NSC has centralised all the anti-corruption resources.[4] As a result, the Anti-corruption Investigation Department was removed from the procuratorate and folded into the new anti-corruption agency. This integration has been detrimental to the procuratorate. The change clearly undercut the power of the procuratorate, the loss of which was tantamount to 'a tiger without teeth'.[5] Serving as a compensated authority, in recent years the procuratorate was accorded the power to institute civil and administrative litigations in relation to destruction of the ecosystem and natural resources, safeguarding public interests in state-owned land, public assets, and food and medicine safety.[6] The procuratorate has since actively engaged with public interest litigations and carried out the new function. By September 2016, 1,710 public interest actions had been brought against individuals and private entities in these areas of public concern.[7] Despite prosecutors' lingering 'grudge' over the structural

[2] Li Kai and Zhang Fan, 'Xingshi susong jiandu gongzuo jizhi yanjiu (The Research on the Mechanism of Procuratorate)' in Mu Ping and Zhen Zhen (eds), *Jiancha gongzuo jizhi yu shiwu wenti yanjiu (Research on the Work Mechanism of Procuratorate and Practical Issues)* (China Law Press, 2008) 9.

[3] Han Dayuan, 'Lun guojia jiancha tizhi gaige zhong de ruogan xianfa wenti (On a Number of Constitutional Issues in Relation to the National Supervisory Reform) (2017) 3 *Law Review* 11, 18.

[4] The newly established NSC, as a centralised anti-corruption agency, has replaced the Party's Central Discipline Inspection Committees and the anti-corruption department of the procuratorate, responsible for investigating allegations of bribery, embezzlement or other corruption. See Jinting Deng, 'The National Supervisory Commission: A New Anti-corruption Model in China' (2018) 52 *International Journal of Law, Crime and Justice* 58; Long Zongzhi, 'Jiancha tizhi gaige zhong de shiwu fanzui diaocha zhidu wanshan (Improving the National Supervisory Reform in Professional Crime Investigation)' (2018) 1 *Politics and Law* 1; Tong Zhiwei, 'Dui jiancha weiyuanhui zishen de jiandu zhiyue heyi qianghua (How to Strengthen the Self-Regulation of the National Supervisory Commission)' (2017) *Law Review* 1; Li Hongbo, 'Maixiang jianchaweiyuanhui: quanli jiandu zhongguo moshi de fazhihua zhuanxin (Heading towards the National Supervisory Commission: The Change of Paradigm of Power Supervision in the Chinese Model in Rule of Law) (2017) 3 *Law Review* 150; Wang Haiyan, 'Jiancha zhidu yu xingshi susong fa de xianjie (The Coordination between the Supervisory Commission System and the Criminal Procedure Law)' (2017) 6 *Political Science and Law Forum* 84.

[5] Han Dayuan (n 3) 18.

[6] Standing Committee of the National People's Congress, Decision on Authorising the Supreme People's Procuratorate to Carry out Pilot Work on Public Interest Litigation in Several Regions, www.npc.gov.cn/wxzl/gongbao/2015-08/27/content_1946100.htm (accessed 18 July 2018); Pilot Plans of the Procuratorate Organs in Instituting Public Interest Litigation, www.spp.gov.cn/zdgz/201507/t20150703_100706.shtml (accessed 18 July 2018); Implementation Measures of the Pilot Work of the People's Procuratorate in Instituting Public Interest Litigation, www.spp.gov.cn/flfg/201601/t20160108_110652.shtml (accessed 18 July 2018); Implementation Measures in Implementing Trials of the Public Interest Litigations Instituted by the People's Procuratorate, www.court.gov.cn/fabu-xiangqing-37422.html (accessed 18 July 2018).

[7] The Supreme People's Procuratorate of the People's Republic of China, '1,710 Public Interest Litigations were Instituted by the Pilot Procuratorates' (5 November 2016) www.spp.gov.cn/zdgz/201611/t20161105_171729.shtml (accessed 18 July 2018); The Supreme People's Procuratorate of the People's

reform, it seems that their gain in enforcing public interest law has to some extent compensated for its functional loss in anti-corruption investigations.

As a supervisory agency in the criminal justice system, the procuratorate in many ways inherited the legacy of the demised Soviet procuracy system. The Soviet procuracy was the most authoritative institution in the Soviet legal system.[8] It was entrusted to supervise the observance of laws by all ministries, government agencies, enterprises, social organisations and individuals (general supervision), as well as the application of the law in legal processes (special supervision).[9] The Soviet procuracy has its roots in early eighteenth-century Russia, and was reintroduced by Lenin in 1922 as a centralised, hierarchal, legal institution 'to watch over the establishment in reality of a uniform conception of legality in the whole republic'.[10]

The Soviet procuracy system was widely adopted by many former Socialist countries due to political allegiance.[11] Transplanting the Soviet-style procuracy into the Chinese system was predominately a political choice. The fact that the newly founded People's Republic of China in 1949 was a communist regime, isolated by Western countries, suggests that following the Soviet model was the only option available at the time.[12] By sending legal experts to China, the Soviet Union played an important role in the early construction of country's legal system, building a similar procuracy system.[13] Like many other legal transplants, copying the Soviet model was not an easy task, so it was not transplanted into China in its entirety. Thus, the Soviet procuracy's general supervisory function has not been adopted, leaving the function of the Chinese procuratorate limited to supervising the enforcement of legal institutions. Meanwhile, the procuratorate has been structured to have a dual leadership, subordinated to the congress at the local level and the procuratorate at a higher level, rather than the 'vertical leadership' of the Soviet model.[14] This adaptation is largely due to the lack of funding

Republic of China, 'Cao Jianmin's Mid-term Report on the Pilot Work of the Public Interest Litigations Instituted by the Procuratorate' (5 November 2016) www.spp.gov.cn/zdgz/201611/t20161105_171728.shtml (accessed 18 July 2018). For an analysis, see Hu Weili and Tian Kai, 'Jiancha jiguan tiqi xingzheng gongyi susong shidian qingkuan yanjiu (Research on the Public Interest Litigation Pilot Work Instituted by the Procuratorate)' (2017) 2 *Administrative Law Studies* 19, 21–22.

[8] GB Smith, 'The Impact of Socialism on Soviet Legal Institutions and Procedures' (1984) 23 *Columbia Journal of Transnational Law* 315, 320–22.

[9] ibid 76–77.

[10] ibid.

[11] H Oda, 'The Procuracy and the Regular Courts as Enforcers of the Constitutional Rule of Law: The Experience of East Asian States' (1986) 61 *Tulane Law Review* 1339.

[12] G Xu, 'Jianchayuan zuowei "falv jiandu jiguan" de lishi jieshi yu sikao (Historical Explanation and Rethink about the Procuratorate as a Supervisory Institution)' (2013) 10 *Dongyue Review* 142, 144.

[13] Han Dayuan and Yu Wenhao, 'Fayuan, jianchayuan he gongan jiguan de xianfa guanxi (The Constitutional Relationship between the Courts, the Procuratorate and the Police)' (2011) 3 *Legal Studies* 3, 10.

[14] Oda (n 11). Leng Shao-chuan and Chiu Huangdah, *Criminal Justice in Post-Mao China: Analysis and Documents* (SUNY Press, 1985) 69.

in the central procuratorate and a shortage of professional staff in many deprived regions.[15]

The early development of the procuratorate was fraught with difficulties. Socialist legality, which was highly regarded in the Soviet Union, was treated with suspicion by the Chinese Party leaders.[16] As China's relationship with the Soviet Union deteriorated in the late 1950s, the Soviet bureaucratic model was replaced by Maoist mass mobilisation and 'politics in command'.[17] During the Anti-Rightist Movement between 1957 and 1965, the procuratorate's supervisory function was criticised for 'weakening and denying the dictatorship of the proletariat'.[18] Prosecutors were purged as 'right deviationists and revisionists', and attacked for making a 'fetishism of law'.[19] The procuratorate essentially ceased to function in the late 1950s and the Party Committees completely controlled the criminal process. During the Cultural Revolution, it continued to be targeted for being a hindrance to the 'proletarian revolution', eventually being abolished in the early 1970s.[20]

After the Cultural Revolution, the Constitution Law 1978 restored the legal status of the procuratorate and its supervisory power to oversee the criminal justice institutions.[21] It was tasked with detecting and investigating corruption crimes,[22] sanctioning arrests,[23] prosecuting criminality,[24] and checking the legality of trial proceedings and courts' decisions[25] at different stages of the criminal process. These roles were undertaken by different departments of the procuratorate. The Department of Anti-corruption Investigation, as mentioned, was responsible for detecting crimes related to public servants in office. The Department of

[15] Xie Pengchen and Ren Wensong, 'Sulian jiancha zhidu dui woguo de yingxiang (The Influence of the Soviet Procuracy on Our Legal System)' (2010) 7 *Hebei Legal Studies* 195, 197; Zhao Xiaogeng and Liu Tao, 'Lun zhonghua renmin gongheguo jiancha jiandu zhineng de xingcheng yu fazhan(The Shaping and Development of the Procuratorate of the People's Republic of China)' (2006) 3 *Jurist* 39, 44; Sun Qian, 'Renmin jiancha de guanghui lichen: jinian renmin jianchayuan huifu chongjian 30 zhounian (The Glory Journey of the People's Procuratorate: In Memory of the Recovery of the People's Procuratorate for 30 Years)' (2008) 11 *The People's Procuratorate* 5, 8.

[16] Chiu Huangdah, 'China's Criminal Justice System and the Trial of Pro-democracy Dissidents' (1992) *New York University Journal of International Law and Politics* 1181; Leng Shao-chuan and Chiu Huangdah (n 14) 16.

[17] Leng Shao-chuan and Chiu Huangdah (ibid) 16.

[18] Oda (n 11) 1344; Han Dayuan and Yu Wenhao (n 13) 10; Xie Pengchen and Ren Wensong (n 15) 197–98; Zhao Xiaogeng and Liu Tao (n 15); T Hsia and WI Zeldin, 'Recent Legal Developments in the People's Republic of China' (1987) 28 *Harvard International Law Journal* 249.

[19] T Hsia and Zeldin (ibid).

[20] Leng Shao-chuan and Chiu Huangdah (n 14) 17–18; Min Shan, 'Jianchaquan peizhi de lishi bianqian yu fansi (The Historical Change and Rethink about the Power of the Procuratorate)' (2010) 5 *Journal of National Prosecutors College* 52, 62.

[21] The Constitutional Law 1978, Art 43; the procuratorate's legal standing was preserved in the subsequent Constitutional Law: see Art 129 of the Constitutional Law 1982 (last amended in 2004).

[22] CPL 2012, Art 18.

[23] CPL 2012, Art 78.

[24] CPL 2012, Art 167.

[25] CPL 2012, Arts 203 and 217.

Prosecution had the duty of bringing criminal charges to trial and overseeing the court by counter-appealing (*kangsu*) judgments containing errors to a higher court.

This model of supervision, in addition to various procedural commitments, embodies an extraordinary concentration of power. This is justified by the distinct socialist ideology, which is considered to be divergent from the doctrine of the separation of powers.[26] Wang Guiwu explained that because other forms of prosecutorial power arrangements invariably belong to the capitalist discourse and thereby should be abandoned completely, setting up the procuratorate directed by Leninist legal thought was the historical destination.[27] The configuration of procuratorial power was believed to conform to the socialist polity of the People's democratic dictatorship, which should be organised through the principle of democratic centralism (*minzhu jizhongzhi*) rather than 'the hypercritical capitalist parliamentary system'.[28] This democratic centralism provides the divisions of functions and powers between the central and local state organs and gives 'full scope to the initiative and enthusiasm of the local authorities under the unified leadership of the central authorities'.[29] The organisational structure guided by this socialist principle features a combination of vertical and horizontal modes of supervision which gives the rubric form to the relationship between democracy and centralism.[30] As an organisational principle, democratic centralism combines legislature and administration, and suggests that communist institutions exercising sovereign power are entrusted with the protection of the general public. The centralised controlled institutions are 'represented by subordination to higher level agencies, [and] are more important than democratic controls represented by accountability to the people's congresses'.[31] In this regard, the operation of the state should be prioritised as a matter of expediency, rather than as a question of principle.[32] The procuratorate is mainly concerned with the enforcement of the rule of the political regime,[33] which is not necessarily equivalent to safeguarding the rights of individuals.

As the procuratorate is simultaneously committed to several basic tasks in the criminal process, the extent to which this respects a blurring of roles is a point of

[26] See Xie Pengcheng, 'Lun jianchaquan de xingzhi (The Nature of the Power of Procuratorate)' (2000) 2 *Studies of Law* 34.

[27] Wang Guiwu, *Zhonghua renmin gongheguo jianchazhidu yanjiu (A Study of the Procuratorate in the People's Republic of China)* (China Law Press, 1991) 164.

[28] Zedong Mao, *Mao Zedong Wenji (The Selection of Mao Zedong's Works)*, vol 4 (People's Press, 1991) 1480.

[29] The Constitutional Law of the PRC 1982, Art 3(4).

[30] For more discussion about democratic centralism, see S Biddulph, 'Democratic Centralism and Administration in China' in Fu Hualing et al (eds), *Socialist Law in Socialist East Asia* (Cambridge University Press, 2018) 205.

[31] ibid.

[32] DA Loeber, 'The Soviet Procuracy and the Rights of the Individual against the State' (1958) 1 *Journal of the International Commission of Jurists* 59, 60.

[33] Oda (n 11).

tension. When Western jurisprudence was introduced into China in the 1990s, scholarly criticism was levelled at the nature of the power of the procuratorate, and its triple identity of the investigator, prosecutor and supervisor.[34] Chinese academics, such as Chen Ruihua, argued that the procuratorate's role as a criminal investigator and prosecutor inevitably undermined its status as an independent supervisor since it was driven by the ambition of winning cases in the courts.[35] Even though the procuratorate is defined as an official body of supervision by the constitutional law,[36] this primary function is often influenced by its secondary, albeit dominating, role as a partisan advocate.

The procuratorate's role in court is also a subject of concern. In light of the prosecutors' supervision, issues regarding the ceremonial ritual of the courts, such as 'should the prosecutor stand up when judges enter the court?', have invoked widespread discussion that begs the question 'who is actually in charge at trial?'[37] Some scholars have argued that the supervision of the courts has sabotaged the authority of the court, establishing the prosecutor as 'the judge over judges' and causing uncertainty in adjudication.[38] As the debate has progressed, it has probed the nature of the power of supervision, begging the critical question of who should supervise the supervisor: a paradox which seems to have no resolution under the current system. These considerations have given rise to a more general observation: the power of supervision has created an irreconcilable and fundamental conflict with the criminal prosecution principle, both in theory and in practice. Apparently, this tension is derived from the Soviet legacy. As Chen Ruihua put it:

> It is a Utopian-like myth that a State institution with the responsibility to prosecute and detect crimes is given the mission to supervise and guarantee the uniformity of

[34] There is a substantial body of Chinese literature discussing the nature of the power of the procuratorate. See, eg Wan Yi, 'Jianchaquan ruogan jiben lilun wenti yanjiu (Basic Study on the Power of Procuratorate)' (2008) 26 *Political Science and Law Forum* 91; Long Zongzhi, 'Lun jianchaquan de xingzhi yu jiancha jiguan de gaige (The Nature of the Power of the Procuratorate and the Legal Reform)' (1999) 10 *Studies of Law* 2, 6; Hu Xiabing, 'Woguo jiancha jiguan zhiquan de jiantao yu chonggou (Rethink and Reconstruct the Power of the Procuratorate in China)' (2001) 10 *Legal Research and Exploration* 43; Chen Weidong, 'Woguo jianchaquan de fansi yu chonggou: yi gongsuquan wei hexin de fenxi (Rethink and Reconstruct the Power of the Procuratorate in China: Based on the Prosecution Power)' (2002) 2 *Legal Studies* 3; Hao Yinzhong, 'Jianchaquan zhiyi (Questioning the Power of the Procuratorate)' (1999) 3 *China Renmin University Review* 71.

[35] Dong Hao, 'Woguo sifa jiguan duochong zhineng gaige zhi sikao (Thoughts about the Multiple Functions of the Judicial Institutions in China)' (1997) 4 *Legal Studies* 27; Chen Ruihua, *Zhongguo xingshi susong de qianyan wenti (The Fronting Edge of Chinese Criminal Justice)* (China Renmin University Press, 1999) 530.

[36] Pursuant to Art 129 of the Constitutional Law, the People's procuratorate is the institution responsible for legal supervision.

[37] Long Zongzhi, 'Jianchaguan gaibugai qili: dui tingsheng yishi de yizhong sikao (Should the Prosecutor Stand Up? Some Thoughts about the Court Rituals)' (1997) 3 *Studies of Law* 44, 45; He Weifang, 'Yizai suowei jianchaguan jiqi wenti zhe: yu longzongzhi xiansheng shangque (The Surprising Question of Whether the Prosecutor Should Stand Up: A Discussion with Mr Long Zongzhi)' (1997) 2 *Legal Studies* 58.

[38] Chen Weidong (n 34).

> the enforcement of the law, and to rectify the wrongs that are made by other legal institutions.[39]

Facing this theoretical dilemma, an effort has been directed towards reframing the power of supervision, and academic views on the actual nature of the power of the procuratorate have differed. Hitherto, four categorisations have been advanced to define its nature:

(i) an executive power. This school of academics believes that the power of the procuratorate should belong to the executive. Compared to judicial power, this proposition argues that the procuratorate lacks an independent status; its decision is not legally binding, nor does it have the effect of a final resolution.[40]
(ii) a judicial power. Directly opposed to the aforementioned position, this viewpoint believes that prosecutors serve as guardians of the criminal justice system; their prosecutorial decisions are based upon evidence and facts, the function of which should place it alongside the judiciary.[41]
(iii) double ascriptions. This view argues that the power of the procuratorate embodies the characteristics of both the executive and the judiciary: the vertical leadership of the procuratorate makes it closer to the executive and its activities concerning prosecution resemble the judicial power.[42]
(iv) a supervisory power. This proposition affirms that the power of the procuratorate should preserve its Soviet heritage and operate as a supervisory body. It argues that the function of supervision should be perceived as a unique form of state power, despite it presenting certain features similar to the executive and the judiciary.[43] As Zhang Zhihui argued:

> The fundamental reason why the constitutional law juxtaposes the procuratorate's power of supervision with the power of government and the power of adjudication is not that it wants the procuratorate to share the power of the executive with the government, nor does it want the procuratorate to share the power of the judiciary. The constitutional law does so purely because it wants the procuratorate to supervise the government and the judiciary.[44]

While these proposals might be useful in exploring the controversial function of the procuratorate, certain crucial issues, such as the independence of the

[39] ibid 531.
[40] ibid; Hao Yinzhong (n 34).
[41] Long Zongzhi (n 37).
[42] Wan Yi (n 34) 92.
[43] Xie Pengcheng (n 26); Zhang Zhihui, *Jianchaquan yanjiu (A Study of the Power of the Procuratorate)* (China Procuratorate Publishing, 2007) 34. Zhang Zhihui, 'Zhongguo Tese Jiancha Zhidu de Lilun Tansuo – Jianchaquan Jichu Lilun 30nian Yanjiu Pingshu (The Theoretical Exploration of the Procuratorate System with Chinese Feature: A Literature Review over the 30 Years' Procuratorate Theory)' (2009) 16 *China Law Studies* 150, 155.
[44] Zhang Zhihui, 'Jianchaquan yu falv jiandu (The Power of Procuratorate and its Supervisory Nature)' (2004) 3 *The Procuratorate of Shanxi* 76, 76.

procuratorate, have been sidelined in the debate. The *UN Guidelines for Prosecutors* (*UN Guidelines*) and *The Standards of Professional Responsibility and Statement of the Essential Duties and Rights of Prosecutors* (*The Standards*) require that prosecutors perform their duties without prejudice, favour or intimidation.[45] Regarding this standard, how to adjust prosecutors' affiliation to different branches of the state, so that prosecutors can maintain neutrality, has often been a focal point in Western academic discussion. For example, criticism has been levelled at the affinity between prosecutors and judges in Italy after the Constitutional Law severed the link between the prosecution and political bodies and attached the power of the prosecution to the judiciary.[46] In France, academic attention has been given to a conflict between the independence of *procureurs* and the requirement that prosecutors be democratically accountable to the Minister of Justice, thereby being susceptible to interference in sensitive cases.[47] In England and Wales, prosecutors' impartiality is projected in articulation between the long-established police force and the relatively new creation of the Crown Prosecution Service (CPS). Even though the CPS has a sphere of responsibility, which is independent, it has been criticised for a lack of objectivity due to its subordination to the police.[48]

In China, the procuratorate's independence from executive bodies, organisations or individuals is explicitly stated in the Constitutional Law.[49] Yet the procuratorate's 'dual subordination' has placed the procuratorate in a vulnerable position in dealing with various political bodies whilst maintaining its independence. For instance, the procuratorate's subordination to the local congress is reflected in the reality that the local council controls the personnel and the operational budget of the procuratorate.[50] Local influences are able to interfere

[45] *UN Guidelines* 4 and 13; *The Standards* 3.

[46] M Caianiello, 'The Italian Public Prosecutor: An Inquisitorial Figure in Adversarial Proceedings?' in E Luna and M Wade (eds), *The Prosecutor in Transnational Perspective* (Oxford University Press, 2012) 255.

[47] JS Hodgson, 'Hierarchy, Bureaucracy, and Ideology in French Criminal Justice: Some Empirical Observations' (2002) 29 *Journal of Law and Society* 236. See also J Hodgson, *French Criminal Justice: A Comparative Account of the investigation and Prosecution of Crime in France* (Hart Publishing, 2005).

[48] See B Hancock and J Jackson, *Standards for Prosecutors: An Analysis of the United Kingdom National Prosecuting Agencies* (Willen-Jan Van Der Wolf, 2006) ch 4; F Belloni and J Hodgson, *Criminal Injustice: An Evaluation of the Criminal Justice Process in Britain* (2000) ch 6; Andrew Sanders et al, *Criminal Justice* (Oxford University Press, 2010) ch 7.

[49] Constitutional Law, Art 131.

[50] Zhang Xiaohui, 'Qiantan jiancha jiguan renshi guanli zhidu gaige (On Reform of the Personnel Management of the Procuratorate)' (2010) 6 *Legal Space and Time* 162; Feng Zhifeng, 'Jiancha jiguan renshi guanli gaige sanshinian gailan (Overview of the 30-year Reform of the Personnel Management of the Procuratorate)' (2008) 19 *The People's Procuratorate* 21; Tian Cui, 'Jiceng jiancha jiguan jingfei baozhang wenti tanxi (The Financial Safeguards of the District Procuratorate)' (2012) 8 *Law and Economy* 95; Ge Lin, 'Jingfei baozhang shiyexia de jianchayuan yunzhuan: jiyu liangge jiceng jianchayuan butong jingfei zhuangkuang de fenxi (The Operation of the Procuratorate in the Context of Financial Safeguards: Analysis of the Financial Situation of Two District Procuratorates)' (2013) 26 *Journal of Yunnan University Law Edition* 113; Chen Meijing, 'Jianxi jiancha jiguan jingfei baozhang wenti: Yi guanxi hezhoushi babuqu jianchayuan wei li (The Financial Safeguards of the Procuratorate: An Example of the Babu District Procuratorate in the City of Hezhou, Guangxi Province)' (2010) 11 *Law and Economy* 54.

with prosecutors' actions in individual cases via higher ranked officials within the procuratorate.[51] Meanwhile, the procuratorate's political accountability to the Communist Party also allows certain Party institutions to intervene in prosecutors' decision-making. Thus, the Political-Legal Committee, a Party institution responsible for coordinating the relationship between different legal institutions, has, historically, created a tension between the independence of the procuratorate and the requirement that the procuratorate follows the Party's leadership.[52] This has been demonstrated most clearly in the exercise of the Political-Legal Committee's power to issue directions to prosecutors in influential cases that resulted in miscarriages of justice. After a negative social response, the Political-Legal Committee has gradually suspended its power to issue instructions in individual cases in recent years. Nevertheless, Party institutions still have an overriding authority over the procuratorate, and influence the procuratorate in a less formal way.[53]

II. The Role of the Prosecutor

With regard to the procuratorate's supervisory function, the Chinese prosecutor is not only responsible for preparing and presenting a case against individuals on behalf of the state, but also ensures the legality and fairness of the criminal process.[54] In this legal rhetoric, prosecutors are expected to review the police case objectively and to assiduously give appropriate instructions in relation to correct enforcement of the law.[55] Perceiving themselves primarily as reviewers of the investigative case, many prosecutors emphasised their commitment to fairness, albeit conceding that undue influences were unavoidable:

> Prosecutor: My main job is to review the evidence rather than gathering the evidence.[56]
>
> Prosecutor: Although the prosecutor was originated as a party, the arms between the prosecution and defence are too unbalanced. So, we have to be fair to them. Just follow the truth. We are not investigative officers; we only review the cases from the police. We must be objective.[57]

[51] See Mou Yu, 'Beyond Legitimate Grounds: External Influences and the Discretionary Power not to Prosecute in the People's Republic of China' in M Caianiello and J Hodgson (eds), *Discretionary Criminal Justice in a Comparative Context* (North Carolina Press, 2015) 121.

[52] ibid.

[53] ibid. See also 'Self-Reform of the Central Political-Legal Committee: No Interference with Individual Cases', *News.ifeng* (14 July 2013) http://news.ifeng.com/mainland/detail_2013_07/14/27479910_0.shtml (accessed 3 November 2014).

[54] Prosecutors are usually subject to certain rules to ensure the fairness of the criminal process. This is not only demonstrated by their judicial role in inquisitorial systems, but can be generally found in adversarial systems. For example, in the USA, rule 3.8 of the ABA Model Rules of professional conduct requires prosecutors to 'make timely disclosure to the defence of all evidence or information … that tends to negate the guilt of the accused or mitigates the offense.' Similar rules can also be seen in England and Wales.

[55] See Art 7 of CPL 2018.

[56] Interview APS-2.

[57] Field note APU-3.

Prosecutor: Generally speaking, I was taking the role of an independent supervisor. But when I was reviewing the case, I have been influenced by some external factors, which is unavoidable.[58]

From time to time, they expressed sympathy towards a suspect who pleaded guilty and who showed remorse. In those cases, they readily welcomed evidence that would mitigate the sentence of the accused, especially evidence in connection with voluntary surrender and meritorious performance.[59] This neutral image of the prosecutor, however, was premised on the condition that the accused was willing to confess and her conviction was certain. Unfortunately, their role as neutral officers safeguarding fair play had not extended to circumstances where the accused's prospective verdict was in question. Whenever the prosecutor's objective of swiftly securing a successful prosecution was thwarted, impartiality was no longer evident. This was acknowledged by two prosecutors whose comments seemed to have contradicted the remarks of their colleagues mentioned earlier.

Prosecutor: Frankly speaking, as a prosecutor in China, it is impossible to be a neutral officer. Our job is to accuse and charge the suspect. It is very hard to be neutral because our workload is very heavy and we feel under pressure all the time. Therefore, I think our position is that of an accusing party. Also, I don't think we can be a neutral officer because our job is to fight against crime.[60]

Prosecutor: In mainland China, our role should be defined as an accusing party. However, during the criminal procedure, we would try our best to be fair with all cases, which is not contradictory to our role. We cannot work as a neutral officer in the court as the Western countries do.[61]

The limit of being even-handed in Chinese prosecution was to a large extent associated with the Appraisal System. As noted in chapter one, over a long period of time, the prosecutor's performance was evaluated by a matrix of criteria that were connected with prosecutors' career success in their tenures. Prosecutors were required to meet the targets set out by the procuratorate at a higher level, such as a high rate of conviction, successful counter-appeal verdicts against erred court judgments and processing cases in a cost-effective manner.[62] In this arrangement,

[58] Field note APU-5.
[59] Field note APU-23 (*CASEA* 23).
[60] Interview APS-3.
[61] Interview APS-2.
[62] Zhu Tonghui, 'The Appraisal System in the Criminal Justice System' (2009) 1 *Law and Social Science* 5; Li Enshen, 'The Li Zhuang Case: Examining the Challenges Facing Criminal Defense Lawyers in China' (2010) 24 *Columbia Journal of Asian Law* 129, 164; Wu Meilai and Gui Ouli, 'Xingshi susong zhineng de yihua yu zhili: yi gongjianfa xingshi susong guanlian jixiao kaohe wei zhongxin (Alienation and Management of the Function of Criminal Proceedings: Analysis of the Appraisal System Applied to the PSB, the Procuratorate and the Courts in China)' (2013) Award Winning Essay at the 25th Academic Conference in the Judiciary, Research on Justice and Administrative Implementation, 348–58; Xie Xiaojian, 'Jiancha jiguan yewu mubiao guanli kaoping dui xingshisusong de yingxiang (Influence on Criminal Justice over the Management of the Procuratorate's Tasks)' (2014) 6 *Anhui University Journal* 119; Wan Yi and Shi Qingzheng, 'Jianchayuan jixiao kaohe shizheng

acquittal avoidance was at the heart of the work of the prosecutor. At an individual level, an acquittal could have a significantly negative impact on a prosecutor's career. At an institutional level, a procuratorate with a relatively high acquittal rate was likely to be affected in the overall ranking in that region, which would lead to a subsequent financial punishment. Collateral consequences of the acquittal also involved state compensation for the wrongfully charged defendant and the implication of a tarnished reputation.[63] The sanctions imposed on the procuratorate then percolated through the hierarchical layers and spread out to the individual prosecutors. In avoiding the adverse effect, prosecutors' tasks were consciously directed towards avoiding potential acquittals.[64] Priorities were set out to meet the target, superseding other legal obligations.[65]

Discontent over the rigid assessment method was widely expressed within the procuratorate. A number of prosecutors argued that the goal to maintain consistently high conviction rates was unreasonable, as it obliterated the division between the prosecution and the adjudication.[66] Given that judicial discretion was an integral part of adjudication, requiring prosecutors to be completely in line with the judges' view was an arbitrary imposition.

> Prosecutor: They (the policymakers of the Appraisal System) want the conviction rate to be 100%, which is so ridiculous. Having different opinions with evidence is so normal. Everyone should be allowed to have different judgements toward the evidence. But they want us to win every case. This is so ridiculous.[67]

> Prosecutor: I think acquittals are very normal. I think the Appraisal System should be discarded. I think the law is a discipline in which there exist differing viewpoints on the same issue. Everyone thinks differently and the criterion of the judgement varies. For the same quality and quantity of evidence, a group of people may think it is sufficient to prove the fact that the suspect is guilty whilst another group may think that there are alternative explanations. I think the acquittal is absolutely normal practice. Due to the assessment, we are not allowed to make any mistakes or have any acquitted cases. Now 'everyone turns pale when acquittals are mentioned'.[68] This is not right.[69]

Prosecutors' disgruntlement also originated from their supervisory role. As an authority entrusted with the job of overseeing the criminal justice system, the procuratorate was supposed to be in an exalted position over and above other legal institutions, including the courts.[70] The fact that the work of the procuratorate

yanjiu: yi S shi jianchajiguan wei yangben de fenxi (Empirical Study on the Appraisal System for the Procuratorate: Analysis of the Procuratorate in S city)' (2009) 1 *Oriental Law* 28.

[63] Field note APU-23.

[64] Wan Yi and Shi Qingzheng (n 62).

[65] Field note APU-31. For some criticism, see Wan Yi and Shi Qingzheng (n 62).

[66] Field notes APU-4, 5 and 7.

[67] Field note APU-4.

[68] This is from the Chinese idiom, 'when people are talking about the tiger, their face turns pale' (*tanhu sebian*), meaning that the subject (here, the tiger) is so daunting that it becomes taboo.

[69] Interview APS-2.

[70] As discussed earlier, this remains a heatedly debated and controversial topic. Many prosecutors nonetheless held the view that they were supposed to be superior to judges: Field notes APU-4 and 5.

had to be evaluated and decided by the courts suggests that the legal status of the procuratorate was, in fact, inferior to their judicial peers.

> Prosecutor: Those who designed the assessment model should think about these problems … due to the appraisal model, the law has been undermined or hollowed … You know that legal work is mostly subjective. So, when I have a case, as a prosecutor, if I think the suspect has committed a crime and should be prosecuted, I will prosecute it. When I prosecuted the case to the court, the judge who thinks differently may acquit the case. We are different legal personnel and have a different way of thinking. The result is absolutely normal. But the consequence is, once he made an acquittal, our work is whitewashed due to the assessment. This has a great effect on us. So, we have to be nice to the court even though we have the supervisory power.[71]

Nevertheless, the Appraisal System made perfect sense from the party-state's perspective. The legitimacy of the state draws heavily from the performance of its criminal justice system in effectively delivering the social control tenet, and maintaining an exceptionally high conviction rate was deemed to be necessary, as the chief purpose of the criminal justice system was to be known as a deterrent and punitive.[72] Over the last two decades, the acquittal rates in China have been less than 1 per cent.[73] This operational mechanism has fundamentally shaped the role of prosecutors, their working culture, their ethos and their relationships with other legal actors, particularly the police and judges. Even though the Appraisal System has officially been abolished, its impact in practice is still highly relevant today. Noticeably, the acquittal rates since 2015 are still extraordinarily low – even lower than the 2000s, according to the official statistics.[74] The status quo seems unlikely to change in the near future.

III. Overseeing the Police Case

If the role of supervision accords with the logic of the criminal procedure, it would be best demonstrated in its oversight of the police. Supervision of the legality of the police investigation has been perceived as an essential part of the function of

[71] Interview APS-4.

[72] Xu Jianhua, 'Legitimation Imperative: The Production of Crime Statistics in Guangzhou, China' (2018) 58 *British Journal of Criminology* 155, 171; S Trevaskes, 'Severe and Swift Justice in China' (2007) 47 *British Journal of Criminology* 23, 47; Xie Xiaojian (n 62); Wan Yi and Shi Qingzheng (n 62).

[73] The acquittal rates from 2001 to 2018 were 0.88%, 0.7%, 0.65%, 0.44%, 0.26%, 0.19%, 0.15%, 0.15%, 0.14%, 0.12%, 0.1%, 0.08%, 0.06%, 0.071%, 0.66%, 0.084%, 0.088%, 0.09% and 0.057%, respectively. Data produced by *The China Law Year Book* (China Law Year Book Press, 2001–2018); The Work Report of the Supreme People's Court 2001–2018; The Work Report of the Supreme People's Prucuratorate 2001–2018.

[74] The numbers of acquitted defendants from 2015 to 2018 were 1039, 1076, 1156 and 819, respectively, significantly lower than in the 2000s. From 2001 and 2009, the numbers of acquittal were 6597, 4935, 4835, 3365, 2162, 1713, 1417, 1373 and 1206, respectively. Data derived from *The China Law Year Book* (ibid).

the prosecution service in many countries and is endorsed by the International Association of Prosecutors. For example, *The Standards* require prosecutors to 'ensure that the investigation services respect legal precepts and fundamental human rights' when supervising a police investigation.[75] Prosecutors' control of the police in the investigation is a common feature in countries with an inquisitorial tradition. Prosecutors in adversarial systems do not have any substantive involvement in the investigation phase.[76] Nevertheless, in jurisdictions such as England and Wales, the police may seek appropriate advice from prosecutors to facilitate the effectiveness of an investigation and prosecution.[77]

In countries with an inquisitorial influence, the level of prosecutors' involvement in police investigations varies, depending on the specific police–prosecutor relationship mandated by law. Thus, Dutch prosecutors are responsible for 'all aspects of criminal investigation', ensuring that the police comply with the law.[78] Likewise, in France, the *procureur* oversees the majority of the police investigation, including the questioning of suspects held in police custody (*garde à vue*).[79] Although the effectiveness of this supervisory model over the conduct of investigations has been criticised, it is designed to provide a safeguard to suspects, preventing intrusive infringements of an individual's liberty.[80] The Italian prosecutor's involvement with the police investigation is less prominent compared to other inquisitorial countries, yet they can still exercise authority over certain units among the police corps.[81] Japanese prosecutors perhaps possess the highest level of control over the investigation, and routinely 'interact with the police during the pre-charge investigation', rather than simply relying on the police for information.[82] Their proactive stance illustrates that prosecutors are the dominant partners in the police–prosecutor relationship.

Comparative empirical research suggests that the effectiveness of the public prosecutors' authority to direct the investigation should not be overstated. Mathia's study of prosecutorial supervision in Germany, Belgium and France reveals that prosecutors can do little about the investigation because the police seldom inform

[75] *The Standards*, 4.2(b). See also 19 and 22(a), *Recommendation of the Commmittee of Ministers to Member States on the Role of Public Prosecution in the Criminal Justice System*, adopted by the Committee of Ministers on 6 October 2000 at the 724th meeting of the Ministers' Deputies, Council of Europe.

[76] Hancock and Jackson (n 48) ch 4; Belloni and Hodgson (n 48) chs 2–4; DA Harris, 'The Interaction and Relationship between Prosecutors and Police Officers in the United States, and How this Affects Police Reform' in Luna and Wade (n 46) 56.

[77] CPS, 'Prosecution Policy and Guidance' www.cps.gov.uk/legal/a_to_c/cps_relations_with_the_police/ (accessed 27 June 2016).

[78] Although, in practice, the police are in charge of most investigations due to the limited prosecution resource. See PJP Tak, 'The Dutch Prosecutor: A Prosecuting and Sentencing Officer' in Luna and Wade (n 46) 141.

[79] Hodgson, 'Hierarchy' (n 47); see also Hodgson, *French Criminal Justice* (n 47) 144.

[80] Hodgson, *French Criminal Justice* (n 47) 146.

[81] Caianiello (n 46) 252.

[82] DT Johnson, *The Japanese Way of Justice: Prosecuting Crime in Japan* (Oxford University Press, 2002) 51–55.

them until the inquiry is almost over.[83] Chinese prosecutorial supervision, similar to this practice, is passive and has an 'after-event' model. Most police investigations are carried out solely by the police.[84] Only when the police have completed their investigation and have transferred the case to the procuratorate can prosecutors intervene, and issue further directions and guidance to the police if the evidence requires, thereby prolonging the investigative phase.[85] This procedural arrangement cuts short the prosecutorial supervision, leaving the main police investigation free from any sort of direct external scrutiny.[86] Rather than monitoring how the investigation is conducted, the prosecutorial oversight focuses on the end product of the police work, mostly by examining the investigative dossier, interrogating suspects and occasionally interviewing victims. Prosecutors are also allowed to gather evidence, for example by interviewing the victim and witnesses, to evaluate the case independently, but this is restricted to limited categories of circumstances.[87]

A. Examining Investigative Dossiers

Reviewing the investigative dossier and scrutinising the admissibility and probative value of the evidence contained therein are arguably the most critical parts of the prosecution work. This process is particularly important within the context of China, given that witnesses are seldom called to give evidence at trial, and defence lawyers have limited recourse to investigating the way police evidence is collected. Scrupulous reviewing of the police case without prejudice is pertinent to the prosecutor's role as the guardian of the criminal process, and prosecutors are expected to oversee the police work and safeguard the rights of the accused. At any rate, diligently inspecting police activities in relation to case construction falls squarely into the ideology of prosecutorial supervision. It may furnish a timely remedy to the victim of police misconduct and ensure the integrity of the criminal process. Congruent with this rationale, Article 171 of the Criminal Procedure Law 2018

[83] E Mathias, 'The Balance of Power between the Police and the Public Prosecutor' in D-M Mireille and J Spencer (eds), *European Criminal Procedures* (Cambridge University Press, 2002) 459–87.

[84] Chen Weidong and Hao Yinzhong, 'Zhen jian yitihua moshi yanjiu: jianlun woguo xingshi sifa tizhi gaige de biyaoxing (A Study of the Integration of the Investigation and the Prosecution: On the Necessity of Reforming the Criminal Justice System in China)' (1999) 1 *China Legal Studies* 58, 64; Chen Lan, 'Woguo jianjing guanxi de fansi yu chonggou (Reconsideration and Reconstruction of the Police–Prosecution Relationship)' (2009) 6 *Legal Studies* 110; Liu Jihua, 'Jianjing yitihua moshi zai jiedu (Reinterpretation of the Integration of the Investigation and the Prosecution)' (2013) 6 *China Law Studies* 147; Lyu Ping, 'Xingshi lian chengxu de dulixing zhiyi (Enquiry on the Independence of the Case Filing Process in the Criminal Procedure)' (2002) 3 *China Law Studies* 142.

[85] According to Art 171 of CPL 2012, the procuratorate can require a maximum of two further investigations conducted by the police to gather further evidence.

[86] Although the police must request the authorisation from the procuratorate in order to remand suspects in custody, the procuratorate does not monitor other police work.

[87] This is often subject to local practices. For example, at site A, prosecutors only interview the victims in rape and assault cases.

(CPL 2018) sets out the tasks that the prosecutor should discharge at the preparation stage, which comprises:[88]

1. whether the facts and circumstances of the crime are clear, whether the evidence is reliable and sufficient, and whether the charge and the nature of the crime have been correctly determined;
2. whether there are any crimes that have been omitted or other persons whose criminal responsibility should be investigated;
3. whether it is a case in which criminal responsibility should not be investigated;
4. whether the case has an incidental civil action; and
5. whether the investigation of the case is being lawfully conducted.

In compliance with this legal provision, prosecutors are expected to check whether the evidence has been gathered in a lawful manner and whether the case is strong enough to be convicted by the court. Despite the supposition, oversight in practice seemed to be confined to how the case dossier was presented, viz whether the basic written evidence was completed and whether the formalities of the evidence complied with legal requirements. Thus, prosecutors spent a substantial amount of time ensuring that the duration of the interrogation was within the proscribed legal time period, the notification about the suspect's rights was included in the dossier and the suspect's signature was in the right place.[89] Indeed, these are errors that occurred frequently. Some of the common 'oversights' included, but were not limited to, the absence of important procedural documentation (such as the arrest warrant);[90] the suspect's criminal record;[91] mistakes in spelling the suspect's name due to carelessness;[92] and a poorly executed recording of the victim statements.[93]

Prosecutors complained about the quality of case dossiers almost on a daily basis in site A. However, the deficiency of the police work was innocuous: as long as the written documents were lawful in format, they were most likely to be accepted by the prosecutor, no matter how the documents were created. For example, in a drug trafficking case (*CASEA* 47), the prosecutor found that the quantity of the drug had not been recorded in the case. As an important piece of evidence determining the accused's criminal responsibility and future sentence, it is required that the police weigh the drug as soon as practically possible, the record of which must be made in the presence of the suspect, who would be asked to validate the record by signing it. In this case, the quantity of the drug had somehow not been weighed according to the procedure. This mistake was unlikely to be rectified due to the lapse of time. This procedural slip-up seemed to have not worried the prosecution

[88] This article remains the same under the framework of CPL 1996. See Art 137 of CPL 1996.
[89] Field notes APU-18, 19 and 20.
[90] Field note APU-18.
[91] Field note APU-17.
[92] Field note APU-19.
[93] Field note APU-45.

at all. When asked how the police were going to remedy this issue, the prosecutor responded calmly: 'it is ok. I will ask the police to sort it out tomorrow.' On the following day, a police officer sent a record of the quantity of the drug, with the suspect's signature in place and the date matched perfectly. In a subsequent conversation with the officer, I learnt that the record had been 'patched' after they had received the instruction from the prosecutor.[94]

The tactics employed to resolve procedural mistakes of all types are apparently familiar to the prosecutors. There was clearly no desire to investigate the legality or authenticity behind the lawful presentation. So long as these official documents bore an image recognised by law, they were deemed as proper evidence with probative value. In another instance, a prosecutor discovered that the police had mistakenly put an unsigned form of notification regarding the suspect's rights and duties (*quanli yiwu gaozhishu*) in the dossier. Then the following conversation ensued:

> Researcher: According to the law, the form needs to be signed as soon as the suspect was arrested. So how can the suspect sign it now?
>
> Prosecutor: Don't worry. The police can get it done. Sometimes they won't bother to ask the suspect to sign it. They would sign it by themselves or ask a clerk to sign. Then they would thumbprint it by themselves. No one would really check.[95]

In Hodgson's research on French prosecutors, she found that the *procureur*'s oversight of police investigations was merely a paper exercise. Since the *procureur* aligned herself with the police, the police were given a free hand in constructing the case against suspects.[96] Clearly, there was a parallel in the Chinese context, where the primary concern of the prosecutor was not the process, but the end product. Compared to their French peers, the Chinese prosecutor went further. They were proactive in terms of the way they accommodated illicit practices, and they assisted the police in various ways to achieve this outcome. On one occasion, a prosecutor found that the date on the report of the suspect's arrest did not match the date on the suspect's statement. When asked about the discrepancy, the police officer explained the 'dilemma' they faced and sought advice.

> Police: After we apprehended the suspect, we were caught up in another drug case. We detained the guy in the police station for about three days before we interrogated him and transferred him to the detention centre. Do you have any suggestion as to illegal detention?
>
> Prosecutor: What about making a statement explaining that there was bad traffic or the vehicle broke down? The clock won't tick until the time the suspect arrives at the police station. So, you can straighten up the discrepancy of time.
>
> Police: Good idea.[97]

[94] Field note APU-32.
[95] Field note APU-17.
[96] Hodgson, *French Criminal Justice* (n 47) ch 6.
[97] Field note APU-18.

Evidence obtained in an illegal way was rarely excluded by the prosecutor, nor used as an exculpating factor favourable to the suspect. Whilst prosecutors perceived themselves as case reviewers, it seemed that they had defined their own role in a narrow way, which is more of a proofreader of the case dossier, rather than an authority capable of expressing criticism of their own conduct to guarantee the reliability of the evidence produced. Most prosecutors were willing to give legal advice to enhance the weight of the written evidence, and to make a procedurally flawed case appear persuasive. Their instructions were always constructive: the essence of overseeing the police case was to enhance the quality of the prosecution case rather than being critical:

> Researcher: Have you ever excluded any illegal evidence when you review the police dossier?
>
> Prosecutor: So far, I have never come across any evidence that has been excluded since I started working as a prosecutor in 2009. But I excluded a piece of evidence when I worked in the department of authorisation of arrestment [custody] of the procuratorate. It was a drug trafficking case. On the list of seizures, there was no signature of the suspect. That evidence was not accepted.
>
> Researcher: What happened to that evidence?
>
> Prosecutor: They sent it back to the police and the police made the suspect sign on the list.[98]

Despite the supervisory role of overseeing the legality of the police investigation, the actual relationship between the prosecutor and the police was more of mutual cooperation built on the bureaucratic coalition. Prosecutors generally acquainted themselves with the police who worked in the same jurisdiction. Some of these work relationships even developed into friendships. There were occasions when the police officers who worked closely with the prosecutors went out to play badminton or football with them after work.[99] One police officer who frequently visited the prosecutor's office for advice helped a prosecutor's friend to cancel his speeding penalties.[100] One prosecutor invited a number of police officers whom he often contacted for case preparation to his birthday dinner party.[101] Exchanges of personal favours between the prosecutor and the police officers abounded, which strengthened their alliance. In this harmonious working relationship, police could openly contact a prosecutor for advice when a certain legal requirement was breached, and the prosecutors were ready to help.

Before the Appraisal System was abolished, part of the police audit was linked to the prosecutor's decision not to prosecute.[102] When prosecutors chased the

[98] Interview APS-3.
[99] Field note APU-18.
[100] Field note APU-45.
[101] Field note AP-34.
[102] Fan Bonai and Ma Yanjun, 'Woguo gongan jingwu jixiao pingjia shijian ji pingjia tixi de goujian yanjiu (The Practice of the Police Evaluation and the Construction of the Evaluation System in China)' (2006) 4 *Journal of Xiangtan University* 15; Wu Meilai and Gui Ouli (n 62) 348–58.

police for additional materials to ensure that all required legal documents were included, their requests were usually responded to efficiently. After all, the police needed their cases to be successfully processed. The success of the police case was based on the clear-up rate according to the Appraisal System in site A. Depending on the type of offence, the clear-up rate could be calculated by the number of cases in which the suspect was charged or by the number of suspects who were approved to be remanded in custody (*pizhu baidu*). The prosecutors found that their instructions to the police were not always diligently followed. The police sometimes stopped responding to the prosecutor's requests as soon as it was decided that a case should be prosecuted. The police also tended to ignore instructions from the prosecutor if they believed that the outcome of the case would not adversely affect their own appraisal.

> Researcher: Do you think the police respond to your instructions promptly?
>
> Prosecutor: When we send an outline of the evidence to the police, the police are obliged to gather further evidence. Due to the appraisal policy, the police are reluctant to respond to our instructions once their tasks have been fulfilled. For those cases in which the suspects are in custody, once the custody department has authorised their application, the police have finished their task. If we were to ask them to gather further evidence after the suspect had been approved to be remanded in custody, they would be annoyed. Their mentality is such that they think the evidence gathering for the case has been completed and there is enough evidence to prosecute the case. They would not bother gathering further evidence.[103]
>
> Researcher: Do the police follow your instructions?
>
> Prosecutor: This issue is related to our appraisal model … For the police, they have the assessment which will set a goal of how many suspects they have arrested. It is not orientated with the citizen's satisfaction. It purely pursues the goal of how many suspects they have 'fought with'. Then the problem is they are utilitarianly motivated. All they want is to fulfil their task. (Their task is) for instance, how many people have been approved for custody each year. Once the suspect has been in custody, their task is achieved. So, the problem occurs that when a case has come to the point that the suspect is authorised to be remanded in custody, it is very hard for us to ask them to gather further evidence. We have no further effect on them. They feel that they are doing a favour for us. But for those cases when the suspect is not detained and in custody, there is no problem to ask them to gather additional evidence. Therefore, this problem is caused by the Appraisal System.[104]

What can easily be drawn from the prosecutor's grudge against the Appraisal System was the frangibility of the police–prosecutor relationship. It is true that there was a mutual dependence between the police and prosecutors, for which trust and cooperation were central to success. Yet the police's dependence was apparently anchored on the interests attached to the internal evaluation. This audit framework created the authority of the prosecutor over the police. Since the

[103] Interview BPS-1.
[104] Interview APS-4.

Appraisal System was overhauled in 2015, prosecutors have found their control over the police to be diminished:

> Prosecutor: Situations get more difficult after the abolishment of the Appraisal System. Police have lost their motivation to work hard as before. It is more difficult to direct them and instruct them to collect further evidence these days.[105]

When their instructions were ignored, prosecutors were powerless and frustrated.[106] To keep the case progressing, sometimes prosecutors decided to gather evidence by themselves:

> Prosecutor: I have to gather the evidence by myself. The police are reluctant to get the evidence, as their task is done. For those cases, I sometimes have to get the right evidence on my own.[107]

Disregarding their directions was not the only thing about the police that prosecutors complained about. In many instances, prosecutors were not satisfied with the quality of the case, even though cases were repeatedly returned to the police for further investigation.[108] According to some prosecutors, the complementary investigations were often conducted in a perfunctory manner, or not carried out in the way that the prosecutors had hoped for. There were a number of cases in which the police produced misleading information, or newly obtained evidence was clearly fabricated.[109] Botched police work increased the prosecutor's workload,[110] making them frustrated about the prospect of the cases and their weak 'teammates':

> Prosecutor: I asked the police to re-conduct the victim's statement and confirm that it was the suspect who assaulted the victim on his leg in the skirmish, but all they did was copy and paste the victim's previous statement and add one extra line saying that the suspect did the kick. They did not even bother to re-do a new statement![111]

The prosecutors' dissatisfaction was very often aimed at a group of inexperienced police officers, whose investigative skills were regarded as 'not being up to scratch'.[112] Unfortunately for the prosecutors, these 'green hands' constituted the bulk of the police force, becoming the mainstay of the crime investigation in the region. In a conversation with a senior prosecutor, he attributed the deterioration in the quality of police cases to the reformation of police recruitment.

> Prosecutor: The police recruitment reform since 2008 was disastrous. The PSB recruited far more graduates from universities who knew nothing about law and

[105] Interview GPS-1.

[106] A similar finding is documented in Mike McConville et al, *Criminal Justice in China: An Empirical Enquiry* (Edward Elgar, 2011) 386–95.

[107] Field note APU-23.

[108] Field notes APU-35, 39 and 42. It is worth noting that the prosecutor can return the case back to the police a maximum of twice.

[109] Field notes APU-36 and 37.

[110] Field note APU-38.

[111] Field note APU-22.

[112] Field note APU-31.

> had no professional training. They may be qualified to do something else, but some of them are not competent to be a policeman. The training is inadequate. All they had is a limited six-month on-the-job training. Imagine that, the new recruits just out of school, learnt geography or history, are now dispatched to gather evidence, with literally no legal knowledge or work experience![113]

With limited first-hand material, I was in no position to verify the reliability of the information. Were it true, the new police generation would be of great concern. The case dossiers assembled by some of the newly recruited officers, however, did leave obvious traces of manipulation and fabrication in the suspects' statements.[114] Their lack of experience was also visible in that some of the statements contained basic mistakes, such as spelling mistakes in witnesses' names, or the wrong dates of events.[115] Out of frustration, one prosecutor decided to gather evidence himself on a few occasions:

> Prosecutor: I was very disappointed with the police. As you have seen, this evidence dossier is quite thick at the moment. Actually, when the case was just given to me, the dossier was very thin. I read the dossier and developed lots of doubts … I have interviewed the victim, but I was still in doubt as to the fact that the evidence has presented. I started to gather more evidence myself … The messages I gathered have become the decisive evidence in this case. I dropped the case eventually due to these text messages. It is really a thorny problem that nowadays the police are not adequately trained.[116]

Despite the dissonance, the police were generally cooperative. As part of the Iron Triangle, the police and prosecutors were closely aligned and collaborated with each other. The police's lack of professionalism and the poor quality of the work that they produced was a headache to the prosecutor. But this did not change the position of the two legal actors as 'allies fighting against crime'.[117] The supervisory role that was greatly valued by the prosecutor seemed to have little substance. Prosecutors could not entirely control the police. Their authority very much derived from the performance indicators, which were ironically disapproved of by the prosecutors themselves.

B. Prosecutorial Interrogations

As part of the review process, the prosecutor is required to interrogate the suspect pursuant to the law.[118] It is believed that prosecutorial interrogation is

[113] Field note APU-30.

[114] This included again cutting and pasting the suspect's or witnesses' previous statements. Field notes APU-22, 34, 35 and 49.

[115] Field note APU-22.

[116] Field note APU-24.

[117] McConville et al (n 106) 386.

[118] According to Art 173 of CPL 2018, when examining a case, a people's procuratorate shall interrogate the criminal suspect, consult the defence lawyer, the victim and his or her agent ad litem, and record their opinions in writing. Any written opinion of the defence, the victim and his or her agent ad litem shall be attached to the case files.

an essential step in taking account of the suspect's story, verifying the accuracy of the confessions maintained in the record and gaining a sense of the suspect's attitude (especially contrition) in preparing the trial.[119] The interrogation practices in site A varied dependent on the habit of each prosecutor. Most prosecutors interrogated the suspect after they had reviewed the case dossier.[120] The prosecutorial interrogation took place either in the detention centre, if the suspect was placed in custody, or within the interrogation room inside the procuratorate's workplace, if the suspect was granted bail or was placed under residential surveillance. In both instances, defence lawyers were not allowed to be present during the process.[121]

(i) The Interrogation Room

The layout of the interrogation rooms, which I had a chance to observe, was typically accusatory. They highlighted the authority of the interrogators and the debased social status of the accused. The interrogation rooms in the local detention centre in site A were squalid, windowless rooms, separated into two parts by iron bars. Behind the bars was a plastic stool for the suspect, which was attached to the floor. On the other side of the bars was a desk facing the stool, where interrogators could type out statements. The room was barren and the walls were smeared with dirt or unrecognisable Chinese characters. Like other areas of the detention centre, the rooms reeked of a mixture of damp, urine and disinfectant. In the summer, mosquitoes swarmed so thickly that they blackened the ceilings. A ceiling fan was installed, but the slowly rotating blades could hardly deliver much air flow to ease the heat.[122]

The layout of the interrogation rooms in other detention centres in site A was roughly the same. Suspects were invariably questioned behind iron bars. However, compared to the local detention centres, the sanitation of the central detention centre was significantly better. Its facilities were well maintained and there were more security guards. Apparently, the operational funds for the higher-level detention centre was more sufficient than for the local ones.[123]

The arrangements of the interrogation rooms inside the procuratorate were different from those in the detention centres. All the walls in the interrogation

[119] See Chen Weidong, *Xingshi Susong Fa (Criminal Justice Law)* (China Renmin Press, 2004) 294.

[120] According to McConville et al (n 106) 122, the interrogation periods varied from prosecutor to prosecutor; whilst some preferred to interrogate the suspect before they read the dossier, others would interrogate within 3 days after they had received the case.

[121] CPL 1996 and CPL 2012 are silent as to whether defence lawyers are allowed to be present during pretrial interrogations. However, in legal practice, their presence has been explicitly rejected by legal institutions on the grounds that there is no legal provision supporting this practice.

[122] Field note APU-3.

[123] The human and financial resources were allocated according to the size of the detention facility and the number of detainees. Lei Cheng and E Nesossi, 'China's Pre-trial Detention Centres: Challenges and Opportunities for Reform' in E Nesossi et al (eds), *Legal Reforms and Deprivation of Liberty in Contemporary China* (Routledge, 2016) 101.

room were covered with soft materials to protect the suspect from self-harming. A CCTV camera was installed, although it was always switched off. The rooms were spacious. Although all the windows had iron grates, there were no iron bars dividing the rooms. A long desk and three stately judges' benches were positioned on a raised platform about 60 cm above the floor at one end of the room. At the other end of the room was placed one of the most gruesome contraptions in Chinese criminal justice – the tiger chair. The tiger chair is a notorious instrument for interrogational torture.[124] It is made of solid wood and has a bar lying across its arms to prevent the suspect from standing up. When a suspect sits in the chair, she is completely trapped: her hands are tightly buckled and feet fastened – and being forced to sit in the chair for a long period could be sheer agony, as the design of the chair puts tremendous strain on the body. The tiger chairs in the procuratorate building were employed by the former anti-corruption department for extracting confessions from suspects who were involved in corruption-related crimes; they were not used to interrogate suspects reviewed by prosecutors. Suspects for prosecutorial interrogations were led to sit on a normal wooden chair next to the tiger chair. Albeit not in use, the presence of the tiger chair could provoke an immediate spine-chilling reaction. A suspect from a middle-class background expressed his fear when he caught sight of the tiger chair:

> Suspect: I just came into this room and saw the chair (he pointed to the tiger chair next to him). It sent shivers down my spine … My hairs stood up. I have not seen anything so grisly for a long time.[125]

The set-up of these interrogations rooms (both those in the detention centres and those inside the procuratorate) did not follow the advice of Inbau et al, who suggested that a sense of privacy should be a priority for interrogation settings.[126] These rooms were clearly created for a different purpose. They were reminiscent of the torture chambers in medieval Europe.[127] The overlooking podium, the

[124] 'Tiger Chairs and Cell Bosses: Police Torture of Criminal Suspects in China', *Human Rights Watch* (13 May 2015) www.hrw.org/report/2015/05/13/tiger-chairs-and-cell-bosses/police-torture-criminal-suspects-china (accessed 1 August 2016). See also S Doughty, 'Our Torture Chair is a Comfy Chair, China Insists: Nobody Expected Beijing to Copy the Spanish Inquisition for Its Interrogations', *Mail Online* (29 January 2016) www.dailymail.co.uk/news/article-3421938/China-claims-notorious-torture-chair-comfortable.html (accessed 1 August 2017); 'Interrogation Chairs "Padded for Comfort", Claims Chinese Official as Beijing Denies Torturing or Holding Political Prisons', *South China Morning Post* (19 November 2015) www.scmp.com/news/china/policies-politics/article/1880506/interrogation-chairs-padded-comfort-claims-chinese (accessed 1 August 2017); E Reynolds, 'Tiger Chair: Sick Torture Tactics in Chinese Prisons', *News* (17 May 2015) www.news.com.au/world/asia/tiger-chair-sick-torture-tactics-in-chinese-prisons/news-story/c6681dd9ad-c7a45ac7681d18d5af5816 (accessed 1 August 2017); 'Report Details Widespread Chinese Torture in Police Detention', *BBC News* (12 November 2015) www.bbc.com/news/world-asia-china-34786336 (accessed 1 August 2017); Amnesty International, *China's Trade in Tools of Torture and Repression* (Amnesty International Publications, 2014).

[125] Field note APU-20.

[126] F Inbau et al, *Criminal Interrogation and Confessions*, 3rd edn (Williams & Wilkins, 1986) 29–34.

[127] JH Langbein, *Torture and the Law of Proof: Europe and England in the Ancient Regime* (University of Chicago Press, 1976) 14–26.

cage-like device and the presence of a tiger chair are all elements that symbolised power and compound the captive image of the suspect. They convey an unequivocal message that the interrogators have absolute control over the suspect; the suspect has no choice other than to show obedience. In this context, the rationale underpinning the interrogation tactics in twenty-first-century China bears little difference from that of the European interrogators of the Middle Ages.[128] The interrogations in China are still heavily dependent upon coercion and oppression.[129] Any observer who has seen these interrogation rooms could easily understand why torture as an entrenched practice is so difficult to eradicate – it was befitting of the oppressive surroundings.

(ii) Prosecutorial Interrogation

The physical conditions made it unpleasant to visit the local detention centres on a regular basis. As a result, the prosecutors in site A had reduced their number of visits to a minimum.[130] This routine practice applied to most prosecutors in site A. Cases were accumulated until they reached a certain total (ranging between 3 and 10). Then the prosecutor would conduct a batch of interrogations in a one-off undertaking. However, these visits did not always go smoothly for the prosecutors. For one thing, the time available for interrogation was limited, especially when the prosecutors intended to process a number of cases in one visit. The amount of time available for visits to detention centres was inflexible and subject to contingencies. Visits must obey the centre's own schedule, which normally allowed interrogations to take place between 09:30 and 11:30 in the morning and between 14:00 and 16:00 in the afternoon – after which time the suspect had to be escorted to their cell for lunch or dinner.[131] In addition to that, certain routine and logistic matters could aggravate the time pressure. The prosecutors needed to collect the case dossiers, laptops and portable printers from her office,[132] request an official vehicle for dispatch,[133] and travel to the far-away detention centre in rush hour. Official cars were not always available, and prosecutors could be stuck in a traffic jam for a long time. The bureaucratic management system in the detention centres could also be considerably time-consuming. Official documents must be exchanged and registered before a detainee was fetched. When a glitch occurred in

[128] MR Dutton, *Policing and Punishment in China: From Patriarchy to 'the People'* (Cambridge University Press, 1992) 114–17.

[129] For empirical research on Police Torture in China in recent years, see Amnesty International, *No End in Sight: Torture and Forced Confessions in China* (Amnesty International Publications, 2015).

[130] Field notes APU-11, 14 and 47.

[131] Like most institutions, the detention centres were closed between 12 and 2 pm in China for the siesta.

[132] As the most important asset in the criminal process, case dossiers must be securely stored in the prosecutor's office. They were not allowed to be taken home.

[133] The official procuratorate cars were often shared by several prosecutors, who made the journey together.

the computer system, interrogations had to be put on hold. Also, fetching a suspect from her cell alone could take a considerable amount of time – sometimes as long as an hour – for no good reason.

In light of these constraints, efficiency was paramount. To maximise the number of cases in a short space of time, a time slot was scheduled for each suspect, allowing more time occasionally for certain complicated cases or cases in which the suspect refused to plead guilty. Interrogation preparations were crucial in streamlining the interrogation process, and prosecutors had always typed up formulated questions and answers.[134] These questions and answers were copied from the accused's statements in the police interrogation. Then, once the suspect pleaded guilty, a confirmative statement would be printed out ready to sign. This seamless work strategy had significantly shortened the interrogation duration. On one occasion, a highly 'productive' prosecutor completed nine interrogations within two hours, with every interrogation lasting less than five minutes and most of that time being spent on checking the suspect's personal information.[135]

Such practice was desirable for easing the workload that the prosecutors faced. After working in the procuratorate for a while, many prosecutors came to the realisation that no one really wanted to do a proper and thorough interrogation – it was seen as a box-ticking exercise, serving no particular purpose. Experienced prosecutors, who prosecuted the same range of crime categories day after day, found the criminal cases to be homogeneous, with only the names and details varying. Their limited contact with suspects certainly made them feel that criminal cases were mainly about processing 'piles of paperwork', and there was 'very little human temperature' in that setting.[136] On that note, they certainly did not think that their job could significantly influence the lives of the 'worthless people' they dealt with:

> Prosecutor: For me, interrogations, as well as other work, are just those repetitive chores you have to fulfil with monotonous regularity. There are not many legal technicalities involved, although we do have to remember to confirm certain basics … For example, the questions for drug trafficking are like this: first, you should ask them about the fact. Ask what's happened and how were they arrested. Then ask them about the expert report and whether they have any disputes. Thirdly, ask them what profit they gained from the business. The profit includes the drugs that they might get for themselves. So, it is not limited to the money. Fourth, ask them why they sold the drugs. Also, remember to confirm the weight of the drug and ask whether they have any disputes.[137]

> Prosecutor: I think our work is pretty boring. On the TV dramas, there are always exciting plots surrounding investigating horrific and sophisticated crime; in reality, I am pretty disappointed. We are just repeating the same formulas day in and day out.

[134] Field note APU-34.
[135] Field note APU-36.
[136] Field notes APU-35 and 36.
[137] Field note APU-8.

> As you asked about interrogations. I won't say that is exciting at all. You have already seen our work routine. First, we copy the facts that the police have got in the dossier. For example, for these illegal trading receipts, we should ask what types of receipts the accused has sold. Then confirm whether she knows the number of the receipts and whether she has any disputes against the authenticity of the receipts. Then ask the suspect about the face value of the receipts and their resources. Anyway, you should make sure that all the elements of the crime have been supported by her statement. Another example is the drug cases. You should ask them what is the motivation of drug trafficking. You should exclude the fact that the suspect was working as an agent for the drug dealer. The expert report is important. Always ask them whether they have any disputes against the expert reports. Also remember to confirm that they have no disputes against the weight of the drugs. We have to be scrupulous, but I don't find our work is fulfilling.[138]

One strict rule that the prosecutor ought to follow was that the suspect must be interrogated in a way that corroborates her previous confessions. As far as prosecutors were concerned, the principle of assumption of guilt was unshakeable, regardless of whether it was decided to prosecute the case or not. The whole interrogation process was set out to uphold this premise. To confirm the guilt of the suspect, corroboration was a key step. In the following field note excerpt, an experienced prosecutor was coaching a junior prosecutor on how to effectively solicit a guilty account:

> Prosecutor: You must not ask questions at your will. You should lead questions to what the victim said. If the suspect's confession can reflect what the victim and the witnesses said, the statement of the witnesses will be corroborated. Then we can use it against him (the suspect). All the questions you asked should not be too subjective. They should be based on the evidence in the dossier.[139]

Under this guidance, the prosecutorial interrogation was often carried out in a way to validate the account in the investigative dossier. Questions were designed to encourage the suspect to confess and to dovetail with narratives presented by the police. Instead of asking 'did you conduct the theft?', the prosecutor simply asked 'how did you conduct the theft?', implying that the crime (theft) in question was not in dispute.[140] Similarly, the suspect was asked how much profit she had received from the drug transaction, rather than whether the illegal transaction took place or had generated any profit at all.[141] Many of the questions were constructed in such a way as to leave an impression that the prosecutorial interrogation was merely a repetition of police questioning. A consistent answer was hence expected, and any discrepancy of the story was dissuaded.

The end product – the official statement produced by the prosecutor – was always presented in a neat and brief format, with a clear and concise selection of

[138] Field note APU-7.
[139] Field note APU-18.
[140] Field note APU-34.
[141] Field note APU-12.

words. Judging from the interrogation record, it appeared that the process was carried out in a smooth, civil and even considerate manner, where hesitations, uncertainties or disputes were out of the question. This was in contrast with the actual interrogation, where the exchanges between the prosecutor and the accused were constantly muddied with confusion, contradiction and tension. Very often, the suspects clearly did not understand the legal concept used by the prosecutor, or the legal intricacies of the situation. They might well have entered a guilty plea without fully understanding the substance of what had been accepted and the legal consequences it entailed. With no access to a defence lawyer advising her how to proceed without incriminating herself involuntarily, the suspect was often left confused, signing statements with no legal assistance being available to her. For instance, one female suspect accused of illegally possessing narcotic drugs was a 21-year-old girl. Her manner was agreeable and it seemed that she was making some effort to please the prosecutor. Judging from her response, she was completely at a loss and did not truly understand the crime she was accused of:

> Field note-APU 23 (*CASEA* 33) Illegal Possession of Narcotic Drugs:
>
> Prosecutor: 7 bags of Magu[142] were found by police in your apartment in the evening of 5th November. These drugs belonged to your friend, but you decided to keep them for your own use. Is that true?
>
> Suspect: They were my friend's property. All I agreed was to hold something valuable for him – he never told me what's inside. I did not know what they are as they were kept in a locked suitcase. He was travelling to the North to do some business and his condo was not a safe place.
>
> Prosecutor: But you did know that he was a drug user. It must have occurred to you that he might leave some drugs in your possession. And most importantly, they were found in your apartment.
>
> Suspect: He gave all sorts of things for me to look after temporarily. Sometimes jewellery and car keys etc. He trusted me.
>
> Prosecutor: So, you know that it is possible that he might give you some drugs someday.
>
> Suspect: I don't know what was inside. He only told me something valuable. So, I guess it was some expensive stuff. It could be anything expensive.
>
> Prosecutor: I am not here to hear all these pretexts. Do you plead guilty of possessing drugs? You will be better off if you do so. These drugs were found in your apartment. That is the fact.
>
> Suspect: As you said, they found them in my apartment. So, yes, I plead guilty.

Here the suspect was apparently unaware of the law that knowledge of narcotic drugs was a prerequisite for the offence of drug possession.[143] No explanation

[142] A type of drug that is composed of methamphetamine mixed with caffeine.

[143] See Art 3 of Judicial Interpretation of the Supreme People's Court's Application of the Decision of Prohibition of Drugs Made by the National People's Congress Standing Committee No 30 (20 December 1994).

was offered by the prosecutor throughout the interrogation in relation to this crucial legal component. It can be seen from the conversation that the *actus reus* of the offence, that is, the drug found in the suspect's possession, was repeatedly emphasised as if that alone could have led to the conviction of the guilt. Clearly, the suspect did not fully understand the implications of the guilty plea either. Her account seems to suggest a lack of the corresponding *mens rea* on her part, but this was not recorded in the statement. Instead, the prosecutor simply adopted the story constructed by the police, stating that the suspect had a knowledge of the contents of the suitcase and the drug was intended for her own use.

This was not the only case where the suspect admitted a crime without understanding its legal implications. Suspects sometimes asked the prosecutor questions during an interrogation. The most frequent questions asked included how long they would be sentenced for,[144] what sentence discount they would get if they pleaded guilty,[145] what would happen if they claimed innocence, what would the consequences be of retracting their earlier confessions[146] and how long would they have to wait for the trial.[147] The answers provided by prosecutors varied significantly. While some prosecutors gave a straightforward estimation, others chose to be tight-lipped, or to answer in an ambiguous and diplomatic way, such as 'it is difficult to say and it is subject to the judge's discretion',[148] 'it is inappropriate for me to answer',[149] 'it depends on how you behave'[150] or 'I have to review other evidence to make a comprehensive judgement first'.[151] Any question that might have indicated that the accused was going to retract her confession and plead not guilty was strongly discouraged, and was always accompanied by a warning that the suspect would be punished with the most severe sentence she could possibly get.[152]

Compared to those compiled in the police case dossier, the prosecutorial interrogation record carried less weight in criminal proceedings. These statements were mainly for internal use. Their main purpose was to assess the strength and persuasiveness of the police case and to justify the prosecutor's decision-making. For such a limited function, it was expected that the interrogation record conducted by the prosecutor could faithfully mirror the prosecutor–suspect conversation. After all, hearing the story from the suspect's perspective could be helpful in knowing the facts in question and reaching a rational decision. It could also offer an opportunity to oversee the police work, given that the prosecutor has the obligation to

[144] Field notes APU-11, 13, 24, 29, 35 and 37.
[145] Field notes APU-11, 13, 24, 29, 36, 37, 42, 45 and 48.
[146] Field notes APU-12, 13, 27, 29, 35, 36 and 37.
[147] Field notes APU-12, 13, 14, 29, 45 and 48.
[148] Field notes APU-11, 13, 29 and 48.
[149] Field notes APU-11, 14, 29, 45 and 48.
[150] Field notes APU-14 and 37.
[151] Field notes APU-12, 13 and 27.
[152] This point will be discussed at greater length in ch 5.

do so. However, as I have shown in the examples, the reality was quite different from this percept. Most of the prosecutorial interrogation records were merely a refined version of the suspect's earlier accounts made in front of the police. Prosecutors carefully maintained the gist of the case constructed by the police, unless the suspect openly protested. Prosecutors occasionally made minor changes to reflect the suspect's adjustment of the story, adding a few details, selecting different words or highlighting certain facts, provided that the modifications did not alter the established case facts.

In general, the interrogation record was an edited and attenuated version, rather than a verbatim account of the conversation between the prosecutor and the suspect. Noticeably, the prosecutors preferred to use certain words or fixed phrases that were clearly more familiar to them. But it was a thin line between the facts told by the suspect and those presented in the statement, which might have contained inaccuracies and misunderstandings. There were instances in which the facts documented in the statements were distorted by the prosecutor, although the contortion did not directly affect the accused's criminal liability. For example, in one drug trafficking case, *CASEA* 47, a middle-aged woman was suspected of being an accomplice of a drug seller. The suspect's boyfriend was charged as the principal offender (*zhufan*) of drug trafficking. One of the purposes of the prosecutorial interrogation was to identify whether the suspect had a knowledge of her boyfriend's illegal transaction. The suspect had received little education, although she was articulate enough to express herself well. Throughout the interrogation, the prosecutor abruptly interrupted her several times to paraphrase her words:

> Field note APU-31 (*CASEA* 47) Accessory to drug trafficking
>
> Prosecutor: Your friend Tang said he wanted 10 grams of ice.[153] So, you told that to Mao, your boyfriend. After that, your friend Tang came to your rented apartment and bought the ice. The business was finished in your rented apartment. Is that correct?
>
> Suspect: Yes.
>
> Prosecutor: What is the relationship between you and Mao? He is your boyfriend, isn't he?
>
> Suspect: You could say that. We have only lived together for a short period of time. We knew each other in a teahouse. We cohabited together shortly after we met. But funny enough, till now I still have no idea where his home address is.
>
> Prosecutor: [Typed 'Mao is my partner and we lived together'] Tang is your friend, and you call him 'your brother'. How did Tang know Mao?
>
> Suspect: Mao was running the business of the teahouse. I introduced Tang to Mao. They knew each other for a week.
>
> Prosecutor: [Typed 'I called Tang my brother, so Mao knew him'] How did Tang know that Mao was selling drugs?

[153] It is a purified form of methamphetamine.

Suspect: They were chatting while they were playing cards. I heard that.

Prosecutor: How did you know Mao was selling drugs?

Suspect: Because he is a drug user. He said he could get drugs.

Prosecutor: [Typed 'I told Tang that Mao could get drugs as he is a drug user'] How did Mao, your boyfriend, give the drug to Tang?

Suspect: I was cooking at the time. Our apartment is very small. The chairs were in the left corner …

Prosecutor: [Stopping her] So you wanted to say that you did not see that.

Suspect: Yes.

Prosecutor: [Typed 'I did not see how they were selling the drugs but I know they were doing the transaction.']

As soon as the interrogation was over, the prosecutor packed up the computer and printer and was ready to go. They pointed out a place on the interrogation record and asked the suspect to write a declaration which stated 'I have read the record, which is exactly what I said'. The suspect was also asked to sign her name and write the date, all of which were finally sealed with her thumbprints. If a suspect was illiterate, a sample of the declaration would be produced and they would be asked to replicate the wording. Despite the unambiguous declaration, the vast majority of suspects simply signed their names as demanded without actually reading the statement, as if checking the statement constituted an affront to the prosecutor's integrity.

The prosecutors whom I had observed rarely allowed the suspect to read the interrogation record at the end of the process. The hastiness in packing up the typing devices and the complex signing procedure clearly made it difficult for the suspect to make a request to check the content of their own statement. As far as the suspects were concerned, making such a request was highly inappropriate, as it would cause a delay in the process and implied distrust of the authority, who had the power to influence their cases. Nevertheless, there was a strong desire on their part to verify the details of the recording, as could easily be ascertained from their body language. Some of them quickly glanced at the record while signing their names, with a facial expression that did not divulge any suspicion. Others deliberately slowed down the signing process while quickly skimming the written account of the dialogue. Only a very small number of suspects (6 out of 67) were brave enough to openly ask if they were able to read the interrogation record. The responses from the prosecutors were either a censure, with noticeable vexation, stating that 'there is nothing for you to worry about; it is just what we talked [about]',[154] or absolute outrage, which often constituted an extension of an already deteriorated suspect–prosecutor relationship following from an antagonistic interrogation.[155] In either case, perseverance was needed if the request

[154] Field notes APU-35, 37 and 44.

[155] Field notes APU-20, 45 and 65.

was turned down by the prosecutor. In *CASEA* 64, the suspect was a 40-year old woman, investigated and detained for sheltering prostitutes (*rongliu maiyin*). She already had a criminal record for procuring others to engage in prostitution (*jieshao maiyin*) 4 years ago. The prosecutorial interrogation itself was fraught with belligerent arguments. It was apparent that the suspect had lost trust in state officials. When the interrogation ended, the suspect refused to sign the statement, the accuracy of which she fundamentally disputed.

Field note APU-65 (*CASEA* 64): Sheltering for prostitution

Prosecutor: How many houses have you rented?

Suspect: I rented four rooms. One of the rooms which I rented for a long time was too hot to live in during the summer.

Prosecutor: Did your husband charge the prostitutes?

Suspect: No. I always excluded my husband from this business. He is not involved at all.

Prosecutor: [Shouting] Not involved? Prostitutes Shasha and Zhang had confessed to the police and they said they gave money to your husband.

Suspect: Shasha and Zhang were tortured by the police. Hot chilli water was poured into their noses and ears until they said what the police wanted. I met the 'misses'[156] when I was asked to provide my fingerprints. They told me that they were interrogated in the same room and they have seen what the police did to each other. Even a man could not bear the pain, not to mention the fragile women. The 'misses' did not tell the truth. I asked them whether they read the interrogation record before they signed, and they said they did not. The police did not give them a chance to read the interrogation record. The interrogating officer promised that 'I honestly wrote what you said, why to bother reading it'. I did not read every word of the record of my police interrogation but I read some. The police officer did not write what I said. They made it up. They interrogated me twice, but they have five records of interrogation. How can that be possible? They just copied and pasted what they fabricated in my account. Why do they do this to me? I honestly confessed what I did and I trusted the government. But why are they not doing things honestly …

Prosecutor: [Angrily stopping the suspect] Enough. The police do not torture these days. It is illegal to do so. How did the customer find you?

Suspect: I don't understand.

Prosecutor: [Shouting loudly and used certain swear words] You don't know? Everything has reasons. How can the customer find your place rather than other houses?

Suspect: I see what you meant. The place I rented used to be a brothel. From time to time, there was someone knocking our door and asking for a 'miss'. It used to be a lot. But now the number of customers has become much smaller because the police check our places so frequently.

Prosecutor: On the day you were arrested, a man, Zhou, called you and asked for a prostitute. You told him that 'fast food' (the one-off business) was 150 yuan and 'staying overnight' was 230 yuan. He asked for a bargain. Then you reduced the price of 'fast food' to 130 yuan, didn't you?

[156] The Chinese way of saying prostitutes.

Suspect: No, officer. I have never said that. The other night, I was half asleep when Zhou called. I only knew him after I was arrested. I answered the phone and the man, Zhou, asked 'is there anyone in'. I said 'you can come in and have a look'. I did not say anything about 'fast food' or 'overnight'. They were made up by the police. As soon as the man came in, the police knocked on the door and arrested them at the staircase. I did not know this until later when I met Shasha in the police station. She told me that Zhou was working for the police. Because the police did not know which room I rented, they sent him to entrap me.

Prosecutor: [Shouting loudly] You are making things up. The police won't use entrapment apart from the drug trafficking cases. This is impossible.

Suspect: Officer, I told the truth. Shasha told me that …

Prosecutor: [Interrupting her words] If you dare say that again, I will charge you with a new offence. Do you want to try?

Suspect: [A few seconds of silence] Officer. I really wanted to be cooperative. I have told you everything I know. We have been arrested by the police already and it is so easy for them to get the evidence against me.

Prosecutor: Will you pick up the business again when you are released in the future?

Suspect: No. Never! I have been punished and I will look for a legal job … The community centre had advised me to work in a supermarket. I will work legally after I am out. My husband and I are both in custody. I am really worried about my child. I have been in the detention centre for a whole month and I have no idea what has happened to my child. Is she in school? Who takes care of her? She is only 15.

Prosecutor: [Printed out the record and gave it to the suspect to sign and thumbprint] Copy this sentence and sign your name here. What are you looking at? It is the same as you said. Quickly sign your name and put the date on. I am running late.

Suspect: [Read the record of interrogation carefully] Officer, you typed a mistake, I rented four rooms but you wrote I rented four houses. Also, I did not say anything about 'fast food' and 'overnight'. This was made up by the police. On that night, I was half-asleep when the man called me. I only asked who he was. You copied what the police wrote in my statement. I corrected the mistake and the police officer changed this in my second interrogation. Can you change this, please?

Prosecutor: [Using a lot of swear words] I have packed the computer and printer away already. I cannot change that for you. I told you, the fact is clear now and you cannot get away with it. Why do you argue about such trivial details? The fact is very clear now.

Suspect: Officer, I know nothing about law, but I think it is very important that we should get the facts straight. I have confessed to what I know and I have told you everything. I don't know what are the main facts or detailed information. I only know that what you wrote was not what I said.

Prosecutor: [Shouting] What an attitude you have! I tell you that sheltering prostitution will be sentenced to from one-year to five-year imprisonment. If you behave well, your sentence will be mitigated. However, if you have such an attitude, I tell you, the judge will put a maximum sentence on you! You quibble with me. I tell you, this is not worthwhile. You cannot get away with this. Quickly sign your name and put your thumbprint on that!

Suspect: No. It is not what I said and I will not sign my name.

> Prosecutor: I told you that the difference you talk about is not the main facts. Sign your name here.
>
> Suspect: I am sorry but I will not sign unless these words are changed.
>
> Prosecutor: It is ok that you do not sign. I can put a note on the record of interrogation, which also is valid. You cannot get away with this!

As can be seen from the extract, the suspect reported the use of torture. However, this was dismissed by the prosecutor, who showed no interest in investigating the alleged police malpractice. Of the measures designed to combat interrogational torture,[157] prosecutors were given high hopes of being able to independently investigate the abuse of police power.[158] However, I was not aware of any official enquiry into police misconduct being carried out by the prosecutor during my visit to the field site in 2013, given the good relationship between the police and the prosecutors.[159] There were a good number of cases that involved allegations of police brutality in investigations.[160] Only one case in relation to torture was taken seriously by the procuratorate. In that case, the procuratorate decided to exclude a confession statement which was believed to have been obtained by torture. The exclusion of the statement, however, did not make much difference to the case, since the suspect made a total of seven confessions, and the remaining incriminating statements were sufficient to secure the conviction.[161] Despite the strong suspicion of interrogational torture, no police officer was investigated for committing the crime nor was disciplined for the inappropriate misconduct. Nevertheless, most prosecutors still emphasised the important

[157] Other approaches to combat torture include the exclusionary rule, detention centre regulations and police interviewing skills. See Chen Weidong and T Spronken, *The Three Approaches to Combating Torture in China* (Intersentia Publishing, 2012).

[158] See Chen Guangzhong et al, *Zhonghua Renmin Gongheguo Xingshi Susongfa Xiaogai Tiaowen Shiyi yu Dianping (Annotations and Comments on the Revised Articles of the Criminal Procedure Law of the People's Republic of China)* (People's Court Press, 2012) 242; Wang Mingming, 'Dui woguo ezhi xingxun bigong falv jizhi de kaocha yu fansi (Reconsideration of the Legal Mechanism of Curbing Tortures in China)' (2012) 4 Jiangsuo jingguan xueyuan (Journal of Jiangsu Police Officer College) 21. Wan Yi, 'Jiancha jiguan zhengju guize de xiugai yu wanshan: dui renming jianchayuan xingshi susong guize zhengju zhang xiugai jianyi (Revision and Perfection of the Evidence Rule in Relation to the Procuratorate: Revision Suggestions on the Evidence Chapter of the Criminal Procedure Law in Relation to the Procuratorate)' (2014) 3 *China Criminal Law Magazine* 61; Chen Ruchao, 'Xingxun bigong de guojia zhili: 1979–2013 (The State Governance of Torture: From 1979 to 2013)' (2014) 5 *China Law Studies* 5, 22.

[159] However, other empirical research has shown that procuratorates elsewhere were relatively effective in identifying police misconduct in practice. Yang Guanyu and Guo Xu, 'Feifazhengju paichu guize shishi kaocha baogao: yi J sheng jianchajiguan wei shijiao (Empirical Report on the Implementation of the Illegally Obtained Evidence: From the Perspective of the Procuratorate in J Province)' (2014) 22 *Evidence Science* 5. According to Art 171 of CPL 2012, when the procuratorate believes that the evidence is illegally obtained, it may ask the police to give an explanation regarding the lawfulness of the evidence.

[160] Out of the 64 cases that I closely monitored, 27 cases were alleged to have involved malpractice (from overbearing behaviours to torture) by the police.

[161] Unfortunately, I was not able to obtain more details of that case for pragmatic reasons.

role of prosecutorial interrogation in identifying the issue of torture and fulfilling their supervisory function. According to them, it was a unique way to reveal police wrongdoing:

> Researcher: How do you review the legality of the evidence?
>
> Prosecutor: For example, I would check whether there were two officers during the interrogation and whether the interrogation took place at a legal time and in a legal place. On the other hand, we would listen to the suspect's defence. For example, if a suspect told us that he was tortured during the investigation, then we would ask him for further information such as the names of the interrogation officers, the time that the interrogation took place and the methods that were employed. Based on the information, we would gather further evidence such as the officers' statements, the suspect's statements after detention and the medical reports before he had been admitted to the detention centre. By reviewing all the evidence above, if we believe there is some illegal evidence, we would exclude such evidence and charge it.[162]
>
> Prosecutor: … We have to prove that all the evidence we have received has been legally obtained. The legality of the evidence is the precondition to the admission of the evidence. If the evidence in question is not legally obtained, we have to exclude it. The most important way to review the legality of the evidence is by questioning the suspect. The suspect will tell us how the evidence (the confession) was gathered. After the interrogation, we would communicate with the police. If the evidence (the suspect's confession) is claimed to be illegally obtained, we would gather evidence regarding his (the suspect's) status before he was put into the detention centre.[163]

In reality, illegally obtained evidence reported by suspects, such as that seen in the sheltering for prostitution case (*CASEA 64*), was rarely investigated by prosecutors. The alleged maltreatment of suspects was disregarded by the prosecutor when the issue of torture, other unlawful means or tactics was brought up by suspects. Where a suspect made such assertions, the reaction of the prosecutor was either to show outright scepticism or to ignore it. In *CASEA 34*, the suspect's complaint that 'I was hung up and beaten by the police' was greeted with indifference by the prosecutor. A similar explanation by a suspect in *CASEA 37* – 'the police asked me to cooperate, otherwise my wife would be in trouble' – was responded to with an accusation that the suspect was lying. In fact, none of the prosecutors in site A had any experience of undertaking a prosecution of torture against the police; they had rarely requested an explanation regarding the lawfulness of the evidence from the police.[164] Based on my conversations with some of the prosecutors, it was

[162] Interview BPS-4.

[163] Interview APS-4.

[164] During the interview, two prosecutors said that the police were asked to produce an explanation of the lawfulness of the evidence gathering. However, this was obviously rare: Interview BPS-4. It should be noted that my observation was conducted between 2012 and 2013. Since 2013, there has been a top-down policy to enforce the exclusionary rules in line with the criminal justice reform in China. In research on exclusionary rules conducted by Guo Zhiyuan, prosecutors in recent years have been more active in uncovering the illegality of evidence. Guo Zhiyuan, 'The First Step of the Long March: Implementing the Exclusionary Rule in China' (2017) 25 *Asia-Pacific Law Review* 48.

clear that they shared a similar work model and had a comparable attitude towards suspects. This attitude was derived from the understanding of the status quo of the police investigation and the fact that the criminal justice system was weighted heavily in favour of confessions. To date, confessions are still the most persuasive pieces of evidence in any given case:[165]

> Prosecutor: Our forensic techniques are really weak. Ordinary evidence such as fingerprinting is rarely used in the court. We rely too heavily on the suspect's statements. When I went to interrogate the suspects, they have said to me 'look! The police beat me up. It is still hurting.' Then I have asked them 'do you have evidence that you were beaten by the police?' They don't have of course. So, I have to say 'I have no way of helping you. Now confess what you did.' But, in my opinion, some of the suspects are really in need of a good beating. They would not tell the truth until they have learned a lesson.[166]

For that reason, prosecutors showed little enthusiasm in vigorously checking the means by which evidence was obtained in police investigations. The supervisory task was kept to a minimum, if it could not be avoided completely. One of the supervisory tasks of the prosecutor entails identifying whether there is any neglected offence or offenders.[167] Struggling with a heavy caseload, the prosecutors in site A had played down this obligation. Thus, when an inexperienced prosecutor intended to embark on a new investigation which was concerned with fraud as confessed by the suspect during the prosecutorial interrogation, his referral to the senior prosecutor encountered strong disgruntlement:

> The junior prosecutor reported a fraud case to the head prosecutor. During a prosecutorial interrogation, the suspect confessed a new offence of fraud which he committed. This case was not known by the police.
>
> Head prosecutor: Did you put down what the suspect confessed?
>
> Junior prosecutor: Yes, I did.
>
> Head prosecutor: If you don't want too much hassle or make things difficult, you should not have recorded what he confessed. As long as the paperwork cannot indicate the extra transactions, you don't need to be involved in the trouble. However, since you have written it down, you have no choice now. You have created trouble for yourself. Next time, don't bother getting the trouble again.[168]

Following that advice, when another suspect claimed that the crime she was charged with was a direct result of her being a victim of illegal gambling, which she had reported to the police but had got no response (*CASEA 15*), this report of a crime was completely disregarded by the prosecutor, who showed no interest in

[165] See also McConville et al (n 106) 337–40.

[166] Field note APU-30.

[167] As mentioned earlier in this chapter, Art 168 of CPL 2012 (Art 171 of CPL 2018) provides that the procuratorate must ascertain whether there are any crimes that have been omitted or other persons whose criminal responsibility should be investigated.

[168] Field note APU-16.

the police negligence or the offence that had not been investigated. In that case, the suspect, a female accountant in her 20s, tried to offer a full account of the accused offence but was consistently stopped by the prosecutor, who wished to end the interrogation as quickly as possible. As far as the prosecutor was concerned, once the case was ostensibly matched with the facts provided in the police case, there was no point in exploring further details.

> Suspect: I was an accountant. But when I was employed in X company, I was a financial manager. I was doing both the accountant's job as well as working as a cashier. You see, this is flawed, as …
>
> Prosecutor: [Stopping her] OK, I understand what you mean. [Speaking very loudly] Listen to me! The financial system of the company is none of our business. Our job is to prosecute crimes.
>
> Suspect: OK. I was managing all the financial issues of the company. Then I was involved in a Lottery account one day and I checked it on the website …
>
> Prosecutor: [Stopping her] Stop! I don't want to hear so many details of what you said. Now let me just read what you said in the police station. The fact is you were involved in this gambling game and you had to use the money of the company to invest in this fraudulent trick. How did you invest the money?
>
> Suspect: I used my salary to buy it initially because I believed what it said. On the website, it is said the Public Security Bureau and the Taxing Bureau have given credits to the lottery company. So, I really trusted it. However, after I was registered as a member of the website, someone kept calling me for money. They even threatened me that if I did not send them the money, they would stop me from taking the National State Official Exams. All that I said can be found in my mobile recordings.
>
> Prosecutor: [Stopping her] All that you said is nothing to do with this case. They are nothing to do with the case.[169]

During my fieldwork, I had not witnessed any meaningful supervision of the police work undertaken by the prosecutors. For the majority of cases, suspects' previous statements in the police questioning, which might have been obtained by illegal or an inappropriate manner, were further utilised to buttress the prosecution case.

C. Interviewing Victims

Prosecutors occasionally interviewed criminal victims as part of the review process. This ascertaining procedure, however, was not extended to all criminal cases. There were only two criminal offences for which interviewing the victim was mandatorily required in site A, namely intentional assault (*guyi shanghai*)

[169] Field note APU-15.

and rape.[170] When asked why these two offences were singled out a prosecutor answered hesitantly:

> Prosecutor: To be honest, I have no clue why only those two types of crime. It is our practice. But I am thinking that [it is] because the rape case is the so-called 'one to one' case (*yi dui yi an jian*), meaning that only the offender and the victim knew what happened. In the rape case, usually, only the rapist and the victim know what happened. Interviewing the victim can make us convinced. We can understand the facts of the case as well. For assault cases, we have to inform the victim of his right to compensation.[171]

This was confirmed by another prosecutor, who felt that interviewing the victim was a waste of time:

> Prosecutor: I am not sure why we have to do this for assault and rape cases. The most important part of interviewing the victim is informing them of their legal rights because the victim of the assault is entitled to compensation. Actually, I think if they are given a notice of their rights that should be sufficient. Therefore, I don't think it is necessary to interview victims either. I think the court can inform the victim of his rights which should not be our job. Most of the evidence has been gathered by the police, I cannot see any point why we need to do it again.[172]

These two explanations are far from convincing. First, there are many other offences which can be categorised as the 'one to one' type but where interviewing the victim is not required. A typical example is bribery. Bribery takes place privately between two parties. However, the prosecutor seldom interviews the briber, who can be categorised as a victim according to Chinese law if the property was extorted by a state official who the person was forced to bribe in order to protect her rightful interests.[173] Secondly, interviewing victims in rape and assault cases cannot guarantee that prosecutors will get a better picture of the case. Like any other offence, the victim in assault and rape cases might be intoxicated, unconscious or unaware of the situation, thereby being incapable of offering useful information. Thirdly, it seems illogical and unjustifiable that assault and rape victims are given notice of their special rights via an interview, whereas victims of other crimes are not. It also seems unnecessary for the notification to take the form of an interview, if the prosecutor only intended to deliver a message of the victim's entitlement to compensation; a simple notice would normally suffice.

There are, however, other reasons to explain why prosecutors are specifically required to interview rape and assault victims as a local procuratorate work policy. As far as rape is concerned, prosecutors are expected to thoroughly

[170] There is no official document suggesting that interviewing rape and assault victims is a widespread practice in other procuratorates in China. The intentional assault should be interpreted broadly, including sexual assault.

[171] Interview APS-2.

[172] Interview APS-1.

[173] According to Art 389 of the Criminal Law, only those who bribe in order to seek unlawful interests are guilty of bribery.

ascertain the lack of consent (which is also known as 'against the will of the female victim', as the law stipulates) as a crucial element of a crime, which can be very complicated, depending on the circumstances.[174] For intentional assault, the prosecutor has the discretion to decriminalise the offence by deciding not to initiate prosecution, if the injury is minor or the circumstance is not serious according to Article 177 of CPL 2018. Therefore, the victim's account is an indispensable means by which the prosecutor can assess the harm caused, taking account of the various circumstances.

Although this may be a better interpretation of the procuratorate's local policy, it is not difficult to see that this policy is problematic. The problem lies in the lack of clarification of the policy. There was genuine confusion amongst the prosecutors as to why a compulsory interview was needed for those two categories of victim. The consequence of this was that interviewing of the victim (especially assault cases) was always executed perfunctorily. Aside from corroborating the victim's account with the suspect's statement, the questions were merely a repetition of those that had been asked by the police.[175] For example, one interview I observed concerned a 9-year old schoolgirl who had been sexually assaulted by a man who had trespassed in her mother's flat.[176] The police also reported that the man had also stolen 900 yuan from the flat. The girl and her mother, a woman in her late 30s, both attended the interview. Although the victim was the 9-year-old girl, the questions were mainly addressed to the mother, who answered most of the questions. In the course of the interview, it became clear that there were some discrepancies between the police statements and the account given by the victim's mother.

> Prosecutor: Did your daughter tell the truth in the police station?
>
> Victim's mother: Yes.
>
> Prosecutor: When was that? On the 9th of June?
>
> Victim's mother: I cannot remember the exact date.
>
> Prosecutor: Then I will copy what you said in the police's interview. [Started to copy the record of the interview in the dossier] What happened then?
>
> The victim's mother told the prosecutor what she witnessed on that day. However, the prosecutor concentrated on copying her previous statement in the police station. Differing from what was recorded in the dossier, which maintained that the suspect only sexually assaulted the victim once, the victim's mother reported that the man sexually assaulted her daughter twice, on two different occasions, and stole 2000 yuan, rather than 900 yuan from her flat. The prosecutor, however, ignored the discrepancies and did not record the new information in the statement.

[174] See Art 236 of the Criminal Law. See also The Supreme People's Court, the Supreme People's Procuratorate and the Ministry of Public Security on Answers to Specific Issues of Implementation of Law on Processing Rape Cases (26 April 1984), Fayanzi [84] No 7.

[175] This is also found in McConville et al (n 106) 125.

[176] In China, there is no such crime as burglary or offences equivalent to trespass with the intention to commit a sexual offence, as in the UK.

Prosecutor: Do you have any requests for us?

Victim's mother: We are worried if he is released in the future from the prison, he will hurt my child again. He knows my child, where we live and I don't want my child to be hurt.

[The prosecutor seemed uninterested in exploring her request]

Prosecutor: So, you hope the law punishes him. [Typed 'I hope the law punishes him'] OK, Come and sign it here.

After the interview, I asked the prosecutor about her stolen money and the second sexual assault.

Researcher: She said the guy had done this twice to her daughter and he stole more money than was recorded. But you did not ask her any more detail?

Prosecutor: There is no evidence in the dossier. So, it is useless.[177]

According to the law, the prosecutor should heed the opinions of the victim and the victim's needs or requirements when ascertaining whether the evidence is reliable and sufficient for a prosecution.[178] In reality, as long as a written record was produced to show that the victim's statement matched the defendant's confession, the prosecutor's task was discharged, disregarding any contradiction or disputes. In this regard, interviewing victims was mainly seen as serving the same corroborative purpose as the other prosecutorial activities being undertaken.

IV. Conclusion

The Chinese procuratorate's responsibility for overseeing the enforcement of the law by other criminal justice institutions is undoubtedly controversial in the light of democratic legal rationales. As a divergent approach from Western legal systems, the procuratorate in China and its Soviet prototype were designed to facilitate the centralised Socialist authority and the highly controlled justice system in their particular sociopolitical contexts. In this perspective, the judiciary, the police and other legal institutions are treated equally as law enforcement agencies despite their distinctive functions, whereas the procuratorate is entrusted as a guardian of justice. This special legal status of the procuratorate embodies remarkable confidence of the state in the procuratorate's ability in maintaining the socialist legal order and ensuring strict observance of the socialist law.

Despite the official rhetoric, the actual role that the procuratorate has played in supervising other criminal justice institutions is somewhat different from this expectation. The procuratorate's oversight of the police investigation is perceived as essential to ensure the quality of the police case and compliance with legal procedures. However, as an after-event review model, prosecutors are unable to

[177] Field note APU-43.
[178] See Art 170 of CPL 2012.

direct the investigation effectually until the police inquiry is over. More problematically, the chief objective of the prosecutor is to offer professional guidance to the police and to help them construct a legally coherent case dossier. Prosecutors' actions are largely driven by a concern of the presentation of investigative dossiers that are capable of withstanding the scrutiny of the court, rather than the legality of the investigation process or the reliability of the evidence produced. The tactics employed by the police to resolve all sorts of procedural errors are familiar to the prosecutors, but they rarely demonstrate any desire to investigate the legality of the investigation process. The authenticity or reliability of the legal documents is rarely questioned. In fact, the prosecutors constantly give constructive legal advice to the police, helping them enhance the probative value of the written evidence and making a procedurally flawed case appear persuasive. When an unlawful issue is identified, their action is to assist the police in recycling the tainted evidence.

Prosecutors have a duty to interrogate suspects and interview victims of certain types of crime in order to verify the veracity of their accounts and to supervise the investigation process. These interviews and interrogations are largely routinised, and prosecutors hardly explore the potential anomalies in the police-dominated investigation. These procedures are mainly carried out in a way to corroborate the suspect and victim statements contained in the investigative dossier. Since prosecutors are aligned with the police in their common objective of securing convictions, their actions are geared towards shoring up the case prepared by the police, including providing legal advice to cover up illegally obtained evidence or procuring guilty pleas from suspects to confirm their earlier confessions gained through a range of oppressive tactics. Oversight in this context is to help the police conceal or legitimise their malpractices, even to the extent of teaching them how to falsify evidence. In this regard, prosecutors are complicit in the misconduct and procedural irregularity, which may very well be one of the causes of miscarriages of justice.

5

Pre-trial Decisions Concerning Prosecution

Following the analysis of the prosecutor as supervisor of police investigations, this chapter embarks on the examination of the prosecutor's role as a decision-maker, who determines whether or not to prosecute. In considering whether the prosecutorial discretion works effectively in weeding out weak cases, it examines the operation of the power of 'not to prosecute' in prosecutors' day-to-day practice, taking account of how they handle external influences. I will investigate what prosecutors do to ensure conviction, when weak cases fail to be screened out of the system. This involves the acquisition of guilty pleas during the prosecutorial interrogation, a process that facilitates an efficient disposition of large volumes of cases. The difficulties that the defence lawyer has to confront at this stage will also be explored. The prosecution review period is crucial to defence lawyers, during which time they are allowed to access the prosecution evidence or gather further evidence to construct the defence case.

I. The Discretionary Power Not to Prosecute

A. Prosecutorial Discretion

Prosecutorial decision-making, as a type of professional judgment of the prosecution organisation, consists of a decentralised professionalism approach and a more rigid bureaucracy approach.[1] The decentralised professionalism model is characterised by ample autonomy of prosecutors as legal professionals, who are certified by an adequacy of professional training and ethical disposition on entry, only loosely supervised by their peers. As an alternative, the bureaucratic paradigm implies regimenting compliance with stable and hierarchically promulgated rules. Prosecutors tend to be substantially overseen by their superiors, who 'tolerate low-visibility rule departures either because of the limits of their capacity to monitor

[1] William Simon identified a third model, that is, the post-bureaucratic approach, which enhances greater transparency and greater potential for stakeholder participation: W Simon, 'The Organisation of Prosecutorial Discretion' in M Langer and DA Sklansky (eds), *Prosecutors and Democracy: A Cross-National Study* (Cambridge University Press, 2017) 176.

or because they favour the benign departure'.[2] Being a difficult-to-define concept, prosecutorial discretion treads on the two contrasting paradigms and is associated with a process that allows a constrained authoritative decision to be made within the ambit of formal rules, as well as many social, economic and political disciplines that act upon the exercise of choice.[3] In what aspect and to what extent prosecutors are able to exercise discretion are pertinent to the way prosecutors are defined in a given system and its sociolegal calibration. In jurisdictions where prosecutors are regarded as one of the leading figures of the criminal justice system (such as the USA, France and Japan), they enjoy high social status and are entrusted to apply 'a discrete body of university-based knowledge to a particular situation',[4] with no obligation to justify its correctness. The controlling mechanism is internally entrenched in their belief in law as well as the professional community. In contrast, the bureaucratic paradigm relies on the bureaucratic systems to offer control of the prosecutorial power.[5] In such a model, prosecutors are usually no more privileged than a civil servant whose job is to faithfully apply the law. William Simon suggests that although this model is 'superficially compatible with public accountability' for its purporting to 'operate in a hierarchical, rule-governed manner described by Max Weber and Frederick Taylor', it actually provides abundant room for low-visible frontline discretion.[6]

The Chinese prosecution system largely falls into the bureaucratic category in which regimenting judgment and observance of the bureaucratic order are prioritised. Newly qualified prosecutors nowadays are required to have a minimum of a bachelor's degree, and to have passed the tough National Judicial Examination and political integrity scrutiny. Despite the high academic threshold on entry, prosecutors are more like civil servants than legal professionals. Prosecutors are not always accustomed to making independent decisions based on their judgement of a case in a given situation.[7] In fact, their job is primarily concerned with the strict application of criminal rules without resorting to diversionary considerations. Political allegiance to the Party leadership is also of paramount importance. The incumbent Chief Prosecutor Zhang Jun defined the Supreme People's Procuratorate as, above

[2] ibid, 181.

[3] See L Gelsthorpe and N Padfied, *Exercising Discretion: Decision-Making in the Criminal Justice System and Beyond* (Routledge, 2003) 5.

[4] Simon (n 1) 176.

[5] See S Boyne, 'German Prosecutors and the Rechtasstaat' in Langer and Sklansky (n 1) 138–74.

[6] Simon (n 1) 181.

[7] X Sun, 'Faxue jiaoyu de zhidu kunjin yu tupo: guanyu faxue jiaoyu yu sifa kaoshi deng falv zhiye zhidu xiang xianjie de yanjiu baogao (The Dilemma of the Legal Education and How to Break Through: A Report on the Connection of Legal Education and The National Justice Examination System)' (2012) 9 *Studies of Law* 108; M Qian, 'Guojia tongyi sifa kaoshi zhidu shishi qinianlai cunzai de wenti yu sikao (Problems on the 7-year Implementation of the National Justice Examination)' (2009) 4 *Rule of Law Research* 98; X Zhang and L Xu, 'Guanyu wanshan guojia sifa kaoshi de yanjiu yu sikao (Research on the National Justice Examination)' (2011) *China Justice* 77–78.

all, a 'political institution and a legal institution with strong political orientation',[8] whose cardinal principle is the Party's absolute leadership and centralised authority.[9] In following this guidance, prosecutors are expected to be legal experts with correct political awareness, who use 'political ideology to deal with intricate and complex legal issues to achieve the best political, social and legal result'.[10]

As discussed in the preceding chapter, there is a strong hierarchical ordering within the procuratorate. This hierarchical structure of authority seeks to ensure certainty and uniformity of decision-making where the exercise of official discretion is kept to a minimum in order to satisfy their accountability to the law and higher levels of authority, eliding arbitrariness and undue personal interests. The Chinese prosecution system primarily follows a mandatory prosecution principle.[11] The bulk of the prosecution system (which does not deal with juvenile suspects or victim–suspect reconciliation) follows the legality principle, for which prosecutors' discretion over non-prosecution decision-making is minimised. Criminal Procedure Law (CPL) 2012 and CPL 2018 inherited the non-prosecution rules from their predecessor, in which three gateways are set out through which the decision not to prosecute can be made. The non-prosecution absolute (*juedui buqisu*) – the first gateway – stipulates that the prosecutor must discontinue a case in circumstances such as no crime, cases involving a statutory time bar on the institution of proceedings and deceased or exempted suspect(s).[12] The other two gateways allow prosecutors to exercise limited discretion in deciding whether or not to proceed with a case in relation to evidence inadequacy (*zhengju buzu buqisu*) and *de minimis* offences (*zhuoding buqisu*). Thus, prosecutors may decide not to prosecute if the evidence is deemed to be insufficient or unreliable, or the police's supplementary investigation fails to provide adequate evidence.[13]

[8] See Zhang Jun, 'Weirao sange biaoshuai zhahao zuigao jiancha jiguan dang de jianshe (Focusing on the Party Construction of the Supreme Procuratorate by Grasping the Three Initiatives)' (The Supreme People's Procuratorate of the PRC, 17 July 2018) www.spp.gov.cn/spp/tt/201807/t20180717_385182.shtml (accessed 16 September 2018).

[9] Zhang Jun, 'Chi er bu xi zhuahao jiancha jiguan dang de zhengzhi jianshe (Grasping the Party Construction With No Rest)' (The Supreme People's Procuratorate of the PRC, 1 July 2018) www.spp.gov.cn/spp/tt/201807/t20180701_383424.shtml (accessed 8 August 2018).

[10] ibid.

[11] For a different view see Wang Jiancheng, 'Lun qisu fading zhuyi he qisu pianyi zhuyi de tiaohe (The Reconciliation between the Principle of Legality and the Principle of Opportunity)' (2000) 2 *Peking University Review* 90; Wu Xiaohui, 'Lun gongsu cailiangquan de yunxing yu chengxuxing kongzhi (On the Operation and Procedural Control of the Prosecutorial Discretion)' (2016) 1 *China Criminal Law Magazine* 70, 72.

[12] CPL 2018, Art 16 (CPL 2012, Art 15).

[13] According to Art 175 of CPL 2018 (Art 171 of CPL 2012), the prosecutor may decide not to prosecute the case if the case has been returned to the police once, the prosecutor believes that the evidence is insufficient and there is no need to conduct a supplementary investigation. See Art 403 of The Criminal Procedure Rule Applicable to the People's Procuratorate (Amended by the Supreme People's Procuratorate in the 80th Meeting of the 11th Procuratorate Committee on 16 October 2012, No 2012(2)). Pursuant to Art 172 of CPL 2012, the prosecutor should place a charge on the accused only if she is satisfied that the fact is clear and the evidence is reliable and sufficient. A straightforward interpretation

They are also at liberty to drop a case when the crimes committed are regarded as so trivial that the law is unlikely to impose criminal punishment on the defendant.[14]

Further control of the prosecutorial discretion is reflected in a series of complicated bureaucratic procedures in which the prosecutor has to seek permission from the Prosecutors' Committee or the Chief Prosecutor.[15] This mechanism aims to afford a unified and coordinated approach to ensure that no cases are filtered out of the system unless they are regarded as weak or trivial at the top echelon. In site A, when a case was considered to be discontinued by a prosecutor, she initially had to discuss the case with the head prosecutor first, who was in charge of all the important decisions of the criminal cases in the team. If the non-prosecution suggestion was endorsed, the prosecutor would prepare a case report and present it to the deputy chief prosecutor.[16] The deputy chief prosecutor might then take time to consider the appropriateness of the decision, and if non-prosecution was to be pursued she would submit the case to the Prosecutors' Committee for discussion.[17] Only if the Committee and the deputy chief prosecutor reached a consensus not to bring the case forward for prosecution would the decision be officially validated.[18] Any veto that occurred in the course of the deliberation would result in the case being prosecuted straight away.

The reason why the prosecutors' discretionary decision not to prosecute is subjected to bureaucratic examination is, to a large degree, to prevent individual prosecutors from being interfered with by external forces. The system has undoubtedly incubated a distrust of its own legal agents. In a legal culture emphasising the punishment of the offender, the arrangements of the prosecution system revolve largely around an entrenched assumption of guilt, the instrumental function of the criminal process and the prosecutor's role as an accusing party. Corresponding with that, there is a perceived public desire for retribution against the accused in China.[19] Many prosecutors have affirmed that their major concern is to

of this provision is that the prosecutor must decide not to prosecute if the evidence is unreliable or insufficient. The inadequacy of evidence may be temporary, as the prosecutor has the opportunity to ask the police to collect additional evidence. But a legal constraint is placed on the undertaking of the extra investigation pursuit. Specifically, the prosecutor is allowed to return the case dossier to the police a maximum of twice for further investigation, which should be carried out within a one-month period. If, after exhausting the means of supplementary investigation, the prosecutor is still unconvinced with the sufficiency of the evidence, she has no choice but to make a non-prosecution decision.

[14] CPL 2018, Art 177 (CPL 2012, Art 173).

[15] See Art 401 of The Criminal Procedure Rule Applicable to the People's Procurorate (Amended by the Supreme People's Procuratorate in the 80th Meeting of the 11th Procuratorate Committee on 16 October 2012, No 2012(2)).

[16] A deputy chief prosecutor (and the chief prosecutor) are responsible for all the prosecution cases within the procuratorate.

[17] The Prosecutors' Committee's discussion and the final decision not to prosecute would be filed on record for future review. Field note APU-12.

[18] See Arts 288 and 289 of The Criminal Procedure Rule Applicable to the People's Procurorate (Amended by the Supreme People's Procuratorate on 21 September 1999, No 1999(1)).

[19] Cai Huifang, *Xingshi sifa ji sixing shiyong: ruogan yinan wenti shili poxi (Criminal Justice and the Application of the Death Penalty: Analysis of Complex Cases)* (China Law Press, 2009) 45.

combat crime.[20] Therefore, when a decision is made in favour of a suspect, there is a suspicion that this is motivated by corruption.

> Prosecutor: What is very strange in China is if you decided to drop a case and you report it, people will think you have gained some benefit from the suspect … So, we are always cautious.[21]

The complexity of the bureaucratic review has certainly put off some prosecutors' desire to pursue a non-prosecution. The authorisation process has been streamlined to some extent since the implementation of CPL 2012.[22] In some local procuratorates, individual prosecutors have been given greater power to make a final decision not to prosecute.[23] For the vast majority of procuratorates in China, however, prosecutors do not have complete power to discontinue a case even if the case in question fits perfectly into a non-prosecution category. The decision not to prosecute still resides with the apex of the hierarchy. In contrast, every prosecutor is fully empowered to proceed with prosecution without any procedural restriction. The presumption of guilt is saliently marked here. Virtually all prosecutors, regardless of their work experience and rank, can independently make a decision in relation to prosecuting a case. In fact, prosecuting an accused has been such a run-of-the-mill routine that many prosecutors did not even feel it was a real power.[24]

Against this background, the proportion of case withdrawals prior to the trial has been kept at a low level. Take those suspects who were processed by the procurorate in site A, for example. From 2009 to 2012, the number of suspects who were dealt with by the procuratorate were 2489, 1900, 2693 and 2484, respectively. The number who were not prosecuted in those years were 68, 72, 69 and 78.[25] This gives the non-prosecution rates between 2009 and 2012 of 2.73, 3.79, 2.56 and 3.14 per cent, respectively. These figures are roughly in line with national statistics, as well as with corresponding calculations in other local procuratorates during the same time period.[26] The reasons for such low non-prosecution rates are

[20] Interview APS-2; Field notes APU-3 and 5.

[21] Interview APS-4.

[22] See Art 401 of The Criminal Procedure Rule Applicable to the People's Procurorate (Amended by the Supreme People's Procuratorate in the 80th Meeting of the 11th Procuratorate Committee on 16 October 2012, No 2012(2)). The practices vary depending on local procuratorate policy.

[23] In the Beijing City procuratorate, the individual prosecutors are given a final decision as to whether or not to prosecute, apart from major and influential cases. 'Jiancha jiguan "buqisuquan de heli shiyong" guandian jijin (The Compiled Views on the Reasonable Application of Non-prosecution by the Procuratorate)', *Fazhi ribao* (*Legal Daily*) (15 May 2019) www.spp.gov.cn/spp/zdgz/201905/t20190515_418339.shtml (accessed 3 June 2019).

[24] Field note APU-13.

[25] It should be noted that in this statistical calculation, the number of cases (as opposed to suspects) registered by the procuratorate and the cases that were decided to be withdrawn were not considered. In site A, the number of cases registered from 2009 to 2012 were 1893, 1590, 2406 and 2298, respectively; the corresponding number of cases that were decided not to prosecute were 68, 63, 65 and 72.

[26] It should be noted that nationwide rates of non-prosecution have increased to around 5% since those years. The national non-prosecution rates from 2013 to 2015 were 5.1%, 5.4% and 5.2%, respectively, according to the Supreme Procuratorate's Report to the National Congress. In more recent

multiple. Aside from the bureaucratic control, perhaps the most immediate cause was the Appraisal System.[27] For a long period of time, the procuratorate's non-prosecution rates were linked to the evaluation of the police performance. Police stations with a higher number of cases being discontinued by the corresponding procuratorate (hence a non-prosecution rate above average for the region) were unlikely to be in contention in the upcoming competition for the best Public Security Bureau (PSB) unit, resulting in a potential loss of bonuses for the police officers and promotion prospects for the leader of the PSB. Therefore, the police had strategically withdrawn cases from the procuratorate when the prosecutor indicated that certain cases might not be prosecuted. In so doing, they could minimise the negative impact on the official statistics.[28]

This procedural manipulation might not cause any major practical problems for the accused[29] as long as the identified weak cases are sifted out of the system. But police officers who have invested a lot of time searching for evidence and apprehending the suspect sometimes do not give up easily. Various tactics have been employed to pursue the prosecution of such cases. In one instance, the police in site A repackaged a dismissed old case under the disguise of a different offence without producing new evidence. The prosecutor had previously advised that the case be withdrawn, as he believed that the case was too trivial to be prosecuted. In commenting on the police's second attempt, the prosecutor expressed his disapproval:

> Prosecutor: The suspect cannot be convicted as it is a civil dispute rather than a real criminal offence. This case was investigated in relation to an offence of creating a disturbance of the public (*xunxin zishizui*) a few months ago and I asked the police to withdraw the case. Now the same case was sent to me under the offence of assault, using the same evidence. This is such a waste of time and public resource – it may have something to do with the police officer's ego unless the police officer has some personal interest in it. I understand that the police put a lot of energy in investigating a case which turned out to be not good enough, but they simply don't want to let it go.[30]

years (since 2015), the non-prosecution rates have been increased to between 5% and 10%. 'Jiancha jiguan "buqisuquan de heli shiyong" (n 23). See also Guo Shuo, 'Zhuoding buqisu zhidu de zai kaocha (Reconsideration of Discretionary Decision Not to Prosecute)' (2018) 3 *China Law Studies* 228. See Zhang Shaobo, 'Gongsu huanjie chengxu fenliu jizhi de fansi yu wanshan: yi 2009 zhi 2012 nian D jianchayuan buqisu zhidu yunxing zhuangkuang wei fenxi shijiao (Reconsideration and Perfection of Divisionary Mechanism in the Public Prosecution: Analysis of D Procuratorate's Non-prosecution Operation between 2009 and 2012)' (2013) 8 *China Criminal Law Magazine* 93; Chen Yiping, 'Xingshi buqisulv piandi zhi shizheng fenxi: yi moudi 2003–2010 nian xingshi buqisu anjian wei fenxi duixiang (Empirical Analysis of the Low Non-prosecution Rate: On the Basis of Non-prosecution Cases between 2003 and 2010)' (2011) 8 *China Criminal Law Magazine* 73; Wu Xiaohui (n 11); Li Ci, 'Lun futiaojian buqisu yu zhuoding buqisu de guanxi (On the Relationship between Conditional Non-prosecution and Discretionary Non-prosecution)' (2014) 4 *Legal Forum* 115, 117.

[27] M McConville et al, *Criminal Justice in China: An Empirical Enquiry* (Edward Elgar, 2011) 142.

[28] Field note APU-15. See also Chen Yiping (n 26) 78.

[29] Apparently, this is a problem of statistical manipulation. Clearly, the integrity of the criminal justice system is compromised.

[30] Field note APU-23.

The non-prosecution principle has been relaxed in recent years, with signs indicating that the system is gradually accommodating more latitude in the disposition of cases as well as having accorded prosecutors with greater responsibility in the development and implementation of criminal justice policy. This trend is specifically reflected in low-level criminal cases (the newly introduced reconciliation agreement between the suspect and the victim) and the juvenile prosecution system, which has been reformed since CPL 2012. The prosecution system now enables the prosecutor to make a conditional decision not to prosecute in relation to juveniles who are suspected of committing certain types of offences punishable by a fixed-term imprisonment of less than a year, provided that the suspect has shown repentance over their crimes.[31] Although this new juvenile prosecution principle has been heavily criticised for its limited scope of application,[32] a significant level of diversionary discretion has now been placed in the hands of prosecutors, who are no longer obliged to prosecute all juvenile cases where sufficient evidence is present.

The limits of the discretionary role of the prosecutor are also extended to the field of sentencing. In particular, prosecutors are able to advise the court to mete out lenient punishment if a reconciliation agreement has been reached between the suspect and the victim.[33] This new change confers a proactive diversionary power on prosecutors, allowing them to partake in the sentencer's role. This may have far-reaching implications in the prosecution system and adjudication.[34]

[31] These types of crimes are only limited to those provided in ch 4 (Crimes of Infringing upon Citizens' Right of the Person and Democratic Rights), ch 5 (Crimes of Property Violation) and ch 6 (Crimes of Obstructing the Administration of Public Order) under the special provisions of the Criminal Law. See Art 282 of CPL 2018 (Art 271 of CPL 2012).

[32] Liu Xuemin, 'Jiancha jiguan futiaojian buqisu cailiangquan yunyong zhi tantao (The Exploration of the Operation of the Conditional Non-prosecution Discretions)' (2014) 6 *China Lawl Studies* 205; Cheng Xiaolu, 'Futiaojian buqisu zhidu de shiyong (The Application of the Conditional Non-prosecution Discretion)' (2013) 6 *Journal of National Prosecutors College* 22; Zhang Zhongjian, 'Jianshi yu wanshan: Woguo weichengnianren futiaojian buqisu zhidu ruogan wenti tantao (Review and Perfection: Exploration of the Conditional Non-prosecution System of Juvenile Cases)' (2013) 7 *China Criminal Law Magazine* 84; Chen Xiaoyu, 'Chongtu yu pingheng: Lun weichengnian ren futiaojian buqisu zhidu (Conflicts and Balance: On the Conditional Non-prosecution Decisions in Relation to Juvenile Cases)' (2012) 12 *China Criminal Law Magazine* 60. Regarding early empirical research of the pilot scheme of the Conditional Non-prosecution prior to 2012, see The People's Procuratorate of Haidian District of Beijing, 'Futiaojian buqisu zhidu shizheng yanjiu (The Empirical Study of the Conditional Non-prosecution Decisions regarding Juvenile Cases)' (2009) 6 *Journal of National Procurators College* 74.

[33] CPL 2018, Art 282 (CPL 2012, Art 279).

[34] Dong Lintao, 'Woguo futiaojian buqisu zhidu ruogan wenti de fansi yu wanshan (Reconsideration and Perfection of the Conditional Non-prosecution System of Juvenile Cases)' (2015) 1 *Jinan University Journal* 42; Du Wenjun and Shi Mingqing, 'Weichengnianren futiaojian buqisu zhi shiyong (On the Application of the Conditional Non-prosecution System of Juvenile Cases)' (2012) 3 *Oriental Law* 111; Huang Jingping, 'Xingshi hejie de zhengcexing junxing dao fazhihua yunxing: yi dangshiren hejie de qingshang anjian wei yangben de fenxi (From the Policy Operation to Legal Operation of the Criminal Reconciliation: Analysis of the Parties' Reconciliation of Minor Injuries)' (2013) 3 *China Law Studies* 163; Wang Hongyu, 'Zhongfa bijiao shiyu xia woguo gongsu anjian hejie chengxu zhi

These two special procedures will not be addressed at length in this book due to the scope of this study. Nonetheless, they are important issues that indicate that the prosecution policy is developing in a direction that is less punitive than it used to be.

B. Cases Considered for Non-prosecution

In this section, I examine some of the cases that the prosecutors decided not to pursue, expounding on the factors that have influenced their decision-making. Disposing of cases that are *de minimis* or evidentially inadequate is an exercise of the prosecutorial discretion which ensures that only those cases conforming to the legal prerequisites are to be tried. How to interpret the criterion of 'minor' and under what circumstances the accused can be exempted for a lack of evidence that is 'faithful to the substance of legislated penal statutes and to the values underlying the large criminal law project'[35] are quite obscure in practice. I had no access to the Prosecution Committee meetings or internal reports of proposed non-prosecution cases in the field site. Hence, the yardstick that was applied by prosecutors to withdraw a case was not clarified unless certain cases were openly discussed. Nevertheless, what was certain was that those cases that it was decided not to prosecute were not always the so-called weak cases – cases with feeble evidence or cases concerned with minor offences that there was little value in prosecuting. Paradoxically, a good proportion of cases that had been prosecuted could be easily identified as inherently weak and could have been dropped had there been a rigorous screening system in place.[36] As I shall show, the factors that had an impact on the prosecutor's decision-making sometimes departed from legal norms, and mostly concerned institutional interests or extra-legal considerations.

(i) The Implicit Rule of Non-prosecution

Public prosecutors are bound by an internal rule that demands consistency of decisions across different departments within the procuratorate, embodying uniformity of procuratorate policies. With the high custodial rate in pretrials in China, the majority of suspects who are remanded in detention centres are dealt with by at least two departments of the procuratorate, namely the Department of Investigation Supervision (*zhengcha jiandu bumen*) and the Department of

zai wanshan (Further Perfection of the Reconciliation of Public Prosecution Cases in a Comparative Context Between China and France)' (2013) 6 *China Law Studies* 131; Yao Xianseng, 'Lun xingshi hejie anjian sifa gongxinli de fazhi baozhang (On the Legal Safeguard of the Judicial Credibility of Criminal Reconciliation)' (2014) 5 *China Criminal Law Magazine* 67.

[35] DC Richman, 'Accounting for Prosecutors' in Langer and Sklansky (n 1) 45.

[36] This issue will be discussed in the next section of this chapter.

Public Prosecution (*gongsu bumen*). The Department of Investigation Supervision is responsible for approving remands (*pizhun daibu*) on the request of the police[37] – a decision that is normally made at an early stage of the police investigation and within a relatively short period of time.[38] The approval itself, which has little to do with the prosecution of the accused at the time of authorisation, has significant implications on the decision whether to prosecute later on. In site A, it was an unwritten rule that the public prosecutor 'ought to' prosecute if the accused had been remanded in custody. This was to avoid potential state compensation claims from the wrongfully imprisoned suspect.[39] In vindicating the 'erroneous judgement' made by the Department of Investigation Supervision when a state compensation action was brought, the procuratorate took the consequences, preventing the damage of a tarnished reputation that collectively affects all the state officials within the organisation.

Compliance with the internal rule meant that the public prosecutor's autonomy in the prosecution of cases in which the suspect was remanded was further constrained. Prosecutors hence had lost the initiative in a good proportion of cases. They had no choice but to slavishly follow the decisions made by their colleagues in the other department. Such practice undoubtedly led to unfair treatment of suspects. When assessing the police's requests for remand, the Department of Investigation Supervision might take into account factors such as the suspect's migrant status, age and health, and their relationship with the victim. These considerations focus on the dangerousness of the suspect or the gravity of the offence committed, as well as the suitability of custody as a compulsory measure. Quite differently, the prosecutor from the Department of Public Prosecution would tend to focus more on the seriousness of the crime and would play down other irrelevant circumstances. Thus, it was common in site A that a migrant worker would be approved to be remanded in custody mainly due to the fear that she might abscond;[40] this decision, however, dictated that non-prosecution was out of the question, even though the case may have perfectly fulfilled the criteria for case discontinuation, according to which the case should have been screened out of the system.[41]

There were a few occasions when prosecutors from the two different departments consulted with each other to reconcile their divergent views. Such communication was conducive to appreciating the reasoning of the initial decision of the remand of the suspect, but there was little hope that the prosecutor would

[37] As noted earlier, in Chinese criminal justice, arrest (*daibu*) is equivalent to remand in custody in England and Wales, and the suspect will be kept in the detention centre pending trial. The Department of Custody Necessity Review in the procuratorate shall make the decision whether or not to remand a suspect in custody on the request of the police.

[38] The procuratorate must decide whether or not to remand the suspect in custody within 7 days. See Art 91 of CPL 2018.

[39] State Compensation Law of PRC 1994, Art 17(1).

[40] For the circumstances under which a suspect must be remanded in custody, see Art 81 of CPL 2018.

[41] Field notes APU-32, 34 and 45.

drop the case. In one theft case (*CASEA 27*), the suspect stole a pair of cheap earrings and a pair of socks. The prosecutor from the Department of Public Prosecution intended not to place a charge on the accused, as the value of the stolen items was minimal. This, however, was inconsistent with the earlier decision made by the Department of Investigation Supervision, who granted the police's application of remand on the ground that the suspect had a criminal record of theft from 3 years ago. The prosecutor in charge of approving the application insisted that the suspect showed no remorse and was too dangerous to be on the loose. After a brief conversation exchange over lunch, the public prosecutor agreed to charge the suspect, based on the fact that the accused had been kept in the detention centre for two months.[42]

Despite being deferential, the public prosecutor would sometimes make an effort to remedy the seemingly irreversible situation, albeit in a compromised way. For example, in a case involving creating a disturbance of the public (*xunxin zishizui*), the suspect was a destitute porter who struggled to earn enough money to live. Being drunk, he kicked some flowerpots near the local government building out of frustration. The prosecutor was sympathetic to the porter and intended to withdraw the case due to the minor nature of the criminal damage. Unfortunately, the suspect had been remanded in custody, therefore non-prosecution was not an option. A charge was eventually placed to comply with the implicit rule. As a compromise, however, the prosecutor recommended a custodial sentence equivalent to the term that the suspect would have already served pending trial, meaning that he would be released as soon as the trial was over. The prosecutor explained her decision:

> Prosecutor: There is no chance to exculpate him. All the suspects who have been remanded in custody must be convicted. Otherwise, we have to admit that we made a mistake and state compensation is likely to be triggered. I personally really feel sorry for these poor people. Life is too harsh for him. I don't want to charge him. That's all I can do to help him.[43]

Here the prosecutor transferred her prosecutorial discretion to the sphere of sentencing, and creatively circumvented the dilemma between obeying the prosecution rule and sticking to her own view. Whereas this seemed to be a perfect solution that satisfied both sides, it illustrates the disabled function of the procuratorate in the observing the law and the contorted effort made in thwarting the exercise of the rights of the accused in calling the institution into account.[44] Since the issue was inappropriately diverted to the ambit of punishment, the decision of the prosecution has stretched to other branches of the criminal justice system, with ramifications on the penal system.

[42] Field note APU-18.
[43] Field note APU-22.
[44] A Duff, 'Discretion and Accountability' in Langer and Sklansky (n 1) 14.

(ii) External Interference

Chinese prosecutors are not immune to external interference. There are charges that prosecutors are corrupt and may have abused their discretionary power to cover up serious offences in an unscrupulous manner.[45] As far as most prosecutors were concerned, the undue influence was an unavoidable factor in the operation of the criminal justice institution. As one prosecutor put it, 'external influences are like a disease – we hate it, but we have to live with it'.[46]

This concentration of the power not to prosecute failed to be a disincentive to abuse prosecutorial discretion. Some of the cases that were withdrawn based upon inappropriate considerations in site A were in fact initiated at the top echelons.[47] External influences regularly interfered with prosecutors' actions via higher ranked officials within the procuratorate. It sometimes became imperative for the leader of the procuratorate to entertain the needs of various stakeholders and to coordinate necessary relationships within the polity. This paved the way for external intervention. The most common form of interference was the department leaders of the procuratorate giving instructions to the responsible prosecutor through telephone calls or, occasionally, a private meeting. As directions were given by the officials at the top of the hierarchy, prosecutors had no choice but to follow them. On those occasions, the prosecutorial decision not to prosecute was usually based upon an account that fits into the gateway of *de minimis* cases or insufficient evidence. Prosecutors were also required to report the progress and the way the case was handled to the leaders on a regular basis.

In spite of the pressure from the leaders, prosecutors were reluctant to cede their authority. Although they had no power to challenge the instruction from the leaders, they were not entirely deferential to their interference. 'Speedy prosecution' was one of the strategies adopted by prosecutors in site A to avoid potential intervention. Since the prosecutor's decision on prosecution did not require permission from officers at a higher level, if prosecutors had knowledge that special instructions would be likely in a given case, they would accelerate the progress of the prosecution review, so that the suspect could be charged within a very short period of time. When the belated instruction arrived, the case would have already been transferred to the court, beyond the possibility of interference from the Chief Prosecutor. Such tactics to address external influence were covertly acknowledged by the Chief Prosecutor or the department leaders of the procuratorate, as they were the very officials taking responsibility for the decision-making. One prosecutor noted that 'none of the leaders, especially the Chief Prosecutor, wish to be

[45] See, eg 'Mudianjiang jianchayuan gongran baobi yanzhong fanzui, yiyu hewei (Why Mudanjiang Prosecutors Cover Up Serious Offences)' (Sina Weibo Website, 20 February 2018) www.weibo.com/ttArt/p/show?id=2309404209449643444827&infeed=1 (accessed 1 September 2018); Wu Xiaohui (n 11) 72.

[46] Field note APU-22.

[47] Field note APU-24; Interview APS-4.

involved with this interference or take a risk with their careers'.[48] Prosecutors were willing to make a decision on their own, rather than be directed by intervening forces.

Nevertheless, the prosecutor's discretion not to proceed with a prosecution was certainly not applied equally to all suspects. Rent-seeking with power (*quanli xunzu*), or utilising public power for private interest, often occurs in its prosecution process as well as other sectors of society where personal relationships are highly valued and override the legal system.[49] With a dramatically widening social stratification,[50] those disempowered people who do not have the resources to evade the prosecutorial process are charged as a means to maintain the stability of the party-state.[51] At the other end of the scale, the elites who are in possession of social and financial capital have plenty of resources available to negotiate their journey (including corruption) through the justice system.[52]

(iii) Dangerous Driving Cases

In this section, I will use dangerous driving cases as an example to illustrate how prosecutorial discretion was exercised in practice. My main reason for selecting dangerous driving cases is the large number of such cases being processed and observed in the field site. Some of these cases were openly discussed in the prosecutor's office, which enabled me to gain an insight into their decision-making process. Ever since drink-driving was criminalised (under the umbrella offence of dangerous driving) in 2011,[53] there has been a massive crackdown on the new motoring offence, with a vast number of drivers being intercepted and prosecuted for consuming alcohol over the prescribed limit and then driving.[54] Drunk driving cases were a major source of prosecution work in site A between 2011 and 2013, when this type of offence constituted 38 per cent of all prosecution cases.[55] A good proportion of these cases were relatively minor and, in theory, could fit squarely

[48] Field note APU-36.

[49] Rent-seeking of power is an economic term of corruption, which has popularly been used in the Chinese social context. It means that people in possession of public power use that power to gain a personal advantage. M McConville, 'Criminal Justice in China and the West' in M ConConville and E Pils (eds), *Comparative Perspectives on Criminal Justice in China* (Edward Elgar, 2013) 66.

[50] In recent years, China has had Gini coefficients of 0.491 (2008), 0.490 (2009), 0.481 (2010), 0.477 (2011) and 0.474 (2012), respectively, according to data from the official statistical department of China, www.economy.caijing.com.cn/2013-01-18/112444588.html. The minimal international warning level of the divide between the rich and the poor is 0.40. In China, the wealthiest 10% of Chinese families earned 55 times more than the least fortunate 10%. The average wage in the best-paid industry was almost 16 times that of the poorest paid. ibid 65.

[51] ibid 69.

[52] ibid 65.

[53] Art 22 of the Amendments to the Criminal Law 1997, which came effect on 1 May 2011.

[54] See Art 133 of Criminal Law 1997. The limit of alcohol consumption for dangerous driving is 80 milligrams per 100 millilitres of blood.

[55] Field note APU-35.

into the non-prosecution criteria.[56] One would expect many of these misdemeanours to be diverted on the *de minimis* ground, not least because many motorist offenders were middle-class residents, who had no criminal record and posed no danger to society. Another reason would be that the drink-driving offence carries a sentence of fines or penal servitude (*juyi*), and the suspect cannot be kept in custody pending trial. These cases could thus easily be discontinued by prosecutors without any scrupulous concerns of state compensation. Nonetheless, the vast majority of drink-driving cases proceeded to trial. These decisions seemed to be policy driven. As a newly codified offence that was introduced to answer the public outcry over drink-driving, the criminal justice system was determined to show the authority of the law and its deterrent function.[57]

It was still possible to withdraw minor drink-driving cases according to the policy circulated within the procuratorate. These non-prosecution requirements included a borderline level of alcohol (less than 100 milligrammes per 100 millilitres of blood), the vehicle carried no passengers and no accident occurred. Very few cases satisfied these prerequisites. For those cases that did fulfil all the elements, they were closely scrutinised and sometimes heatedly debated. One of the cases (*CASEA 8*) that the prosecutor decided not to pursue concerned a man who had parked his car in front of the house of a neighbour whom he knew was on holiday. When his neighbour cut short his holiday and returned home unexpectedly, the accused was asked to move his car at a time when he was already in bed after consuming some alcohol in the evening. Since the drink-driving offence requires a *mens rea* of intention to endanger the public,[58] it was surprising that the police decided to arrest the suspect in the first place, given that the circumstance of the case was so insignificant, in that the suspect was only parking the car rather than intending to drive the car on a public road. The prosecutor who handled the case, however, focused on a different issue, that is, whether the parking space was on a public road – his turning on of the ignition would be perceived as driving only if the place where the car was situated was recognised as a public road according to the Road and Traffic Safety Law.[59] This case was submitted to the Prosecutors' Committee, where a debate took place as to whether the communal area surrounding the accused's house should be categorised as a public road. In the end, the case was dropped primarily due to the disagreement on how 'public road' should be interpreted.[60]

[56] See Xu Miao, 'Zuijia yilu ruzui de chuzui lujin tanxi (On the Exculpation of Minor Drunk Driving Cases)' (2013) 15 *Journal of Wuhan University of Science & Technology* 202.

[57] Zhao Binzhi and Yuan Bin, 'Zuijia ruxing zhu wenti xin tantao (Exploration on Issues Concerned with Criminalisation of Drunk Driving)' (2012) 8 *Law Magazine* 15; Chen Wei, 'Zuijia: "yilv ruxing" hai shi "qubie duidai" (Drunk Driving: All Being Criminalised or Differentiated)' (2012) 1 *Legal System and Social Development* 119.

[58] Criminal Law, Art 133.

[59] Road Traffic Safety Law 2003, Art 119.

[60] Field note APU-18.

It is true that prosecutors had little liberty to interpret what could be counted as 'minor' in this type of motor offence, given the standardised guidance issued from the top of the bureaucratic pyramid. Yet, situations like this still allow the prosecutor to narrate the case in an independent and justificatory manner to demonstrate that the prosecution path may not be the best option to achieve a desirable result. Instead of evaluating the insignificant circumstance, the prosecutor's prime approach was to search for instrumental rules and normative details to determine the outcome. Such a technocratic approach was consistent with the bureaucratisation of the procuratorate, where decision-making was always made under the watchful eyes of superiors, lest the decision makers' power was being abused.[61] As far as these prosecutors were concerned, their role as a legal professional was to mechanically apply the law to ensure the fidelity to the applicable legal standard.

In contrast to the intense scrutiny of non-prosecution cases, low-visibility rule departures abounded in cases that were decided to be prosecuted – so much so that comprehensive supervision was almost non-existent. Discretions in favour of prosecution were occasionally made on personal grounds, seeking to punish suspects whose behaviour was out of line in the opinion of that particular prosecutor. A bizarre example of drink-driving (*CASEA 38*) was a man who was accused of driving under the influence of alcohol and the person who reported the offence was his wife. According to the police record, his wife made a telephone call to the police to report the drink-driving crime. Shortly after the call, the police found the car, which was stationary on the street. The alcohol saturation test indicated that the man's alcohol consumption level was 200.8 ml/100 mg, well above the prescribed legal limit of 80 ml/100 mg. There was CCTV footage showing that a similar car drove out of a nearby car park. However, the footage was of such poor quality that it was impossible to identify the driver or the number plate. Up until that point, the case appeared to be an ordinary drink-driving case, with enough evidence to suggest that the man had consumed a significant amount of alcohol and drove under such an influence. The law-abiding wife who was concerned about their safety reported the offence to the police. However, this case took an unexpected turn during the prosecutorial interrogation when the accused provided a story that challenged the narrative presented in the case dossier. The interrogation indicated what happened from the suspect's perspective:

> Prosecutor: In the evening of 29th of May, where did you drink?
>
> Suspect: In a small restaurant, with my wife. My wife got a phone call from her sister who was taking care of our child. Her sister said that our child was sick and we had to take her to the hospital. So, we decided to go home.
>
> Prosecutor: Who was driving?
>
> Suspect: My wife. I was sitting on the passenger seat. I was dozing off on the way home. Since I drank too much, my wife said that if I drove, she would call the police. So, I did

[61] MJ Damaška, *The Faces of Justice and State Authority: A Comparative Approach to the Legal Process* (Yale University Press, 1986) 21–23.

not drive. It was she who drove all the way. However, we had an argument about child care. I became angry and I said to her 'I will drive'. She was agitated, so she called the police.

Prosecutor: Did you actually drive or not?

Suspect: No, I did not. I was just in a fit of pique. As the argument went on, she stopped the car and we swapped seats. Although I was on the driver's seat when the police came, I did not drive at all.

Prosecutor: [Flipping the dossier and shouting] Liar! The toll collector said he saw the car window was put down and you were driving. How do you dare to make up stories! Look, I have got a CCTV recording. I will give you another chance: did you drive or not?

Suspect: I honestly did not drive that night. I was mad with my wife and it was my wife who drove the car.

Prosecutor: [Paged through the file for about 2 minutes] Where did you sit when the police came?

Suspect: I was on the driver's seat.

Prosecutor: Anyone else in the car?

Suspect: No. Just my wife and me. She was sitting on the passenger seat after we swapped.

Prosecutor: [Angrily] How did you swap your seats inside the car without coming out of the car?

Suspect: My wife came to my seat and I stepped into the driver's seat.

Prosecutor: [Shouting] Rubbish! I don't believe you can swap your seats just inside the car! This was impossible.[62]

This scenario offered by the accused apparently denies the allegation that he was driving under the influence of alcohol. If what the suspect said was true, the prosecution case would have collapsed. None of the other pieces of evidence in this case could unequivocally prove or disprove whether the man actually drove the car: the quality of CCTV footage was too bad to tell who was driving; the toll collector at the parking lot could not remember who was in the driving seat; the telephone recording from the wife's report to the police did not specify that the husband was the actual driver (as there are no different tenses in the Chinese language). The wife later retracted her report and claimed that her husband did not drive at all. The only evidence that could have proved that the man drove out of the car park was his own confession after he was arrested by the police and was taken to the police station. But this again was retracted, as the man claimed that he was under the influence of alcohol and was not in possession of his full capabilities.

Given that there was no evidence to support the *actus reus*, discontinuation of the case was probably the most reasonable solution – otherwise, the prosecutor have had to have obtained new inculpatory evidence to build a prosecution case.

[62] Field note APU-22.

Gathering more evidence would have been time-consuming and could have been difficult under the circumstances; however, it would have been worth pursuing if the prosecutor had fundamental doubts about the competing version offered by the accused. The prosecutor decided to pursue the charge nonetheless. In order to secure a 'truthful' confession and to teach the suspect a lesson, the prosecutor pressurised the wife by sending her a warning that if her husband refused to tell the 'truth', she would be investigated for perjury.[63] On receiving the message, the suspect pleaded guilty. The case was soon prosecuted and the man convicted. When asked why the prosecutor took the trouble to prosecute such a minor case given the overwhelming lack of evidence, the prosecutor responded:

> From the evidence's point of view, I may have no solid evidence against the suspect … But I am not resigned to the fact that those liars can get away from punishment by denying their guilt. The excuse he offered does not make any sense. Why did two well-built persons swap their seats inside the car with a high degree of difficulty, while it is much easier to complete the change if they opened the door and left the car momentarily? As a driver, I would not change my seat with someone sitting as a passenger without leaving the car – it would be awkward. There is no other way to explain this. I have not wronged the man. I am upholding justice … I feel very angry because the suspect dared lie to me. Who does he think he is?[64]

It is certainly problematic that cases like this were pursued in the court primarily because of the prosecutor's 'sense of justice', rather than a justice that was demonstrated by producing persuasive and reliable prosecution evidence that was collected in a legitimate and appropriate manner. This drink-driving case was not the only example where an overzealous prosecutor had taken on certain suspects due to the way justice was understood or the feeling that their authority was challenged, in spite of the bluntly weak cases. On several occasions, the prosecutors were observed to have been emotionally carried away with incipiently weak cases. In *CASEA 40*, the prosecutor decided to charge a drink-driver suspect mainly because he 'could not bear the suspect's arrogance and complacency'.[65] In an assault case (*CASEA 59*), it was decided to prosecute the suspect because of 'his noxious personality'.[66] In a theft case (*CASEA 60*), the prosecutor pressed the charge since the young suspect, who was from a privileged background, 'responded [to] the prosecutor's questions with absolute contempt' and 'told nothing but lies'.[67] What these cases had in common was that the suspects did not 'behave like a suspect' or pay enough respect to the prosecutor. These 'degraded people', who refused to be awed by the authority of the prosecution, had somehow hurt the prosecutor's pride, which they deeply valued.[68] To some degree, the prosecution decisions in those cases was tainted with personal retribution.

[63] Field note APU-31.
[64] Field note APU-31.
[65] Field note APU-38.
[66] Field note APU-42.
[67] Field note APU-43.
[68] This will be discussed later in this chapter.

II. Decisions on the Modes of Trial

A sound, efficient system that has a built-in succession of separate and independent checks is expected to weed out a good proportion of cases in the process before reaching the critical stage of the trial. The fact that the prosecution in China fails to offer a vigorous screening mechanism is bound to have ramifications, with the courts having to deal with a good number of cases without adequate evidence. Prosecutors are not overly concerned about processing weak cases as long as the suspect pleads guilty. Nowadays, if the accused admits her guilt, most of these cases can be easily processed through fast-tracked procedures,[69] namely the simplified procedure (*jianyi chengxu*) and the expedited procedure (*sucai chengxu*).

A. Leniency for Pleading Guilty and Accepting Punishment

Admittedly, it is in no one's interest to take many cases to full trial if the defendant's guilt is straightforward. It has been a widespread, but still controversial, practice across a number of different criminal justice systems for the system to 'reward' a defendant with a measure of lenity and 'save' her from facing a lengthy contested trial if she voluntarily pleads guilty.[70] Dealing with large backlogs of cases in an expeditious and cost-effective manner seems to be the main, if not the only, cause for various forms of plea bargaining. By the same token, the procedural economy seems to be the reason why the rule of leniency for pleading guilty and accepting punishment (*renzui renfa congkuan zhidu*, hereinafter referred to as leniency for a guilty plea) was introduced by CPL 2018.[71] According to the newly added Articles 15 and 201, the Chinese criminal justice system has fully incorporated the policy of plea negotiation, enabling the accused to receive a sentence reduction in consideration for her guilty pleas.[72] It is clear that the bargaining is currently confined to sentence reduction, rather than extending to charge bargains and fact bargains, which have been a common practice in adversarial systems.

[69] See Richard L Lippke, *The Ethics of Plea Bargaining* (Oxford University Press, 2011) 191–92.

[70] A large body of literature exists in the field of plea bargaining. For criticism regarding the US practice, see Lippke (ibid) 193. For criticism of the British example, see M McConville and L Marsh, *Criminal Judges: Legitimacy, Courts and State-Induced Guilty Pleas in Britain* (Edward Elgar, 2014). For other jurisdictions, see SC Thaman, *World Plea Bargaining: Consensual Procedures and the Avoidance of the Full Criminal Trial* (Carolina Academic Press 2010).

[71] Zhou Xin, 'Renzui renfa congkuan zhidu lifahua de zhongdian wenti yanjiu (Research on the Central Points of the Legislation of the System of Leniency for Pleading Guilty and Accepting Punishment)' (2018) 6 *China Law Studies* 172, 180; Han Xu, '2018 nian xingsufazhong renzui renfa congkuan zhidu (The System of Leniency for Pleading Guilty and Accepting Punishment in CPL 2018)' (2019) 1 *Rule of Law Research* 35, 35.

[72] Sun Changyong, 'Wanshan renzui renfa congkuan zhidu de liangge zhongdian (Two Essential Points of the System of Leniency for Pleading Guilty and Accepting Punishment)' (2018) 11 *The People's Procuratorate* 5, 6; Peng Haiqing and Zhang Jindan, 'Renzui renfa congkuan zhidu de hexin jiazhi quxiang bianxi (The Central Value of the System of Leniency for Pleading Guilty and Accepting Punishment)' (2018) 1 *Police Science Research* 68, 69.

This amendment will certainly have a profound impact on the administration of criminal justice, ranging from investigations all the way up to trials.[73] Unfortunately, a full discussion of the implications is beyond both the ambit and the length of this book.

On a brief note, leniency for a guilty plea differs significantly from the well-established guilty plea procedure, ie the simplified procedure,[74] in three aspects, despite the fact that both procedures allow the defendant's sentence to be reduced when the defendant admits her guilt. First, leniency for a guilty plea has expanded the scope of cases where the defendant's guilty plea may have an impact on the sentencing. Unlike the simplified procedure, which deals with low-level offences, such as minor drug crimes, petty property crimes, drink-driving cases, public disorder offences, assaults and the like,[75] leniency for a guilty plea is applicable to all criminal offences across the board.[76] Secondly, leniency for a guilty plea has been defined as a general *principle* of the criminal process that is predominantly linked to the sentence reduction of the defendant. It is not linked to any specific trial procedure, but at the same time could apply to any mode of trial.[77] This suggests that a guilty plea from the accused does not necessarily trigger a quick disposition of criminal cases through one of the fast-tracked procedures. Leniency for a guilty plea is treated as a procedural safeguard of the corresponding criminal principle of 'leniency for confession' (*zishou tanbai congkuan*).[78] In other words, the defendant might undergo the full adjudication, but she is still 'entitled to' a lesser sentence if she pleads guilty. Finally, and perhaps most importantly, Article 174 of CPL 2018 has added a critical condition to leniency for a guilty plea, requiring the suspect to sign a recognisance to admit guilt and accept punishment (*renzui renfa jujieshu*) in the presence of her own defence lawyer or a publicly funded duty lawyer if she is willing to opt for leniency for a guilty plea, except for circumstances in which a recognisance is not otherwise needed.[79]

[73] Han Xu (n 71) 26.

[74] The simplified procedure originated from the judicial interpretation 'Several conditions of the application of the guilty plea procedure by the Supreme Court, the Supreme Procuratorate and the Department of Central Justice in China in 2003', which was introduced as an alternative to the full adjudication. The judicial rule 2003 was fully incorporated into CPL 2012, substituting the previous simplified trial procedure under the framework of CPL 1996.

[75] See Art 214 of CPL 2018.

[76] Yang Lixin, 'Renzui renfa congkuan zhidu lijie yu shiyong (The Interpretation and Application of the System of Leniency for Pleading Guilty and Accepting Punishment)' (2019) 1 *National Procuratorate College Journal* 51, 55.

[77] Kun Huijuan, 'Lun Renzui renfa congkuan zhidua zai zhencha jieduan de shiyong (On the Application of The System of Leniency for Pleading Guilty and Accepting Punishment at the Investigation Stage)' (2019) 4 *Legal System and Society* 33. Yang Lixin (ibid) 55.

[78] See Fan Chongyi, 'Renzui renfa congkuan yu zhishou tanbai (The System of Leniency for Pleading Guilty and Voluntarily Surrender Oneself and Confession) (2018) *People's Rule of Law* 54; Zhou Mengjie, 'Renzui renfa congkuan zhidu yu zishou tanbai shiyong lujin tansuo (The Applicable Pathways of the System of Leniency for Pleading Guilty and Voluntarily Surrender Oneself and Confession)' (2019) 2 *Jiangxi Broadcast University Journal* 65.

[79] These exceptions include: (i) the suspect suffers vision, hearing or speech impairment, or is mentally disabled; (ii) the legal representative or the defence lawyer of a juvenile suspect raised an

Thus, for the first time in Chinese criminal justice, a counsel is permitted to check the voluntariness of the suspect's procedural choice, thereby making her role one of safeguarding in this critical part of the criminal justice process.[80] As a compulsory requirement of the procedure, leniency for a guilty plea as a way for disposing of guilty plea cases can only be validly pursued with the signature of a counsel on the recognisance. There has been a debate as to whether duty lawyers under the newly established legal aid scheme should be counted as being defence lawyers, as their function is limited to offering specific legal advice to the suspect at a certain stage (the prosecution review phase in particular) of the criminal process, rather than representing their case in general.[81] To safeguard the rights of suspects in the streamlined process of leniency for a guilty plea, the duty lawyer scheme is set up to ensure that suspects who have not retained a defence lawyer can access legal advice, and make informed decisions on whether or not to enter a guilty plea. Hence, tailored advice from a counsel relating to the consequences of entering a guilty plea after analysis of the suspect's case is anticipated. However, empirical research conducted by Li Yonghang in the city of Chongqing found that the reality is far removed from the expectation: the duty lawyers were overloaded with cases; they had no time to communicate with suspects and provided no meaningful support as a result. They signed the recognisances without even meeting the suspects, and their signatures were obtained as a formality to fulfil the legal requirement.[82]

Given that leniency for a guilty plea was designed as a mechanism to avoid a full-blown trial, the lack of procedural ascription is puzzling. One reasonable explanation for the paradoxical interpretation of the law is that the defendant's admission of guilt *should* enable the case to be resolved by one of these streamlined dispositional mechanisms if the case fulfils the prerequisites of the specific procedure; if an offence does not meet the requirements of the fast-tracked procedures, especially if the case involves serious crime that carries a heavy sentence, leniency

objection to the juvenile's admission of guilt and acceptance of punishment; and (iii) the signing of a recognisance to admit guilt and accept punishment is otherwise not required. See Art 174(1)–(3) of CPL 2018.

[80] Li Yonghang, 'Renzui renfa congkuan zhidu xia de youxiao falv bangzhu wenti yanjiu (Research on Effective Defence in the Context of Leniency for A Guilty Plea)' (2019) 2 *Western China Law Review* 30, 32.

[81] Gu Yongzhong, 'Wanshan renzui renfa congkuan zhidu de qinli guancha yu sikao jianyi: yiju fuqingshi dengdi xingshi susong chengxuzhong renzui renfa congkuan zhidu de diaoyan (Observation on the Programme to Improve Leniency for a Guilty Plea, Reconsideration and Suggestions: Empirical Studies on the Pilot Project in Fuqing City etc)' (2017) 1 *Rule of Law Research* 56; Tan Shigui and Lai Jianping, 'Xingshi susong zhidu gaige beijing xia zhiban lvshi zhidu de goujian yantaohui zongshu (Symposium of the Construction of the Duty Lawyer System in the Context of Criminal Procedure Law Reform)' (2017) 6 *China Justice* 24; Chen Ruihua, 'Renzui renfa congkuan zhidu de ruogan zhengyi wenti (Several Disputed Issues Regarding Leniency for A Guilty Plea)' (2017) 1 *China Law Studies* 35; Xiong Qiuhong, 'Shenpan zhongxin shiye xia de lvshi youxiao bianhu (Effective Defence in the Context of Trial Centred Criminal Justice Reform)' (2017) 6 *Contemporary Law* 14; Li Yonghang (ibid).

[82] Li Yonghang (n 80) 38. This is also confirmed in Xiao Zhimin's study. See Xiao Zhimin, 'Zhiban lvshi zhidu zai renzui renfa congkuan shiyu zhong de wanshan (The Improvement of the Duty Lawyer's Role in Leniency for A Guilty Plea)' (2019) 4 *Legal System and Society* 32.

for a guilty plea may still apply if the defendant admits her guilt and is willing to receive the penalty. This understanding of the law seems to be supported by the existing practice since the rule was rolled out. According to Yang Lixin, the Chief Justice of the Supreme People's Court, cases tried by the simplified procedure and the expedited procedure constitute 92.11 per cent of all the cases in which leniency for a guilty plea was employed. A relatively small proportion of major and serious offences (8.19 per cent) have also cautiously applied the rule in the ordinary trial procedure.[83] Despite the ambiguity of the law, it seems that leniency for a guilty plea has been utilised to encourage admissions of guilt and to streamline criminal processes.

There is no doubt that the prevalent application of leniency for a guilty plea has eased the burden of caseloads for the prosecutor. As well as being able to swiftly dispose of large volumes of cases, leniency for a guilty plea affords both the prosecution and the courts a managerial system to process cases with or without conclusive evidence. Since CPL 2018 came into force, there has been debate as to whether cases that employ the new rule should have a lower standard of proof. In Yang Wenge's empirical research on leniency for a guilty plea, 73 per cent of judges, 68 per cent of prosecutors and 86 per cent of police officers in his questionnaire sample indicated that a lower standard of proof should be employed in cases in which the accused pleads guilty.[84] This view is countenanced by some scholars as well. For example, Wang Jianchen argued that the principle of 'the Two Basics' – that is, the defendant can be convicted so long as the case contains 'basic facts that are clear and basic evidence that is conclusive'[85] – should be referred to in dealing with minor offences and disposed of via the expedited procedure.[86] Likewise, Xie Dengke suggested that the standard of proof in the simplified procedure should be lower than beyond reasonable doubt.[87] Although such a view is disputed by certain Chinese academics, the idea that the abbreviated procedures do not require strong evidence has been firmly entrenched in practice. In fact, the simplified procedure, as the only guilty-plea-based procedure prior to CPL 2018, has long been utilised to dispose of weak cases.

> Prosecutor: the investigation is not quite up to the standard. For example, with real evidence, such as the application of forensic evidence, it is still a weak area. Therefore, if the suspect does not confess, we have to let him go. This is a very important feature in

[83] Yang Lixin (n 76) 55.

[84] Yang Wenge, 'Shilun renzuirenfa congkuan anjian de zhengmin biaozhun (An Argument on the Standard of Proof in Relation to Cases Applying Leniency for Pleading Guilty and Accepting Punishment)' (2019) 3 *Changbai Journal* 73, 74.

[85] It should be noted that 'the Two Basics' is a controversial policy, implemented in the Strike Hard campaigns, which significantly relaxed the standard of proof during the crackdown period. It is believed that 'the Two Basics' has led to miscarriages of justice. S Trevaskes, 'Severe and Swift Justice in China' (2007) 47 *British Journal of Criminology* 23, 28.

[86] Cited from Yang Wenge (n 84) 74.

[87] ibid.

> China that we rely on the confession. If you look at all the cases we have dealt with, in 80% of the cases the suspect has pleaded guilty. All the cases rely a lot on the suspect's guilty plea. The most sophisticated evidence we deal with every day is the expert report such as the value assessment of the stolen goods. We rarely use DNA comparison. Even for murder cases, forensic evidence plays a minor role … Due to the weakness of the forensic evidence, lots of cases should not be convicted. That's why there are so many claims of the use of torture in the detention centre. The true reason is that we do not have the real evidence to prosecute him. We have to lead him to plead guilty so that the chain of evidence can be formed. If we exclude the suspect's guilty plea, then many cases could not be convicted … This is also the reason why we need guilty pleas to get rid of a large number of cases via the simplified procedure.[88]

Securing guilty pleas from the suspect, therefore, is the key to swiftly disposing of cases through the guilty plea procedure. In site A, the prosecutor always read the case dossier and asked the police whether or not the suspect had admitted her guilt before she set out to meet the suspect. Negotiation was crucial in attaining guilty plea procedures by any means. As a low-visibility action, the negotiation process was embedded in the prosecutorial interrogation.[89] For this reason, guilty plea acquisition was always on the agenda for prosecutorial interrogations.

B. Taming the Suspect: Tactics to Procure Guilty Pleas

Although CPL 2018 has expanded the defence lawyer or the duty lawyer's involvement in the case review process, such as allowing her to submit her defence opinion to the prosecution[90] and to provide legal advice to her clients, as well as signing the recognisance, such lawyers are still excluded from the core of the prosecution process, ie prosecutorial interrogation, which, to a large extent, determines whether or not the suspect decides to plead guilty. For the vast majority of cases, the prosecutorial interrogation was the first and only face-to-face encounter between the prosecution and the accused. It was during this critical meeting that prosecutors obtained guilty pleas and accelerated the process on most occasions, turning suspects into convicts. A typical prosecutorial interrogation usually started with the prosecutor establishing his authority, using either his body language or the tone of voice, to overwhelm the accused.[91] In one instance, a prosecutor shouted at a suspect before the interrogation commenced when the suspect was playing

[88] Interview APS-2.

[89] As noted in the previous chapter, this is mainly due to the fact that prosecutors were reluctant to visit detention centres in many instances.

[90] CPL 2018, Art 173.

[91] Or the procuration may take place in a later interrogation, if the suspect has been interrogated more than once. There is no limitation of times for the prosecutor to interrogate the accused. If the accused refuses to plead in the interrogation, it is likely that the prosecutor may try more than once.

with her telephone and had her legs crossed.[92] She did not realise the prosecutor had come in:

> Prosecutor: [loudly shouting] Put down your legs and switch off your phone. The interrogation is solemn and you are a suspect![93]

In common law countries where plea negotiation has been a mature and common practice, there is a nuanced but important distinction between guilty pleas and confessions. A guilty plea is a procedural response to the offence charged, indicating that the accused admits each and every element of the offence charged against her. This admission enables a court to bypass the fact-finding process and move directly to sentencing. To qualify as a guilty plea, the admission of guilt must be 'unequivocal, free from duress and personal to the defendant'.[94] A confession, on the other hand, is a notion that does not pay any tribute to the trial model. In England and Wales, the Police and Criminal Evidence Act 1984 defines a confession to include 'any statement wholly or partly adverse to the person who made it, whether made to a person in authority or not and whether made in words or otherwise'.[95] In other words, confessions and guilty pleas are concepts of different natures, and confessions do not necessarily lead to guilty pleas. For a long time, the dissimilarity between the two concepts in China had never been clarified.[96] Either form of self-condemnation could successfully trigger the same legal consequence of the case being disposed of in a cost-effective way. The situation has started to change since CPL 2018 came into force, and a suspect's signature on the recognisance to admit guilt and accept punishment now indicates that she has made a voluntary and unequivocal admission to the fact as well to the elements of the offence charged.[97] However, whether this distinction in law can actually translate into practice so that the suspect fully appreciates the implications of a guilty plea hinges on the effectiveness of the defence advice. At the time of writing, the duty lawyer scheme is still at the early implementation stage.[98] A shortfall in the number of qualified defence lawyers enrolled in the duty lawyer scheme means that the burgeoning needs of suspects who want to be advised can rarely be met.[99]

[92] In China, crossing legs in front of people is sometimes regarded as haughty.

[93] Field note APU-39.

[94] McConville and Marsh (n 70) 62.

[95] Police and Criminal Evidence Act 1984, s 82(1).

[96] For a definition of the guilty plea in the Chinese context, see Yang Lixin (n 76).

[97] Sun Changyong, 'Renzui renfa congkuan zhidu de jiben neihan (The Basic Connotation of Leniency for a Guilty Plea)' *Law Daily* (Beijing, 14 August 2019) 3.

[98] Han Xu (n 71) 37; Song Lihong, 'Zhiban lvshi zhidu yunxing de fumian xingtai ji duice (The Negativities and Solution to the Operation of the Duty Lawyer Scheme)' (2019) 4 *Legal Exhibition* 5; Zhu Yuling and Li Ning, 'Xingshi falv yuanzhu zhiban lvshi gongzuo zhize tangxi (Exploration of the Obligations of Duty Lawyers in Criminal Legal Aid Work)' (2019) 32 *Journal of Shanxi Politics and Law Institute for Administrators* 62; Lu Xu and Xu Rui, 'Renzui renfa congkuan zhiruxia zhiban lvshi zhidu de wanshan (The Perfection of the Duty Lawyer Scheme in the Context of Guilty Plea and Sentence Mitigation System)' (2019) 36 *Journal of Political Science and Law* 92.

[99] See Li Yanfei, 'Zhiban lvshi zhidu de shizheng kaocha yu gaige zhanwang (Empirical Research and Reform Prospect of the Duty Lawyer Scheme)' (2019) 3 *Administration and Law* 90.

As far as prosecutors are concerned, this conceptual ambivalence is useful to elicit guilty pleas. This is illustrated in prosecutorial interrogations, where the prosecutors always started with the straightforward question – whether the suspect would like to make a confession or, in a slightly euphemistic way, whether the suspect had 'told the truth' in the police station. Detailed facts were rarely enquired about at the beginning of the interrogation; it followed only after the suspect's position was clear. If the suspect pleaded guilty, the prosecutor would acknowledge the suspect's 'wise' choice by reassuring her of the benefits of that decision. The interrogation process would then accelerate by quickly confirming the key facts.

> Prosecutor: Will you plead guilty or not?
>
> Suspect: Yes, I do.
>
> Prosecutor: Good. Normally if you are well behaved and you would like to pay the fines, the penalty will be light.[100]
>
> Prosecutor: Do you plead guilty or not? If you plead guilty, you will be sentenced lightly. So, behave and confess what you have done.
>
> Suspect: OK.[101]
>
> Prosecutor: Did you tell the truth in the police station?
>
> Suspect: Yes.
>
> Prosecutor: OK. It is good that you plead guilty, as your case will be dealt with quickly. Now I will read what you said in the police station. [The prosecutor quickly read one of the confessions in the dossier] Is that what you said?
>
> Suspect: Yes.
>
> Prosecutor: Come and sign your name here.[102]

Over 70 per cent of the suspects I observed in my fieldwork pleaded guilty in the prosecutorial interrogation. For the majority of suspects who did not have a defence lawyer offering them advice, it was difficult to assess whether they truly understood what guilty pleas meant to them, apart from the vague idea that they might get a lesser sentence. Worryingly, those who pleaded guilty included several suspects who seriously disputed the facts established by the police. Some of them clearly entered into an agreement without even knowing the crimes that they were to be charged with. This was exemplified in the following two accounts, one of which has been mentioned in chapter four.

> Field note-APU 23 (*CASEA* 33) Illegal Possession of Narcotic Drugs:
>
> Prosecutor: 7 bags of Magu[103] were found by police in your apartment in the evening of 5th November. These drugs belonged to your friend, but you decided to keep them for your own use. Is that true?
>
> Suspect: They were my friend's property. All I agreed was to hold something valuable for him – he never told me what's inside. I did not know what they are as they were kept

[100] Field note APU-28.
[101] Field note APU-36.
[102] Field note APU-18.
[103] A type of drug that is composed of methamphetamine mixed with caffeine.

in a locked suitcase. He was travelling to the North to do some business and his condo was not a safe place.

Prosecutor: But you did know that he was a drug user. It must have occurred to you that he might leave some drugs in your possession. And most importantly, they were found in your apartment.

Suspect: He gave all sorts of things for me to look after temporarily. Sometimes jewellery and car keys etc. He trusted me.

Prosecutor: So, you know that it is possible that he might give you some drugs someday.

Suspect: I don't know what was inside. He only told me something valuable. So, I guess it was some expensive stuff. It could be anything expensive.

Prosecutor: I am not here to hear all these pretexts. Do you plead guilty of possessing drugs? You will be better off if you do so. These drugs were found in your apartment. That is the fact.

Suspect: As you said, they found them in my apartment. So, yes, I plead guilty.

Field note-APU 26 (*CASEA* 16) Drug trafficking

Prosecutor: Do you plead guilty?

Suspect: Yes.

…

Prosecutor: How much drug did you sell? How much profit did you earn?

Suspect: I did not earn any profit. Many accounts were made up by the police. I did a favour to my friend. I did not gain any profit.

Prosecutor: [Shouting] Why did you say something different from what you said in the police station? You said you went to the market and got 200 yuan for the drugs. He also paid you 50 yuan for your benefit. [Speaking very loudly] The 50 yuan is your profit, isn't it?

Suspect: That is the way it was – but I wouldn't say that is the profit. That did not even cover the cost. I was doing a favour to my friend.

Prosecutor: Stop using 'that is the way it was'. Yes or no?

Suspect: Yes.

Prosecutor: You said what you said in the police station was not true, then why did you sign your name on each page? Did you sign them?

Suspect: Yes.

Prosecutor: Well then. Look, if you plead guilty, your sentence will be mitigated. As long as you behave in the court and plead guilty, you will not be sentenced long. It is over, come out and sign your names.

Fourteen suspects challenged the accounts in the case dossier and claimed innocence. The denial of guilt undoubtedly posed a dilemma for the prosecutor. These cases could be too weak to prosecute; however, non-prosecution was an undesirable option given that these suspects had been remanded in custody for a period of time. The suspect could easily tell from the prosecutor that a guilty plea was demanded. Unsurprisingly, the denial of the request quickly led to an escalation of tension between the prosecutor and the accused. In one drug trafficking case in which the prosecutor's suggestion of a guilty plea was not appreciated, pressure was exerted by shouting and the use of aggressive language by the prosecutor.

> Prosecutor: Did you tell the truth in the police station?
>
> Suspect: I didn't … I said nothing.
>
> Prosecutor: [Stopped typing the statement and looked at the suspect] The crime you committed does not carry a heavy penalty.
>
> Suspect: It has nothing to do with the punishment. I am innocent.
>
> Prosecutor: [Looking at him angrily] What?
>
> Suspect: [Explains that he was arrested whilst waiting for his friend].
>
> Prosecutor: [Shouting] What did you say in the police station?
>
> Suspect: I said the same thing in the police station.
>
> Prosecutor: [Flipping the evidence dossier and speaking angrily] You said clearly what happened! Why did you plead guilty in the police station?
>
> Suspect: [Speaking loudly] I didn't.
>
> …
>
> Prosecutor: [Angrily] I tell you, if you don't plead guilty now, you cannot do that in the court.
>
> Suspect: What? Speak louder?
>
> Prosecutor: [Shouting] Let's see who will win! You will receive a very heavy sentence! You deserve it! [Angrily] Come out and sign your statement!
>
> The suspect was given the statement and he started to read carefully. The prosecutor was very angry.
>
> Prosecutor: [Shouting] Sign it!
>
> Suspect: I haven't finished reading!
>
> Prosecutor: [Angrily] So slow. Can you read more quickly? Why haven't you finished?
>
> Suspect: It is my right to read it!
>
> The prosecutor became so angry that she went out of the interrogation room and called in security. When security came, the suspect had almost finished signing the statement.
>
> Security: Behave! What a manner![104]

For the prosecutors, the negation of guilt or retraction of early confessions was a deviation – suspects should always be deferential to authority, especially the authority who possessed the power to decide their fate.[105] Rather than being perceived as a way of exercising their right to defending themselves, confrontation from the suspect was always depicted as 'a wish to escape punishment by not telling the truth', which should be tamed by exemplary norms. As far as these prosecutors were concerned, procuring guilty pleas became part of their routine job and a basic work skill that must be mastered to secure convictions.

[104] Field note APU-16.

[105] For relevant analysis, see McConville (n 49) 49–50.

If a prosecutor was good at gaining guilty pleas from suspects, it would be a talent to boast of. This meant overbearing and oppressive 'strategies' should be adopted whenever possible. Failing to do so was seen as a form of incompetence, as the prosecutor was not aggressive enough to undertake the job. On one occasion, I conversed with an experienced prosecutor, who had just come back from an interrogation;

> Researcher: How was your interrogation? Did all the suspects plead guilty?
>
> Prosecutor: Yes. Even those that didn't plead guilty in the police station; they would plead guilty in front of me.
>
> Researcher: Why? Do you have any special techniques?
>
> Prosecutor: Very easy. You just tell them the consequences. You can let them know that you have sufficient evidence to make the accusation. If they do not plead guilty, the result would be adverse to them. They all understand it.
>
> It turned out his technique was not that simple. Later that day, the prosecutor told us (another two prosecutors and myself) what happened:
>
> Prosecutor: Initially the suspect did not plead guilty. He was so confident and arrogant. I was polite to him in the beginning. But then, I was pissed off at his manner … I shouted at him. I gave him a dirty look when he came to sign. I saw his hands were shaking … He was so scared! He pleaded guilty finally. These people should be scorned. They need a good beating before they admit what they have done.[106]

All prosecutors, both male and female, were supposed to be iron-fisted when confronting the suspect during the interrogation. This had the effect of shaping their characters. This point was elaborated by a senior prosecutor, who opined that female prosecutors must lose their femininity to become capable prosecutors:

> Prosecutor: I don't think ladies should work as prosecutors … This work will cause a personality change. Just have a look at the able female prosecutors I know. They are all very aggressive and talk like trumpeting … I still remember X (a female prosecutor) when she was just recruited into our department, such a sweet girl! But now, I don't even think she is a woman.[107]

I did not observe any physical violence being used directly against suspects in my fieldwork. However, bitter tones, foul languages, intimidating body gestures and slamming furniture were all used as measures to press for guilty pleas. Facing such an aggressive interrogative manner, some of the suspects gave in with resignation. One trainee prosecutor described how a suspect was compelled to plead guilty in the face of a prosecutor's heavy-handed interrogation tactics:

> At first, the suspect did not plead guilty. The prosecutor was so angry. He thumped the desk and threatened the suspect. Then the suspect was scared. He said his wife was beaten up by the police. He was too angry to tell the truth. But eventually, he confessed and pleaded guilty.[108]

[106] Field note APU-32.
[107] Field note APU-63.
[108] Field note APU-32.

As far as prosecutors were concerned, pleading guilty was primarily for the suspect's benefit. On one occasion, a prosecutor declared that convincing the suspects to confess was a way to 'improve their well-being', as they could come out of the prison quickly and look after their families. This implied that the suspects were presumed to be guilty and should be convicted by the courts. As the following conversation between a senior prosecutor and a trainee suggested:

> Prosecutor: Did the suspect plead guilty?
>
> Trainee prosecutor: No. He didn't. He said the police treated him badly, so he did not want to plead guilty.
>
> Prosecutor: This is so ridiculous! Pleading guilty is for his own sake! It has nothing to do with the police station. Once he is done [has been convicted and sentenced], he can come out of the prison quickly.[109]

Compared to the police, the prosecutor's manner was considered to be civil by some suspects.[110] There were hardly any reports from suspects that physical violence had been applied during the prosecution review stage. This 'better treatment' seemed to have been conducive to the suspect's admission of guilt. For some suspects, pleading guilty was a sign of trust and should be based on a degree of mutual respect. Knowing that such a mindset existed, some prosecutors were able to formulate tactics to enhance the chances of procuring guilty pleas. In one instance, a prosecutor passed his wisdom that suspects were willing to plead guilty because of his moderate manner of interrogation:

> Prosecutor: Sometimes the suspects who did not admit guilt in front of the police would plead guilty before us (prosecutors). They said they did not want to make a confession before the police because they were cruel. They (the suspects) like us because they said we were polite and nice. I think that is interesting.[111]

Coercion and coaxing were often employed alternatively to 'crack' difficult cases. The two ingredients to securing a guilty plea – 'waiver rewards' and 'trial penalties' – were tactically mingled to compound each other and to maximise the effect. This strategy was found to be successful particularly for risk-averse suspects. In executing this technique, the prosecutors always used the suspects' early signed confessions as a bargaining chip. In verifying the suspect's prior confessions recorded by the police, shouting or beguiling was used to exert pressure.

> A suspect claimed that he was wrongly identified by the police in a drug trafficking case.
>
> Prosecutor: You said what you said in the police station was not true, then why did you sign your name on each page? Did you sign them?
>
> Suspect: Yes, I did.
>
> Prosecutor: [Shouting] Then that is what you have said honestly! You have admitted to the police officer and you want to change your statement now. [Speaking very

[109] Field note APU-37.
[110] Field notes APU-32 and 33.
[111] Field note APU-32.

loudly] I have to tell you, it is useless! You have confessed in the police station and you cannot change it now! You have signed on each page of your statement. Discipline yourself! You cannot get away with it! Now I ask you, where did the 'ice' (the drug) come from? … Are you going to admit your guilt?

Suspect: Fine. I am guilty.[112]

In a drug trafficking case, the suspect denied that he owned the drugs or participated in any drug transactions.

Prosecutor: Did you admit this when you were interrogated in the police station and when deciding whether or not you should be remanded in custody?

Suspect: [Silence]

Prosecutor: Look. It is totally useless to deny that now. If you have admitted to the authorities, it means these people believe the evidence in this case is enough to investigate you and keep you in custody. In that case, it is in vain for you to withdraw what you have said in the police station. Now, do you plead guilty or not?

Suspect: This is such an injustice! This is totally corrupt!

…

Prosecutor: It is really bad luck. You have no choice now. Did you sign the record?

Suspect: They did not let me read what they wrote. They forced me to sign my name.

Prosecutor: OK. This is too late. To be honest, there is no other option for you. Your signed records will bite you.

Suspect: So, I have no choice, but to plead guilty?

Prosecutor: Yes.[113]

Prior to CPL 2018 there was little prospect that a suspect could retract a guilty plea and maintain her innocence in the future, once she had admitted her guilt and signed the statements. While the withdrawal of a guilty plea has now been permitted in the new legal regime, the recognisance signed earlier could still be used as valid confession evidence against her at court, even though the discount of sentence cannot be 'awarded' if she is found guilty.[114] In light of such a detrimental effect of withdrawal, few defendants can afford to run the risk of changing their mind once a recognisance is signed. The logic behind the retraction of written statements is that the defendant must 'pay a price' for an ostensible inconsistency induced by herself.

This principle could even extend to written confessions claimed to be signed under duress by means of threat, oppression or even torture. Inquiry into the police conduct during the investigation was rarely carried out in an independent and transparent way. Instead, the prosecutor's own interrogation records were conducted in line with the investigative work of the police to ensure that the case

[112] Field note APU-15.
[113] Field note APU-17.
[114] The Procuratorate of the City of Guangzhou, 'The Notification of the Legal Recognizance to Plead Guilty and Accept Punishment' (The Internet Procuratorate of the City of Guangzhou, 26 July 2018), www.jcy.gz.gov.cn/gsjwxz/714.jhtml (accessed 18 September 2019).

was ironclad. In so doing, the suspect's previous statement in the investigation was not only unchallenged but was used as a basis to reinforce its own probative value. For example, in one drug possession case, the prosecutor intended to make the suspect admit that she kept the drugs for her own use. This suggestion was rejected by the suspect, who insisted that the drugs did not belong to her.

> Prosecutor: So, the police found 10 small bags of 'ice' and 1 bag of Magu.[115] You said you wanted to keep them for yourself because you had a quarrel with your ex-boyfriend who had these drugs.
>
> Suspect: No, it is not true. I did not say anything like that. It is made up by the policeman. They were my boyfriend's and I did not know how to deal with them, so I kept them where they were.
>
> Prosecutor: I have to warn you that if you constantly change your statement, your penalty will be aggravated.
>
> ...
>
> Prosecutor: Why is the statement you give today different from the one you gave in the police station?
>
> Suspect: I did not confess in the police station. Then they (the police) were very furious. They shouted at me. The reason why I kept the drugs was not that I did not want to throw them away but because the drugs are not mine. I didn't know how to deal with it. At least they are not mine.
>
> Prosecutor: Why did you sign the record of interrogation in the police station?
>
> Suspect: They interrogated me for a long time. They forced me to sign it ... I had no choice. They wrote down that 'I kept the drug because I wanted to take some whenever I want'. It is not what I said. They persuaded me and explained to me that such writing does not necessarily mean that I wanted to use drugs.
>
> Prosecutor: What you said now is useless. You have signed it and it is too late. You have to say the same thing. Otherwise, your punishment will be aggravated.[116]

Claiming innocence or disputing the accuracy of the statements during the prosecutorial interrogation turned out to be not always helpful to the defence case – the prosecutors had methods to remedy those matters in order to salvage the case before it was sent for trial. For instance, when a suspect declared that she decided to withdraw her confessions, an inquiry would be made to find out the reasons behind this. In several instances, the suspect reported that her earlier confessions were extorted by torture in the police station. Instead of investigating the alleged police torture independently, the prosecutors sent a message to the police, asking them to produce evidence to refute the allegation and to shore up the validity of the written confessions. After all these matters were taken care of, the case would be sent to the court. This time, the suspect had no choice but to plead guilty.

[115] Magu is methylamphetamine and caffeine. 'Ice' is highly purified methylamphetamine.
[116] Field note APU-21.

> Researcher: What happens if they (suspects) do not plead guilty even if they admitted this in the police station? Say, if they totally deny the whole fact?
>
> Prosecutor: Then you should ask them why they say such things in the police station. Ask why they change their statement and the reason that they change their statement. If they totally deny the fact, tell them that if they plead guilty, the abbreviated procedure will be applied so they will be imposed with a lesser punishment. Write down their defence in detail. Then try to eliminate the possibility of their claimed facts by further investigation.[117]

In the past, some academics and legal practitioners argued that the guilty plea procedure offers an extra option for suspects, without which the accused could always resort to the alternative solution: the full adjudication.[118] This argument is still relevant even since CPL 2018 came into force, given that the vast majority of cases in which the accused pleaded guilty have been resolved primarily by guilty plea procedures and sentence discounts are largely linked to the abbreviated trial models.[119] In theory, the accused's rights are better safeguarded and her case would be better contested if the case were tried by the common procedure. In reality, the existence of the full adjudication itself amounted to oppression. The uncertain prospect of conviction and a sentence without mitigation constituted a package of coercion that forced the accused to plead guilty.[120] Quite often, a simple comparison of the potential outcomes between a simplified trial and a full adjudication was sufficient to persuade the accused to opt for self-condemnation.[121]

> Prosecutor: [Shouting] Do you plead guilty or not? If you don't plead guilty, the ordinary procedure will be applied. Then you will be given a long sentence – close to the maximum sentence. Do you know that? If you plead guilty, the simplified procedure will be used and you will get a sentence discount. You will come out of prison quickly. Do you enjoy staying in the detention centre?
>
> Suspect: [A few seconds of consideration] I will plead guilty.[122]

[117] Field note APU-8.

[118] For example, Li Yingmin argues that, as an alternative to full adjudication, the simplified trial process offers the defendant the right to choose trial procedures: Li Yingmin, 'Xingshi jianyi chengxue de xinxiuzheng jiqi shiyong tanxi (The Revision of the Simplified Criminal Trial and its Application)' (2012) 9 *The Chinese Procurators* 33, 35. Similarly, Zhang Lu acknowledges that the set-up of simplified trials based upon defendants' guilty pleas is an improvement in the protection of human rights: Zhang Lu, 'Xingshi jianyi chengxu de gaige yu wanshan: yi woguo Taiwan diqu xiangguan lifa wei cankao (The Reform and Perfection of the Simplified Criminal Trial: In Comparison with Taiwan Legislations)' (2012) 10 *Faxue zazhi* (*Law Magazine*) 160, 161.

[119] See Yang Lixin (n 76) 55.

[120] This has also been a well-documented understanding in relation to the US plea bargaining system. See Lippke (n 69) 10–38; O Bar-Gill and O Ben-Shahar, 'The Prisoners' Plea Bargain Dilemma' (2009) 1 *Journal of Legal Analysis* 737, 738; WF McDonald, 'From Plea Negotiation to Coercive Justice: Notes on the Respecification of a Concept' (1979) 13 *Law and Society Review* 385.

[121] Apparently, there is a realistic problem that the prosecutor might overcharge the suspect by recommending a higher sentencing range. As noted earlier, the expedited procedure now allows a 10–30% sentence discount. See the Supreme Court No 1 Criminal Tribunal, 'Considerations on Certain Issues of the Pilot Scheme of the Expedited Procedure of Criminal Cases' (2016) 4 *Legal Application* 18, 21.

[122] Field note APU-18.

C. Sentence Discounts

According to Article 67 of the Criminal Law, if the suspect honestly confesses her guilt, the court may consider a mitigated sentence. This article is mirrored in Article 15 of CPL 2018, which states that the accused may receive a lighter sentence if she voluntarily confesses her guilt, admits the facts charged and is willing to accept the punishment. Due to the discretional 'may' and the fact that judgments in China are often drafted in a brief and vague way regarding the reasoning for sentencing, it was difficult to assess whether a lesser sentence is truly meted out when the accused pleads guilty.

The status quo has ameliorated in recent years, with the reduction rates of a sentence being delegated to local judiciaries, making the sentence discount standards more specific at a policy level. For example, the judiciary in Zhuhai district, Guangzhou city adopted a staged incentive scheme to encourage early guilty pleas. It allowed up to 20 per cent sentence discount if the accused pleaded guilty in the police investigation and a diminished 15 per cent discount if guilty pleas were made at a later stage.[123] Likewise, a 'sliding scale' of discounts was implemented in Jimei district, Shamen city, enabling the accused to receive a 33 per cent reduction in sentence when the guilty plea was entered in the police investigation, a 20 per cent reduction in the prosecution evaluation period and a 10 per cent reduction when the defendant pleaded guilty after the trial began.[124] To encourage suspects to enter an early admission, a defendant in Jimei was entitled to a 40 per cent sentence discount if there existed other mitigating circumstances (such as the accused voluntarily turning herself in).[125] The most lenient sentencing policy has been documented in Mo city, Shandong province, where a defendant was exempted from criminal penalties after voluntarily pleading guilty and offering a substantial sum of damages to the family of the deceased victim in a dangerous driving case.[126] Cases like this do, however, raise a concern that sentence negotiation could become a monetary business in the shadow of the guilty plea policy. Since the defendant's willingness to compensate the victim has been widely

[123] 'Guangzhou Zhuhai sifa bumen lianhe guifan shiyong renzui renfa congkuan zhidu: yi lingkougong beigaoren dangting renzui beijianxing yicheng (Guangzhou City, Zhuhai Judicial Institutions Issued Joint Regulations on Guilty Plea-Lenity System: A Defendant without Confessions were Awarded 10 per cent Discount in Court)', *Post of People's Courts* (24 March 2017) http://rmfyb.chinacourt.org/paper/images/2017-03/24/04/2017032404_pdf.pdf (accessed 25 September 2018).

[124] This sliding scale sentencing model has been championed by Liu Weiqi, who suggests that delayed guilty pleas are tactics employed by hard-core defendants who calculate the chances to 'confront the norms'. Liu Weiqi, 'Renzui renfa de "321" jietishi congkuan niangxin jizhi (The Sliding Scale Sentencing Mechanism of 3–2–1 in Guilty Plea Cases)' (2018) 12 *Huibei Social Science* 147, 148.

[125] 'Zuiduo kejianxing 40%! Renzuirenfa congkuan zhidu de Jimei shijian (A Maximum of 40% Sentence Discount! The Jimei Practice of Guilty Plea-Lenity System)', *Sohu* (18 July 2017) www.sohu.com/a/158155018_410224 (accessed 25 September 2018).

[126] See the Criminal Judgment (No Lu 0282 Crim Initial Judgment No 1168) Issued in Mo City People's Court, https://wenshu.court.gov.cn/ (accessed 25 September 2018).

recognised as consideration for sentence mitigation in practice,[127] defendants from a privileged background could benefit from the system, whereas those from the lower social class who cannot afford a handsome amount of compensation have to serve the actual sentence. In this context, the outcome of the policy implementation has been a reflection of stratified social classes where resources, power and treatment are unfairly distributed.

It is far from clear whether a suspect will truly benefit from the promised sentence discount, given that prosecutors can strategically overcharge the suspect or recommend a greater sentence within their discretionary range. Most suspects do not have sufficient legal knowledge to know precisely how long the sentence imposed on them is likely to be. Only a small number of suspects could afford defence lawyers to provide such advice. Therefore, to ensure that the guilty plea is 'bargained' on a level playing field, a comprehensive legal aid system in which suspects can have access to legal counsels is necessary, so that the suspect can be advised as to the highest sentence that is likely to be imposed on the basis of the facts, the potential sentence discount and the possible sentence settlement on their behalf. As the duty lawyer scheme is still in its inception, whether changes can be brought to the practice so that the suspect is effectively advised has yet to be seen.[128]

With limited avenues to information and to assess their own preferences, some of the suspects sought advice from prosecutors. In site A, prosecutors' replies were strategically formulated in responding to such enquiries. Hence, if a suspect gave little resistance to the prosecutor and showed a willingness to enter a guilty plea, the prosecutors would often understate the seriousness of their offence and give an indication of their potential sentence range. Whenever hesitation was visibly detected in considering whether or not to plead guilty, or the suspect was simply making a general enquiry, prosecutors usually played up the uncertainty and refused to offer any helpful guidance. If the circumstance was such that the prosecutor had sensed that the suspect was going to retract his previous confessions or was unlikely to plead guilty, the gravity of the crime in question and severity of the potential penalty would be emphasised or exaggerated.

> [A theft case]
>
> Suspect: I surrendered myself voluntarily. I was so afraid and upset. I have never stolen anything before in my life. I feel so guilty and I feel I owe a lot to that guy. He did not do anything wrong and I stole his laptop. I was so guilty, so I went to the police station by myself. I feel I am so stupid. Do you think I will be sentenced?

[127] See Zhou Qiang, 'Congkuan zhidu shidian gongzuo qingkuang de zhongqi baogao (The Mid-term Report of the Work in Relation to the Pilot Project of Mitigating Sentencing Regime)' *The People's Court Post* (Beijing, 24 December 2017) 1.

[128] Han Xu (n 71) 37; Song Lihong, 'Zhiban lvshi zhidu yunxing de fumian xingtai ji duice (The Negativities and Solution to the Operation of the Duty Lawyer Scheme)' (2019) 4 *Legal Exhibition* 5; Zhu Yuling and Li Ning, 'Xingshi falv yuanzhu zhiban lvshi gongzuo zhize tangxi (Exploration of the Obligations of Duty Lawyers in Criminal Legal Aid Work)' (2019) 32 *Journal of Shanxi Politics and Law Institute for Administrators* 62; Lu Xu and Xu Rui (n 98); Li Yanfei (n 99) 90.

Prosecutor: You only stole less than 2,000 yuan and you have turned yourself in. So, you should be sentenced for less than a year.[129]

[A dangerous driving case] The suspect pleaded guilty.

Suspect: How long I will be sentenced to?

Prosecutor: Shouldn't be too bad. Your serum test result was not high. But the problem is you had a passenger in your car. It will aggravate your sentence. If you want to be given a short sentence, request the court to impose a fine on you.[130]

[A dangerous driving case]

Suspect: I am guilty. I thought I could get away with it. How long will I be sentenced for?

Prosecutor: Don't worry. As long as you have pleaded guilty, your punishment will be very light – a maximum of penal servitude.[131]

[A theft case]

Suspect: I knew nothing about the proceeds. X (the accomplice) has got all the things we had stolen. How long do you think I will be sentenced?

Prosecutor: You have served as an informant and the police have arrested another two thieves. So, you have performed the meritorious service. As long as you plead guilty and behave, you shouldn't be sentenced too long.[132]

[A drug trafficking case] The suspect was silent and refused to indicate whether or not he was going to plead guilty.

Suspect: How long will be the sentence?

Prosecutor: I cannot tell you the exact length. But it is not a big issue. As long as you pay the fines, behave and plead guilty in the court, your penalty will be mitigated for sure.[133]

[A drug trafficking case]

Prosecutor: Do you know how long they (the accomplices) have known each other?

Suspect: I am not sure. How long will I be in prison?

Prosecutor: I don't know. I am not the judge.[134]

[A fraud case] The suspect was still hesitant, hoping to glean more information before making the decision.

Prosecutor: So, now the things are quite clear. Are you going to plead guilty then?

Suspect: How long do you think I will be sentenced for?

Prosecutor: As a prosecutor, I cannot tell you. You can check the Criminal Law by yourself. There were a lot of factors that will be taken into consideration.[135]

[A credit card fraud case] A suspect was investigated for credit card fraud: he was investigated for owing the bank 12,000 yuan with no intention to pay.

[129] Field note APU-19.
[130] Field note APU-51.
[131] Field note APU-25.
[132] Field note APU-17.
[133] Field note APU-15.
[134] Field note APU-31.
[135] Field note APU-15.

> Suspect: I don't think I can afford to be put in prison. If so, my sick mother will be dying. How long will I be sentenced for?
>
> Prosecutor: Based on my experience, your case is serious. I am thinking about 5 to 8 years in prison.[136] But if you plead guilty and pay off the money, you will be able to get three-year imprisonment which could be reprieved (*huanxing*). Do you know what reprieve is? Reprieve is that you can do whatever you are doing now normally. However, if you commit a crime during the three years' probation period, you will be put in prison to execute your full actual sentence.[137]
>
> [Forging stamps of public institutions (*weizao shiye danwei yinzhang zui*)] The suspect retracted his early confessions in the police station and claimed innocence.
>
> Prosecutor: The co-offender in this case, your boss said you had a chat with him, how could you say you did not know what it was? I have to warn you that if you change your statement, the case will be tried in the ordinary procedure. What you said will be used as evidence against you, because you are dishonest. You have been remanded in custody, which means there was no problem in the evidence. So, what you have told me now is in vain. Which version do you want me to record? The one you said in the police station or the new one you gave just now?
>
> [The suspect was hesitant]
>
> Suspect: How long will I be sentenced for?
>
> Prosecutor: It depends on how you behave. Last time I processed a similar case, the defendant was sentenced for three years. Your case is more serious than that one.[138] So, you may wish to weigh the consequence here.[139]

Richard L Lippke noted that state officials in the USA offer suspects charge and sentence concessions in exchange for guilty pleas 'because they suspect that the evidence they have falls short of meeting the rigorous standard of proof required by the criminal law'.[140] This is also true of the Chinese criminal justice system. It is difficult to fathom the precise scope of cases in which the evidence has not reached the standard of proof but which have been dealt with by guilty plea procedures. Yet it is common knowledge that guilty plea procedures have been prevalently utilised to dispose of cases in which the evidence is not conclusive beyond a reasonable doubt. A senior prosecutor in site A estimated that one in three prosecution cases would be dropped if guilty pleas were not available.[141] The veracity of this statement may need further confirmation, but the possible proportion concerned was not far off. Of the 64 cases closely monitored in this study, 16 cases

[136] According to Art 196 of the Criminal Law, the offence of credit card fraud with a sum less than 50,000 yuan should be sentenced to a maximum of 5 years' imprisonment, penal servitude and a fine of between 20,000 yuan and 200,000 yuan.

[137] Field note APU-59.

[138] According to Art 280 of the Criminal Law, the offence of forging stamps of public institutions carries a maximum sentence of 3 years' imprisonment. The prosecutor's words were very tactical, as he hinted that the suspect was likely to be sentenced with a minimum of 3 years' imprisonment.

[139] Field note APU-21.

[140] Lippke (n 69) 191.

[141] Field note APU-41; Interview APS-1.

(25 per cent) could be identified as hopelessly weak (with little evidence to support the charged facts aside from their pleas). Yet, all of them proceeded successfully to trial in the form of a simplified procedure.[142]

Almost all of the 64 cases followed in this study can be categorised as low-level crimes, mostly concerned with a small amount of drug trafficking, drink-driving offences, property offences with relatively low value and offences against the person with relatively minor bodily harm. A district criminal judge informed me that serious crimes and minor offences were classified and treated somewhat differently; whereas minor offences were sometimes disposed of perfunctorily by the courts, major and serious offences were investigated 'in a more thorough and responsible manner'. According to him, the 'quality of evidence with which the intermediate court proceeded was distinctive from the cases they (district judges) dealt with on a daily basis'.[143] The scope of my research prevented me from undertaking such comparisons in the field. But even if this remark were true, it does not justify the belief that low-level crimes do not 'deserve' thorough investigations but should be processed in a cost-effective way. It is common sense that if the state does not have enough evidence to prove the guilt of an individual, it is the state officials' responsibility to discontinue the proceedings, rather than putting the accused through a needless ordeal.

III. Constructing the Defence Case at the Pre-trial Prosecution Review Stage

A. Accessing Case Files in the Prosecutor's Office

Gaining an understanding of the prosecution case as early as possible is crucial for defence lawyers to respond to the prosecution and to construct defence cases.[144] Since the prosecution case is presented in the form of investigative dossiers, accessing case files is essential for defence strategies. CPL 2018 stipulates that the earliest point that defence lawyers are able to access the case dossier is when it has been transferred to the procuratorate.[145] The defence lawyer is allowed to

[142] Field note APU-44.
[143] Interview ATJ-1.
[144] See McConville et al (n 27) 176.
[145] CPL 2018, Art 40. This Article was intact in CPL 2012. However, prior to CPL 2012, the defence lawyer was not able to access substantive prosecution evidence against the accused until the case was transferred to the court (see Art 36 of CPL 1996). In practice, such rights were further curtailed as prosecutors were not supposed to send the entire case dossier to the court before trial: prosecutors' 'pick and choose' tactics placed the defence at a great disadvantage. In addition, defence lawyers reported denials of access in criminal cases due to a high charging fee for photocopying files. In the face of the outcry of the highly restricted access to the prosecution case, CPL 2012 reversed the situation, allowing the defence to examine the prosecution evidence. See Sida Liu and TC Halliday, *Criminal Defence in China: The Politics of Lawyers at Work* (Cambridge University Press, 2016) 54.

photocopy, scan or take photographs of the case dossier at the procuratorate.[146] Albeit enshrined in law, the right to access case dossiers is not always guaranteed. Defence lawyers have reported that some prosecutors were reluctant to assist them in revealing all the evidence in certain cases; they deliberately placed obstacles in their way when defence lawyers approached the procuratorate for evidence.[147] The practices of the procuratorate varied from region to region, and defence lawyers were told to follow the 'local rules'. Most crucially, there was no remedy available to defence lawyers when such a right was denied.

> Defence lawyer: It is almost impossible to see the dossiers in the Procuratorate (in site B)! The Procuratorate only provides the so-called 'objective evidence' to us. The so-called objective evidence includes the authorisation of custody, extension of the procedure, writ of detention and the expert report. Not substantive evidence. They (prosecutors) do not allow us to see the suspect's confession and other statements. So far, I have never seen any statements in the Procuratorate (in site B) ... There is nothing we can do about it.[148]

> Defence lawyer: They would create some hurdles for us in site J ... In site J, if we request to photocopy the dossier, we are asked to bring the A4 photocopy paper with us. In one procuratorate, we are not allowed to photocopy the dossier and we are only allowed to take pictures of the dossier with our camera, whilst with another procuratorate, they have a regulation completely the opposite: we are only allowed to photocopy the dossier but we are not allowed to take pictures. The practice in the court and the procuratorate varies. Sometimes in the prosecutors' office, we are only allowed to access the dossier A which contains the warranties and the writs only. That's meaningless for us. We are not allowed to see the dossier B (evidence dossier) which contains the suspects' confession, witnesses' statements and other real evidence. If we wish to read the dossier B, we have to write an application letter to the leader of the Procuratorate.[149]

On the positive side, many defence lawyers acknowledged that their access to case dossiers has been less restricted since CPL 2012 was implemented. However, not all evidence was treated equally. For example, digital forms of evidence, especially audio and video records of the police interrogation, were usually unavailable to defence lawyers, which made it difficult to apply for the exclusion of evidence.[150]

> Defence lawyer: If the case has been passed to the procuratorate, it would be easier for us (to access the case dossier). There are two working models to access the dossier in site C. The first one is that the Procuratorate gives us a notice and all the dossiers will be available. Another model is that they select some evidence in both dossier A (document dossier) and dossier B (evidence dossier) for us to photocopy. But they will let us see

[146] See Art 47 of 'The explanation of the application of the Criminal Procedure Law 2012 provided by the Supreme People's court'.

[147] Sida Liu and Halliday (n 148) 55. Beijing Shangquan Law Firm, 'The annual report of the implementation effect of the new criminal procedure law 2013' (2014) www.sqxb.cn/content/details16_1644.html (accessed 9 March 2014).

[148] Interview DBL-1.

[149] Interview CDL-3.

[150] See also Sida Liu and Halliday (n 148) 55.

more evidence just before the case is sent to the court. Some procuratorates allow us to take photos of the evidence, which is good I think because we are allowed to see most of the evidence in the dossier. It used to be that they would give us some selected evidence in the dossier to be photocopied. Therefore, we are not allowed to see all the evidence. However, we are not allowed to see the videos.[151]

Defence lawyer: As far as the evidence in the dossier is concerned, the videos, CDs and other digital recordings are not allowed to be seen by the defence as well. [Laughing] Last time we requested to watch the videos, they (the procuratorate) showed us the door! I think this is very problematic – the court does not allow us to see the videos either.[152]

B. Gathering Defence Evidence

As noted in chapter 3, defence lawyers gathering evidence in the pretrial stage is likened to 'working in a minefield'.[153] In engaging with defence preparation, defence lawyers' liberty, career and finances are constantly at risk. CPL 2012, as well as its 2018 progeny, ostensibly reinforces the defence right by stating that defence lawyers are entitled to take statements from the witnesses if the witnesses explicitly agree.[154] In reality, defence lawyers are advised not to conduct any evidence gathering, especially when the evidence acquired by the defence contradicts that relied upon by the prosecution. The direct danger is from Article 306 of the Criminal Law, which has been used by police and prosecution against the active defence.[155] Fu Hualing noted that when exculpatory evidence was sought by defence lawyers against the prosecution case, prosecutions were 'immediately switched to Article 306, abandoning the former charge practice'.[156] With 90 per cent of the cases against defence lawyers prosecuted under Article 306 resulting in acquittal,[157] legal scholars have believed that prosecutions based on

[151] Interview CDL-1.

[152] Interview BDL-1.

[153] ibid 57–58.

[154] CPL 2012, Art 41 and CPL 2018, Art 43. Alternatively, they can apply for evidence collection via the procuratorate or the courts. If the evidence that the defence lawyer gathered contains the incapacity of the suspect or alibis, she is obliged to inform the criminal justice institutions promptly.

[155] For a discussion of Art 306, see ch 3.

[156] Fu Hualing, 'When Lawyers Are Prosecuted: The Struggle of a Profession in Transition' (2007) Social Science Research Network, www.papers.ssrn.com/sol13/papers.cfm?abstract_id=956500 (accessed 3 September 2013).

[157] Due to the high acquittal rate in this category of cases, Art 306 is deemed as a 'bad article that damages the judicial system': Hou Shumei and Ron Keith, 'The Defence Lawyer in the Scales of Chinese Criminal Justice' (2011) 20(70) *Journal of Contemporary China* 379, 393. The acquittal rate of cases prosecuted under Art 306 is confirmed as being slightly lower in other studies, which may be based upon different sample years. For example, Du Xiaoli claims that 'according to the All Chinese Lawyers Association (ACLA), between 1997 and 2007 108 defence lawyers were prosecuted under Art 306, but only 32 of them were convicted': Du Xiaoli, 'Lun "lvshi weizhengzui" zuizhi dulixing de xiaojie: yi xingshisusongfa de xiangying xiugai wei jinglu (The Nature and Deconstruction of the Crime Relating

this provision were primarily motivated by professional retaliation.[158] Defence lawyers were prosecuted because they challenged the prosecutorial evidence. Accordingly, the peril they face in pretrial defence construction comes directly from the prosecutor.[159] As a result, cautious defence lawyers rarely exercise this right to obtain defence evidence in case it potentially becomes 'a trap used by their rival' against them.[160]

> Defence lawyer: We have to be very cautious about the crime of producing false evidence – article 306, which is very intimidating. No lawyers can afford such setbacks. Just imagine that if a lawyer has been thrown into the detention centre for three months, can he undertake more work for a suspect when he comes out? Even if the lawyer has been acquitted and compensated, no one would take such a big risk. Once the prosecutor has seen some evidence advantageous to the suspect, we are suspected of doing something illegal. Prosecutors often play a big role in persecuting us. Based on these suspicions, if the suspect or the witness gives in due to the use of coercive measures and gives an adverse statement against us, we will be trapped … If the suspect and the witness both cannot resist the stress and tell them it is the lawyer who taught them what to say, very soon it would become a disaster for us.[161]

Facing an outcry to abolish Article 306,[162] which is believed to be formulated purely to criminalise defence lawyers,[163] CPL 2012 responded by attenuating the direct antagonism between the prosecutor and the defence lawyer.[164] This measure has blunted the tooth of 'the big stick 306' since its implementation in 2013.[165] However, its far-reaching ramifications have led to the self-censorship of many defence lawyers. Evidence acquisition remains the 'high voltage zone' that they keep away from.[166]

For many defence lawyers, case construction is restricted to the evidence accessed from the official case dossier. The 2014 Shangquan survey indicates that the majority of defence lawyers (65.1 per cent) have shied away from collecting evidence. For those defence lawyers who had undertaken evidence-gathering activities, 30.4 per cent of them were interfered with by state officials.[167]

to the Forge of Evidence by Defence Lawyers: Based upon the Reform of the Criminal Procedure Law)' (2013) 4 *Studies of Law* 112, 114.

[158] Fu Hualing (n 159).

[159] ibid 41.

[160] Sida Liu and Halliday (n 148) 58.

[161] Interview BDL-1.

[162] See Hou Shumei and Keith (n 160) 392.

[163] ibid.

[164] For more details, see ch 3. To diminish the negative effect of Art 306 of the Criminal Law, particularly after the high-profile case of *Li Zhuang* in 2009, Art 42 of CPL 2012 stipulates that 'the defence lawyer suspected of a crime shall be handled by a criminal investigation authority other than the one handling the case in which the defence lawyer provides representation'.

[165] Sida Liu and Halliday (n 148) 60.

[166] ibid. Sida Liu and T Halliday, 'Dancing Handcuffed in the Minefield: Survival Strategies of Defence Lawyers in China's Criminal Justice System' (2008) SSRN working paper, http://ssrn.com/abstract=1269536.

[167] Beijing Shangquan Law Firm (n 150).

The fear generated by the professional risk has resonated in some of the interviews conducted in this research.

> Defence lawyer: Gathering evidence by ourselves would be very dangerous and indeed it is a great risk in our country. If we look for the victim or his family and try to seek their pardon, this will be detrimental to us. There are a lot of cases in this country where the defence lawyers have been arrested when they tried to gather evidence. So, it will be a very dangerous activity in this profession.[168]

> Defence lawyer: We are advised not to ask someone to give his testimony in the court. If we have rebutted the evidence that was gathered by the prosecutors and the police in the dossier, they would accuse us with perjury. When we ask someone to go to the court to testify, we have to communicate with the witness. For example, if we ask the witness to go to the court, we may have to pay for his subsistence etc. We don't know the witness personally even though he may be known by the defendant's family. The prosecutors and the court may treat our communication with the witness as bribery or corruption. If the police or the procuratorate do not believe in our evidence, they may find the same witness and force him to give a very hostile statement relating to any change in the statement being due to an act of bribery. The procuratorate and the police are very powerful and they can employ all sorts of coercive measures to mislead the witness. Once the witness has been forced to give a statement against us, we would be in serious trouble. Therefore, if I have to gather further evidence, I would only gather the real evidence which is impossible to concoct.[169]

> Defence lawyer: It is too dangerous to try to gather your own evidence. There are a lot of reasons … So my defence will mostly be focused on the evidence we have accessed from the dossier.[170]

Despite the risk in active defence preparations, there are some defence lawyers who have been strategically gathering evidence whilst protecting themselves from falling prey to the professional retaliation. Since testimonial evidence is more likely to be targeted by the state officials, defence lawyers find it safer to collect 'objective evidence', such as official documents in the possession of state agencies. As far as oral evidence is concerned, they would either apply to the courts or the procuratorate to collect the statements on their behalf[171] or take reasonable steps to ensure that the evidence in question does not raise any suspicion. The following extract from an interview with a defence lawyer illustrates how a defence lawyer has protected himself from potential risks:

> Defence lawyer: I do not gather new evidence by myself during the criminal proceedings. If I have to gather new evidence, I would gather the documentary evidence or real evidence. I would not touch the oral evidence, as it is too risky. There are lots of cases in

[168] Interview CDL-3.
[169] Interview CDL-2.
[170] Interview CDL-1.
[171] But such a request may very well be rejected on spurious grounds. See Zuo Weiming et al, *Zhongguo Xingshi Susong Yunxing Jizhi Shizheng Yanjiu er: Yi, Shenqian Chenxu wei Zhongxin (The Empirical Study on the Operational Mechanism of the Chinese Criminal Justice II: The Focus of Pre-trial Stage)* (China Law Press, 2009) 223–33.

> which the defence lawyers were arrested by their opponents in the court! As soon as a lawyer had finished his defence work in the court, he was arrested by his opponent prosecutors. The risk to our career is beyond our control. If I dared to gather oral evidence, firstly as a safeguard, I would apply for the full CCTV coverage to show the procedure of my evidence gathering. If I know of a key witness who might have known some facts favourable for my client, I would give this information to the police and request them to gather the evidence. Otherwise, we could bring the witness to the police station and ask the police to do the interview. That is a safeguard to gather further evidence. I think if we do it in this way, it may help to some extent. But the result may not be ideal. The limitation in the law gives too little room for defence lawyers to practice. How can we lawyers be enthusiastic about our work?[172]

In taking such guarded steps, some defence lawyers have managed to collect pieces of evidence without exposing themselves to great dangers. Gathering defence evidence and challenging the prosecution case are highly precarious practices in China. Even if they are successfully done, they do not automatically transfer to an outcome that is beneficial to the defendant.[173] Despite all the challenges, a few skilful defence lawyers have proved that it is still possible to engage in robust defence through evidence acquisition. In one of the interviews, a defence lawyer passed on his experience of how to fulfil such tasks in an assault case.

> Defence lawyer: For example, with the acquittal case that I mentioned just now, the crime happened during the course of an evening. An eyewitness in this case said he saw the fight from a distance of 30 metres. There was a big fishing lake between the witness and the crime scene. The witness could not have stood in the middle of the lake because the lake was quite deep. As there was no light at the crime scene, it would have been impossible for the witness to see my client's face. Therefore, it was illogical to accept that the witness could recognise the defendant and identify him later. So, I drew an on-site record of the crime scene and its surrounding environment. I also went there at about the same time of night and made a video of that area. The on-site record of the crime scene made by the police was not as precise as the one I submitted … In this case, I used the google map and the satellite map to corroborate my drawing. I also took into consideration the weather as well. I submitted the weather information on that given night which was without any moonlight. Eventually, the judge acquitted my client based upon my evidence.[174]

Chinese defence lawyers are facing greater jeopardy in their defence activities compared to their peers in Western jurisdictions. A successful defence requires much more courage, experience, commitment and sometimes even luck. In such a hazardous professional environment, defence lawyers are either forced to withdraw from the territory of evidence gathering or develop coping strategies to protect their own safety and the interests of their clients.[175]

[172] Interview BDL-1.
[173] McConville et al (n 27) ch 12.
[174] Interview CDL-2.
[175] Interviews CDL-2 and BDL-1.

C. Prosecutor–Defence Lawyer Relationship

It is no surprise that many prosecutors viewed themselves as the rival of defence lawyers. Their antagonistic attitude towards defence lawyers seemed to be fostered by the unfavourable light cast on defence lawyers in the statist discourse. Despite being part of the legal profession, the defence has traditionally been portrayed as an individual who intermeddles in the legal process on behalf of others, stirring up litigation and interfering in politics.[176] Even today, defence lawyers are still occasionally depicted as unethical and corrupt pettifoggers who do nothing but exploit legal loopholes and set free criminals.[177] For most defence lawyers who have no political connections or official standing,[178] they are marginalised by the criminal justice system. With no power to match other professional opponents, they are sometimes derided by prosecutors. One prosecutor referred to defence lawyers as follows:

> Prosecutor: Frankly speaking, the defence lawyers that I came across are really of low ethics! They are really of low morality. I do not have any prejudice against lawyers. But I don't see any good defence lawyers. I think most lawyers are at the mercy of the bureaucratic institutions. They are of low self-esteem. If they come to the Procuratorate to photocopy the dossiers, we can bully them as much as we want.[179]

Controlling the source of evidence and the power of prosecution, prosecutors have been used to defence lawyers being humble. In site A, prosecutors would remind defence lawyers of their subservient role whenever necessary. On one occasion, a defence lawyer intended to take photographs of the case dossier using his telephone. This was disallowed by a senior prosecutor, who admonished him that the only way he was permitted to retain a copy of the dossier was to photocopy the documents.[180] The prosecutor's reprimand was finished by the following remarks:

> Remember that the case dossier is an important legal instrument. Although we have the mercy to lend it to you momentarily, it does not mean that you can do whatever you

[176] In ancient China, lawyers were portrayed politely as 'litigation tricksters' or 'pettifoggers', and less politely as tigers, wolves or demons. See G MacCormack, *The Spirit of Traditional Chinese Law* (University of Georgia Press, 1996) 25.

[177] During my observation in site A, one common 'pastime' of the prosecutors was to denounce the defence lawyers. Field note APU-12. Such common labels used by the prosecutor can also be seen in Hou Shumei and Keith (n 160) 389. See also Fu Hualing (n 159).

[178] As mentioned in ch 1, the procuratorate, the police and the courts were deemed 'the institutions of the people's democratic dictatorship'. Unlike state officials, most individual defence lawyers do not have a political background. However, a considerable proportion of defence lawyers are engaged in politics, such as congressional deputies. See Fu Hualing (n 159). There are a number of successful defence lawyers who have connections with the criminal justice institutions. Many of them formerly worked in one of the state agencies in the criminal process. For defence lawyers' political engagement, see Sida Liu and TC Halliday, 'Political Liberalism and Political Embeddedness: Understanding Politics in the Work of Chinese Criminal Defence Lawyers' (2011) 45 *Law and Society Review* 831, 832–54; Sida Liu and Halliday (n 148) 73–79.

[179] Interview APS-6.

[180] This admonishment was in fact against regulation. See Art 47 of 'The explanation of the application of the Criminal Procedure Law 2012 provided by the Supreme People's court'.

> want. You are a defence lawyer and you are on our turf. So, you obey our rule and do what you are told.[181]

This incident aside, interactions between prosecutors and defence lawyers in site A appeared to be polite. Prosecutors were observed to be ostensibly cooperative in assisting defence lawyers to photocopy the dossiers they requested. They answered defence lawyers' questions with clarity; their attitudes were civil and pleasant in general. In spite of the seemingly amicable relationship, prosecutors poured scorn on their courtroom rivals relentlessly behind their back. One of the prosecutors' pastime pleasures in the office was to ridicule the 'useless' defence lawyers they encountered: how they were humiliated by prosecutors or judges in the courtroom.[182] In so doing, they appeared to empower themselves in order to gain self-esteem. On one occasion, a defence lawyer brought no change with him to pay a small amount for a photocopying fee (about 5 yuan) in the procuratorate and asked the prosecutors in the office for help. With no one else responding, I volunteered to lend him the money, so that he could finish his job in time. After the defence lawyer left, I was reproved by the prosecutors for 'helping a defence lawyer'. Albeit being an independent researcher, I had worked with the prosecutors for an extended period of time and was treated 'as one of them', implying that I was expected to join them in despising defence lawyers. The senior prosecutor's comment illustrated their profound prejudice against defence lawyers: 'I cannot believe that you helped a defence lawyer. I was also shocked that he (the defence lawyer) even dared to ask for help from us. He was so ignorant of his own status (*buzhi tiangao dihou*).'[183]

The fact defence lawyers had to approach prosecutors 'on their turf' to access case dossiers certainly made them vulnerable. On one occasion, a young defence lawyer was waiting for a senior prosecutor in order to request a photocopy of a case dossier. Initially, the defence lawyer waited nervously outside the office. He was then invited to sit inside the office to wait, which apparently made him more intense. Every time someone came into the office, he immediately stood up and showed his respect. This awkward situation lasted for two hours until the prosecutor returned the office. Commenting on his behaviour, one prosecutor later likened him to 'a sheep tumbled into the wolves' territory'.[184]

Defence lawyers' debased status seemed to have derived from the fact that they were acting on behalf of the criminal suspects. In contrast, lawyers who represented the victim were treated with greater respect by the prosecutor.[185] In one instance, a lawyer representing the victim of a fraud case came to the procuratorate to check on the progress of the case. Hearing that the case was yet to be

[181] Field note APU-14.
[182] Field notes APU-43, 44 and 45.
[183] Field note APU-18.
[184] Field note APU-12.
[185] Field note APU-20. This was obviously due to the experience that many victims were furiously protesting in the procuratorate.

prosecuted, the lawyer openly criticised the prosecutors for 'being inefficient', which kept her client waiting. The prosecutor in charge of the case kept making apologies, begging her to understand the heavy caseload he had to cope with.[186] Such a response would simply have been unthinkable had it been a defence lawyer.

The prosecutor–defence lawyer relationship not only comprised contempt, but was also mingled with discontent and jealousy, which ultimately contributed to the disdain the prosecutors nurtured against their more 'wealthy' opponents. Although prosecutors 'would like to project themselves as an authority with social respect',[187] the mundane prosecution work was commonly described as 'dull' and 'uninspiring', with depressingly large caseloads rewarded by a modest salary, which offered them neither self-respect nor a sense of honour. Working for long hours and combating deadlines and ever-growing workloads, many prosecutors suffered from burnout, becoming disillusioned, cynical or wretched over time.[188] Prosecutors often dismissed themselves as 'working machines' and 'paperwork slaves'.[189] Resentment against the drudgery of their work was a constant theme in office conversations, and they were 'fond of criticising defence lawyers for how much they take for doing so little; then complain how much they, as prosecutors, have to do to make so little'.[190] In spite of their profound disdain for defence lawyers, ironically some prosecutors expressed their admiration of their former colleagues who decided to become defence lawyers eventually.

> Prosecutor: I am really tired of my work. We are just a machine and we only got about 3,000 yuan per month. The defence lawyers can earn 10,000 yuan for each case. That is such easy money. B (a former prosecutor) used to work in our office and he left last year. He was an able man, so he is a lawyer now. He is so courageous! I just stick to this 'safe' work and do not dare to take a risk.[191]

In one instance, a prosecutor had a hushed conversation with me before a court trial commenced:

> Prosecutor: You can understand why we don't have a passion for our work now. For a whole month, we have to process about 15 cases, but we are paid so little. Defence lawyers charge 10,000 yuan for one case, and we are paid 3,000 yuan for an average of 15 cases each month. How can we guarantee quality? If we are paid as much as the defence lawyers, I will work so hard on each case.[192]

[186] ibid.
[187] McConville et al (n 27) 389.
[188] See CJ Ogletree, 'Beyond Justifications: Seeking Motivations to Sustain Public Defenders' (1993) 6 *Harvard Law Review* 1239; BS Otey, 'Buffering Burnout: Preparing the Online Generation for the Occupational Hazards of the Legal Profession' (2014) *South California Interdisciplinary Law Journal* 147; L Norton et al, 'Burnout and Compassion Fatigue: What Lawyers Need to Know' (2015) 84 *University of Missouri at Kansas City Law Review*. 987.
[189] Field notes APU-2, 11 and 44; Interview BPS-1.
[190] See Fu Hualing (n 159); Field notes APU-34, 36 and 40.
[191] Field note APU-15.
[192] Field note APU-47.

Such comments seemed to seek justification of the slippage in the quality of prosecution cases and their mindless work style. Working in a bureaucratic setting with limited autonomy, prosecutors were pressured by performance indicators and other managerial arrangements. This made them jealous of the defence lawyer's free work style as well as their high salary, even though they were aware of the hazards that the defence lawyer's job entailed. In the meantime, they were loath to lose the power they have, which was the asset that sustained their self-esteem, making their opponent defence lawyers subservient. In this understanding, they tended to use it to the fullest extent.

IV. Conclusion

The Chinese prosecution system seems to fit squarely into Parker's crime control model in that the majority of cases can easily pass the prosecution criteria and the entry of guilty pleas has been strenuously sought to secure a high rate of conviction.[193] Decisions to prosecute criminal cases can be made unimpededly by any prosecutor regardless of her work experience, whereas prosecutors' discretion to discontinue a case is cautiously exercised and carefully scrutinised by layers of bureaucratic schemes. The prosecution system has no screening mechanism to rigorously filter out incipiently weak cases. As a result, cases in which the evidence falls short of the required standard of proof abound. With the criminal justice system zealously promoting 'swift justice', these weak cases have been disposed of in an industrial scale through the ever faster guilty plea procedures.

Most of these weak cases are now channelled through the formalised plea negotiation that has been integrated into the revised CPL 2018. The law holds out the incentive of a reduced sentence to those who plead guilty, and a variety of sentence discount schemes have been designed to encourage the accused to admit her guilt as early as possible. The new plea system certainly contributes to a lower cost of the operation of the system, saving resources needed to deal with a growing number of criminal cases. Meanwhile, it ensures a conviction and avoids uncertainties in an otherwise contested trial. However, the sentence discount, the lack of sufficient defence lawyer's advice and the prosecutor's authoritative form of communication to suspects exert a considerable pressure towards pleading guilty. A report published by the Royal Commission on Criminal Justice in England and Wales noted that 'it would be naïve to suppose that innocent people never plead guilty because of the prospect of a sentence discount'.[194] This statement can equally be applied to the Chinese context: it is foolish to assume that innocent people in China would act differently in a similar sentence discount regime. As has been shown in some of my empirical accounts, the process in which guilty pleas

[193] HL Packer, *The Limits of the Criminal Sanction* (Stanford University Press, 1968) 162–63.
[194] RCCJ, *The Royal Commission on Criminal Justice* (HMSO, 1993) 110.

were entered was not always based on voluntary and informed considerations. The authoritativeness of the prosecutorial indication and the coercive nature of the communications exert enormous oppression on the guilty and innocent alike. It is doubly ironic that after years of reflection on the mass production of miscarriages of justice known to be caused by false confessions, the criminal justice system now feverishly persuades the accused to enter guilty pleas in the name of efficiency.

As a murky area of the law, prosecutorial discretion does not neatly follow the binary sense of being within or outside of what is permitted by the law. Hidden rules are given priority over formal laws. The prosecution criteria are not always applied equally to all suspects. With a dramatically widening social stratification,[195] those socially and financially deprived groups become the bulk of the population regulated by the criminal law. At the other end of the spectrum, the elites who are in possession of the social and financial capital have resources to negotiate their journey (including corruption) within the justice system. Just as McConville summarised in 2013, the task of the state is 'simply to control the majority of its population which is economically disadvantaged, socially and politically disempowered and without legitimate avenues to rectify injustices'.[196]

The prosecution review stage is a reflection of the accusatory role of the prosecutor, the debased status of the accused and the marginalised defence within the sociopolitical context of China. It is clear that the superior legal status derived from their supervisory function fails to translate into the self-esteem of prosecutors or to commit to their duties. Many prosecutors have experienced burnout due to high caseloads and constant time pressures. With a lack of motivation, their dissatisfaction is sometimes vented on suspects through aggressive demands for guilty pleas in prosecutorial interrogations. The ability to subjugate suspects has become an essential skill for prosecutors. 'Competent prosecutors' are expected to overawe suspects with their 'aura of authority' by the way they behave and talk.[197] In this regard, prosecutors' coercive-compliant interrogative style is no different from that of the police, casting doubt on their capacity to fulfil the supervisory role. In the authoritarian setting of China, where a systemised standard of due process is lacking,[198] defence lawyers are substantially constrained in constructing the defence case during this pretrial phase as a result of various obstacles created by the system. Their access to the prosecution dossier has been restricted by their professional opponents, and their evidence-gathering process is often fraught with hazards.

[195] In recent years, China's Gini coefficients have been 0.491 (2008), 0.490 (2009), 0.481 (2010), 0.477 (2011) and 0.474 (2012), respectively (see n 50). The international warning level of the divide between the rich and the poor is 0.40. In China, the wealthiest 10% of Chinese families earned 55 times more than the least fortunate 10%. The average wage in the best-paid industry was almost 16 times that of the poorest paid. ibid 65.

[196] ibid.

[197] Field note APU-14.

[198] EC Ip, 'The Supreme People's Court and the Political Economy of Judicial Empowerment in Contemporary China' (2011) 24 *Columbia Journal of Asian Law* 367, 370.

6

Trials without Witnesses

Trials are regarded as the last bastion against injustice.[1] Given the way investigative dossiers are constructed and the lack of an efficacious screening mechanism to weed out weak cases, the Chinese criminal justice system's effectiveness in protecting innocent individuals from being wrongfully accused hinges on the courts. For the defendant who has now been formally charged, waiting to be tried, the questions that concern her most are how her case is going to be presented and whether it will be handled impartially. This chapter focuses on these two aspects.[2] As with previous chapters, case dossiers are placed at the centre of the analysis of judicial activities, which determines whether or not the defendant is actually guilty. The mechanism for making this crucial decision deserves close consideration, and judges' relationships with prosecutors are forged surrounding this nexus.

I. Hollowed Criminal Trials and Criminal Case Dossiers

Once the prosecutor hands over the Bill of Prosecution and investigative case dossiers, the 'ownership' of the criminal case is transferred to the court. The case dossiers (including both the evidence dossier and the procedure dossier) are now placed in the custody of the judge responsible for the case, who is going to preside over a forthcoming court hearing and deliver the judgment about whether or not the defendant is guilty.

The way criminal cases are presented may have a major impact on the final outcome of the case. In adversarial systems, jurors and judges are exposed to oral testimonies at trial from both the prosecution and the defence, which allow them to make a rational decision.[3] In contrast, judges in China are used to working

[1] TW Frampton, 'The Uneven Bulwark: How (and Why) Criminal Jury Trial Rates Vary by State' (2012) 100 *California Law Review* 184.

[2] Given the scope of this study, this chapter will focus on first instance trials in basic courts. This is consistent with the subject of this research, which is miscarriages of justice that occur in the routine criminal process. The criminal appeal system and death penalty review system, albeit important in shedding light on this purpose, are not dealt with directly, given the constraint of empirical data and the length of the book.

[3] WL Bennett and MS Feldman, *Reconstructing Reality in the Courtroom* (Quid Pro Books, 2014) 58.

on written case dossiers. The prejudicial effect of evidence presentation had been well acknowledged by Chinese legal professionals. In the wave of reform in 1996, an adversarial-style trial model was advocated to substantialise the hollow court hearing (*tingshen shizhihua gaige*).

A. The Reform of Substantialising the Court Hearing

The so-called reform of substantialising criminal trials (*xingshi tingshen shizhihua gaige*) may sound strange to those who are not familiar with the short history of Chinese criminal procedure law. By saying that the criminal hearing is 'hollow and without any substance', it suggests that the trial does not play a meaningful role in deciding a case. Yet this explanation might still be baffling. If the court hearing is not conducive to judicial decision-making, deciding whether or not the defendant is guilty, why does a court need a trial? If the trial has to take place, what is it for?

In answering these questions, it is necessary to trace back to the first Criminal Procedure Law of the PRC, passed in 1979 (CPL 1979), a predominant feature of which is the educational role of law[4] – a common trait shared by all socialist jurisdictions at the time.[5] In this legal regime, the aims of the trial were not to reach a verdict of guilt or innocence of the defendant, but to reform a flawed person to be selfless, loyal and respectful of the social norms in communal life,[6] and to teach the public at large to be good socialist members.[7] Before the trial, the judge would receive the case dossier with all the evidence relating to the defendant, to decide whether the case should be prosecuted. Once that was done, the case would proceed in one of the following ways: it could be accepted for trial, sent back with an order for supplementary investigation, dismissed or returned with a request that the case be withdrawn.[8] Only when the judges had confirmed the guilt of the accused would the trial proceedings commence. In this model, a trial was symbolic in nature, seeking the propaganda objective of educating the public, 'condemning vice and praising justice'.[9]

In such a 'verdict first, trial second' (*xian ding hou shen*) practice, judges learnt the case facts entirely from the case dossier and established the belief of guilt or innocence beforehand. The trial was nothing but a performance, with no

[4] Interestingly, since the actual trial – the trial by dossier – was not conducted in public, there was no concern that innocent people would suffer public scrutiny. To some extent, the trial was a 'shaming' event.

[5] H Berman, S Cohen and M Russell, 'A Comparison of the Chinese and Soviet Codes of Criminal Law and Procedure' (1982) 73 *The Journal of Criminal Law and Criminology* 238.

[6] DC Clark and J Feinerman, *Antagonistic Contradictions: Criminal Law and Human Rights in China; China's Legal Reforms* (Clarendon Press, 1996) 65.

[7] ibid.

[8] See M McConville et al, *Criminal Justice in China: An Empirical Enquiry* (Edward Elgar, 2011) 134.

[9] Shanghai Municipal Lawyers Association Research Department, 'Shanghai Concentrates on Doing a Good Job of Criminal Defence Work in Turmoil-Related Cases' (1990) 427 *Shanghai Lawyer* 15, 17.

meaningful contribution to the outcome of the case. The dossier-based trial style bore an inquisitorial character; like their counterparts in inquisitorial systems, the credibility of the documents in the dossier were rarely queried by judges.[10] With the influx of Western literature on comparative studies in 1990s' China, this practice was challenged by scholars and forward-looking legal elites alike. Wang Shangxin, a member of the National Congress Legislative Committee, once expressed the negativities of such trials:

> Before the trial, judges have already formed a firm belief of the case and arrived at the conclusion in relation to the verdict and sentencing. The trial is purely a show. The defendant and defence lawyers' opposite views are hardly respected.[11]

Based on suggestions offered by scholars, criminal trials should be reformed to substantialise the proceedings by ending the 'verdict first, trial second' practice.[12] With regard to how the reform should proceed, two proposals were proffered. One suggested that judges should not be allowed to access the dossier at all, in case they develop undue prejudice against the defence.[13] This was seen as a drastic way of severing judges' knowledge of the pretrial information.[14] It aimed to force judges to ascertain the facts through a court hearing, eradicating any residual influence of case dossiers.[15] Compared to this proposal, the other solution was relatively moderate. It strove to reform the trial by modifying the dossier transfer system. In this approach, judges can view limited items of pretrial evidence before trial, checking whether or not the prosecution have put up a prima facie case.[16] But differing from the practice under CPL 1979, evidential scrutiny prior to the trial would not go beyond the procedural aspects, that is, judges only need to be satisfied that there is sufficient evidence in support of the prosecution case.

Compared to the former proposal, which intended to completely restructure the criminal process, the latter solution, which was built upon the status quo of the practice at the time, was supported by most scholars. That proposal was later adopted by CPL 1996. Thus, pursuant to Article 150 of CPL 1996, the prosecution should submit the main evidence (*zhuyao zhengju*) of a criminal case in the form of a photocopy to buttress the indictment when initiating the prosecution.[17]

[10] See JS Hodgson, *French Criminal Justice: A Comparative Account of the Investigation and Prosecution of Crime in France* (Hart Publishing, 2005) 191.

[11] Wang Shanxin, 'Xingshi susongfa xiugai de ruogan wenti (Certain Issues in Relation to Criminal Procedure Law Reform)' (1994) 5 *Legal Studies* 76.

[12] Chen Ruihua, *Xingshisusong de zhongguo moshi (The Chinese Model of Criminal Proceedings)* (China Law Press, 2009) 164.

[13] The only document that would be allowed to be seen from the prosecution is the Bill of Prosecution. This is the so-called 'Single Piece of the Indictment (*qisushu yiben zhiyi*)'. ibid.

[14] ibid 164.

[15] Li Xinjian, *Xingshisusong gouzaolun (The Structure of the Criminal Procedure)* (The China University of Political Science and Law Press, 1992) 238. For comment on this proposal, see also Chen Ruihua (n 12) 164.

[16] Chen Ruihua (n 12) 164–65.

[17] Art 150 of CPL 1996.

This provision was designed to enable the court to strike out a prosecution if the prosecution case was short of prima facie evidence.[18] Despite all the effort to avoid the court viewing the full prosecution case prior to the trial, the case dossier would still be transferred to the court, but *after* the court hearing.[19] The reform, in this sense, was merely delaying the courts' access to the case dossiers. With no mechanism in place to ensure that only the evidence presented and the facts ascertained at trial would form the basis of judgments, judges could read the case dossier to make a final decision.[20] In this regard, there seemed to be no fundamental difference in judicial practice under the two legal regimes, aside from the postponed time frame of dossier viewing. The link between the pretrial investigation and the trial remained, which left the door open for resurrecting the old practice.

B. Prior Belief and Judicial Bias

One of the main concerns under the 1996 criminal justice reform was the judicial bias developed by reading case dossiers. This concern is supported by a number of studies which found that judges need less diagnostic evidence to convict the defendant so long as the dossier was read in advance. For example, Bernd Schünemann showed that judges who read case files containing the prosecution views and inculpating evidence prior to trial had a significantly higher tendency to convict the defendant.[21] This phenomenon is explained by psychologists as confirmatory bias; that is, when people have formulated a 'preconception or hypothesis about a given issue, they tend to favour information that corresponds with their prior beliefs and disregard evidence pointing to the contrary'.[22] The confirmatory bias prompts people to search, code and interpret information in congruence with their early

[18] See Wen Dongfu, 'Woguo gongsu anjian zhengju yisong zhidu zhi fansi yu chonggou (Reconsideration and Reconstruction of the Evidence Transference by Public Prosecution)' (2003) 4 *China Criminal Law Magazine* 81; Sun Yuan, 'Juanzong yisongzhidu gaige zhi fansi (Reconsideration of the Transference of Case Files)' (2009) 27 *Political Science and Law Forum* 167; Zhang Jinde, 'Xingshi shengpan shang de yuduan paichu yuanze yanjiu (Research on the Prevention of Prior Belief in Criminal Trials)' (2005) 10 *Procedure Law Review* 81.

[19] See Art 42 of 'On Several Issues of the Implementation of Criminal Procedure Law' (Issued by the Supreme People's Court, the Supreme People's Procuratorate, the Ministry of Public, the National Security Bureau, the Ministry of Justice and the Legal Committee of the National Congress on 19th January 1998).

[20] It is worth noting that for the vast majority of cases, the judges made a decision after the trial. There was a small proportion of cases in which the judges were required to make a decision at the end of the trial. However, those judgments announced at the end of the trial were predetermined prior to the trial. Given that all the judgments had to be approved by the court leaders before the judicial accountability reform in 2015, it was impossible for a judge to make an independent decision at the end of the court hearing.

[21] B Schünemann, 'Experimentelle untersuchungen zur Reform der Hauptverhandlung in Strafsachen' in J Kerner et al (eds), *Deutsche Forschungen zur Kriminalitätsentstehung und Kriminalitätskontrolle* (Heymanns, 1983) 1109–52.

[22] E Peer and E Gamliel, 'Heuristics and Biases in Judicial Decisions' (2013) 49 *Court Review* 114, 115.

assumption, consciously blindfolding themselves to new leads of inquiry and alternative evidence. Due to such bias, it would be much more difficult for the disadvantaged party to disconfirm the hastily reached conclusion of the judge.[23] The confirmatory bias may be further compounded by the former conviction rate of the court.[24] Hence, if the court had historically high conviction rates, the judge's reading of a prosecution case dossier might confirm the hypothesis that the defendant is more likely than not to be guilty. In criticising the dossier-reading practice in inquisitorial systems, L Fuller eloquently advanced that:

> What generally occurs in practice [as evidence is heard] is that at some early point a familiar pattern will seem to emerge from the evidence; an accustomed label is waiting for the case and without awaiting further proofs, this label is promptly assigned to it. It is a mistake to suppose that this premature cataloguing must necessarily result from impatience, prejudice or mental sloth. Often it proceeds from a very understandable desire to bring the hearing into some order and coherence, for without some tentative theory of the case there is no standard of relevance by which testimony may be measured. But what starts as a preliminary diagnosis designed to direct the inquiry tends, quickly and imperceptibly, to become a fixed conclusion, as all that confirms the diagnosis makes a strong imprint on the mind, while all that runs counter to it is received with diverted attention.[25]

This danger developed by reading the prosecution case dossier prior to the trial appeared to have been noted by Chinese judicial reformers. Article 150 of CPL 1996 was designed to safeguard a neutral trier with minimal knowledge of pretrial evidence. The implementation of the law, however, backfired. One of the problems was the unspecified scope of main evidence (*zhuyao zhengju*). What constituted the main evidence of a case was entirely left to the procuratorate to interpret. With unfettered discretion over the selection of evidence, prosecutors tended to transfer exclusively photocopies of inculpatory evidence to the court, with evidence in favour of the defence usually being held back.[26] A second issue concomitant with the evidence selection was the constrained access to case dossiers by the defence. CPL 1996 states that once a case is referred to court for prosecution, the defence lawyer should view the case from the court.[27] The law completely ignored the fact that

[23] WA Wagenaar et al, *Anchored Narratives: The Psychology of Criminal Evidence* (St Martin's Press, 1993) 27; M Rabin and J Schrag, 'First Impression Matter: A Model of Confirmatory Bias' (1997) UC Berkeley Working Paper No 97-250. For a relevant discussion, see J Kerstholt and J Jackson, 'Judicial Decision Making: Order of Evidence Presentation and Availability of Background Information' (1998) 12 *Applied Cognitive Psychology* 445.

[24] Apparently, this discussion is mainly applied to inquisitorial systems, where judges have the power to decide the guilt or innocence of the defendant as well as her sentences.

[25] LL Fuller, 'The Adversary System' In Harold Berman (ed), *Talks of American Law* (Harvard University Press, 1971) 43–44.

[26] Chen Weidong and Hao Yinzhong, 'Woguo gongsu fangshi de jiegouxing quexian jiqi jiuzheng (The Structural Flaws of the Public Prosecution in China and its Correction)' (2000) 4 *Legal Studies* 101.

[27] CPL 1996, Art 36.

the full case dossier was still in the prosecutor's possession at the time. As a result, defence lawyers could only see photocopies of the selected inculpatory evidence that was transferred to the court. This caused a serious problem for defence lawyers, especially those engaged at a later stage.[28] Unable to gain access to the full case dossier, their rights were significantly curtailed. In many cases, this amounted to an outright deprivation of defence preparation.[29]

Criticism was, therefore, levelled at the poor legislative drafting, which failed to deliver upon the well-intended expectations. As the disapproval of the controversial law of photocopied evidence continued, certain academics began to cast doubt on the impact of prior beliefs on trials, suggesting that it was an unfounded accusation. Mo Danyi, for instance, argued that the negativities of prior belief were exaggerated. In his view, judges who were trained to deal with complicated information were capable of being 'immune' from the 'pollution of biased bilateral evidence'.[30] Likewise, Li Changlin suggested that the quality of first instance trials would be improved were judges to have the opportunity to read the case dossier in advance to identify the key issues of criminal cases.[31] Meanwhile, the extra cost incurred by photocopying large volumes of written documents was also an issue for debate.[32] After years of academic condemnation of the negative impact of the law, the criminal justice reform turned full circle. The revised CPL 2012 eventually restored the discarded practice, requiring that prosecutors send the entire case dossier to the court prior to the trial. This law remains intact in CPL 2018.

To a large extent, CPL 2012's resurrection of the pretrial case dossier transfer was a compromise of judicial practices. Legal reformers' hope of making substantive changes to the trial was defeated by the reality that the vast majority of cases in China were de facto 'tried by dossiers'.[33] Before the revised CPL 2012 took effect, judges usually did not start working seriously on the case until the trial was over and the case dossiers were transferred.[34] When it came to major and

[28] This is particularly the case for the defence lawyers appointed by the court. According to CPL 1996, for legal aid cases, the public defence lawyer will not be appointed until the case has been transferred to the court.

[29] Cai Jie and Liu Jing, 'Xingshi juanzong yisong zhidu de lunhuixing gaige zhi fansi (Reconsideration of the Convertible Reform in Relation to Criminal Case Dossier)' (2014) 1 *Law Review* 156; Hu Lianfang, 'Juanzong yisong zhuyi: dui lixiang de tuoxie haishi dui xianshi de zunzhong: 2012 nian xingshi susongfa queli juanzhong yisong de zhengdangxing (Transferring Files: Compromising the Ideal or Respecting the Reality: The Legitimacy of Establishing Case File Transference System in CPL 2012)' (2013) 43 *Journal of Northwest University* 84; Wang Yu, 'Woguo xingshi juanzong yisong fangshi de kunjin jiqi gaige chulu (The Plight of the Way Case File Transference and its Reform)' (2006) *Contemporary Law Science* 56; Sun Yuan, 'Quanan yisong beijing xia kongfang juzong bilu zai shenpan jieduan de shiyong (The Use of Prosecution Case Dossier at Trial within the Context of Full Transference of Dossiers)' (2016) 6 *Legal Studies* 155.

[30] Mo Danyi, 'Zhiquan zhuyi susong zhong yuduan paichu zhiyi (Reconsideration of Prior Belief in the Inquisitorial System)' (2012) 4 *Politics and Law* 150.

[31] Li Changlin, 'Xingshi yishen caipan zhiliang baozheng tixi lungang (The Systematic Outline of the Quality of the First Instance Criminal Trials)' (2009) 1 *Journal of Political Science and Law* 56.

[32] Chen Weidong and Hao Yinzhong (n 26); Hu Lianfang (n 29); Wang Yu (n 29).

[33] McConville et al (n 8) 242–47, 351–86.

[34] Interview ATJ-1.

serious cases, Article 150 was routinely ignored by both the prosecution and the courts. During my fieldwork in 2012,[35] I noticed that the judges from the basic court frequently telephoned the prosecutors to 'borrow' the case dossiers if a case to be tried was considered to be complex and serious.[36] Their requests were readily satisfied by prosecutors, who took it as a sign of diligence.[37] Such practice was certainly not confined to site A. Chen Ruihua, for example, has observed that prosecutors routinely sent all the case dossiers to the court before trying major and complex cases in Jiangsu province.[38] Flouting the law aside, this provision could also be circumvented under special circumstances. In investigating special cases instructed by the highest echelon of the party-state, specific judges were appointed to join the panel with police and prosecutors. In those situations, the investigative case dossier was shared within the panel, long before the trial took place.[39]

Such non-compliant practices seemed to be widespread in many parts of China. Judges from different regions made no effort to conceal the fact that subverting the law was common. When asked about the reason behind this, they indicated that the purpose of reading the case dossier before trial was to ensure that the trial was conducted in a more effective way.[40] This explanation was often followed by a complaint about the 'ill-consideration of the law'.

> Judge: We would read the dossier before we have the hearing. In the old regime of CPL 1996 the prosecutor only sent the copies of the main evidence to us. The new law of CPL 2012 has ruled that all the evidence should be sent to us. This is necessary, because, for example, we need to know about the defendant's confession. If he has changed his statement, we would list any doubts that we have developed. We need to solve these problems in the trial. The old law was very unreasonable. Now the new law provides that all the dossiers should be sent to the court before the trial. If we don't read the dossiers before the trial, how can we hear the case efficiently? We are not computers. We are just ordinary people. We need to know the basic information before we understand the case.[41]

The judges who concurred with the complaint included those from the intermediate courts who try death penalty cases.

> Researcher: What improvement do you think occurred with the law after the CPL 2012 came into force?
>
> Judge: We can try the case after reading the dossier, which is a huge relief to all of us. The law got it wrong and now it is time to set it straight.[42]
>
> Judge: CPL 1996 was badly drafted in that it did not allow us to read the case dossier [before trials]. In my opinion, this was very unrealistic. We have to try the case on the

[35] CPL 2012 came into effect in 2013.
[36] Field notes APU-17, 22 and 30.
[37] ibid.
[38] Chen Ruihua (n 12) 169.
[39] ibid.
[40] Interviews GTJ-1, FTJ-1, ATJ-1 and GTJ-4.
[41] Interview GTJ-1.
[42] Interview GAJ-1.

> basis of the dossier. The legislature simply had no idea what the practice is like. There is a lot of resentment in the judiciary about this.[43]

When asked whether reading the case dossier may cause an undue bias against the defence, the response was either denial of the possibility[44] or avoidance of the question completely.[45] As far as judges are concerned, case dossiers were indispensable in that they allowed them to go to the trial fully prepared and focus on the issues that needed to be resolved. Two judges made it explicitly clear that they could not make decisions without recourse to case dossiers.

> Judge 1: There is one thing that is absolutely clear: judges in China are responsible for the truth that is embodied by the dossier … Do we dare to make a judgment just by hearing the witnesses' testimony in the court? No. No judge has the courage to do this in China.[46]
>
> Judge 2: The judicial decision must be based on the dossier! All the facts and the evidence come from the dossier. This is the ultimate rule – no matter we read it before or after trial.[47]

Then the question arises: why do judges rely so heavily on case dossiers? This to a great extent relates to the long-term inner working model of the courts, which has significantly shaped the judicial system in China.

C. The Split between the Public Hearing and the Determinative Decision-Making

Up until the judicial accountability reform (*sifa zerenzhi gaige*) was launched in 2015, one of the idiosyncratic features of the courts in China was that the judges who conducted a criminal trial might not have been the ones who decided the case. Criminal cases were ostensibly adjudicated by a collegial bench (*heyiting*) or a single judge. For a long period of time, however, cases were in fact determined by 'faceless judges' – judicial members who were accorded the power to influence judicial decision-making, notably different levels of leaders in the courts and the adjudicative committee.[48] Take a basic court as an example, which exercises jurisdiction over the vast majority of criminal cases in China.[49] The criminal

[43] Interview FTJ-1.
[44] Interviews FTJ-1, GAJ-1, 2 and 4, and GTJ-1.
[45] Interviews ATJ-1 and GAJ-3.
[46] Interview ATJ-1.
[47] Interview GAJ-3.
[48] Almost 95% of the criminal cases were tried by basic courts. Qiang Shigong and Zhao Xiaoli, 'Shuangchong jiegouhua xia de falv jieshi: dui 8 min zhongguo faguan de diaocha (The Legal Explanation of the Dual Structure: An Inquiry on 8 Chinese Judges)' in Liang Zhiping (ed), *Falv Jieshi Wenti (Questions on Legal Explanation)* (China Law Press, 2010) 237.
[49] Basic courts exercise jurisdictions over cases other than national security cases, cases in relation to terrorism or cases that the defendant might be sentenced to life imprisonment or the death penalty. See Arts 19 and 20 of CPL 2012.

chamber (*xingshi shenpanting*) comprised the chief (*tingzhang*), the deputy chief (*fu tingzhang*) and a number of criminal judges. Some basic court judges indicated that judicial opinions formulated by judges used to be routinely reviewed by the leaders – the chief, the deputy chief or the vice president of the court in charge of the criminal chamber (*fenguan yuanzhang*), especially when the case in question was complex or serious, or it might have a certain impact on society.[50] Judgments were not allowed to be officially issued without the signature of the leaders. Practices in different regions varied, but criminal cases were always required to be reported to (*huibao*), and approved by (*pizhun*), the leaders. In site G, for example, where the court processed a large number of cases, the leaders scrutinised cases that were reported to be controversial or serious. For the majority of ordinary cases, they signed off the judgments automatically, leaving the autonomy to trial judges or collegial benches.[51] The situation was different in site F, where the criminal court was located in a rural area, with relatively fewer cases to deal with. The chiefs were much more hands-on. Every single case there used to be reviewed carefully by them.[52]

For ordinary cases, the draft judgments were validated by the leaders fairly quickly, with the sentences of the specific cases being occasionally revised.[53] Major, complicated and controversial cases and cases in which the collegial bench was divided would be submitted to the adjudicative committee for discussion.[54]

[50] The elements to be approved included the verdict, the appropriateness of the sentencing and the wording of the judgments. Interviews ATJ-1 and GAJ-1, 2, 3 and 4.

[51] Interview GTJ-1. Nevertheless, the judgments still require the signature of the leader before it can be issued.

[52] Interview FTJ-1.

[53] Wang Biao, 'Fayuan neibu kongzhi xingshi caipanquan de fangya he fansi (The Methods and Reflection of the Control of the Judicial Power within the Court System)' (2013) 1 *China Criminal Law Magazine* 65, 76.

[54] CPL 2012, Art 180. Again, this needs to be approved by the chief of the chamber, and by the vice president of the court who is in charge of the chamber. Once the submission is approved, the trial judge will draft a case report and send it to the committee for discussion. This also includes cases that may be counter-appealed (*kangsu*) by the procuratorate or cases in which the defendant may potentially be acquitted, exempted from criminal punishment or sentenced to the death penalty, which should be sent to the adjudicative committee for discussion. According to 'The advice of the implementation of the reform and perfection of the adjudicative committee of the People's court issued by the Supreme Court (No 3, 2010)', the following cases must be submitted to the adjudicative committees for discussion: (i) for the Supreme People's Court, criminal judgment that has been validated but there is an error in the decision which requires change; and cases counter-appealed by the procuratorate; (ii) for the High People's Courts and the Intermediate People's Courts, criminal judgment that has been validated but there is an error in the decision which requires change; cases counter-appealed by the procuratorate; cases that are going to be imposed with the death penalty with immediate execution; cases that should be acquitted; cases for which the application of the law requires a legal opinion from the higher court; and serious cases that should be submitted to the higher court for trial; and (iii) for Basic People's Courts, criminal judgment that has been validated but there is an error in the decision which requires change; cases where the sentence imposed should be lower than the legal tariffs or the defendant should be immune from any criminal sentence; cases that should be acquitted; cases where the application of the law requires a legal opinion from the higher court; cases which are likely to incur life imprisonment or the death penalty and should be submitted to the higher court for trial; and serious cases that should be submitted to the higher court for trial. In addition, controversial cases, such as where members of

The adjudicative committee was founded on the idea that 'collective wisdom is better than individual wisdom (*jiti zhihui youyu geren zhihui*)'.[55] The adjudicative committee normally comprised the president and vice president(s) of the court, chiefs and deputy chiefs of various court chambers, leaders of administrative departments and a number of senior experienced judges.[56] In submitting the cases for discussion, trial judges or the collegial bench relinquished their role as adjudicator and 'entrusted' it to the committee.[57]

To some extent, the case dossier is a by-product of the review mechanisms. The written protocols and the way case dossiers (including the courts' internal dossier) were assembled were particularly suitable for future audits in that they incorporated all traces of official activity and materials used for decision-making. The completeness of the information and the fact that the documentation in the file had an authoritative appearance made it an ideal vehicle to be reviewed in the multistage hierarchical process.[58] The presentation of case dossiers, especially their ostensible authenticity of documentation, tends to leave a univocal impression. Such an effect would be produced every time the case dossier was read.[59] In so doing, the interpretation of the evidence and the understanding of the case facts could be repeatedly verified in the hierarchical process, making it possible to evaluate and control decision-making at the very basic level.[60]

The 'faceless judges' and the undisclosed case dossier therefore formed a hidden trial system, which facilitated the key coterie within the court to control the power of adjudication. The leaders of the court and the adjudicative committee who did not conduct the court hearing but relied on internal reports and case dossiers had the power to decide cases.[61] This contravenes some of the well-established

the collegiate bench cannot make a final agreement due to the disputes, cases with wide social influence and cases that involve difficult legal applications, should also be discussed by the adjudicative committees.

[55] Liao Yongan and Li Shifeng, 'Woguo minshi heyi zhidu zhi yunxing xianzhuang: yi yige qianfada diqu jiceng fayuan de minshi shenpan wei kaocha duixiang (The Status Quo of the Civil Collegiate Benches: Based on the Study of a Local District Court in a Less Developed Area in Mid China)' (2007) 3 *Social Science* 85, 93.

[56] A discussion of the adjudicative committee usually followed a set procedure. It started with the trial judge or a member of the collegial bench introducing the basic information of the case, followed by complementary comments from the chief or the deputy chief. Then the members of the committee took it in turns to voice their individual opinions. After that, a debate or discussion ensued between the members, leading to a conclusive decision. Zuo Weimin, 'Shenpanweiyuanhui yunxing zhuangkuang de shizheng yanjiu (Empirical Research on the Operation of the Adjudicative Committee)' (2016) 3 *Legal Studies* 159, 167.

[57] From the accountability point of view, this 'entrustment' is not complete. If the judgment was overturned by the court of appeal and was regarded as 'wrong', it would be the trial judge or the collegial bench that was responsible for the errors that had been made, even though the decision was technically made by the adjudicative committee. Therefore, the adjudicative committee has the power to adjudicate, but bears no corresponding responsibility.

[58] MR Damaška, *The Faces of Justice and State Authority* (Yale University Press, 1986) 50.

[59] Interview ATJ-1.

[60] Wang Biao (n 53) 72.

[61] R Peerenboom, 'Judicial Independence in China: Common Myths and Unfounded Assumptions' in R Peerenboom (ed), *Judicial Independence in China: Lessons for Global Rule of Law Promotion* (Cambridge University Press, 2010) 78.

standards of a fair trial, specifically the principle of orality and immediacy, which requires the judges who are responsible for determining the charge to examine the evidence subject to the oral procedure.[62] This leads to two problems. The first is that the defence right was undermined. The split between the facade of the public trial and the secret 'trial' made it impossible for the defence to challenge the content of the evidence or the manner in which it was obtained.[63] The views put forward by the defence lawyer at trial might not be able to reach the real decision-makers. The second issue is concerned with the system's lack of transparency. The secret trial system apparently contravened the basic principle that 'People's courts shall hear cases in open court' that is enshrined in law.[64] This principle requires that examination and determination of the evidence should take place not only in the presence of the parties, but also in the presence of the judge. In the double-façade trial system, the trial judge appeared to be the authority in adjudicating the case, yet her role was symbolic – 'a deceptive masquerade', with the ultimate power lying somewhere else, beyond the knowledge of the defendant.[65] These internal arrangements resulted in unfettered encroachment on individual judges' autonomy and the blurred responsibility of the fact-finder/decision makers, rendering the whole system open to abuse and unlikely to fulfil the purpose of the discovery of truth.

Given that the 'judges behind the veil' are empowered to determine the outcome of the case, a pertinent question is *who* has the responsibility for assessing the credibility and probative force of the evidence and hence interpreting the facts in question. This is important because it links with the essence of the notion of immediacy, in which the examination of the evidence lies at the very core and by which the basic responsibility of the fact-finder/decision maker is defined.[66] In the Chinese scenario, the answer was indisputable: it was the trial judge or collegial benches (rather than the unseen leaders or the adjudicative committee) who evaluated the evidence at trial and constructed the narratives which formed the factual basis of the judgment. In spite of the absence of witnesses in most trials, the trial judges were able to observe the demeanour of the defendant and evaluate the weight of the evidence adduced. Their briefing contained the ascertainment of the facts which was rarely questioned by the judicial bench or the single judge.[67]

[62] Chen Weidong, 'Sifa zerenzhi gaige yanjiu (The Research of the Judicial Justice Reform)' (2017) 8 *Law Magazine* 32.

[63] SJ Summers, *Fair Trials: The European Criminal Procedural Tradition and the European Court of Human Rights* (Hart Publishing, 2007) 50–58.

[64] Art 11 of CPL 2018. The same Article remains intact in CPL 1996 and CPL 2012.

[65] Summers (n 63) 58.

[66] ibid.

[67] As a result of the growth in the volume of cases, members of the adjudicative committee can only have a glimpse of the case based on the trial judge's debriefing. Thorough deliberation is impossible given the limited discussion time. Therefore, the discussion is eventually guided by the trial judge or the leader of the criminal division who is familiar with the case details. Yan Hao, 'Shenpanweiyuanhui Gongneng de Yihua yu Chongzu (The Alienation and Reconstruction of the Function of the Adjudicative Committee)' (2005) 6 *Journal of Southwest University of Political Science and Law* 95. Empirical studies have indicated that the committee members' discussion on specific cases was far from sufficient. Rather than having a heated debate of the cases, most of the time was spent on trial

In this regard, trial judges performed the fundamental role in the criminal proceedings, even though their final decision-making was routinely tempered.[68]

In light of the central part judges played in ascertaining evidence and constructing narratives, their treatment of the case dossier was crucial. Adjudication has been operating on the assumption that the prosecution case was reliable and admissible.[69] As discussed in chapter three, it has been exceptionally difficult to rebut such assumptions. This was exemplified in how the alleged illegally obtained evidence was handled by the courts.[70] The courts were overly cautious when it came to excluding prosecution evidence. Trial judges were loath to assess the evidence contained in the dossier from a critical perspective. Unless the defence had vigorously challenged the way that the prosecution evidence was obtained, evidence compiled in the dossier would rarely be questioned and, therefore, be automatically admitted. For cases in which evidence was affirmed to have been obtained unlawfully, none of them resulted in acquittal.[71] Some judges have voiced their faith in the case dossier when constructing the judicial narratives and have claimed to be accountable to 'the truth embodied by the dossier'.[72] This seemed to include those cases where the way the prosecution evidence was gathered was disputed.

This dossier-orientated adjudicative model has endured through the reform of judicial accountability. The reform, however, has ended the controversial internal leader review system and has narrowed down the scope of cases eligible to be submitted to the adjudicative committee.[73] For the first time, judges are now

judges introducing the basic information of the cases. Zuo Weimin (n 56); Xu Xianghua Research Team, 'Shenpanweiyuanhui zhidu gaige lujin shizheng yanjiu (Empirical Research on the Perspective of Reform of the Adjudicative Committee)' (2018) 2 *China Law Studies* 28.

[68] The position of the chief or the deputy chief was often held by senior judges proficient in handling cases. Their oversight of the cases might be justified as a mechanism of 'quality control', especially when the trial judge feels a lack of confidence, or the case involved needs to be handled with extra care. Zuo Weimin (n 56). See also R Peerenboom, *China's Long March toward Rule of Law* (Cambridge University Press, 2002) 323–24; Peerenboom, 'Judicial Independence in China' (n 61) 71.

[69] Interviews ATJ-1 and GAJ-1, 2, 3 and 4.

[70] For relevant discussion, see ch 3.

[71] Ye Rui and Wu Qingguo, 'Feifa zhengju paichu guize shiyong wenti shizheng yanjiu: yi S sheng C shi wei yangban (Empirical Research on Exclusionary Rule of Illegally Obtained Evidence: Based on the Sample of S province and C city)' (2015) 6 *Journal of Railway Police College* 78, 79; Xu Jianxing and Fang Binwei, 'Woguo xingshi feifa zhengju paichu guize sifa shijian shizheng yanjiu: yi W shi xingshi shengpan shiwu wei shijiao (Empirical Study of Judicial Practice in the Use of the Exclusionary Rule of Illegally Obtained Evidence) (2016) 24 *Evidence Science* 682, 684; Zhang Jian, 'Shenpai zhongxin gaige beijing xia feifa zhengju paichu guize de luoshi yu wanshan: jiyu 2013nian lai 486 feng xingshi panjueshu de shizheng kaocha (Implementation and Perfection of Exclusionary Rule of Illegally Obtained Evidence Against the Background of Trial Focused Reform: Empirical Research on 486 Judgments since 2013)' (2016) 5 *Journal of Xi'an Electronic and Techonology University* 40, 41.

[72] Interview ATJ-1.

[73] The Supreme People's Court, 'Several Opinions of the Supreme People's Court on Improving the Judicial Accountability System of People's Courts', *China Court* (21 September 2015) www.chinacourt.org/Art/subjectdetail/id/MzAwNEgtMIABAA==.shtml (accessed 19 October 2018). This reform is further strengthened by additional judicial documents, emphasising judges' responsibilities. Cases to be discussed by the adjudicative committee are limited to those concerning national security, social stability, foreign affairs or foreign nationals, and legal application in relation to major and serious cases.

placed at the centre of the judicial activities, being able to form their own working teams around judicial activities and exercise power without interference from their senior colleagues within the court system.[74] Collegial benches and single trial judges are no longer required to report the cases to the leaders of the court, and judgments can be issued without the signature of the chief of the criminal chamber. Meanwhile, an accountability procedure has been put in place to make judges answerable for the decisions they have made.[75] There is no doubt that the judicial accountability reform has enhanced the autonomy of individual judges and made significant progress in terms of the transparency of criminal proceedings. Laudable as it is, the reform made no change to the central part that the case dossier plays in adjudication, nor any meaningful advance in respect of the oral and public hearings and their contribution to the final outcome of cases. Consequently, no structural transformation has been brought to the way the narrative is constructed. Judges are still reliant on the case dossier prepared by the police and the prosecution from the investigative phase.

II. The Judge–Prosecutor Relationship

Why do judges place so much trust on the case dossier? Aside from the internal controlling mechanism within the court system, it is in many ways concerned with the tripartite relations within the Iron Triangle, especially the relationship between the courts and the procuratorate. This relationship, as the official discourse suggested, is one of 'mutual cooperation and mutual supervision (*xianghu peihe, xianghu zhiyue*)'.[76] Despite being the trier of the case, the court's power of adjudication is overseen by the procuratorate through the counter-appealing of erroneous judgments.[77] Thus, when mistakes regarding the ascertainment of fact or application of law are identified,[78] the prosecutor can initiate a retrial by submitting the case to a higher level. If the suspected error is confirmed by the higher court, the responsible judges might be subjected to disciplinary sanctions if the fault identified cannot be justified.[79]

See 'Opinions on Establishing Judges and Prosecutors' Sanction System (Temporary)' (issued in July 2016) and 'Notice on Strictly Implementing Judges' and Prosecutors' Selecting and Appointment and Procedures' (issued by the Central Political-Legal Committee, March 2017).

[74] The Supreme People's Court, 'Several Opinions' (ibid) s 2(1).

[75] See 'Opinions on Establishing Judges' (ibid).

[76] CPL 2018, Art 7 (CPL 2012, Art 7).

[77] CPL 2012, Art 217.

[78] Normally, the counter-appeal should be initiated before the judgment becomes final. However, according to Arts 242 and 243 of CPL 2012, a retrial can also be launched if an error in the verdict or sentence is identified.

[79] Since the judicial accountability reform, individual judges' responsibility regarding overturned judgments have been significantly narrowed. If the reversed judgment is due to a different interpretation of the law or evidence that can be reasonably justified, newly emerged evidence, a change of

The dynamics between judges and prosecutors is designed to identify errors that occur in the judicial system and to ensure the correctness of the enforcement of the law. Key to this model is the independence and impartiality of both legal actors. To be specific, prosecutors assume the role of safeguarding the lawfulness of the criminal proceedings. They have a legal duty to identify potential illegality within the criminal justice process and to challenge and rectify inaccurate judgments. The legal standing of judges is independent of those of the prosecution. Judges are able to review the case in a neutral and dispassionate light. It is worth noting that Chinese prosecutors play a part similar to the *parquet* (the French prosecutor's office) in legal rhetoric, which is commonly regarded as the 'standing judiciary' in the French criminal justice system. Unlike its French counterpart, however, the prosecutor in China has no obligation to follow the exculpatory lines of inquiry, despite its supervisory function in identifying procedural errors.[80]

The way judges and prosecutors have interacted in practice, however, is somewhat different from the legal rhetoric. Their relationship can be observed through the lens of the Appraisal System. In order to avoid undesirable outcomes for both institutions, prosecutors and judges were strategically aligned.[81] Based on a mutual understanding, the courts assisted the procuratorate in avoiding a potential acquittal. In return, the prosecutor avoided using the power to counter-appeal an erroneous judgment. Thus, if a case was likely to be acquitted by the court, the court would inform the prosecutor proactively to withdraw the case[82] or to secretly replace the case with a different one prior to the court hearing in order to avoid the acquittal.[83] If the application of the law was controversially subjective, a discussion would be initiated by judges, followed by a private negotiation between the two

circumstances etc, judges should no longer be sanctioned. See 'The Supreme People's Court on Several Opinions of Perfecting the Judicial Accountability of the People's Courts (zuigao renmin fayuan guanyu wanshan renmin fayuan sifa zerenzhi de ruogan yijian)' (issued in 2015, No 13) s 28.

[80] See Hodgson (n 10) 67.

[81] As noted in previous chapters, all the criminal justice institutions were subject to the Appraisal System before its abolishment in 2015. Under the Appraisal System, one important judicial indicator was the overturned judgment, which might affect judges' career prospects and salary bonuses. Zhu Tonghui, 'The Appraisal System in the Criminal Justice System' (2009) 1 *Law and Social Science* 5; Li Enshen, 'The Li Zhuang Case: Examining the Challenges Facing Criminal Defense Lawyers in China' (2010) 24 *Columbia Journal of Asian Law* 129, 164; Wu Meilai and Gui Ouli, 'Xingshi susong zhineng de yihua yu zhili: yi gongjianfa xingshi susong guanlian jixiao kaohe wei zhongxin (The Alienation of Solution of the Function of Criminal Justice: Based on the Correlation of the Appraisal System in Criminal Justice Institutions)' in R He (ed), *Gongzheng Sifa yu Xingzhengfa Shishi Wenti Yanjiu (Shang Ce) (Judicial Justice and the Implementation of the Administrative Law (Part 1))* (People's Courts Press, 2014) 348; Xie Xiaojian, 'Jiancha jiguan yewu mubiao guanli kaoping dui xingshisusong de yingxiang (Influence on Criminal Justice over the Management of the Procuratorate's Tasks)' (2014) 6 *Anhui University Journal* 119; Wan Yi and Shi Qingzheng, 'Jianchayuan jixiao kaohe shizheng yanjiu: yi S shi jianchajiguan wei yangben de fenxi (Empirical Study on the Appraisal System for the Procuratorate: Analysis of the Procuratorate in S city)' (2009) 1 *Oriental Law* 28.

[82] Withdrawing a case to avoid acquittal is normal practice. See Huang Qiusheng, 'The Research on the Quality of the Cases Prosecuted by Taizhou Procuracy' (2007) 5 *Zhejiang Procuracy* 87, 89.

[83] Field note APU-59.

actors to reach a common understanding.[84] In exchange, prosecutors would courteously hint to the court if errors were found in judgments, rather than launching a counter-appeal.[85] In this reciprocally beneficial relationship, communication resolved actions and cooperation replaced oversight. A harmonious relationship was developed to protect their respective interests, as well as to avoid confrontation and loss of face.

This alliance between judges and prosecutors has significantly influenced the way acquittal has been perceived by judges. Rather than seeing it as a normal outcome that certifies the failure of the prosecution to prove guilt beyond reasonable doubt, acquittals have been taken by a crime control mindset to imply that criminals are set free. During my interviews, some judges indicated that acquittals would cause a distraction to the criminal justice system; as a result, they should be avoided at all costs.

> Judge: An acquittal case has a huge influence on society. If a case is announced as being wrongfully prosecuted, the public power will be affected; if we allow an acquittal, the whole legal system will be changed as a consequence; if a lot of acquittal cases have occurred, the whole political system will collapse.[86]

From the internal audit perspective, an acquittal had no negative consequence on judges' performances. Quite the opposite, a court that issued acquittals would be rewarded by the Appraisal System.[87] However, an acquittal had a detrimental effect on the procuratorate, and hence the relationship between the two institutions could be ruptured. With this in mind, an acquittal must be resolved out of sight. During my field site observation in site A, I witnessed a 'crisis' in the procuratorate caused by the incident of a potential acquittal.[88] The court at the same hierarchical level intended to acquit a defendant due to an inappropriately charged offence of 'public provocation and picking quarrels (*xingxun zishi zui*)'.[89] In that case, a girl in a discotheque was approached by a man, who wanted to buy her a drink. She was awaiting her boyfriend and was a little afraid of the man, so she drank the glass of alcohol bought by the man. Soon after the girl's boyfriend arrived, the girl and the boyfriend went dancing. The man, who was then drunk, approached the girl again, using inappropriate words to tease her. This apparently provoked her boyfriend, and the two started to fight. The man called two other people to help fight the girl's boyfriend. One of them smashed a wine bottle and stabbed the boyfriend in his belly. There was a wound, but the injury was relatively minor. There was, however, a lot of property damage, including smashed glasses and damaged furniture. The prosecutor in charge of the case believed that the nature of the crime

[84] Field note APU-5.
[85] Field note APU-24.
[86] Interview FTJ-1.
[87] Wu Meilai and Gui Ouli (n 81) 348–58.
[88] Field notes APU-6, 7, 8, 9 and 10.
[89] This is a type of public disorder offence.

was an interruption of public order and the offence 'public provocation and picking quarrels (*xingxun zishi zui*)' was selected. All three defendants involved in the fight pleaded guilty, and the defence lawyers did not contest the charge.[90] After the trial, the court suggested that this case should be treated as a personal assault, rather than a public disorder offence. In order to reinforce this argument, the judge indicated an acquittal of the defendants of the offence of 'public provocation and picking quarrels (*xingxun zishi zui*)'. Upon receiving the news, the procuratorate reacted immediately to negotiate with the leaders of the court. Since the trial had been concluded, it was too late to withdraw the case from the court. To minimise the damage, they offered to trade the acquittal for two potential counter-appeals arising from mistakes found in two previous judgments.[91] An agreement was eventually reached that the court would convict the defendants on the condition that the procuratorate would drop the two counter-appeals.[92]

As the interests of the court and the procuratorate were tied up in the audit assessment, neither of them would run the risk of harming each other. This was particularly the case if the leaders of the institutions wished to be promoted. A judge who was interviewed following this event made an observation of the consequence of acquittals:

> Judge: The consequence that this (an acquittal) will lead to is the lack of cooperation with the work between the court and the procuratorate. For example, when we want them to do a favour for us, such as the extension of the legal period, or amend some minor mistakes in the written judgement, it is hard to make sure they will not get you into trouble. If you push someone to the dead corner, you will have continuous problems.[93]

It is worth noting that such a 'trade-off' negotiation was not conducive to their mutually cooperative relationship. It was therefore not commonly seen in daily practice.[94] Nevertheless, it reflects the interplay of the dynamic relations between the two institutions. A senior prosecutor commented that the two institutions are not just bound in a bureaucratic alliance, but are involved in interrelationships that are in the nature of a game:

> Prosecutor: I think we should call this 'mutual games playing' … The two [the procuracy and the court] have some devices and mechanisms to control each other, yet they also have some mutual interests between themselves. The game playing has led to a very special type of relationship.[95]

[90] Field notes APU-6 and 7.
[91] Field notes APU-6 and 7.
[92] Field notes APU-9 and 10.
[93] Interview ATJ-1.
[94] Field notes APU-9.
[95] Interview APS-5.

To maintain a good gaming relationship, cooperation was the key. Unless it was unavoidable, a counter-appeal should never be initiated in case it sabotaged the alliance. Yet, the power of the counter-appeal remained a useful bargaining chip in securing the interests of the procuratorate. The two institutions constantly considered each other's actions and rationalised their own decisions accordingly. Besides offence and defence in protecting their own interests, they were happy to pay tribute to each other, especially in the domain of the court hearing. As far as most judges were concerned, prosecutors have never been regarded, or treated, as a party in the courtroom, but rather as an authority. In an interview with a senior judge, an anecdote was told in relation to the prerogative of the prosecutor.

> Judge: There are many things [that have] happened in China that you [could] never imagine in other countries. Many years ago, when I was still a court clerk working in the court, a prosecutor found that the result of the case was unfavourable to him after the cross-examination. Then he simply stood up, took all the dossiers and stormed away from the court … After that, the court had to adjourn the trial and communicate with the prosecutor. In the end, the case was settled but the prosecutor's behaviour was really shocking … In our country, the prosecutors are really powerful.[96]

This standpoint was endorsed by other judges:

> Judge: The procuratorate is a very robust institution in our country whose power of legal supervision is extremely mighty, which includes the power of prosecution and the power of counter appealing … There is no such powerful procuratorate in any other countries in this world. In Taiwan, the prosecution is only part of the court system (therefore part of the judiciary): a good working model that we should follow.[97]

> Judge: In our minds, we try to treat the procuratorate as a party. However, we know that it (the procuratorate) is not an ordinary party. It is very powerful.[98]

Ever since the criminal justice reform of 1996, the role of trial judges (or the collegial bench) has changed from being active investigators to passive fact-finders. Despite the impartial image, the courts showed extraordinary tolerance of prosecutors' occasional unprofessional behaviour at trial. On several occasions, the prosecutor's speech was so emotionally charged that the denunciation of the defendant in the court could be classified as abusive. Foul language and ill-mannered gestures were used by the prosecutor when addressing the defendant. In some cases, they were so disrespectfully inappropriate that the behaviour of the prosecutor clearly fell below basic professional standards. Yet, when the defence protested, the judge remained silent.[99] The court's acquiescence to the prosecutorial behaviour

[96] Interview GAJ-1.
[97] Interview GAJ-2.
[98] Interview ATJ-2.
[99] Field note APU-61.

occasionally led to poorly controlled proceedings. In one instance, two defence lawyers were shouted at by a prosecutor to 'shut up' when it was their turn to proffer an argument.[100] The prosecutor's usurpation of the judge's role clearly suggested who was in charge.

A prosecutor described what happened in the trial.

> Prosecutor: The case was obviously a theft, however, the lawyer insisted it was a crime of embezzlement ... After hearing the stupid comments of the defence lawyers, I was so furious and told the lawyer to shut up. I told him: 'there is no room here for you to give such suggestions. Shut your mouth and be quiet.'[101]
>
> Prosecutor: In this case, my main job in the trial was to prevent the defendant from speaking. The defendant was so defensive. From time to time, when I gave my view, he would refute me with long stories. I was wound up and got angry. So, I asked him to shut his mouth several times ... The defendant asked the judge to change me as a prosecutor! He said I insulted him by using the swear words. I argued back by saying that the 'F' word was not a swearing language, but the local dialect.[102]

The courts' forbearance of prosecutors' unprofessional behaviour largely stems from their self-recognition as part of the Iron Triangle,[103] in which they are allied to the police and procuratorate in the fight against crime. It is well known that prosecutors and judges belong to 'the same family'.[104] Identifying themselves as a state apparatus, judges and prosecutors are in fact different components of the same entity, with no meaningful distinction to be drawn between them.[105] This is exhibited by the fact that judges occasionally stepped in to assist the prosecution at trial.

> Judge: The procuratorate is a very powerful institution. We have to treat them with respect. There was a time when I was still a court clerk, the prosecutor, for some reason, did not appear at the trial – it was a common trial, not those simplified trials where prosecutors were not required to attend. Everyone was waiting. After half an hour, the chief judge decided to continue with the trial. So, he picked up the dossier, read the Bill of Prosecution and started to play the role of the prosecutor while managing to preside the trial. Now you would think the judge's behaviour might be a bit problematic. For some of us it was so natural.[106]

Beyond the trial, judges made no secret of their befriending of prosecutors. The prosecutor and judge at the same level in site A knew each other very well.

[100] Field notes APU-12 and 64.
[101] Field note APU-12.
[102] Field note APU-62.
[103] This term has often been used by scholars who study the Chinese criminal justice system, see Li Enshen (n 81) 161.
[104] H Tanner, *Strike Hard: Anti-crime Campaigns and Chinese Criminal Justice, 1979–1985* (Cornell University East Asia Program, 1999) 31–32.
[105] McConville et al (n 8) 398.
[106] Interview ATJ-2.

The buildings of the prosecutor's office and the court were adjacent, and prosecutors were given free access to the courtrooms and the offices of judges. Prosecutors were generally familiarised with their neighbouring judges' work style, and many of them were good friends. The importance of cooperation was emphasised repeatedly during my observation of and interviews with these two legal actors. Their collaboration was reflected mostly in their frequent communications over the telephone, through which legal opinions, issues concerning evidence and sentencing were all informally exchanged and discussed.[107] Decisions of the criminal cases were often made based upon such casual telephone conversations, in which chit-chat, negotiations and compromises were blended.[108] If a charged fact was unclear, the judge would call the prosecutor to request supplementary evidence or to return the case for further investigation. When a judge ran out of the legally proscribed adjudication period, a private call between the judge and the prosecutor would allow her to 'borrow' extra time from the earlier stage of prosecutorial review. This inevitably involved falsification of the registration documents.[109] As far as prosecutors were concerned, the entire adjudication process was open and transparent. The following extracts from private conversations between a judge and a prosecutor elucidated how their informal exchange had influenced the outcome of the case.

> A prosecutor was having a conversation with the trial judge on the phone.
>
> Prosecutor: [Speaking to the judge] I did not want to prosecute this suspect initially. I did this because I was pressurised … I know that it is very hard to convict him just based upon the case fact. But I must prosecute him, I have no choice, you know … Since I have already charged him, why not impose a very light sentence on him, such as the suspension of imprisonment, so that he can come out quickly? As long as he is convicted, it will be alright … You agreed? That's good.[110]
>
> A prosecutor was discussing a case with the judge on the phone before the trial.
>
> Prosecutor: [Speaking to the judge] I was sympathetic to the suspect. He was poor and he could not earn enough money for his living. So, he did some criminal damage out of frustration … You may consider imposing a light sentence on him so that he can get out of the prison quickly.

[107] Field notes APU-24, 35 and 45.

[108] Field notes APU-24, 34 and 35.

[109] According to Art 202 of CPL 2012, the court must announce the judgment within 3 months after the court has filed the case. For death penalty cases, cases involving civil litigation or cases concerning other difficult situations (see Art 156 of CPL 2012), the adjudication period can be extended for another 3 months after authorisation by the Supreme Court. After the enforcement of CPL 2012, the court is less likely to 'borrow' the legal period from the prosecution due to the extended period permitted by the law. Such practice was very frequent before CPL 2012 came into force. Before CPL 2012, however, the court only had 1 month (or at the most 1.5 months) to deliver the judgment after the case has been filed.

[110] Field note APU-59.

After the phone call, the prosecutor said to his colleague:

> Prosecutor: The judge agreed to what I said and the suspect should be released next month. I like such a work style with the judge whom I am familiar with so that we can discuss the case and then make a decision together.[111]

In such a relationship of mutual dependence, trust and cooperation are engrained within the working culture of the courts and the procuratorate, taking the place of real supervision and oversight. This alliance is embodied in the way the investigative dossier was used for adjudication. The bundle of evidence selected and scrutinised by the prosecutor was treated as trustworthy. In this context, the case dossier is not only the evidence presented by the prosecution to buttress the criminal charge, but a test of the interinstitutional bond. A trial model based on critically examining and verifying the investigative work of the police would certainly create antagonism and undermine this harmonious relationship. Consequently, excluding any prosecution evidence would amount to an explicit denial of the work of the prosecutor and the police. This explains why the courts are reluctant to exclude evidence even though the prejudicial weight of the evidence exceeds its probative value.[112] To maintain the trust and the relationship, judges use the case dossier as the primary source of information for determining the charge. Their endorsement of the case dossier has therefore resulted in the absence of witnesses at trial.

III. Trial without Witnesses

In common law countries, witnesses' statements taken from the pretrial investigation are generally categorised as hearsay evidence.[113] In England and Wales, for example, subject to exceptions, statements not made in oral evidence in court which are adduced as evidence of any matter stated are treated as hearsay evidence.[114] The rule against hearsay is embedded in jury trial systems, which place a premium on orality. In the adversarial tradition, witnesses are expected to take an oath and deliver their testimony in person, which makes it perfectly natural that one witness is forbidden from giving testimony on behalf of others.[115] The justifications for the general exclusionary rule against hearsay, accordingly, tend to revolve around the anxieties about hearsay. These concerns include that out-of-court statements are not usually made under oath; the unfairness of

[111] Field note APU-34.

[112] For a discussion of excluding inappropriately and unlawfully obtained evidence, see ch 3.

[113] However, the hearsay rules are subject to a number of exceptions. For example, in England and Wales, under the Criminal Justice Act 2003, four categories of situations are set out to allow the hearsay evidence to be admitted in the court, such as parties' agreement and the court's discretion. See Criminal Justice Act 2003, s 114(1).

[114] Criminal Justice Act 2003, s 114(1). See also *R v Twist* [2011] EWCA Crim 1143.

[115] R Munday, *Evidence* (Oxford University Press, 2017) 369.

depriving a party of the opportunity to cross-examine the witness; and the risk of information distortion through repetition.[116] Moreover, there is an emotional resentment that people sometimes make unpleasant claims behind a person's back that they would not make to their face. Hearsay, therefore, is against this human nature that the accused wishes to directly question his accuser.[117] In *Teper v R* [1952], Lord Normand famously elucidated why hearsay evidence is inherently unreliable:

> [Hearsay evidence] is not the best evidence and it is not delivered on oath. The truthfulness and accuracy of the person whose words are spoken by another witness cannot be tested by cross-examination, and the light which his demeanour would throw on his testimony is lost.[118]

While some of these concerns are now seen as exaggerated (such as observing the demeanour of witnesses), others have been recognised as valid in recent decades. A report by the Law Commission in England concluded that oral evidence is preferable to hearsay principally because it can be challenged in cross-examination.[119] It also raised the worry that hearsay may be deliberately concocted for forensic use, and the loss of nuance and subtle meaning may result in errors produced by repetition.[120] At the fundamental level, the anxieties of this exclusionary rule lie in the fear of an unjust conviction.[121] Due to human fallibility (such as defects in the perception, memory, sincerity or ability to articulate of the maker of the statement),[122] it is believed that the rule against hearsay can operate to reduce the risk of admitting evidence of doubtful reliability that might otherwise lead to miscarriages of justice. This rule is also designed to safeguard the right to confrontation, which allows the accused to question witnesses in court, thereby protecting the defendant against coercion and restraining the capricious use of public power.[123]

In spite of the sound rationale, the hearsay rule, or the due process principle that underpins the rule, has never been recognised by the law in China. Hence, the accused's right to confront witnesses is not appreciated by the criminal justice system. On the contrary, court hearings without witnesses' oral testimony have been the norm in judicial practice. Certain safeguards were stipulated to encourage witnesses to appear in court, which encompassed offering general protection

[116] *R v Jenkins* (1869) LR 1 CCR 187.

[117] *Coy v Iowa* 487 US 1012 (1988), 1017.

[118] *Teper v R* [1952] AC 480, 486 (Lord Normand).

[119] Law Commission Report, *Evidence in Evidence in Criminal Proceedings: Hearsay and Related Topics* (Law Com No 245, 1997) 1.29.

[120] G Durston, *Evidence: Text and Materials* (Oxford University Press, 2011) 244.

[121] *R v Horncastle* [2009] UKSC 14; *R v Riat* [2013] 1 WLR 2592.

[122] ALT Choo, *Hearsay and Confrontation in Criminal Trials* (Clarendon Press, 1996) 17–29.

[123] An example of this is the Sixth Amendment to the US Constitution, known as the Confrontation Clause, which states: 'In all criminal prosecutions, the accused shall enjoy the right … to be confronted with the witnesses against him'. See also Summers (n 63) 147; M Berger, 'The Deconstitutionalisation of the Confrontation Clause: A Proposal for a Prosecutorial Restraint Model' (1991) 76 *Minnesota Law Review*, 560; *Coy* (n 117) 1017.

for the safety of the witnesses who testify; punishment of witness intimidation or retaliation; and enhanced protection measures (such as anonymisation of the identity of a witness, shielding a witness from the view of the accused at trial and issuing restriction orders to prevent potential retaliation) for witnesses who testify in cases concerning national security, terrorism, gang-related organised crimes and drug crimes.[124] However, these measures brought no fundamental changes to the way trials are conducted. Case dossiers remain the centrepiece of trials, and witnesses who should give key evidence are nowhere to be seen.[125]

Over the last two decades, a large body of literature has emerged to identify the reasons that have led to the absence of witnesses at court. Witnesses' fear of revenge and lack of protection, for instance, have long been acknowledged as among the principal reasons.[126] The entrenched institutional culture, the judges' stereotypical dossier-reading working model, in particular has made judges react negatively to the idea that witnesses should be cross-examined.[127] The lack of financial support, the inadequacy in law of witness protection and the compellability of witnesses have been noted as other contributory factors.[128] China's anti-litigation tradition seems to have dampened people's enthusiasm in testifying at court as well.[129]

[124] CPL 2018, Arts 63–65.

[125] See ch 1.

[126] Shi Limei, 'Zhenren chuting zuozheng zhidu yanjiu (The Study of Witnesses' Attending to Courts)' (2002) 10(2) *Legal Review of National Prosecutor's College* 60; Zhou Guojun, 'Xingshi anjian zhenren chuting zuozheng zhidu yanjiu (The Study of Testifying Witnesses' Testimony in Criminal Cases)' (2002) 2 *China Criminal Law Magazine* 14; Wang Li, 'Xingsufa xiugaihou zhengren chuting zuozhenglv rendi de yuanyin (The Reason Why Witnesses Still Do Not Go to Court after the Revision of CPL)' (2013) 4 *Daqing Social Science* 116; Ye Yang, 'Xinxingsufa shishi hou de zhengren chuting zuozheng wenti yanjiu (Research on Witnesses Giving Testimonies after the Implementation of CPL 2012)' (2014) 9 *Social Scientist* 111; Zhao Li, 'Xinxingsufa shishi hou zhengren chuting zuozheng zhidu zai tantao (Reconsideration of Witnesses Giving Testimonies at Trial after the Implementation of CPL 2012)' (2014) 5 *Legal System and Society* 47; Hu Yunteng, 'Zhengren chuting zuozhengnan jiqi jiejue silu (The Difficulties and Solution of Witnesses Come to Court to Testify)' (2006) 28 *Global Law Review* 557.

[127] Chen Weidong, 'Rang zhengren zouxiang fating: xingshi anjian zhengren chuting zuozheng zhidu yanjiu (Let Witnesses Go to the Trial: Research on Witnesses Giving Testimonies at Trial)' (2007) 19 *Journal of Shandong Police College* 40; Mao Yixiao and Yan Jihong, 'Xinxingshi susongfa shiyexia zhengren chuting shixiao guancha: yi Z sheng fayuan wei yangben (Observation of Witnesses Giving Testimonies at Trial after the Implementation of CPL 2012: Based on the Sample of the Courts in Z Province)' (2015) 1 *Journal of Jiangxi Police Institute* 107; He Li, 'Xinxingsufa shijiaoxia zhengren chuting zhidu shilling wenti de jiejue jianyi (Suggestions on the Failure of Witnesses Attending Trial under the CPL 2012)' (2013) 6 *Hebei Legal Studies* 186; Zuo Weimin and Ma Jinghua, 'Xingshi zhengren chutinglv: Yizhong jiyu shizhengyanjiu de lilun chanshu (The Rate of Witnesses' Attendance: An Empirical Analysis)' (2005) 6 *China Law Studies* 164; Wang Li (ibid).

[128] Wang Li (ibid); Hu Yunteng (n 126); Zhao Li (n 126); Li Miao, 'Qianxi woguo xixingsufa zhengren zuozheng zhidu de jingbu yu chizhi (On the Improvement and Stagnation of Encouraging Witnesses to Attend the Trial)' (2015) 21 *New West* 84; Chen Weidong (ibid).

[129] Zhao Li (ibid). It is worth noting that papers written by Chinese academics were not focused on one reason, and the reasons they were focused on were all numerated. Long Zongzhi, *Xingshi Tingshen Zhidu Yanjiu (The Research on the Trial of Criminal Process)* (China University of Political Science and Law Press, 1998) 51; Chen Weidong (n 127); Xu Xin, 'Faguan Weishenme Bu Xiangxing Zhenren? Zhenren zai Zhuanxing Zhongguo Sifa Guochengzhong de Zuoyong (Why Judges Do Not Trust Witnesses? The Witnesses' Role in the Transition of Chinese Criminal Justice)' (2006) 18 *Peking University Law Journal* 337.

Perhaps more crucially, research has alluded to the fact that judges and prosecutors have the mentality of wanting to block live testimony in order to control the result of the trial.[130] As a matter of judicial reality, the extensive application of the guilty plea procedures also renders it unnecessary to call witnesses to testify.[131]

These explanations have been used to rationalise the underlying reasons that result in the absence of witnesses at court. Almost all the research on witnesses in China indicates that witnesses' absence at trial has been a multifaceted phenomenon behind which are various prevarications motivated by considerations and calculations from many quarters. Arguably, it is true that all these aforementioned reasons are somehow relevant to, and have contributed to, the idiosyncrasy of Chinese courtrooms. Nevertheless, it is worth noting that the question of why witnesses do not testify at trial is in fact a conglomeration of two different questions. The two essential aspects to the question, namely witnesses declining to testify at trial and the courts' reluctance to call witnesses, are somewhat disparate in nature and need to be answered from different perspectives. To untangle the issue, it is necessary to address these two aspects separately.

A. Reluctant Witnesses?

Several Chinese studies on witnesses have attempted to calculate the number of witnesses who actually attended a trial and then worked out the rate of witness attendance.[132] Despite the useful numerical illustration of the problem, the witness attendance rate, as a concept, is flawed and has little value in capturing the actual situation. To be specific, there are witnesses in almost every criminal case, but not every witness needs to be summoned to testify at court. Most noticeably, if the defendant pleads guilty, admitting all the elements of the offence charged, it is unnecessary to call any witnesses to repeat the facts.[133] Likewise, the parties – both the defence and the prosecution – may not wish to procure a witness to attend the trial if the veracity of that witness's account has already been agreed. There might also be situations where witnesses attend the trial but are reluctant to testify. On the other hand, a witness may not be able to appear at the trial for legitimate reasons but has provided prerecorded statements for testimony. Additionally, there might be issues concerning the competence of witnesses.

[130] McConville et al (n 8) 246; Zhao Li (ibid).

[131] McConville et al (ibid) 245–46.

[132] Zuo Weimin and Wu Weijun, 'Dangdai zhongguo xingsu faxue: yanjiu yangshi de shanbian yu qianzhan (The Transition of Research Model and Chinese Legal Reform: Debate Based on Empirical Study' (2001) 1 *Legal Review* 62; Yi Yanyou, *Zhongguo Xingsu yu Zhongguo Shehui (The Chinese Criminal Process of Chinese Society)* (Peking University Press, 2010) 79; Zuo Weimin, 'Xingshi zhengren chuting zuozheng chengxu: Shizhengyuanjiu yu lilun chanxi (The Legal Process of Witnesses Appearing at Criminal Courts: Empirical Research and Theoretical Analysis)' (2005) 6(17) *Peking University Law Journal* 641.

[133] McConville et al (n 8) 243.

Even if a witness attends the trial to testify, he or she may not be qualified to do so. The core issue here is not about the number of witnesses who appear in court, but is about effectively summoning those witnesses who can produce material evidence, especially to establish the facts in question. To define who those witnesses are must be based on the circumstances of each individual case. As a general matter of principle, it seems that only in those cases in which the witness's statement is disputed by the parties, or the court thinks that the material facts need to be ascertained by examining the witness, does the witness's appearance to testify at trial become a real issue. Currently, the law states that physically or mentally handicapped people, or minors who cannot distinguish between right and wrong or cannot accurately articulate, cannot serve as witnesses.[134] Yet there is no formal hearing to decide whether or not a person is competent to be a witness. While most of the people who were summoned to attend are assumed to satisfy the prerequisites, this may not always be the case.

That a key witness may refuse to cooperate with the courts and decide not to participate in the trial process has not been a cause of concern for common law countries, where witnesses can be legally compelled to attend. In England and Wales, for example, competent witnesses are obliged to testify at trial, whether they wish to do so or not. Pursuant to the Criminal Procedure (Attendance of Witnesses) Act 1965, witnesses who refuse to be summoned to court to testify can be prosecuted for contempt of court, with a punishment of a custodial sentence.[135] The compulsory power of the courts seems to be soundly justified, as the trial process should not be unduly disrupted or undermined because of a witness's inconsiderate decision.[136]

This is not to say, however, that legal compulsion is the perfect solution to tackle the problem of witnesses being reluctant to testify in court. Even in England and Wales, witnesses have been found to be increasingly reluctant to come forward to testify.[137] Even if they do appear at trial, they may withdraw their previous statements, stand mute or develop a loss of memory in the witness box due to a number of reasons, especially witness intimidation.[138] Home Office Research has found that witness intimidation occurred in about 15 per cent of criminal cases; there were 785 convictions of cases involving 'witness nobbling' in 2005.[139] This problem has now been effectively overcome by enforcing the criminal law and setting up devices to anonymise the identity of the witness.[140] For instance, the Criminal Justice and Police Act 2001 criminalises those who intimidate witnesses with the

[134] See Art 62 of CPL 2018.
[135] See s 2D of the Criminal Procedure (Attendance of Witnesses) Act 1965.
[136] See *R v Yusuf* [2003] 2 Cr App R 32.
[137] C Tapper, *Cross and Tapper on Evidence*, 12 edn (Oxford University Press, 2010) 229.
[138] Munday (n 115) 149–50.
[139] ibid. Sources from Home Office Research, Development and Statistics Directorate, Research Findings, No 124; *The Times* (5 April 2008) 4.
[140] Munday (n 115) 150.

intent to obstruct, pervert or interfere with the course of justice, as well as those who subsequently harm witnesses who have appeared at trial.[141] To deter witness intimidation, the courts have pledged to take such offences 'extremely seriously', meaning that a harsh sentence is likely to be imposed upon conviction.[142] In addition to tough laws, technologies have been employed to alleviate witnesses' fear to give evidence in public. For example, a witness can give testimony behind an erected screen.[143] Witnesses may also apply for anonymity, by using pseudonyms or by disguising their voices or concealing their features.[144]

In China, witnesses are reluctant to appear at trial for roughly the same reasons as in England and Wales, primarily witness intimidation.[145] As mentioned earlier, similar measures, such as anonymisation of the identity of a witness, disguising a witness's features or voices, have now been incorporated in law. However, the reluctance of witnesses to testify in court is still a persistent phenomenon. During my interviews, a few judges elaborated on the difficulty of summoning witnesses to court who were fearful of revenge.[146] Interestingly, however, these frightened witnesses had previously assisted the police by giving evidence and their testimonies were consolidated in written statements compiled in the case dossier. If a witness had cooperated with the police by giving a statement early in the investigation, her refusal to appear in court to testify would be unlikely to ameliorate her situation because her identity would be revealed and her pretrial statement would be read out. The defendant would know the name of the person who produced evidence against her anyway, especially if the defendant knew the witness in person. It should be noted that witnesses' identities (aside from police informers) are rarely anonymised in Chinese criminal justice practice.[147] Nor is any other safeguarding procedure in place to deter identification, hence prosecution witnesses are at risk of future revenge. Not attending the trial to testify would be a loss of the chance to correct any mistakes made or clarify an imprecise narrative in hindsight. In this regard, the witness may be in greater jeopardy if those mistakes were inadvertently made and the defendant takes the inaccurate account to be a deliberate fabrication.

The very fact that the majority of criminal case dossiers contain witnesses' inculpatory statements indicates that witnesses have taken the risk of giving evidence against the accused. Thus, fear of retaliation or other personal concern would seem to be illogical if witnesses know that their identities and their statements will be announced publicly during the court hearing. In Zuo and Ma's empirical research, they found that most of the witnesses (44 out of 53) in the study were willing to

[141] Criminal Justice and Police Act 2001, ss. 39 and 40.
[142] *R v Mark Williams* [1997] 2 Cr App R (S) 221, 221.
[143] *R v Richards* (1999) 163 JP 246.
[144] Coroners and Justice Act 2009, ss 88 and 89.
[145] Interview ATJ-2.
[146] Interviews ATJ-1, 2 and 3.
[147] Interviews APS- 5 and 6.

cooperate with the court and give oral testimonies at trial after being contacted.[148] This confirms that the reluctance of witnesses has not been the main reason for their absence at trial. It also suggests that witnesses' reluctance to testify at trial can be addressed if the courts make an appropriate effort.

B. Reluctant Courts

In their research on Chinese criminal justice, Mike McConville et al observed that judges and prosecutors endeavoured to keep witnesses away from the trial in order to control the result of the trial.[149] With the contents of the witness statements being settled, judges have been able to scrutinise them in advance and make a decision accordingly.[150] This view was endorsed by some of the judges and prosecutors that I interviewed. Their objections to witness cross-examination appear to focus on the untrustworthiness of witnesses' oral testimony.

> Prosecutor: Sometimes the defence lawyer applies for witnesses to attend the court. If we prosecutors do not think the witness's testimony is conducive to uncovering the crime, we would make an objection to the application … Due to the defence lawyer's private negotiation with the witnesses, they (the witnesses) would go to the court to change their previous statements against us. In such cases, we would be in a very passive position. If the witness's previous statements can be corroborated with the defendant's confession, we would make a request to the court not to admit the witness's live testimony. The court would always grant our objections.[151]
>
> Researcher: Have you ever tried any cases that the witnesses came to the court to testify?
>
> Judge: Yes, we have, but very few … I think there is only one case per year. There were some requests on the witnesses' appearance by the defence lawyer, but I did not permit it. Why? Witnesses would change their statements in the court due to their private negotiation with the defence lawyers. They wanted to overturn the case.[152]

The logic here is clear and is in congruence with the operation of the dossier system: the case dossier as the centrepiece of the criminal process was produced and reviewed by their allied police and prosecutors; its facts are well constructed and its reliability is unquestioned. When a witness is permitted to be cross-examined, the presented facts may become detached and altered from the finely constructed narratives. The memories of the witness are fluid and malleable, vulnerable to interference and weakened by the passage of time.[153] In any event, it would be

148 Zuo Weimin and Ma Jinghua (n 127) 167.
149 McConville et al (n 8) 246.
150 ibid.
151 Interview BPS-1.
152 Here the judge implied that there has been a negotiation to persuade the witness to tell the truth or to lie in order to support the accused.
153 See WA Wagenaar, *Identifying Ivan: A Case Study in Legal Psychology* (Harvard University Press, 1988).

difficult to procure a well-matched recollection from the witness. Without any training to confidently handle the discrepancy between the documentary record and the oral statement, the witness's testimony will throw the adjudication into confusion. In this context, the witness's testimony at trial may open up the scrutiny process of the written case dossier, allowing the working practices of the police and the prosecutor to be assessed publicly. It should be noted that investigations have been a closed, dark world, without sufficient regulation. It is this secrecy of the case-making process and the official image attached to it that legitimise the probative value of the evidence contained in the case dossier. Calling witnesses to testify in a public trial would allow the credibility of the evidence to be challenged. The prosecution evidence may be proved to be untrustworthy and the official narrative discredited. If this can of worms is opened up, it is certainly capable of damaging the bond between the judge and the prosecutor. Taking all the unmanageable factors into consideration, proactively excluding witnesses out of trial would be in the courts' and the procuratorate's best interest.

In this understanding, there is the possibility of conspiracy between the three criminal justice agencies to pervert the course of justice. The courts might doubt that the evidence contained in the case dossier is truthful or reliable. Therefore, the conviction based on the evidence dossier is unsafe. They may nevertheless choose to support the false credence in the dossier rather than permit the evidence to be challenged in public, including by refusing witnesses to be summoned. Such speculated motivations would appear to be reflected in situations where the defendant has reported that the evidence was unlawfully gathered. When the way the evidence is obtained is cast into doubt, the judges, again, are reluctant to open an enquiry that might lead to the thorough examination of the insulated investigative practices.[154]

The courts are supposed to be the locus where justice is upheld, denouncing evils and appraising morality. This is particularly true to the Chinese scenario, in that the educational function of trials lies at their heart. With this in mind, the trial is meant to be a process of moral communication with both the defendant and the public at large. However, when a court refuses to call witnesses to testify, disguising the reality that the evidence constructed by the police might be unreliable or might have been obtained in an inappropriate or unlawful manner, its moral authority is undermined. It is also trapped in the moral dilemma that the court condones potentially illegal behaviours by the police while simultaneously condemning the unlawful conduct of the defendant.[155] Judicial integrity, in this regard, is seriously compromised and public confidence eroded. It would be hard to put faith in the judicial system because the courts fail to look into wrongdoing by the authorities and refuse to vindicate harms caused to the accused. As a result, the lack of moral legitimacy may bring the administration of justice into disrepute.[156]

[154] Interview GAJ-4. In relation to the discussion of unlawfully obtained evidence, see ch 3.

[155] A Ashworth and M Redmayne, *The Criminal Process*, 4th edn (Oxford University Press, 2014) 346.

[156] The argument of judicial integrity was articulated in the Canadian case of *R v Grant* (2009) SCC 32.

Without witnesses to be cross-examined, more sophisticated examination skills (such as impugning witnesses) have not been adopted as the art of advocacy in Chinese courtrooms.[157] Judges are short of relevant knowledge to preside over sophisticated cross-examinations. To prevent the defence from discrediting the prosecution witness publicly at trial, requests advanced by the defence would often be dismissed on the grounds that bringing the witness to court would mislead the court.[158] Such an official pretext is risible and unconvincing. As a more pragmatic solution, judges often suggest that the prosecutor conduct further investigation in relation to a disputed witness.[159] In doing so, the challenge from the defence has been tactically converted into refined prosecution evidence.

> Defence lawyer: In a white-collar case I got a clue about getting some information that would be useful for our client. So, we approached the witness and took a statement from the witness. We presented the witness's statement to the court before the trial. However, the court did not subpoena the witness to the court. On the contrary, the court exposed the evidence to the prosecution and asked the prosecutor to check the witness's statement. Therefore, it is mainly about how the prosecution would examine the evidence unilaterally. Only when the prosecutor has approved the evidence may the court admit the evidence.[160]

On the other hand, judges' preference for written statements could be seen as a consequence of the long-term internal review mechanism of the judiciary. As previously noted, the judges who heard the trial were not the ones who ultimately decided the case. This kind of inner-working practice could only work effectively with written documentation, which enabled the court leaders to repeatedly scrutinise the case and arrive at a settled decision. Compared to witnesses' oral testimonies, the static, documentary records are better suited to hierarchical review within the institution. Information extracted from particular oral testimonies, the demeanour of witnesses and verbal exchanges between the opposing parties is difficult to convey to the superiors. As a result, the individualised experience of trial judges is downplayed and removed from the collective decision representing the court.

The internal review mechanism of the courts, which rejects decisions based on an individualised justificatory ground, was compatible with the corroboration rule, which focuses on the ostensible coupling of evidence, as discussed in chapter three. The more pieces of evidence that exhibit conspicuous episodes connecting the purported case facts, the greater the weight that will be attached to the evidence

[157] This is similar to the unfavourable and hostile witnesses in English evidence law. See s 3 of the Criminal Procedure Act 1865, s 6 of the Civil Evidence Act 1995 and s 119 of the Criminal Justice Act 2003.

[158] Interview CDL-3.

[159] Interviews ADL-1 and CDL-3.

[160] Interview ADL-1.

and the more likely that the facts in question will be regarded as the truth.[161] The propriety of the bureaucratic scrutiny is to evaluate the facts in accordance with this perceptibly objective standard of corroboration. The facts recognised by the court are established through evidence alignment, by identifying the correlation of the statements and the cohesion between the different pieces of evidence in the case dossier. As long as the purported facts demonstrated in different pieces of evidence are consistent, and keywords and details are perfectly matched, there is no point in recoursing to the trial judge's inner conviction to decide whether the charged facts are beyond reasonable doubt. The constructed version of the facts in the dossier that was internally approved has then become the judicially recognised truth.

> Judge: What is important in China is that the evidence must be corroborated so that a chain of proof can be established. The effect of this kind of proof system is that it can be examined and checked repeatedly. Therefore, if you see it you will make a conclusion; if I see it I will make the same conclusion. [That is] the mechanism of the control of judicial power in China. It emphasizes the repeatable examination of the same judicial result. It (the system) is based on this.[162]

> Judge: We cannot just believe what they (the witnesses) said in person. We have to review other evidence. If what they have said in the police station was confirmed to be true, we have to admit their previous statements. If the witnesses' statements and other evidence, such as the real evidence, can corroborate the defendant's confession, we have to admit what they said in the statements instead of what they said in person (in court). The most crucial thing is that the fact must be ascertained by the chain of evidence. If the witnesses' statements and other evidence are against the defendant, we will make a decision which is detrimental to the defendant.[163]

As noted in chapter three, to convict the defendant, the *corpus delicti* must be clear and the incriminating evidence should be 'reliable and sufficient' (*queshi chongfen*). The element of reliability and sufficiency (*queshi chongfen*) requires that evidence adduced to prove the charged facts must be lawfully obtained and corroborated

[161] Cai Yuanpei, 'Lun Yinzheng yu xinzheng zhi ronghe: Yinzheng moshi de loudong jiqi mibu (The Merging between Corroboration and Ascertainment: The Loophole of the Corroboration Rule and Its Solution)' (2016) 3 *Legal Science* 171; Zuo Weimin, 'Yinzheng zhengmin moshi fansi yu chongsu: Jiyu zhongguo xingshi cuoan de fansi (Rethink and Recast of the Corroboration Rule: Rethink about the Miscarriages of Justice)' (2016) 1 *Legal Science* 162; Yang Jiwen, 'Yinzheng zhengming de lixing jiangou: Cong xingshi cuoan zhili lunzheng chufa (Construction of Corroboration Rule: From the Argument of Miscarriages of Justice)' (2016) 6 *Law and Social Development* 173; Zhou Hongbo, 'Zhongguo xingsh yinzheng lilun pipan (Criticism over the Corroboration Rule)' (2015) 6 *Legal Studies* 136; Long Zongzhi, 'Xingshi yinzheng zhengmin xintan (Exploration of the Corroboration Rule)' (2017) 2 *Legal Studies* 149; Luo Weipeng, 'Yinzheng yu zuijia jieshi tuili: Xingshi zhengming moshi de duoyuan fazhan (Corroboration and IBE: The Pluralistic Development of Criminal Proof)' (2017) 5 *Jurists* 117; Mou Lvye, 'Lun feifazhengju paichu guize he yinzheng zhengming moshi de chongtu ji mihe lujing (The Conflict between Exclusionary Rule of Inappropriately Obtained Evidence and Corroboration Rule and Its Solution)' (2017) 29 *Peking University Law Review* 1068.

[162] Interview ATJ-1.

[163] Interview GAJ-1.

by other evidence.[164] The law casts confession evidence in a suspicious light.[165] Confessions are seen as a class of evidence that has inherent defects and the law has looked towards corroboration as a means of redress to enhance their reliability. Thus, no conviction can be sustained on the basis of confession evidence alone and the facts ascertained must be proved beyond reasonable doubt.[166] Although corroboration appears to be an obvious remedy for the potential risk of false confessions, the efficacy of the corroboration rule employed by the current system cannot be overstated. As discussed previously, the law does not specify to what extent the evidence must be corroborated, or whether the supporting evidence should come from an independent source. The corroboration rule also fails to clarify whether confessions can be corroborated by the facts mentioned by the accused in the course of the interrogation if these facts could have been known only to the perpetrator of the crime as a result of her participation in it. The practice in site A was that confessions can be relied upon to secure a conviction, so long as *some* of its details are matched by other types of evidence.[167]

> Judge: If the details of one piece of evidence are shown in another piece of evidence, the evidence is corroborated. The details may not be exactly the same, for example, the time. That is because the witness and the defendant may have different perceptions. As long as they are roughly matched and it is convincing. For example, if the victim said his phone was stolen and gave a description of the phone. If the detail of the phone could be reflected in the defendant's confession and he also confessed how he stole the phone, he could be convicted.[168]

Another weakness of the corroboration rule is that it does not require the supporting evidence to have come from an independent source. Thus, the so-called 'self-corroborating confession' can be employed to prove the guilt of the defendant; it allows the facts known only to the defendant as a result of her participation in the crime to be admitted as supporting evidence.[169] This implies that evidence derived from confessions (such as the identification of the crime scene) can be used as the supporting evidence to bolster up the confessions in question.[170] Taking such a *sine qua non* into account, this rule seems to impose an unacceptably low threshold on the part of the prosecution. I have shown in chapter three that some of the confession evidence was constructed in such a way that it has almost become

[164] See Art 200 of CPL 2018. The reliability and sufficiency of the evidence is explained in Art 55 of CPL 2018, which elucidates that 'all facts leading to the conviction and sentencing should be proved; the inculpatory evidence is proved to be true based upon legal procedure, and the guilty fact has been proved beyond reasonable doubt on the basis of the overall evidence adduced'.

[165] CPL 2018, Art 55.

[166] See Art 55 of CPL 2018.

[167] This was found in almost all the dossiers at site A during my period of observation. The evidence of the accused's confession forms the crucial part of the dossier (Field notes APU-17, 18 and 22). Without confessions from the accused, the prosecution's case would usually fall apart, as other types of evidence cannot meaningfully prove alleged crimes. This is also shown in McConville et al (n 8) 70–97.

[168] Interview GAJ-2.

[169] The detail of the self-corroborating confession, ibid.

[170] See ch 3.

imperative that it is dovetailed with witnesses' accounts to begin with. The corroboration rule has been internalised to guide the police and the prosecution on how to construct evidence. In this context, it affords little meaningful protection to the accused.

A close examination of the case dossiers in site A shows that the level of corroboration manifested was far from sufficient. Of all the monitored cases (64), about one-third (21) had no evidence other than the defendant's confessions to prove that it was the defendant who committed the crime. In other words, the uncorroborated defendant's confessions were the only evidence that proved the identity of the offender in the case. Although other evidence might have proved that the crime happened, it possessed no information that could connect the defendant to the crime. Interestingly, there were two cases in which the witness statements contained noticeable contradictions. In one of the cases, two witnesses described how the crime (an assault) happened. However, some of the details about the offender were disputed by another witness.[171] In the other case, the victim and the defendant disagreed on one of the criminal transactions.[172] Yet, the issued judgments stated that all these cases had satisfied the corroboration rule and provided no detailed explanation to address any of the inconsistencies or inadequacy of corroboration. In cases that contained an expert's report, the judgments always made it specific that the expert report constituted corroboration. Most of the expert reports only proved to be the peripheral issue of the case (such as an assessment of the value of the stolen items in a theft case). Some of them were relevant to the crime (such as an expert opinion on the degree of personal injury), but none of the expert's statements were pertinent to the involvement of the defendant in the offence. With no exception, the police's statement that described how the arrest was carried out (*zhuahuo jingguo*) was mentioned in the judgments as evidence that supported the defendant's confessions. It was regarded by the court as part of the proving of the chain of evidence, even though it had no immediate bearing on the commission of the crime in most instances.[173]

IV. Managerialism and Abbreviated Trials

Alongside the courts' preference for written dossiers, the managerialism in Chinese criminal justice is amongst the most salient reasons accounting for

[171] One of the cases (*CASEA* 2) involved an assault of a man in a market. According to one witness, the victim and the accused had a fierce argument before the assault took place. However, according to the victim, he (the victim) did not say anything when the accused hit him.

[172] This case (*CASEA* 12) was about illegal trading in receipts, in which the victim stated that the transaction occurred twice, whilst the defendant maintained that the transaction took place only once.

[173] This is reflected in a number of judgments that I saw in the field. Without giving detailed reasons why the evidence was believed to be corroborated, in all the judgments of convicted cases, almost in a set format, the judge wrote 'the court believes that the fact is clear and the evidence is reliable and sufficient, the evidence is corroborated'.

witnesses' absence. Managerialism, as a set of organisational practices that emphasise efficiency and rapid turnover,[174] is not just a criminal justice policy; it has taken over the criminal justice system, becoming a predominant institutional culture. With a growing number of criminal cases year on year,[175] efficiency and case closure rates (*jie'anlv*) have been relentlessly emphasised in the last few years. Since 2012, the number of cases that have been disposed of via the defendant's guilty pleas has steadily risen.[176] From 2013 onwards, over 50 per cent of the criminal cases were processed by simplified procedures.[177] The expedited procedure was incorporated in CPL 2018 to fast-track minor offences carrying a penalty of less than three years' imprisonment, causing a greater expansion of guilty plea procedures. There is no need to call witnesses to the trial if it has been settled that the defendant pleads guilty. Confessions and the case dossier are sufficient for the conviction, and the court hearing is nothing but a paper-based trial.

Currently, two forms of abbreviated trial procedures are officially enacted, namely the simplified procedure (*jianyi chengxu*) and the expedited procedure (*sucai chengxu*).[178] The simplified procedure, as the only trial procedure based on guilty pleas before 2018, was introduced by CPL 2012. It was grafted and reformulated from a less frequently used summary trial under the framework of CPL 1996, allowing a lesser sentence to be imposed in exchange for the defendant's admission of her guilt.[179] It has been widely applied to cases where the defendant has no dispute over the facts and admits her guilt. As the law stands, the simplified procedure only applies to cases tried in the basic courts,[180] where the majority of cases are channelled and disposed of by this means. Approximately 72 per cent of the prosecution cases in site A were tried by the simplified procedure in the first instance. My interviews with legal actors from wider geographical areas of China confirmed this general trend of application in the basic courts.[181]

Key to the simplified procedure is efficiency. In the courtrooms in site A, it was a normal practice for a judge to try 5–10 guilty plea cases in one sitting, with each case lasting between 5 and 20 minutes.[182] Cases were disposed of as if on a

[174] A Freiberg, 'Managerialism in Australian Criminal Justice: RIP for KPIs' (2005) 31 *Monash University Law Review* 12, 14.

[175] See *China Yearbooks 1986–2017* (China Year Book Press, multiple years: 1986–2017). Between 1986 and 2016, there were only two occasions when the number of cases received by the courts was lower than the previous year: 1987 and 2013. In 1986, the courts accepted 461,778 criminal cases. This number was nearly halved in 1987 (289,614). In 2012, the criminal courts received 996,611 criminal cases, and this number dropped to 971,567 in 2013.

[176] See *China Yearbooks 1987–2017* (China Year Book Press, multiple years: 1987–2017).

[177] Noticeably, in 2014, the percentage reached 62.2% (520,555). *China Yearbook 2015* (China Year Book Press, 2015) 1019.

[178] It is also translated as the fast-track sentencing procedure.

[179] Chen Guangzhong, *Annotations and Comments on the Revised Arts of the Criminal Procedure Law of the People's Republic of China* (People's Courts Press, 2012) 292–94.

[180] See Arts 208–213 of CPL 2012.

[181] Interviews APS-1, GAJ-2 and 3 and FTJ-1.

[182] This is based on my observations of court trials. Field notes APU-29, 33, 35–39 and 40–47.

fast-operating conveyor belt. The simplified procedure did not require the judge to delve into the defendant's voluntariness in relation to the admission of guilt prior to CPL 2018.[183] As soon as the defendant pleaded guilty, the case would reach the ultimate issue of sentencing expeditiously, no matter how the guilty plea was procured and whatever consequence it meant to the accused. This guilty plea procedure under the 2018 regime is now conditional upon the defendant having previously been afforded an opportunity to take legal advice and the defendant and the legal advisor both signing the recognisance to plead guilty and accept the sentence.[184] Albeit this safeguard seemingly ensures the voluntariness of the defendant in accepting the simplified procedure, the under-resourced and overloaded legal aid scheme and the poor quality service they provided were identified in empirical research and indicated that their 'valid' choice may not be an informed decision.[185]

With the minimal time spent on each case, the trial procedure was significantly condensed. A simplified trial started from checking the basic information of the defendant, after which the judge would ask the defendant whether or not she wished to plead guilty.[186] Once a positive response was confirmed, the prosecutor would read out the Bill of Prosecution, which consisted of a brief description of the defendant's alleged criminal conduct and the charge(s) of the defendant. This was followed by an abridged courtroom investigation, which involved the adducing of evidence. This part of the hearing, in most instances, was about the prosecutor selectively reading out the contents of the evidence in the case dossier. With a simplified format, her reading was often reduced to a catalogue of the evidence, with no detailed information on the specific evidence. Courtroom debate was confined to a restatement of the positions of the parties. The prosecutor then suggested an appropriate sentence to be imposed on the defendant, taking into account the defendant's plea. At the end of the process, the defendant was routinely urged to give a final statement, expressing her remorse, pleading for leniency or proposing an opportunity to reform her life. The hearing was concluded with the judge's final remarks on the case in general, and informing the defendant of her right to appeal.[187]

[183] The defendant's voluntariness was not the prerequisite of the application of the simplified trial according to CPL 2012. This rule has now changed in CPL 2018. For more discussion, see ch 5. According to Art 4 of the Judicial Rule 2003, the defendant must voluntarily accept the application of the guilty plea procedure if it is applied by the court.

[184] CPL 2018, Art 174. For more discussion on this article, see ch 5.

[185] Li Yonghang, 'Renzui renfa congkuan zhidu xia de youxiao falv bangzhu wenti yanjiu (Research on Effective Defence in the Context of Leniency for A Guilty Plea)' (2019) 2 *Western China Law Review* 30, 38; Xiao Zhimin, 'Zhiban lvshi zhidu zai renzui renfa congkuan shiyu zhong de wanshan (The Improvement of the Duty Lawyer's Role in Leniency for A Guilty Plea)' (2019) 4 *Legal System and Society* 32.

[186] Alternatively, this question can be asked after the prosecutor reads out the Bill of Prosecution.

[187] This is summarised by my observations in the court trials in site A: Field notes APU-5, 32, 40, 46, 47, 50, 52, 53 and 56.

As if the simplified procedure has not been quick enough, an expedited procedure was introduced by CPL 2018 to facilitate the greater disposal of cases speedily. The cases eligible for the expedited procedure largely overlap with those for the simplified procedure; both procedures are applicable to cases where the defendant might be sentenced to imprisonment of not more than three years.[188] Compared to the simplified procedure, which has an abridged version of the fact ascertainment process, the expedited procedure enables a court to move almost directly to sentencing based on the defendant's guilty plea.[189] Most of the oral elements of the hearing have been stripped away in this fast procedure.[190] In this regard, expressed consent in the form of recognisance implies that the defendant has fully agreed to the fact of the case and every element of the charged offence, and carries the legal consequence that her right to challenge the prosecution case has been almost permanently revoked.[191] No courtroom investigation or debate is needed, and the judge will pronounce the judgment immediately after the court hearing.[192] The expedited procedure has a higher demand for fast delivery of the outcome. All the cases to be tried by the expedited procedure are expected to be processed within a short window of time at all stages. Thus, judges are given a turnover period of 10 days to close a guilty plea case.[193] Empirical research on the expedited procedure suggests that judgments rendered on the basis of guilty pleas have been standardised to facilitate rapid delivery of the result.[194]

There is no doubt that the guilty plea procedures are primarily concerned with processing convictions of people. In pursuing this goal, these procedures apparently contravene the corroboration rule, which requires confession evidence to be supported by other evidence. Article 55 of CPL 2018 states clearly that a person should not be convicted upon his confession alone uncorroborated by any other evidence. This suggests that those who were willing to confess and to plead guilty

[188] See Art 222 of CPL 2018.

[189] See Art 224 of CPL 2018.

[190] According to Art 224 of CPL 2018, the judge should take into account the defence lawyer's view and the defendant's final statement. However, such views are unlikely to influence the court's decision-making significantly – there is little time for the judge to deliberate, as she must deliver the judgment on the spot.

[191] As mentioned in ch 4, the accused can make a formal application to the criminal justice institution (usually the procuratorate) to withdraw the legal recognisance to plead guilty and accept the sentence. Once the recognisance is withdrawn, it can no longer be used to facilitate guilty plea procedures and the defendant cannot be awarded with the discount of sentence. However, the withdrawn recognisance can still be used as a piece of confession evidence to prove the guilt of the accused.

[192] See Art 224 of CPL 2018.

[193] For cases in which the sentence might be over 1 year's imprisonment, the turnover time is 15 days. See Art 225 of CPL 2018.

[194] Zhao Heng, 'Xingshi sucai shengxu shidian shizheng yanjiu (Empirical Research on Pilots of the Expedite Procedure)' (2016) 2 *China Criminal Law Magazine* 93; Li Bensen, 'Xingshi sucai chengxu de sifa zaizao (Judicial Re-invention of the Expedite Procedure)' (2016) 5 *China Criminal Law Magazine* 33; Liao Dagang and Bai Yunfei, 'Xingshi anjian sucai chengxu shidian yunxing xianzhuang shizheng fenxi: yi T shi bajia shidian fayuan wei yanjiu yangben (Empirical Analysis of the Operation of the Criminal Expedite Procedure: Based on the Sample of 8 Pilot Courts in T City)' (2015) 12 *Legal Application* 23.

could not be convicted unless or until other evidence of their guilt had been secured. In this regard, these abbreviated procedures have undermined the corroboration rule, creating an exception for cases in which the accused pleads guilty. Since guilty plea cases constitute the majority of criminal cases, the scope of application for the corroboration rule has been substantially reduced. In the guilty plea cases, the suspension of the corroboration rule altogether means that the only counterbalance against false confessions in those cases is the legal advice offered by the defence lawyer or the duty lawyer. Effective defence in this aspect plays a significant role in preventing miscarriages of justice. Whether this objective can be achieved ultimately relies on the sound operation of the legal aid system, which needs sufficient resources and a large number of well-trained and dedicated duty lawyers to function efficiently.

Although CPL 2018 allows the fact-finding process to be bypassed in expedited procedures, certain local courts in China take a more cautious approach and still require their judges to establish 'the clear and correct facts' during the court hearing.[195] Such practice seems to be contrary to the initial purpose of the law and blurs the distinction between the simplified procedure and the expedited procedure. The design of the expedited procedure was completely driven by efficiency and managerialism, with the objective of reducing delays and costs caused by the regimented fact-finding process for relatively minor offences.[196] On the practical level, the defendant has already confirmed her admission to the charged offence as an exchange for a sentence discount. With the defendant and her defence lawyer having no intention to challenge the prosecution case, any further inquiry into the case facts is merely a waste of time. As far as the defendant is concerned, the main focus of the hearing is sentencing: what type of sentence will she get; how long will she lose her liberty; and whether her sentence discount can be fairly and honestly honoured. Accordingly, the court should allow evidence in relation to the defendant's sentence to be adduced, pertinent issues to be brought and relevant debate to be conducted in order to mete out an appropriate sentence. This issue, unfortunately, has so far been ignored both in the criminal justice literature and in practice.

Another matter of concern that has arisen from the guilty plea procedures is the perception that judges believe most defendants are guilty, which may affect their ability to make a neutral decision based on the facts of a case. As noted in chapter three, some of the low-level crimes (such as theft, drug trafficking, assault and dangerous driving) were particularly targeted and constituted the bulk of the criminal cases.[197] The majority of these cases are now channelled into the two forms of guilty plea procedures. A feature of the 'craftsmanship' of the case dossier

[195] Interviews GAJ-2, GTJ-1 and GAJ-3.

[196] J Daum, 'A Bargain at Twice the Speed' (China Law Translate, 21 December 2015) www.chinalawtranslate.com/en/a-bargain-at-twice-the-speed/ (accessed 18 July 2018).

[197] This is not only based upon my observations in site A, but also interviews (ATJ-1, FTJ-1, GAJ-2, GAJ-3) in other regions of China.

in China is that it tended to standardise the crime types. Hence, cases sharing the same crime type ended up with a similar narrative format and repeated categories of evidence.[198] As a result, adjudication became a highly standardised routine. For many judges, the criminal cases that they habitually heard lost their uniqueness; and defendants, no matter how their life circumstances varied, were treated like human shells. Many judges apparently acquired the ability to anaesthetise their hearts when trying a case. They made decisions in their official capacity that may be fundamentally different from those they would make as individuals.[199] In the following courtroom conversation, the judge did not make any effort to disguise his lack of interest in hearing the final statement of the defendant.

> Defendant: I wrote a statement of remorse. Can I read it out? It shows my deep reflection during this period of detention.
>
> Judge: You can read out your remorse. How long is it? ... Don't read it all. Just pick out the most important parts.
>
> Defendant: [Starting to read his confession] I brought harm to the victim and I will voluntarily undertake the punishment imposed on me. I will be a reformed person after this trial ...
>
> Judge: [Interrupting the defendant abruptly] That's enough. The trial is over.[200]

The courts have to make sure that their backlog of cases are moving quickly. Since the judicial reform was initiated in 2015, one of the key performance indicators adopted by the courts in China is the closure rate (*jie'anlv*). It measures the percentage of judgments that have been delivered within the prescribed turnover period.[201] In monitoring the rate, a 'traffic light' case management system has been prevalently employed by many courts to prompt their judges to dispose of cases in a timely manner. Thus, a yellow prewarning signal would remind judges that a case is approaching the deadline; and a red warning signal means that a case has missed the deadline. Like the former Appraisal System, the closure rate is tied up to bonuses and individual judges' career prospects.[202] To fulfil the target, judges

[198] Field notes APU-39 and 40.

[199] Damaška (n 58) 19.

[200] I commonly saw such interruptions from the judge during my observations. Field note APU-56.

[201] Wang Lingfang, 'Jixiao kaoping mang, sikan jieanlv (Busy Appraisals and Reviewing the Closure Rates)', *China Court* (21 January 2019) www.chinacourt.org/Art/detail/2019/01/id/3710203.shtml (accessed 23 March 2019); The Supreme People's Court, 'Diyi jidu quanguo fayuan jieanlv tongbi zengjia 4.02% (In the First Quarter of the Year the Closure Rate Has Increased 4.02% Compared to Last Year)' *China News* (7 May 2018) www.chinanews.com/gn/2018/05-07/8508164.shtml (accessed 23 March 2019).

[202] Chen Jin, 'Lingbao fayuan shixian 2019 nian jieanlv shouyue kaimenhong (The Lingbao Court Has Fulfilled the Work Target of Closure Rate in the First Month of 2019' (Sanmenxia Intermediate People's Court, 1 February 2019) www.smxzy.hncourt.gov.cn/public/detail.php?id=14556 (accessed 23 March 2019); The Supreme People's Court, 'Hubei fayuan banan zhengti zhixiao chixu xianghao jieanlv 99.8% (The General Trends of Case Processing of Hubei Courts Are Excellent, with a Closure Rate of 99.8%)' (accessed 12 February 2019) www.news.sina.com.cn/sf/news/fzrd/2019-02-12/doc-ihrfqzka5059827.shtml (accessed 23 March 2019); 'Xiji fayuan jianlv lianxu sannian ju quanqu jiceng fayuan shouwei (The Xiji Court Topped the Closure Rate amongst All the Basic Courts in the Region

have to keep on top of their workload and case progression, and not to be delayed by adjournments, even though there might be a good reason for doing so.

Before the duty lawyer scheme was formally introduced by CPL 2018, only a small fraction of cases were represented by defence lawyers in simplified trials. The defence lawyers could do little to reverse the conviction outcome or the sentence decision when the defendant entered a guilty plea. With regard to sentencing, the court was faithfully compliant with the procuratorate's recommendations.[203] There was little elbow room for the defence to work in favour of their client.[204] Despite the predetermined trial decisions, a group of defence lawyers in site A were 'specialised' in representing guilty plea cases. With little preparation, their defence strategy, however, seemed to be restricted to the elaboration of the hardship of the defendants, who were almost invariably low-paid and poorly educated, but were dedicated to family obligations.[205] Unfortunately, these personal circumstances had little relevance to the defendant's criminal responsibility. Therefore, they were seldom accepted by the court in relation to mitigation.[206]

> Defence lawyer: Please do consider that the defendant has written a letter of apology. His parents are very poor peasants and they are not in good health. They are in need of a carer …
>
> Judge: [Interrupting the defence] Defence lawyer, make your statement brief![207]

Such a defence strategy can be understood against the general background of the system in which an acquittal is tremendously difficult to achieve.[208] On this note, challenging the prosecution case can be extremely demanding, or can even be deemed not worthwhile by some defence lawyers. However, the difference between risk aversion and confusion of roles should be noted. In interviews with some defence lawyers, I found that a small number of defence lawyers shared a presumption of guilt and had an equivocal or even negative attitude towards their clients.[209] The high conviction rate apparently played a role in the ambivalence of

for Consecutive 3 Years)' (Ningxia Courts, 18 January 2019) www.nxfy.gov.cn/xwzx/2018fyyw/201901/t20190118_4572997.html (accessed 23 March 2019).

[203] Field notes APU-32 and 49.

[204] Based upon my observations in site A, only 15% of guilty plea cases were represented. Currently I have no data for other regions in China. However, I believe this to be a fair assumption because the defendant who is not represented is more likely to plead guilty.

[205] This is shown in a few cases that I observed when the prosecutor interrogated the suspect. For example, in *CASEA* 23, the accused complained that the defence lawyer did not support him to 'tell the fact' whereby he denied the guilty charge but, rather, focused on his cooperative attitude. In another case, *CASEA* 33, the accused told the prosecutor that his defence lawyer had asked him to 'confess truthfully' rather than 'arguing the unnecessary minor details', including the inconsistences of the witness's statements, so that he could obtain mitigation.

[206] This is also noted in McConville et al (n 8) 320.

[207] Field note APU-5.

[208] Sida Liu and Terence C Halliday, *Criminal Defence in China: The Politics of Lawyers at Work* (Cambridge University Press, 2016) ch 3.

[209] See also McConville et al (n 8) 318.

defence lawyers' perception. Ironically, one of the successful defence lawyers with an excellent record of defending major cases openly endorsed the presumption:

> Defence lawyer: The police will initiate the investigation only when the suspect's conduct is highly suspicious. For example, many fraud cases are not investigated by the police because these cases are not up to the standard of requiring investigation. There are many criminal cases that are not investigated. For those cases that are investigated, most of them are certainly criminal acts and the defendants are guilty. That is why there are very few acquittals. There are some miscarriages of justice, but they are exceptional. The best thing they (the accused) should do is to tell the truth and plead guilty.[210]

It would be hard to imagine that the defendant could resist the pressure from her own defence lawyer when making the big decision as to whether or not to plead guilty.[211] When the defence lawyer's efforts are directed towards persuading the accused to plead guilty, the defendant has little chance to dispute the disposition of her case in which a consensus has been reached by the other courtroom actors. This role confusion could potentially be a pitfall for the accused to plead guilty to a charge of which she may be innocent. Against the backdrop of the comprehensive duty lawyer scheme at the pretrial stage, there is a real concern that defence lawyers who are affiliated with the criminal justice institutions (such as detention centres and the procuratorate) may not diligently check the legal constituents of the charge and the available defences or robustly test the correctness of a plea.[212] According to CPL 2018, the trial judge must now confirm that the defendant admits guilt, accepts punishment and agrees with the application of the expedited procedure before initiation of the abbreviated procedure.[213] However, if the defendant was inadequately informed and misled to believe that pleading guilty is the only choice, an affirmative answer to these questions at the beginning of the expedited procedure means nothing other than the capitulation of the defendant.

V. The Full Adjudication: Trial without Witnesses

With the vast majority of minor offences being expected to be processed by the abbreviated procedures, the full adjudication, or the ordinary procedure, is supposed to be employed mainly to deal with complicated, serious offences or other cases that cannot be justifiably disposed of via a simple guilty plea. The ordinary trial procedure can be broken down into five sections: the opening section;

[210] Interview ADJ-1.

[211] This finding is very similar to the defence practice in England and Wales, see McConville et al, *Standing Accused* (Clarendon Press, 1994).

[212] This concern is also intimated in Han Xu, '2018 nian xingsufazhong renzui renfa congkuan zhidu (The System of Leniency for Pleading Guilty and Accepting Punishment in CPL 2018)' (2019) 1 *Rule of Law Research* 35, 37.

[213] See Art 222 of CPL 2018.

the courtroom investigation; debate; the defendant's final statement; and the court's final remarks. The trial procedure starts with a brief formalised introduction, in which the defendant's background information and her rights at the trial are checked and pronounced. After that, evidence from both parties is produced and contested. The defendant and summoned witnesses, if there are any, would be questioned and cross-examined.[214] The parties then argue their legal views, focusing on the main issues, and this is followed by the final statement of the defendant, expressing her remorse or pleading for leniency.[215] The trial draws to a conclusion with the court's final remarks.

The ordinary procedure, as the most formal proceedings that the criminal justice system can offer, is sometimes assumed to be conducted in an aggressive form of questioning and cross-examination. Such dramatic confrontation between the prosecution and the defence, however, is not often seen in real life. The vast majority of trials that took place in site A, for instance, were rather prosaic. There were no witnesses to be cross-examined, and the court hearing was essentially about presenting the written statements in the case dossier.[216] The evidence adduced by the prosecutor often included the interrogation records, statements taken from witnesses, expert conclusions, autopsy reports, photographs of the crime scene, etc.[217] About 60 per cent of defendants that appeared at trial in site A were not represented by defence lawyers. Of those defendants who were represented, only a small number effectively challenged the prosecution case. As a result, most of the court hearings were tightly controlled, devoid of heated debate or courtroom drama.

Differing from adversarial trials in common law countries, where scientific evidence and the testimony of scientific experts play a vital role, there is no forensic tradition in China. In many cases, forensic evidence presented in the form of the expert's conclusion in basic courts were disappointingly perfunctory. The court proceedings were entirely paper-based. Even with important evidence, such as a weapon discovered at the crime scene, the evidence that was adduced at trial was not in its original form, but rather a documentary reproduction.[218] The production of expert evidence usually entailed the prosecutor reading out the final conclusion of a report shrouded by scientific jargon. No explanation as to the materials provided, the methodology employed or the way the conclusion was reached was offered. Nor did the prosecutor provide any extracts of literature or materials that might assist the defence or the court in understanding the analysis.[219] These expert

[214] See Art 192 of CPL 2012.

[215] This is summarised by my observations in the court trial in site A: Field notes APU-5, 32, 40, 46, 47, 50, 52, 53 and 56.

[216] Field notes APU-46, 47, 48, 50, 51 and 53.

[217] Field notes APU-46, 47, 48 and 50.

[218] Field notes APU-46, 47, 50 and 54; Interviews APS-1, 2, 3 and 6.

[219] Field notes APU-46, 47, 48 and 50.

reports were simply announced in an authoritative manner before being fully accepted by the court.

> Prosecutor: Yesterday's trial was so long-winded. I had such a thick dossier and I read statement after statement. The judicial assessor told me that I should have prepared a cup of tea to keep myself awake.[220]

> Prosecutor: It was a case with lots of thick volumes of the dossier. The court borrowed a trolley from the supermarket to carry the dossiers. There were three trolleys! I had to read the evidence out in the court, which made my throat so sore.[221]

> Prosecutor: I have to admit that if I listen to a case tried by the ordinary procedure that is not prosecuted by myself, I would doze off easily. I understand why some judges fall asleep in court.[222]

Before CPL 2018 came into force, the proportion of defendants who were represented in court in China was small: Ira Belkin estimated this to be only about 20 per cent.[223] The traditional legal aid scheme covers a limited category of criminal cases,[224] and retaining a defence lawyer was often too expensive for defendants.[225] For defendants who come from the lower social classes, the lawyer's fee is simply unaffordable. In a sample of 144 defendants (involved in 120 criminal cases) tried in the basic court in site A, only 24 defendants (involved in 19 cases) were assisted by defence lawyers in the ordinary procedure.[226] These cases represented by defence lawyers were concentrated on 'white collar' crimes – bribery and embezzlement in particular. The ratio of representation in the intermediate court was significantly higher; here, the defendants were entitled to free counsel due to the seriousness of their cases (which carry a penalty of death or life imprisonment).[227] It is to be seen how the duty lawyer scheme will change the status quo in the future.

> Judge: Only 10% to 20% of defendants are represented (in site A) … Those economic crime cases have more defence lawyers involved. For most theft and robbery cases, the defendants are usually in a very bad financial situation. They cannot afford a lawyer.

[220] Field note APU-63.

[221] Field note APU-48.

[222] Field note APU-46.

[223] It is estimated that roughly 80% of defendants in China are not represented by counsel at all. See I Belkin, 'China's Tortuous Path Toward Ending Torture in Criminal Investigation' in M McConville and E Pils (eds), *Comparative Perspectives on Criminal Justice in China* (Edward Elgar, 2013) 97.

[224] According to Art 34 of CPL 2012 (Art 35 of CPL 2018), only juvenile cases, or cases in which the defendant has limited or no capacity, is blind, deaf or dumb, or might be sentenced to life imprisonment or the death penalty, can be appointed a free defence lawyer by the state. However, in a particular province in the East of China, the legal aid scheme covers a much wider remit. According to my interviews in site G, all the defendants in the second instance trial are appointed with defence lawyers (Interviews GAJ-1, 2, 3 and 4).

[225] In site A, a less well-developed area in China, a defence lawyer charges 10,000 yuan (about £1000) minimum per case. Interview GAJ-3.

[226] This sample was drawn from the criminal court (including juvenile cases) between June and July 2012. This figure is similar to the finding of McConville et al (n 8) 293.

[227] As mentioned in n 72, a defendant who is likely to be sentenced to life imprisonment or the death penalty should be appointed a duty lawyer by the state. However, no official data were accessible to the researcher.

> All juvenile cases are represented.[228] Apart from those cases, most defence lawyers are retained privately by the defendant or his family.[229]

Since most defendants were not represented, the strength between the prosecution and the defendant was severely unbalanced. The defendants sometimes sought advice from other inmates during detention, which could be misleading. With no support from the legal professionals, these defendants were extremely vulnerable in court. The following excerpt from a courtroom observation is an example of the typical responses of an unrepresented defendant.

> (A case of provocation and disturbance.)
>
> Judge: Defendant, do you have any evidence to adduce.
>
> Defendant: [Behaving confused] I don't know … No.
>
> Judge: All the prosecution evidence is legally gathered and they have followed the legal procedure. It is objective and genuine. The court will admit all the evidence that has been adduced by the prosecutor. Now we move on to the court debating.
>
> …
>
> Judge: Defendant, do you have any opinions regarding your conviction of the crime?
>
> Defendant: No.
>
> Judge: Prosecutor, do you have a sentencing suggestion?
>
> Prosecutor: Since the defendant has confessed his guilty behaviour honestly, we suggest Article 67(3) of criminal law should also be applied. Based on all these facts, we suggest the court sentence the defendant to the fixed-term imprisonment of between 6 months and 18 months.
>
> Judge: Defendant, do you have any opinions regarding your sentencing?
>
> Defendant: No.[230]

For cases in which the defendant was legally represented, the quality of the defence services varied, depending on the skill of the defence lawyers and the sense of responsibility of the individual. Mike McConville et al indicated that lawyers retained by the defendant or her family were found to be more diligent and proactive than defence lawyers appointed by the legal institutions.[231] My observation in

[228] According to Art 267 of CPL 2012, the court, the procuratorate and the police must appoint defence lawyers in juvenile cases if the suspect does not retain a private lawyer. It is noteworthy that the revised criminal procedure law has significantly improved the protection for the juvenile suspect, such as the legal aid scheme, the introduction of an appropriate adult and concealment of the suspect's criminal record. For relevant discussion, see S Persson, 'China Talks Juvenile Justice Reform: A Constructivist Case Study' (2014) *Columbia Public Law Research Paper* No 14-374.

[229] Interview ATJ-1.

[230] Field note APU-35.

[231] See McConville et al (n 8) 336. My observations at site A also indicated that retained defence lawyers were generally more active in pretrial preparations and were engaged in activities such as coming to the prosecutor's office to photocopy prosecution evidence and meeting with their clients. In comparison with appointed defence lawyers, retained defence lawyers were more strategic in court and were more persistent in pursuing sentence mitigations. Instead of merely pleading for leniency based upon the defendant's family background, the mitigation requests put forward by retained defence lawyers were usually more evidence-based, centring around facts such as that the defendant turned

site A confirmed the results. The pro bono nature of the legal aid work sometimes deprived legal aid lawyers of the enthusiasm to vigorously defend these vulnerable defendants. The regulation in relation to legal aid has made it compulsory for registered law firms to offer lawyers to advocate for defendants in the prescribed categories.[232] Given the pro bono nature of legal aid work, the defence lawyers were not funded. Quite often, they had no remuneration for their costs, such as travelling expenses.[233] There is no surprise that many defence lawyers were reluctant to take on legal aid cases. If they had to take on an allocated case, the preparation was often less than thorough. It has been observed that some of the performances by legal aid lawyers were below the expected standard.[234] This is worrying, because those who were entitled to benefit from the legal aid scheme before CPL 2018 were defendants who were particularly vulnerable in terms of their age, their physical or mental disability, or the draconian sentences they might have faced.

> Researcher: Are you paid for legal aid cases?
>
> Defence lawyer: No. It is our duty (to do the legal aid work) and we cannot charge fees. It is for the public benefit. It emphasises our duty to do so. So, we must make that sacrifice.[235]
>
> Judge: Defence lawyers are generally useless … Above all, the legal aid lawyers are the worst. They just come to finish off their work by pleading leniency. They cannot give any effective legal opinions in the court for most cases.[236]

Retained defence lawyers, on the other hand, possessed more resources and exhibited greater zeal and defence skills. If they were hired at an earlier stage of the process, they were able to prepare better and therefore had a greater opportunity to help their clients. Despite the advantage enjoyed by retained defence lawyers, the quality of the defence work varied. Whereas some defence lawyers engaged in proactive case preparation, and hence were able to proffer persuasive argument in the court, others acted in a more perfunctory manner. A majority of the defence lawyers observed in site A focused on the defendant's cooperative attitude, such as voluntary surrender, meritorious services or her good attitude in admitting her guilt.[237] These mitigating circumstances were valid defences. However, relying

herself in or had previously done legally recognised meritorious service: Field notes APU-41, 42, 44, 45, 52 and 54.

[232] See 'On Opinions on Lawyers Conducting Legal Aid Work' issued by the Ministry of Justice and Ministry of Finance [2017] No 15, www.gov.cn/gongbao/content/2017/content_5222957.htm (accessed 21 December 2018).

[233] See Legal Aid Regulations of People's Republic of China. According to Art 28 of the Legal Aid Regulations, a defence lawyer who refuses to accept legal aid cases without proper reason, or terminates legal aid cases without authorisation, may be subjected to admonishment or a suspension of licence. However, according to some defence lawyers, the government has started to subsidise their costs in recent years, albeit the funds are still very limited.

[234] McConville et al (n 8) 303–35.

[235] Interview ADL-1.

[236] Interview ATJ-1.

[237] Again, my research finding is very much in line with McConville et al's study, which found that many defence lawyers were found to be generally inactive at trial and were submissive to the prosecution

ceaselessly on these dispositions could hardly lay a solid foundation on which a defence strategy could be laid to engage with the prosecution case in an attempt to deconstruct it. In instances where the case dossier clearly indicated issues in relation to the way evidence was obtained, little effort was made to challenge the legality of the procedure or the admissibility of the prosecution evidence.[238]

The passivity of the defence lawyers, however, should be understood against the sociopolitical background, which is generally hostile to active defence lawyers. Over the years, active defence lawyers (especially those engaged with human rights) have learnt the limited role they are allowed to play in seeking justice and protecting rights in an authoritarian state.[239] Defence lawyers have limited avenues for gathering evidence without endangering themselves, and may face various restrictions on accessing the dossier. In robustly challenging the prosecution case, they may run the risk of retaliatory prosecution against themselves, or 'being disappeared' by the authorities.[240] Proactive advocacy may be treated as 'disturbing court order' if their defence strategy has vigorously challenged the authority of the prosecution. The mass crackdown on human rights lawyers initiated by the party-state in July 2015 was another damaging strike on what was already a weak community.[241] Defence lawyers have exposed themselves to these professional hazards purely because of their commitment to the legal values that they believe in and the fulfilment of their duty to defend the interests of their clients.[242] Certain scholars believe that it is an exaggeration to label Chinese defence lawyers as an 'endangered species'.[243] However, a number of high-profile cases have sent a clear message that 'no lawyer is safe from prosecution if she stands in the way of government conviction of alleged criminals'.[244] The Iron Triangle which dominates the criminal justice system does not appear ready for genuine openness or being challenged;[245] fighting alone in the adverse environment, without judicial independence or safeguards to a fair trial, is exceptionally tough.[246] Being an

and the court, with their main strategy being to enter a plea for leniency. See McConville et al (n 8) 317–50.

[238] Field notes APU-42, 44 and 65.

[239] See Fu Hualing and R Cullen, 'Climbing the Weiquan Ladder: A Radicalising Process for Rights-Protection Lawyers' (2011) 205(March) *The China Quarterly* 40; E Pils, '"Disappearing" China's Human Rights Lawyers' in McConville and Pils (n 223) 411–38; Sida Liu and Halliday (n 208) 157–70; JA Cohen, 'Politics and Criminal Justice', in McConville and Pils (n 223) 439–43; Lan Rongjie, 'Killing the Lawyer as the Last Resort: The Li Zhuang Case and its Effects on Criminal Defence in China' in McConville and Pils (n 223) 304–20.

[240] McConville (n 8) 411–38.

[241] Although defence lawyers and human rights lawyers can be seen as two different groups, the demarcation of the two communities is not always clear. Sida Liu and Halliday (n 208) 157–67; Fu Hualing and Han Zhu, 'After the July 9 (709) Crackdown: The Future of Human Rights Lawyering' (2018) 41 *Fordham International Law Journal* 1135.

[242] Sida Liu and Halliday (n 208) 45–88.

[243] Hou Shumei and R Keith, 'The Defence Lawyer in the Scales of Chinese Criminal Justice' (2011) 20 *Journal of Contemporary China* 379, 395.

[244] Lan Rongjie (n 239) 319.

[245] E Nesossi, 'Compromising for "Justice"? Criminal Proceedings and the Ethical Quandaries of Chinese Lawyers' in McConville and Pils (n 223) 256–75.

[246] Pils (n 239) 415.

outsider of the criminal justice system, the repressions have naturally provoked many defence lawyers to reflect on the vulnerability of the legal profession. Some of them who struggle to find a footing to defend their case effectively have chosen to take a quiescent stance. For the sake of self-preservation, they may have to embrace self-censorship and step away from zealous criminal advocacy.[247]

In this context, active defence strategies were not often seen in the courts. There were a few dedicated defence lawyers who strived to pursue the best possible result for their clients, but the outcomes of adjudication often fell short of their expectation due to the fact that decisions had already been predetermined. In *CASEA 64*, the defendant was accused of selling drugs to a drug user, who turned out to be a police informant.[248] The defence lawyer intended to exclude the defendant's confession, which was the key prosecution evidence, by arguing that the confession was elicited by torture. To prove the lawfulness of the interrogation procedure, the prosecutor produced a video recording of the interrogation, which was played at trial. The videoed interrogation, in which the accused admitted that he sold a substantial amount of heroin to the police informant, was suspiciously short. The defence lawyer then identified that the video recording was a rehearsed and truncated version of the police interrogation, based on the mismatched information of interrogation durations. The details of the video seemed to have supported what the defendant claimed initially, that is, that the confession was extorted by torture. There was a real hope that the disputed confession could be successfully excluded when hearing the arguments advanced at trial.

> Defence lawyer: The video recording was believed to be the record of the first interrogation. It only lasts 10 minutes and 8 seconds. According to the written record of interrogation, the interrogation should have lasted for two hours. From the video, we can see the cigarette, lighter and drug in the picture, which supports what the defendant said just now. The defendant made it very clear earlier that the police used the cigarette to entice him to make a confession. Besides that, the record of drug weight has no other evidence to support it. From what we saw on the video, the defendant had already signed the record when the interrogation was conducted. Therefore, we request the court to exclude the evidence.[249]

The final judgment, however, accepted the prosecution's viewpoint and ruled that the confession evidence was gathered lawfully and was reliable. The final judgment stated that the manipulation of the video recording was 'not convincing enough to exclude the confession evidence in question'.[250] According to the law, when an issue of illegally obtained evidence is raised (usually by the defence), it is incumbent upon the prosecution to prove beyond reasonable doubt that the disputed evidence is obtained lawfully.[251] Whilst the rhetoric appears auspicious for the

[247] Lan Rongjie (n 239) 319.

[248] This case was tried in October 2013 in site A, 10 months after CPL 2012 came into force.

[249] Field note APU-53.

[250] Field note APU-34.

[251] See Arts 56–58 of CPL 2018. Despite the burden to prove beyond reasonable doubt having been introduced by CPL 2012, it is rarely implemented in judicial practice. By the same token, it is highly

defendant, the judicial reality revealed the contrary. After a brief conversation with the prosecutor in charge of this case, I was informed that the outcome of the case was settled prior to the trial:

> Prosecutor: ... This case will be convicted for sure. If the judge was not going to convict the case, she would have communicated with me before the trial. It has been pre-decided, as most other cases are.[252]

The trial was, therefore, a formality in many cases, through which the predetermined outcome is transmitted and legitimised. In this sense, the old practice of 'verdict first and trial second' seems to have prevailed to date.[253] In a sample of 42 cases in site A in which the first instance judgments were scrutinised, I have compared the outcomes of the cases with the Bill of Prosecution (the charges and the sentence recommendation) (Table 1). It is not difficult to find that the decisions, both the verdict and the sentence, were in line with those suggested by the procuratorate in the majority of instances. There were four cases in which the defendants were charged with multiple offences that resulted in partial acquittal. For the remaining cases, the final verdicts of the court obediently followed the recommendation of the procuratorate, and the sentences imposed by the court were perfectly within the sentencing ranges proposed by the procuratorate.

Comparison of the outcomes of the judgments and the Bill of Prosecution in site A, June to September 2012

	n	%
Verdict:		
Total number of cases charged by the procuratorate	42	100
Cases partially convicted by the court	4	9.5
Cases convicted as the charge maintained in the Bill of Prosecution by the court	38	90.5
Sentencing:		
Total number of cases charged by the procuratorate	42	100
Sentence imposed within the recommended range suggested by the Bill of Prosecution	41	97.6
Sentence imposed beyond the recommended range of the Bill of Prosecution	1	2.4

Note: The sample of cases were randomly selected and monitored by the author during the period of observation. The judgments were all made by the basic court in site A. Of these cases, 12 cases were appealed by the defendant. However, the second instance judgments were unable to be tracked in this study.

doubtful whether the same standard of proof can be understood and applied by judges when dealing with the exclusionary rules.

[252] Field note APU-51.

[253] M McConville, 'Criminal Justice in China and the West' in McConville and Pils (n 223) 35.

Table 1 shows that acquittals had occurred if a defendant was charged with multiple offences. According to the prosecutors in site A, acquittals were tolerated by the Appraisal System and no sanction would be triggered as long as the defendant was convicted on at least one account of offence.[254] This suggests that the criminal justice system was designed to target individuals, rather than criminal offences. In this sense, crime control might not be an accurate model to capture the position of criminal justice practices. As we have seen so far, the system is operating on the principle that cases proceed with staged bureaucratic approvals of the previous phase's deliveries. After a person has been labelled as a suspect, the next process is to repeatedly confirm this deviant status. Trials are just another official statement to reaffirm the established deviant's identity.

Trials had not been a forum of information exchange in most instances, given that the prosecution monopolised the sources of evidence. The system has specifically been designed to allow the information to be channelled through and to flow from the prosecution. It is worth noting that the resource of information is not limited to the prosecution dossier. Whenever a doubt had arisen in relation to a certain issue and the judge required additional evidence to address the problem, the judge would send a private instruction to the prosecutor to gather further evidence.[255] Sometimes when the court felt that the evidence might get out of control, arrangements would be made to ensure that the court and the procuratorate had the ability to scrutinise the evidence in advance. This was demonstrated in situations when a controversial witness was requested by the defence lawyer to be cross-examined. On one occasion, the judge in site A responded to such a request by notifying the prosecutor in charge of the case to procure a written statement from the witness.[256] The prosecutor and the court apparently cooperated wholeheartedly. But such a seamless working relationship did not extend to the defence.

> Judge: After the prosecutors have sent us all of the dossiers, we would read the dossiers thoroughly many times. We may have further questions. If the questions cannot be resolved, we would ask the prosecutors to send further evidence to us … If we have any inquiries, they (the police and prosecutor) would respond immediately and give us a satisfactory answer.[257]

Interestingly, some defence lawyers indicated that since judges placed great trust in the prosecution evidence, mitigating evidence would be more easily admitted if they could persuade the prosecutor to accept certain 'harmless' defence evidence.[258] This defence technique was clearly premised on the fact that the main prosecution evidence was not undermined. Compared to the risk that the evidence adduced by

[254] Field note APU-46.
[255] Field note APU-31.
[256] The request was rejected because the witness was not available. Field note APU-31.
[257] Interview ATJ-2.
[258] Interview CDL-2.

the defence might be rejected by the court, diverting the defence evidence to the prosecution evidence could materially reduce the resistance from the court.

> Defence lawyer: The way the judge treats us is completely different from the way they treat the evidence of the prosecutors. If certain issues have been mentioned by the prosecutors, they will definitely be taken into account by the judge. However, if the prosecutors have not mentioned the exculpatory factors, it will be very hard for this to be admitted by the judge, as the judge does not listen to us … Therefore, once we have spoken to the prosecutors, these exculpatory facts would be accepted (by the judge).[259]

Due to the institutional relationship between the courts and the procuratorate, evidence was treated differently depending on the party it came from.[260] Whereas prosecution evidence would be routinely admitted and used as the basis for the judicial decision, evidence produced by the defence, if there was any, would be scrutinised through the strictest possible procedure.[261] As a component of the Iron Triangle, the courts in China play a role that is profoundly different from their counterparts in Western jurisdictions. Independence is absent in this context. Whilst the function of the court is defined as correctly enforcing the law, empirical evidence suggests that it largely translates into assisting the prosecution to convict the defendant in most instances.[262]

> Judge: In fact, in criminal cases, the prosecutor and the defendant are not on the same level. Apart from a few exceptional cases, we would admit the prosecutorial evidence automatically.[263]
>
> Researcher: Do you naturally believe the prosecution evidence?[264]
>
> Judge: No. Not naturally. But sometimes you have to believe it. If you don't believe it, you will have a lot of problems. If you do not believe it, what else can you do? Can you make an acquittal? It is not allowed within this legal system. Well, in most circumstances, it is unnecessary.[265]

In most countries, formal trials (especially jury trials) are the public face of the criminal justice system and a battleground for 'sharply contested affairs in which the case construction techniques used at earlier stages' of the criminal process.[266] Trials are important events loaded with hopes of finding the truth and embodying

[259] Interview CDL-1.
[260] See McConville et al (n 8) 358.
[261] For instance, a number of prosecutors reported that the evidence offered by defence lawyers was disregarded by the court without an explanation being provided: Interviews BDL-1, JDL-1, CDL-2 and CDL-3. This was confirmed by a judge during my interview, who divulged that evidence produced by the defence is usually not given credence unless it is subjected to severe scrutiny: Interview GAJ-4.
[262] See Art 7 of CPL 2012.
[263] Interview GAJ-3.
[264] This question was not designed as a leading question but, rather, was based upon the content of the conversation with the judge, who had, prior to this exchange, talked about her close relationship with the procuratorate: Interview ATJ-1.
[265] Interview ATJ-1.
[266] A Sanders et al, *Criminal Justice*, 4th edn (Oxford University Press, 2010) 554.

fairness and justice. This noble and dignified function has often been dismissed by the Chinese legal professionals, especially prosecutors and defence lawyers. On the part of prosecutors, a court hearing is nothing but a show to outsiders (including the audience, the defendant and the defence lawyer); the core to the outcome lies in their private communications with the judge. Since a conviction has been secured for most cases, the efficiency of the trial is paramount. This turned trials into pro forma exercises.

> Prosecutor: The trial is just a show! There is nothing substantial in it. I remember last time when I was in the trial and I hadn't started to give my prosecution speech, the judge suddenly knocked his judicial mallet and said 'now it is time to close the trial'. Just observe trials. They are so fast … The judges just want to finish the trial as fast as possible. Every time I go to the trial, I don't even prepare … If we want to secure the conviction, communicating with the judge is far more important than the trial.[267]

Defence lawyers are also aware of the symbolic nature of trials. As far as many defence lawyers are concerned, no matter how thorough they have prepared the case and what level of advocacy skills they have demonstrated, the final decision is beyond their control.[268] Defence lawyers have institutionally been discriminated against by judges and prosecutors. This is predominantly demonstrated in a series of direct confrontations between judges and 'die-hard' lawyers (*sike lvshi*).[269] In a number of publicised incidents, the defence lawyers have been abused, attacked and humiliated by the courts.[270] In a high-profile case[271] involving 17 defendants charged with criminal syndicates (*heishehui xingzhi zuzhi zui*), a heated bout of belligerent exchanges took place between the defence lawyers and the judges in the Guiyang People's Intermediate Court when debating whether the prosecution evidence was obtained legally. This conflict resulted in 20 defence lawyers being admonished and four of them being removed from the court.[272] As reported by defence lawyers on social media, their rights at trial have constantly been restricted and their arguments curbed in court. Some defence lawyers recounted their undignified experiences of being forced to subject to a vigorous search of their bodies and briefcases when entering courtrooms.[273] In certain regions of China,

[267] Field note APU-32, which was recorded on 26 July 2012, before CPL 2012 came into force.

[268] Interviews CDL-1, 2 and 3. See also McConville et al (n 8) 376.

[269] For some incidents involving the 'die-hard' lawyers, see Sida Liu and Halliday (n 208) 158.

[270] Many defence lawyers protested that they had to submit their bags and documents for security checks before they were allowed to enter the courtroom, whereas the prosecutors were not submitted to this procedure. Some defence lawyers also indicated that they were badly treated by the court guards, including violent assault, in the courtroom. See Shen Hong (lawyer), 'Micro Blog' (21 January 2014) www.weibo.com/shenhong1020 (accessed 21 January 2014).

[271] This case is also known as *Xiaohe* case.

[272] Zhou Ze, 'Xiaohe an sanzhounian yantaohui tongbao (Report on the Seminar of the 3rd Anniversary of on Xiaohe Case)' (China Citizens Movement, 2015) www.cmcn.org/archives/23494 (accessed 21 December 2017).

[273] 'Weihu lvshi zunyan chenggongshi, Wuhan lvshi jin fating buzhun soushen (It Should Be a Consensus That Lawyers' Dignity Should Be Respected and They Should Not Be Searched before They Entered the Courtroom)' www.legaldaily.com.cn/Lawyer/content/2013-09/13/content_4848615.

defence lawyers were forbidden to bring telephones and laptops, as well as other personal belongings (such as a digital watch and a bottle of water), to the trial.[274] The judges were not always patient enough to listen to all the evidence and arguments produced by the defence advocates. A few defence lawyers recalled that they were penalised for delivering passionate speeches at trial by the imposition of an aggravated sentence on their clients.[275] There were some courts where judges gave an impression of impartiality, and defence lawyers were seemingly treated equally with their opposing party. However, these cases turned out to be predetermined behind the neutral veneer and the defence views were disregarded.[276]

> Defence lawyer: I think my right to speak in court is protected. We can speak a lot in the court and have a lot of opportunities to communicate. But if we analyse the result, the court normally does not accept lawyers' opinions.[277]
>
> Defence lawyer: With the case that I mentioned about to you just now, when we were in the high court, we believed that any person who listened to our view would change the previous conviction or sentence. However, the judge just said the reasons that we gave could not influence the result of the judgment.[278]

Therefore, the final decision of many cases has been arranged in advance in many instances. In the event that a case is deemed to be too unsafe to be convicted, further action would be initiated in private liaison with the prosecutor to resolve the 'crisis'. In so doing, the trial has functioned as the mechanism which has been set to legitimately transform the defendant into a convict.

VI. Conclusion

In this chapter, I have examined the hollow criminal trials in China and their correlation with the courts' reliance on case dossiers. Judicial activities have been sculpted by the case dossier. This includes the verbalisation of the case dossier by the prosecutor, judges' close reading of the case dossier, their referencing of statements prepared by investigators, and the adjudicative committee's review of the

htm?node=32988 (accessed 22 June 2019); 'Guanyu fayuan menwei dui lvshi sousheng soubao de wenti (On Issues in Relation to Searching Defence Lawyers' Body and Briefcases)' www.blog.sina.com.cn/s/blog_5de131770100gtsd.html (accessed 22 June 2019). 'Hebai nv lvshi jujue fajing tuoyi soushen zao jingo (A Female Lawyer Was Detained for Refusing to Cooperate with the Security Guard of the Court in Removing Her Clothes)' www.rfa.org/mandarin/yataibaodao/renquanfazhi/ql2-09052016120028.html (accessed 22 June 2019).

[274] 'Lvshi chuting, pingshenme buneng shiyong ziji de diannao (Why a Defence Lawyer Cannot Use His Own Laptop when Presenting a Case at Trial?)' (Beijing Defence Lawyers, 21 November 2017) www.bjxsdls.com/info.asp?lb_id=2354 (accessed 22 June 2019). The lawyer Zhu Mingyong also noted that defence lawyers were not allowed to bring their laptops, USBs, removable disks, briefcases or bottles of water to the Yibin Intermediate Court (*Wechat* post, 18 June 2019) (accessed 19 June 2019).

[275] Field note BPU-34.

[276] Interviews CDL-1, CDL-2, GAJ-3 and GAJ-4.

[277] Interview JDL-1.

[278] Interview CDL-1.

case dossier.[279] The dossier-studying model would be repeated and continued in the second instance trial if a case were appealed. In the event that the defendant were sentenced with capital punishment, a similar dossier-reading process would be applied in the death penalty review.

Underpinning this dossier-dominated trial system is the intricate institutional relationship between the courts and the procuratorate, which has been a predominant feature in this phase. On the one hand, the procuratorate strategically cooperates with the court to obtain support in fulfilling its institutional target. On the other hand, the supervisory function is occasionally deployed to pressurise the courts in situations where judicial decisions are detrimental to the procuratorate. The result of this special relationship is the impaired autonomy of the court in performing its independent function, an illustration of which is judges assisting the procuratorate to maintain high conviction rates. Whilst there is sufficient exchange of information between the prosecutor and the judge, the defence lawyer has been excluded from the machinations of the bureaucratic coalition. Defence lawyers have constantly found themselves being kept in the dark about the reasoning of the outcome of the case. They are treated as an outsider of the system, and their rights are at risk of being eroded by the courts that are supposed to safeguard them.

The judge–prosecutor relationship apparently plays a role in the judge's reluctance to allow witnesses to enter the courtroom. Although the reasons why witnesses are absent are multifaceted, one of the important factors is that it opens up the public scrutiny of the evidence. The construction of evidence consolidated in the case dossier has been compiled in the dark, avoiding external scrutiny and interventions. Calling witnesses to testify would permit this secret investigation process to be openly inspected, thereby running the risk of undermining the prosecution case. In this sense, the courts are complicit in disguising the fact that the evidence contained in the case dossier might be unreliable. This speculation seems to be confirmed by the judicial practice of the courts in often being reluctant to exclude unlawfully obtained evidence. Clearly, there is a profound concern of judicial integrity here. In lending support to the police and the prosecution, and confirming the work done at the earlier stage, the courts have debased their moral standing and tarnished the reputation of the administration of justice.

With the guilty plea procedures being the mainstream of criminal justice, seeking a rapid case turnover has become the top priority of the court work. These fast-tracked procedures accelerate the progression of criminal cases towards the final conviction. A typical social control model continues to function through the use of swift justice, operated by institutions that are unified in the mission of convicting the accused, with little room for any effective counter checks in this process.

[279] Wang Biao (n 53) 72.

7

Concluding Remarks

As the research on which this book is based was drawing to a close, the amendments to the Criminal Procedure Law were passed by the National People's Congress and came into effect at the end of 2018. CPL 2018 brought in new measures, including (but not limited to) the duty lawyer scheme, leniency for a guilty plea and the expedited procedure. The newly introduced law is likely to shape the landscape of Chinese criminal justice in different ways. While the duty lawyer scheme, which offers free legal advice and assistance to suspects who are not represented, is certainly an important improvement,[1] the system's pursuit of social control in the euphemistic name of efficiency and its instrumental function as the apparatus of the party-state are much more pronounced.[2]

To a great extent, the reforms that have taken place in recent years have led to significant institutional restructuring. Procuratorates and courts, in particular, have undergone transformations to reflect the party-state policy in which debureaucratisation and streamlined functioning of the criminal justice institutions have been requested. Judges appear to have been empowered following the accountability reform,[3] which constrained the role of the adjudicative committee. The procuratorate, albeit losing their 'teeth' in relation to the anti-corruption investigation, was forced to shift their focus on strengthening the prosecution role. This, again, may be conducive to the improvement of the quality of prosecution cases.

These institutional changes, alongside new rules manifesting traces of due process, may constitute welcome advances that aim to solve long-term problems of the system. The reforms in recent years, however, have not identified the core issues, thereby being unable to address the injustice that yields from the system. I have shown in this book that the actions of the police are crucial in making the case against the accused. The origins of most miscarriages of justice could be traced to the early stages of the police investigation, when the case dossiers were constructed. The operation of the criminal justice system relies almost entirely

[1] See Art 36 of CPL 2018.

[2] For example, the Anti-corruption Department of the Procuratorate was carved out and was incorporated into the centralised anti-corruption agency of the National Supervisory Commission. Deng Jinting, 'The National Supervision Commission: A New Anti-corruption Model in China' (2018) 52 *International Journal of Law, Crime and Justice* 58.

[3] See Fu Hualing, 'Building Judicial Integrity in China' (2016) 39 *Hastings International & Comparative Law Review* 167.

on the case dossiers. With no efficacious mechanism in place to ensure the reliability of evidence, the system is functionally flawed. I have also shown that the criminal justice institutions have not been operating properly to pursue rectitude of criminal cases. Rather, state officials have calculated on guarding their institutional interests. The criminal justice system is 'a living organism in constant flux'.[4] It is currently dominated by the three core criminal justice agencies that prioritise their own interests in steering the system on a course in which the fates of those implicated within the system are controlled and predetermined. Criminal cases may be more conveniently and expeditiously disposed of with the advent of leniency for a guilty plea and the expedited procedure. This, nevertheless, may further compound the deep-seated illness of the system, proliferating unsafe convictions based on potentially unreliable confessions and guilty pleas procured in a coercive manner.

For a criminal justice system to work effectively and to minimise injustice, it is a matter of principle that the system must have integrity.[5] Integrity bestows moral legitimacy on the criminal justice agencies that are set up to uphold the law. This moral strength enables the public to have faith in the criminal justice institutions, believing that state officials act decently to pursue crime and are subject to the same rules of conduct that are commanded of citizens.[6] Integrity should be the standard that lies at the heart of the administration of justice, underpinning all important decision-making. If the state becomes a lawbreaker, it 'breeds contempt for law' and invites 'every man to become a law unto himself',[7] which eventually brings peril to the edifice of the entire system.

The quality of this moral principle seems to be lacking in every phase of the process. To secure the conviction of the accused, confession evidence is procured to align with other evidence (the witness statements in particular) and to fit into a constructed narrative of the guilt of the accused. Statements from the suspect and other witnesses are not verbatim records of the interrogations and interviews. Rather the interrogating officers are allowed to collaborate with the suspect to produce details that corroborate with other evidence in creating an inculpatory account. The final record assembled in the dossier is at best an attenuated version of what was recounted, tinged and distorted to reflect the version of truth contemplated by the police. At worst, it may be a statement that was fabricated (mostly by copying and pasting some of the suspect's earlier accounts, together with a staged identification of the crime scene, which the accused cannot even recall). The manipulation of evidence has extended to the video recordings of the police interrogation, which was introduced for the very purpose of supervising the previously unregulated territory of criminal justice in the hope that false confessions

[4] M Zander, 'Where the Critics Got It Wrong' (1993) 143 *New Law Journal* 1364.

[5] M McConville and L Bridges, *Criminal Justice in Crisis* (Edward Elgar, 1994) 14.

[6] *R v Hickey and others* [1997] unreported CA case in England, cited from M McConville and L Marsh, *Criminal Judges: Legitimacy, Courts and State-induced Guilty Pleas in Britain* (Edward Elgar, 2014) 58.

[7] *Olmstead v United States* [1928] 277 US 438, 471.

can be prevented. This regulation measure, however, has ironically been 'regulated' by the police. As I have shown in chapters three and six, ever since the implementation of the video recording of police interrogations, the recordings submitted to the courts have regularly been found to be edited or based on rehearsed interrogation scenarios, defiantly perverting the course of justice.

The inadequacy of integrity continues at the stage of the prosecution review. The procuratorate, as a guardian ensuring the correct enforcement of the law, assumes the responsibility of supervising police investigations and evaluating the strength and persuasiveness of the police case. However, prosecutors were observed to have carried out these functions rather differently in practice. They were subjected to the Appraisal System, which was engineered to maintain an extraordinarily high conviction rate. Their roles and ethos, in reality, had hence been fundamentally shaped by the performance indicators, and their task was no more than to advance the case to the next level in the most cost-effective fashion and to ensure conviction. Issues in relation to how the evidence is constructed and whether the case dossier is truly reliable have rarely been a cause of concern. Prosecutors have teamed up with the police in matters such as shoring up suspects' earlier confessions by securing guilty pleas, tidying up dubious witness statements to consolidate the prosecution case, or recycling tainted evidence to close any avenues leading to exculpation in the future. Oversight in this sense is merely a disguise for assisting the police to repackage their otherwise flawed cases and being an accomplice in legitimising malpractices and misconduct.

When criminal cases finally arrive at the trial stage, the lack of integrity of the system is manifested in the fact that the courts are reluctant to call witnesses to testify. The absence of witnesses at trial is a disguised endorsement of prosecution cases. In preventing witnesses from appearing at trial, the prosecution evidence, no matter how it is gathered and constructed, becomes virtually unchallengeable in most instances. Case dossiers are accorded a high degree of credibility and have been routinely relied upon by the court to determine the guilt or innocence of the defendant. The automatic acceptance of the prosecution evidence is contrasted with the admission of defence evidence, which has to undergo stringent examination by the court. Amongst all the dangers that imperil the system's moral standing, the special relationship between the courts and the procuratorate is perhaps one of the gravest. As I showed in the preceding chapter, the judge–prosecutor relationship is strategically bound to fortify their mutual interests. This institutional trust creates a channel of information exchange, secretly resolving all the procedural irregularities and determining the outcome of the cases. It leaves no room for impartiality, making the trial nothing more than a charade.

In a country where the dialectic truth is enshrined in its political-legal ideology, accurate fact-finding based on reliable evidence is expected to be laid at the centre of the criminal procedures. The evidence law of China, however, makes no reference to the critical issue of evidence reliability or its safeguards. While much emphasis is placed on the external requirement and the presentation of the evidence (especially in the form of the case dossier), the truthfulness of the content of the evidence and its probative value has seldom been rigorously scrutinised or cross-examined. This feature of evidence law is embodied in the employment of the corroboration rule. This important rule on which the establishment of the guilty facts pivots has shaped the investigation strategies. I have shown that witness statements, multiple confessions, identification records and other evidential materials are deliberately selected, aligned and edited in such a way that the guilty narratives are amplified. As noted, criminal evidence is a product of conscious construction by legal actors, and the building of the police case is a partisan process geared towards securing a conviction of the defendant.[8] The police have, at a most fundamental level, the ability and incentives to select, reject and evaluate facts, and to create cases. Devoid of any context within which the information is extracted, the documentary records are susceptible to a construction process in which ploys and coercion of all sorts are likely to play a part.

Case construction is widely regarded as an official activity in China, and the whole system is concerned with officialdom. There is a boundary between 'insiders' and 'outsiders'. Those inside the official coalition, the Iron Triangle institutions, have developed a strong sense of common identity, cautiously guarding against the outsiders, especially defence lawyers. This exclusivity has been an idiosyncrasy of Chinese criminal justice, prevalent in every phase of the process. Therefore, the defence lawyer, who is outside the official circle, is discouraged from taking on any alternative enquiry and is deprived of the opportunity to build a defence case at a parallel level. Active preparation for defence cases, such as evidence acquisition, has proven to be hazardous for defence lawyers in China. Obstacles are set up at different stages to undermine defence work. This includes (and is not limited to) the difficulties in meeting with their clients in the detention centre and accessing the prosecution dossier. Construction techniques, such as proactively gathering defence evidence and verifying the witnesses' statements in the prosecution case, which are generally regarded as good defence preparations in adversarial systems, have been perceived as too 'radical' an approach to be taken on by defence lawyers. Despite the fact that defence lawyers are accorded the right to gather evidence independently,[9] exercising this right in practice may cost them their career, liberty and safety. Those who engage with such defence strategies run a great risk emanating from Article 306 of the Criminal Law and are susceptible to be prosecuted for committing perjury.[10] This constitutes another example in which the system can be described as unethical, in the sense that it set up a double standard to allow for circumvention or removal of defence rights. The system, on the one hand, has turned a blind eye to the malpractices of state officials. On the other hand, when it comes to defence lawyers, the law has no hesitation in criminalising and

[8] M McConville et al, *The Case for the Prosecution* (Routledge, 1991) 11–12.

[9] CPL 2018, Art 43.

[10] M McConville, 'Criminal Justice in China and the West' in M McConville and E Pils (eds), *Comparative Perspectives on Criminal Justice in China* (Edward Elgar, 2013) 55–62; Fu Hualing, 'Human Rights Lawyering in Chinese Courtrooms' (2014) 2 *Chinese Journal of Comparative Law* 270.

prosecuting this marginalised group, even though they are simply exercising a defence right provided by law.

From an adversarial perspective, this official case construction is only half of the process. There should be an alternative interpretation in favour of the defendant. In the Chinese scenario, this other half of the story is indeed missing. Exculpatory evidence is often excluded by the police and the prosecution, and inquiries regarding the potential innocence of the accused have rarely been conducted or pursued.[11] Key evidence, such as statements from witnesses who gave prosecution evidence, is controlled and unimpeachable. With the dominant role played by the police and the prosecution in shaping the evidence, there has been a lack of functional equivalence of case construction in formulating a competing version of fact for the defence. This functional deficiency continues to the trial stage. There are clearly no equal arms between the prosecution and the defence in the courtroom. The vast majority of defendants are not represented. For the small number of cases which are represented, the trial is simply to confirm the content of the case dossier prepared by the police and the prosecution. Cross-examinations rarely take place to ascertain the credibility and veracity of the official records due to the absence of witnesses. As a result, inculpatory evidence assembled in the case dossier, with its reliability unquestioned, is automatically admitted and given weight to convict the accused.

The case dossier that has been heavily relied upon by the system embodies a controlled official truth of criminal cases that is not open to challenge. This truth is formulated and established on the principle of corroboration, which requires no more than external coherence and ostensibly dovetailed statements and documentary records pointing to the single outcome of guilt. It is operated on the bureaucratic mechanism that is concerned with repeated affirmation and approval of constructed versions of the facts by the next individual/institution in the chain. Truth, in this perspective, is not to be clarified by casting doubt on the prosecution. Criminal justice is an *official recognition and confirmation process*. An officially acknowledged fact is automatically authenticated by the agencies of the state and encounters hardly any resistance. In this vein, the expedited procedure best embodies the essence of Chinese criminal justice. With an unequivocal agenda to secure and fast-track convictions, case dossiers and guilty pleas directly and ultimately determine the fate of the defendant.

In processing the semi-bureaucratic approvals, the system has achieved its social control tenet as the apparatus of the party-state. In the sociopolitical context, the criminal justice system is a coercive instrument that gives effect to the will of the party-state.[12] It legitimises the use of penalties against those individuals who

[11] For detailed accounts and analysis, see chs 3 and 4. Despite this, in legal practice, certain mitigating evidence, such as meritorious performance or evidence showing that suspects turned themselves in, has been generally accepted by the police and the prosecutor.

[12] M McConville et al, *Criminal Justice in China: An Empirical Enquiry* (Edward Elgar, 2011) 447.

have been implicated in the criminal justice system. Therefore, those who enter the system for whatever reason become the property of the system. The identity of the accused from a suspect to a guilty person is almost settled from the outset.[13] The criminal process has been designed in such a way that those who are labelled as suspects can hardly get out of the system through any official channel, even though they may potentially be innocent. In this context, there is no surprise that cases cannot be easily weeded out of the prosecution review process despite their weak evidence. Instead, they are dispatched to the next stage based on guilty pleas. To dispose of the vast volumes of cases, procuring guilty pleas has become a necessary case management solution and a critical step in securing convictions. For many suspects, this means subjugation to the coercive power and threats of draconian sentences. Sentence discounts designed to encourage early guilty pleas are utilised as rewards and to stifle the claims of innocence.[14] Most criminal cases proceed to the next phase as a consequence, regardless of the reliability of the evidence or facts that may not be persuasive enough. It is true that there are defendants who have been acquitted, but these cases are extremely few and far between. Criminal trials are hollow proceedings, serving as affirmative formalities to certify prosecution cases. Case dossiers, as the evidential centrepiece of the trial, are assiduously studied by trial judges before court hearings take place. Prior beliefs developed by judges in reading the case dossier render alternative interpretations of evidence or the facts unlikely. The criminal trials are not created to vigorously verify the reliability of the evidence or the manner in which evidence in case dossiers is obtained, nor are the courts willing to do so, despite the high hopes invested in the exclusionary rules. The close alliance between the courts and the procuratorate is so well entrenched that it permits little room to entertain the idea that the prosecution evidence should be robustly testified and cross-examined. The trial has little substantive meaning other than sealing the legal status of the defendant. With an ever-more hollowed adjudication function dependent on guilty pleas, criminal convictions are mass-produced at lower costs.

The criminal justice system in China is thus structurally weak in preventing miscarriages of justice. None of the criminal justice institutions are capable of functioning independently to preclude potentially innocent individuals from being wrongfully accused or convicted. The entire system is built on the ideology of control – control through case construction, control through prosecution scrutiny, control of the adjudication process and control of defence lawyers. It is predominantly about the control of those accused people who are involved in the system. Ultimately, however, it is the party-state using the criminal justice institutions to exert control of the general population. Nonetheless, the system fails

[13] As noted in preceding chapters, the conviction rates in China have been over 99% for more than a decade.

[14] RL Lippke, *The Ethics of Plea Bargaining* (Oxford University Press, 2011) ch 2.

to control the quality of criminal cases. The state officials have monopolised the right to interpret cases. Without robust checks and challenges, narratives that appear to be reasonably persuasive may be falsely bolstered by unreliable or irrelevant evidence. The case dossier may conform perfectly to the corroboration rule, accepted by the prosecution and the courts, but also may well be the seed of a miscarriage of justice.

APPENDIX: DATA SOURCES

Field Site Coding

APU: Field note from a basic procuratorate in site A.
CASEA: 64 monitored cases drawn from site A.
Site A: A central district inside a major city.
Site B: A middle size city, including rural outskirts (approx 1,050,000 inhabitants).
Site C: A middle size city, including rural outskirts (approx 6,446,000 inhabitants).
Site D: A central district inside a major city.
Site E: An urban area in a middle size city.
Site F: A developed urban area in a major city.
Site G: A developed urban area in a major city.
Site H: A rural area in a small town (approx 200,000 inhabitants).
Site I: A central area in a major city.
Site J: A small town in a rural location (approx 2,100,000 inhabitants).

Interviewees (with Biographical Notes where Available)

APS-1: Junior prosecutor in site A – 3 months' experience.
APS-2: Senior prosecutor in site A – 7 years' experience.
APS-3: Junior prosecutor in site A – 2 years' experience.
APS-4: Senior prosecutor and a leader of the prosecution department of a basic procuratorate in site A – 3 years' experience.
APS-5: Senior prosecutor in site A – 7 years' experience.
APS-6: Senior prosecutor in site A – 6 years' experience: floating post, working in different departments of a basic procuratorate in site A, and 3 years' experience working in the department of prosecution in the same procuratorate.
ATJ-1: Senior criminal judge in a district court in site A – 3 years' experience.
ATJ-2: Senior criminal judge in a district court in site A – 5 years' experience.
BDL-1: Senior defence lawyer in site B – 34 years' experience.
BDL-2: Senior defence lawyer who used to be a judge in a basic court in site B – 12 years' experience.
BPO-1: Senior police officer in a district police station in site B – 20 years' experience.
BPO-2: Senior police officer in a district police station in site B – 6 years' experience.
BPO-3: Senior police officer and the head of a district police station in site B – 8 years' experience.

BPO-4: Senior police officer in site B – 9 years' experience.
BPO-5: Senior police officer and the deputy head of a district police station in site B – 10 years' experience.
BPO-6: Senior police officer of a district police station in site B – 22 years' experience.
BPS-1: Senior prosecutor in a basic procuratorate in site B – 6 years' experience.
CDL-1: Junior defence lawyer in site C – 2 years' experience.
CDL-2: Junior defence lawyer in site C – 3 years' experience.
CDL-3: Junior defence lawyer in site C – 2 years' experience.
DDL-6: Senior defence lawyer in site D – 10 years' experience.
DPO-1: Senior police officer in a district police station in site D – 7 years' experience.
EPO-1: Junior police officer in a district police station in site E – 3 years' experience.
FPO-1: Senior police officer in a district police station in site F – 11 years' experience.
FPS-1: Senior prosecutor in a basic procuratorate in site F – experience not known.
FTJ-1: Senior criminal judge in a district court site F – 3 and a half years' experience.
GAJ-1: Senior criminal judge in a district court in site G, the leader of the criminal court – experience not known.
GAJ-2: Senior criminal judge in a district court in site G – 3 years' experience.
GAJ-3: Junior criminal judge in an intermediate court in site G – 3 months' experience.
GAJ-4: Senior criminal judge in an intermediate court site G – 5 years' experience.
GAJ-5: Senior criminal judge in an intermediate court site G – 8 years' experience.
GTJ-1: Senior criminal judge in a district court in site G – 6 years' experience.
HPO-1: Senior police officer in a district police station in site H – over 20 years' experience.
IDL-1: Senior defence lawyer in site I – 7 years' experience.
JDL-1: Senior defence lawyer in site J – 7 years' experience.
JDL-2: Senior defence lawyer in site J – 9 years' experience.
JDL-3: Senior defence lawyer in site J – 18 years' experience.
JDL-4: Senior defence lawyer in site J – 10 years' experience.
JDL-5: Senior defence lawyer in site J – 7 years' experience.
JDL-6: Senior defence lawyer who used to be a prosecutor in the basic procuratorate in site J – 5 years' experience.
JPS-1: Senior prosecutor in an intermediate procuratorate in site J – 9 years' experience.
JPS-2: Senior prosecutor in an intermediate procuratorate in site J – 5 years' experience.

BIBLIOGRAPHY

Amnesty International, *No End in Sight: Torture and Forced Confessions in China* (Amnesty International Publications, 2015).

Amsterdam, A and Bruner, J, *Minding the Law* (Harvard University Press, 2000).

Ashworth, A and Redmayne, M, *The Criminal Process*, 4th edn (Oxford University Press, 2014).

Bakken, B, *The Exemplary Society: Human Improvement, Social Control and the Dangers of Modernity in China* (Oxford University Press, 2000).

Bao, X, 'Xingshi sifa jixiao kaohe de kunjin yu chulu (The Dilemma and Solution of the Appraisal System of Criminal Justice)' (2015) 4 *Shehui Kexuejia (Social Scientist)* 91.

Bar-Gill, O and Ben-Shahar, O, 'The Prisoners' Plea Bargain Dilemma' (2009) 1 *Journal of Legal Analysis* 737.

Baxter, E, *Complete Crime Scene Investigation* (CRC Press, 2015).

Belkin, I, 'China's Tortuous Path toward Ending Torture in Criminal Investigation' in M McConville and E Pils (eds), *Comparative Perspectives on Criminal Justice in China* (Edward Elgar, 2013) 97.

Belloni, F and Hodgson, J, *Criminal Injustice: An Evaluation of the Criminal Justice Process in Britain* (Macmillan Press, 1999).

Bennett, WL and Feldman, MS, *Reconstructing Reality in the Courtroom* (Quid Pro Books, 2014).

Berger, M, 'The Deconstitutionalisation of the Confrontation Clause: A Proposal for a Prosecutorial Restraint Model' (1991) 76 *Minnesota Law Review* 560.

Berger, P and Luckmann, T, *The Social Construction of Reality: A Treaties in the Sociology of Knowledge* (Penguin, 1966).

Berman, H, Cohen, S and Russell, M, 'A Comparison of the Chinese and Soviet Codes of Criminal Law and Procedure' (1982) 73 *Journal of Criminal Law and Criminology* 238.

Bex, FJ and Verheij, B, 'Story Schemes for Argumentation about the Facts of a Crime' in *Computational Models of Narrative: Papers from the AAAI Fall Symposium* (2010) 6.

Bex, FJ and Walton, D, 'Burdens and Standards of Proof for Inference to the Best Explanation: Three Case Studies' (2012) 11 *Law, Probability and Risk* 113.

Bian, J, 'xingshisusongfa zaixiugai mianmian guan (All Perspectives of the Revision of Criminal Procedure Law)' (2019) 1 *Fazhi yanjiu* (*Rule of Law Research*) 3.

Biddulph, S et al, 'Criminal Justice Reform in the Xin Jinping Era' (2017) 2 *China Law and Society Review* 63.

Biddulph, S, 'Democratic Centralism and Administration in China' in Fu Hualing et al (eds), *Socialist Law in Socialist East Asia* (Cambridge University Press, 2018) 205.

Blackstock, J et al, *Inside Police Custody: An Empirical Account of Suspects' Right in Four Jurisdictions* (Intersentia, 2014).

Bowling, B and Phillips, C, 'Disproportionate and Discriminatory: Reviewing the Evidence on Police Stop and Search' (2007) 70 *MLR* 936.

Boyne, S, 'German Prosecutors and the Rechtasstaat' in M Langer and DA Sklansky (eds), *Prosecutors and Democracy: A Cross-National Study* (Cambridge University Press, 2017) 138.

Braithwaite, J, 'The Myth of Social Class and Criminality Reconsidered' (1981) 46 *American Sociological Review* 36.

Cai, G, 'Zhencha xunwen zhenren de jiben celue (Basic Strategies of Interviewing Witnesses during Police Investigation)' (2007) 3 *Shandong Jincha Xueyuan Xuebao* (*Journal of Shandong Police College*) 80.

Cai, H, *Xingshi sifa ji sixing shiyong: ruogan yinan wenti shili poxi* (*Criminal Justice and the Application of the Death Penalty: Analysis of Complex Cases*) (China Law Press, 2009) 45.

Cai, J and Liu, J, 'Xingshi juanzong yisong zhidu de lunhuixing gaige zhi fansi (Reconsideration of the Convertible Reform in Relation to Criminal Case Dossier)' (2014) 1 *Faxue Pinglun* (*Law Review*) 156.

Cai, Q, 'Xiangchang zhiren gai hequhecong (The Future of Crime Scene Identification)' (2015) 5 *Fazhi Bolan* (*Legal Exhibition*) 213.

Cai, Y, 'Lun Yinzheng yu xinzheng zhi ronghe: Yinzheng moshi de loudong jiqi mibu (The Merging between Corroboration and Ascertainment: The Loophole of the Corroboration Rule and Its Solution)' (2016) 3 *Falv Kexue* (*Legal Science*) 171.

Caianiello, M, 'The Italian Public Prosecutor: An Inquisitorial Figure in Adversarial Proceedings?' in E Luna and M Wade (eds), *The Prosecutor in Transnational Perspective* (Oxford University Press, 2012).

Chen, G and Jiang, Y, 'Gongan jiguan "liangfa xianjie" zhong de zhengju zhuanhua yingyou: yi jingcha xingzhengquan wei shijiao (A Concern Over the Use of Evidence in Connection with Two Powers of the Police: From the Perspective of Administrative Powers of the Police)' (2014) 3 *Zhongguo Renmin Gongan Daxue Xuebao* (*Journal of Chinese People's Public Security University*) 28.

Chen, G et al, *Zhonghua Renmin Gongheguo Xingshi Susongfa Xiaogai Tiaowen Shiyi yu Dianping (Annotations and Comments on the Revised Articles of the Criminal Procedure Law of the People's Republic of China)* (People's Court Press, 2012).

Chen, G, 'Jicheng gongan jiguan shixing "zhengkan heyi" gaige de lixing sikao (Rational Rethink of the Reform of Conflation of Investigation and Crime Scene Inspection in Basic Police Organ)' (2006) 6 *Zhongguo Renmin Gongan Daxue Xuebao* (*Journal of Chinese People's Public Security University*) 94.

Chen, G, 'Shixi xunwen zhengren shibai de yuanyin (An Analysis of the Reason of the Failure Occurred during the Interview of Witnesses)' (2008) 1 *Kejiao Wenhui* (*Compiled Documents of Science and Teaching*) 106.

Chen, G, 'Xingshi zhenju zhidu gaige ruogan lilun yu shijian wenti zhi tantao: yi liangyuan sanbu "liangge zhengju guiding" zhi gongbu wei shijiao' (On a Number of Theories and Practical Issues of Criminal Evidence Reform: From the Perspective of the Publication of 'Two Regulations on Evidence') (2010) 6 *Zhongguo Faxue* (*China Law Studies*) 5.

Chen, G, Chen, H and Wei, X, 'Xingshi zhengju zhidu yu renshi lun – jianyu wuqulun, faliu zhenshilun, xiangdui zhenshilun shangque (Criminal Evidence and Epistemology: A Discussion with Confusion, Legal Realism and Truth Realism)' (2001) 1 *Zhongguo Faxue* (*China Law Studies*) 37.

Chen, H and Zhao, W, 'Xianchang zhiren zhaoxiang hefaxing zhiyi (Questioning the Legitimacy of the Photography of the Crime Scene Identification)' (2003) 4 *Guangxi Zhengfa Guanli Ganbu Xueyuan Xuebao* (*Journal of Guangxi Administrative Cadre Institute of Politics and Law*) 13.

Chen, L, 'Woguo jianjing guanxi de fansi yu chonggou (Reconsideration and Reconstruction of the Police-Prosecution Relationship)' (2009) 6 *Zhongguo Faxue* (*China Law Studies*) 110.

Chen, M, 'Jianxi jiancha jiguan jingfei baozhang wenti: Yi guanxi hezhoushi babuqu jianchayuan wei li (The Financial Safeguards of the Procuratorate: An Example of the Babu District Procuratorate in the City of Hezhou, Guangxi Province)' (2010) 11 *Fazhi yu Jingji* (*Law and Economy*) 54.

Chen, R, 'Lun beigaoren kougong guize (On Defendants' Confessions)' 33 (2012) *Faxue Zazhi* (*Law Magazine*) 46.

Chen, R, 'Renzui renfa congkuan zhidu de ruogan zhengyi wenti (Several Disputed Issues Regarding Leniency for A Guilty Plea)' (2017) 1 *Zhongguo Faxue (China Law Studies)* 35.

Chen, R, 'Xingxun bigong de guojia zhili: 1979–2013 (The State Governance of Torture: From 1979 to 2013)' (2014) 5 *Zhongguo Faxue* (*China Law Studies*) 5.

Chen, R, *Xingshisusong de zhongguo moshi (The Chinese Model of Criminal Proceedings)* (China Law Press, 2009).

Chen, R, *Zhongguo xingshi susong de qianyan wenti* (*The Fronting Edge of Chinese Criminal Justice*) (China Renmin University Press, 1999).

Chen, S, 'Lun bianhu lvshi de zaichangquan (On Defence Lawyers' Right of Access to Interrogations)' (2000) 5 *Faxue Pinglun* (*Law Review*) 67.

Chen, T, 'Lun lvshi de zaichangquan (On Defence Lawyers' Right of Access to Interrogations)' (2006) 11 *Susongfa Luncong* (*Procedural Law Review*) 107.

Chen, W and Hao, Y, 'Woguo gongsu fangshi de jiegouxing quexian jiqi jiuzheng (The Structural Flaws of the Public Prosecution in China and its Correction)' (2000) 4 *Faxue Yanjiu* (*Legal Studies*) 101.

Chen, W and Hao, Y, 'Zhen jian yitihua moshi yanjiu: jianlun woguo xingshi sifa tizhi gaige de biyaoxing (A Study of the Integration of the Investigation and the Prosecution: On the Necessity of Reforming the Criminal Justice System in China)' (1999) 1 *Faxue Yanjiu* (*Legal Studies*) 58.

Chen, W and Spronken, T, *The Three Approaches to Combating Torture in China* (Intersentia Publishing, 2012).

Chen, W, 'Rang zhenren zouxiang fating – xingshi anjian zhengren chuting zuozheng zhidu yanjiu (Let Witnesses Go to the Court: The Study of Witnesses' Testimony)' (2007) 19:2, *Shandong Jincha Xueyan Xuebao* (*Journal of Shandong Police College*) 40.

Chen, W, 'Sifa zerenzhi gaige yanjiu (The Research of the Judicial Justice Reform)' (2017) 8 *Faxue Zazhi* (*Law Magazine*) 32.

Chen, W, 'Woguo jianchaquan de fansi yu chonggou: yi gongsuquan wei hexin de fenxi (Rethink and Reconstruct the Power of the Procuratorate in China: Based on the Prosecution Power)' (2002) 2 *Faxue Yanjiu* (*Legal Studies*) 3.

Chen, W, 'Zuijia: "yilv ruxing" hai shi "qubie duidai" (Drunk Driving: All Being Criminalised or Differentiated)' (2012) 1 *Fazhi yu Shehui Fazhan* (*Legal System and Social Development*) 119.

Chen, W, *Xingshi shengqian chengxu yanjiu* (*Research on Criminal Pre-trial Procedure*) (China Rnemin University Press, 2004).

Chen, W, *Xingshi Susong Fa (Criminal Justice Law)* (China Renmin Press, 2004).

Chen, X, 'Chongtu yu pingheng: Lun weichengnian ren futiaojian buqisu zhidu (Conflicts and Balance: On the Conditional Non-prosecution Decisions in Relation to Juvenile Cases) (2012) 12 *Zhongguo Xingshifa Zazhi* (*China Criminal Law Magazine*) 60.

Chen, Y, 'Xingshi buqisulv piandi zhi shizheng fenxi: yi moudi 2003–2010 nian xingshi buqisu anjian wei fenxi duixiang (Empirical Analysis of the Low Non-prosecution Rate: On the Basis of Non-prosecution Cases between 2003 and 2010)' (2011) 8 *Zhongguo Xingshifa Zazhi (China Criminal Law Magazine)* 73.

Cheng, EK, 'Being Pragmatic about Forensic Linguistics' (2013) 21 *Journal of Law & Policy* 541.

Cheng, X, 'Futiaojian buqisu zhidu de shiyong (The Application of the Conditional Non-prosecution Discretion)' (2013) 6 *Guojia Jianchaguan Xueyuan Xuebao* (*Journal of National Prosecutors College*) 22.

China Yearbooks 1986–2017 (China Year Book Press, multiple years: 1986–2017).

Ching-Chi, H and Pugh, MD, 'Poverty, Income Inequality and Violent Crime: A Meta-analysis of Recent Aggregate Data' (1993) 2 *Criminal Justice Review* 182.

Chiu, H, 'China's Criminal Justice System and the Trial of Pro-democracy Dissidents' (1992) *New York University Journal of International Law and Politics* 1181.

Choo, ALT, *Hearsay and Confrontation in Criminal Trials* (Clarendon Press, 1996).

Choongh, S, 'Policing the Dross: A Social Disciplinary Model of Policing' (1998) 58 *British Journal of Criminology* 623.

Choongh, S, *Policing as Social Discipline* (Oxford University Press, 1997).

Clarke, DC and Feinerman J, *Antagonistic Contradictions: Criminal Law and Human Rights in China; China's Legal Reforms* (Clarendon Press, 1996).

Clarke, DC, 'Empirical Research into the Chinese Judicial System' in E Jensen, C Thomas and T Heller (eds), *Beyond Common Knowledge: Empirical Approaches to the Rule of Law* (Stanford University Press, 2003) 164.

Cohen, JA, 'Politics and Criminal Justice' in M McConville and E Pils (eds), *Comparative Perspective Criminal Justice in China* (Edward Edgar, 2013) 439.

Cooke, FL, et al, 'Who Are "Managing" the Lawyers in China? Control and Commitment in an Evolving Institutional and Cultural Context and Gendered Implications' (2013) 24 *The International Journal of Human Resource Management* 3418.

Cornforth, M, *Dialectical Materialism: An Introduction* (Lawrence and Wishart, 1976).

Cui, M and Wang, L, 'Xingshi cuoan gainian de shencengci fenxi (Deep Analysis of the Concept of Cuo'an)' (2009)1 *Fazhi Yanjiu* (*Rule of Law Research*) 10.

Dai, M, 'Policing in the People's Republic of China: A Review of Recent Literature' (2008) 50 *Crime, Law and Social Change* 211.

Damaška, M, 'Truth in Adjudication' (1998) 49 *Hastings Law Journal* 289.

Damaška, M, *The Faces of Justice and State Authority: A Comparative Approach to the Legal Process* (Yale University Press, 1986).

Deng, J, 'The National Supervision Commission: A New Anti-corruption Model in China' (2018) 52 *International Journal of Law, Crime and Justice* 58.

Dennis, LH, *The Law of Evidence* (Sweet & Maxwell, 2013).

Devlin, P, *The Judge* (Oxford University Press, 1979).

Dixon, D et al, 'Realty and Rules in the Construction and Regulation of Police Suspicion' (1989) 17 *International Journal of the Society of Law* 185.

Dong, B and Qiu, J, 'Xingshi cuoan yufang yu jiucuo jizhi yanjiu: jiyu Zhejiang zhangshi shuzhi qiangjianan de qishi (The Mechanism of Prevention and Identification of Miscarriage of Justice: An Inspiration of Uncle–Nephew Zhang Case in Zhejiang) (2013) 5 *Shandong Jingcha Xueyuan Xuebao* (*Journal of Shandong Police College*) 11.

Dong, H, 'Woguo sifa jiguan duochong zhineng gaige zhi sikao (Thoughts about the Multiple Functions of the Judicial Institutions in China)' (1997) 4 *Faxue Yanjiu* (*Legal Studies*) 27.

Dong, L, 'Woguo futiaojian buqisu zhidu ruogan wenti de fansi yu wanshan (Reconsideration and Perfection of the Conditional Non-prosecution System of Juvenile Cases)' (2015) 1 *Jinan Daxue Xuebao* (*Jinan University Journal*) 42.

Dradley, R and Wright, E, 'Reconsidering the Relationship between SES and Delinquency: Causation but not Correlation' (1999) *37 Criminology* 175.

Du, W and Shi, M, 'Weichengnianren futiaojian buqisu zhi shiyong (On the Application of the Conditional Non-prosecution System of Juvenile Cases)' (2012) 3 *Dongfang Faxue* (*Oriental Law*) 111.

Du, X, 'Lun "lvshi weizhengzui" zuizhi dulixing de xiaojie: yi xingshisusongfa de xiangying xiugai wei jinglu (The Nature and Deconstruction of the Crime Relating to the Forge of Evidence by Defence Lawyers: Based upon the Reform of the Criminal Procedure Law)' (2013) 4 *Faxue* (*Studies of Law*) 112.

Du, Y and Zhang, J, 'Research on the Personnel Management of the Procuracy', the 13th Annual Conference Paper of Shanghai Social Science 2015.

Duan, H, 'Dui woguo sixing anjian zhengmin biaozhun de fansi (Rethink about the Standard of Proof of the Death Penalty Cases)' (2007) 2 *Lvliang Jiaoyu Xueyuan Xuebao* (*Journal of LvLiang Education Institute*) 24.

Duff, A, 'Discretion and Accountability' in M Langer and DA Sklansky (eds), *Prosecutors and Democracy: A Cross-National Study* (Cambridge University Press, 2017) 14.

Dunaway, RG et al, 'The Myth of Social Class and Crime Revisited: An Examination of Class and Adult Criminality' (2000) 38 *Criminology* 589.

Durston, G, *Evidence: Text and Materials* (Oxford University Press, 2011).

Dutton, M and Tianfu, L, 'Missing the Target? Policing Strategies in the Period of Economic Reform' (1993) 39 *Crime and Delinquency* 316.

Dutton, M, *Policing Chinese Politics: A History* (Duke University Press, 2005).

Dutton, MR, *Policing and Punishment in China: From Patriarchy to 'the People'* (Cambridge University Press, 1992).

Dworkin, R, *A Matter of Principle* (Oxford University Press, 1986).

Fan, B and Ma, Y, 'Woguo gongan jingwu jixiao pingjia shijian ji pingjia tixi de goujian yanjiu (The Practice of the Police Evaluation and the Construction of the Evaluation System in China) (2006) 4 *Xiangtan Daxue Xuebao* (*Journal of Xiangtan University*) 15.

Fan, C, 'Renzui renfa congkuan yu zhishou tanbai (The System of Leniency for Pleading Guilty and Voluntarily Surrender Oneself and Confession) (2018) *Renmin Fazhi* (*People's Rule of Law*) 54.

Fan, C, *Xingshi shenqian chengxu gaige shizheng yanjiu: xingshi zhengcha chengxu zhong de lvshi zaichang* (*Empirical Research on Pre-trial Reform: Defence Lawyers' Attendance at Interrogations*) (People's Public Security University Press, 2006).

Fan, C, *Xingshi susong faxue yanjiu zongshu yu pingjia (Criminal Procedure Law Research Review and Comments)* (China Political Science and Law University Press, 1991) 222.

Fang, B, 'Lun zhencha xunwenzhong de jiaoliu jiqiao: yi zhengren he beihairen wei (Communicative Skills in Investigative Interviews: A Focus of Witnesses and Victims)' (2013) 1 *Zhongguo Xingshifa Zazhi* (*China Criminal Law Magazine*) 75.

Fang, B, 'Lvshi zaichangquan bentuhua de lilun fansi (Reconsideration of the Defence Lawyer's Right of Access to Interrogations within the Context of China)' (2015) 6 *Chengdu Ligong Daxue Xuebao* (*Journal of Chengdu University of Technology*) 1.

Feng, Z, 'Jiancha jiguan renshi guanli gaige sanshinian gailan (Overview of the 30-year Reform of the Personnel Management of the Procuratorate)' (2008) 19 *Renmin Jiancha* (*The People's Procuratorate*) 21.

Foucault, M, *Discipline and Punishment: The Birth of the Prison* (Vintage, 1979).

Frampton, TW, 'The Uneven Bulwark: How (and Why) Criminal Jury Trial Rates Vary by State' (2012) 100 *California Law Review* 184.

Freiberg, A, 'Managerialism in Australian Criminal Justice: RIP for KPIs' (2005) 31 *Monash University Law Review* 12.

Fu, H and Cullen, R, 'Climbing the Weiquan Ladder: A Radicalising Process for Rights-Protection Lawyers' (2011) 205 *The China Quarterly* 4.

Fu, H and Zhu, H, 'After the July 9 (709) Crackdown: The Future of Human Rights Lawyering' (2018) 41 *Fordham International Law Journal* 1135.

Fu, H, 'Building Judicial Integrity in China' (2016) 39 *Hastings International & Comparative Law Review* 167.

Fu, H, 'Human Rights Lawyering in Chinese Courtrooms' (2014) 2 *Chinese Journal of Comparative Law* 270.

Fu, H, 'When Lawyers Are Prosecuted: The Struggle of a Profession in Transition' (2007) Social Science Research Network, www.papers.ssrn.com/sol13/papers.cfm?abstract_id=956500.

Fu, H, 'Zhou Yongkang and the Recent Police Reform in China' (2005) 38 *The Australian and New Zealand Journal of Criminology* 241.

Fuller, LL, 'The Adversary System' In H Berman (ed), *Talks of American Law* (Harvard University Press, 1971) 43.

Galvin, R, 'Rounding Up the Usual Suspects: Varieties of Kantian Constructivism in Ethics' (2011) 61 *The Philosophical Quarterly* 16.

Ge, L, 'Jingfei baozhang shiyexia de jianchayuan yunzhuan: jiyu liangge jiceng jianchayuan butong jingfei zhuangkuang de fenxi (The Operation of the Procuratorate in the Context of Financial Safeguards: Analysis of the Financial Situation of Two District Procuratorates)' (2013) 26 *Yunnan Daxue Xuebao Faxueban* (*Journal of Yunnan University Law Edition*) 113.

Gelsthorpe, L and Padfied, N, *Exercising Discretion: Decision-Making in the Criminal Justice System and Beyond* (Routledge, 2003).

Ginsburgs, G, 'Objective Truth and the Judicial Process in Post-Stalinist Soviet Jurisprudence' (1961) 10 *American Journal of Comparative Law* 53.

Goody, J, *Logic of Writing and the Organisation of Society* (Cambridge University Press, 1986).

Gotfredson, MR and Hirschi, T, *A General Theory of Crime* (Stanford University Press, 1990).

Gu, Y, 'Wanshan renzui renfa congkuan zhidu de qinli guancha yu sikao jianyi: yiju fuqingshi dengdi xingshi susong chengxuzhong renzui renfa congkuan zhidu de diaoyan (Observation on the Programme to Improve Leniency for a Guilty Plea, Reconsideration and Suggestions: Empirical Studies on the Pilot Project in Fuqing City etc)' (2017) 1 *Fazhi Yanjiu* (*Rule of Law Research*) 56.

Gudjonsson, GH, *The Psychology of Interrogations and Confessions: A Handbook* (Wiley, 1992).

Guo, J, 'Dui xinxiuding xingshi susongfa zhong chengmoquan wenti de yanjiu (Research on the Newly Added Issue of Right to Silence in CPL)' (2015) 1 *Wuhan Gongan Ganbu Xueyuan Xuebao (Journal of Wuhan Public Security Cadre's College)* 69.

Guo, S, 'Zhuoding buqisu zhidu de zai kaocha (Reconsideration of Discretionary Decision Not to Prosecute)' (2018) 3 *Zhuoguo Faxue* (*China Law Studies*) 228.

Guo, S, 'Zuzhi lixing, chengxu lixing yu xingshi sifa jixiao kaoping zhidu (Organisational Rationale, Procedural Theory and the Appraisal System in Criminal Justice)' (2013) 31 *Zhengfa Luntan* (*Political Science and Law Forum*) 69.

Guo, T, 'Xingshi xianchang zhiren bilu de bianhu celv (Defence Strategy of the Crime Scene Identification)' (2010) 10 *Zhongguo Lvshi* (*Chinese Lawyers*) 54.

Guo, Z, 'Feifa zhengju paichu fanwei jieding de kunjing yu chulu (Plight and Way Out for Exclusionary Rule of Illegal Obtained Confessions and a Probe into Reform of Criminal Interrogation)' (2015) 6 *Zhengju Kexue* (*Evidential Science*) 645.

Guo, Z, 'The First Step of the Long March: Implementing the Exclusionary Rule in China' (2017) 25 *Asia-Pacific Law Review* 48.

Guo, Z, 'Torture and Exclusion of Evidence in China' (2019) 1 *China Perspective* 45.

Hagan, J, 'Why Is There So Little Criminal Justice Theory? Neglected Macro- and Micro-level Links between Organization and Power' in ER Maguire and DE Duffee (eds), *Criminal Justice Theory*, 2nd edn (Routledge, 2015) 57.

Han, D and Gu, J, 'Caipan wenshu zhong de tongbu lunying luxiang zhi gongneng yanjiu (Research on the Functions of the Video Recordings in the Judgments)' (2015) 30 *Shanghai Zhengfa Xueyuan Xuebao* (*Journal of Shanghai University of Political Science and Law*) 126.

Han, D and Yu, W, 'Fayuan, jianchayuan he gongan jiguan de xianfa guanxi (The Constitutional Relationship between the Courts, the Procuratorate and the Police)' (2011) 3 *Faxue Yanjiu* (*Legal Studies*) 3.

Han, D, 'Lun guojia jiancha tizhi gaige zhong de ruogan xianfa wenti (On a Number of Constitutional Issues in Relation to the National Supervisory Reform) (2017) 3 *Faxue Pinglun* (*Law Review*) 11.

Han, K, 'Woguo zhongda xingshi yuanan chengyin fenxi jiyingdui celv: yi gongan sifa jiguan de jixiao kaohe jizhi wei shijiao (The Analysis of Major Miscarriages of Justice in China and the Solutions: From the Perspective of the Appraisal System of the PSB)' (2013) 10 *Zhengzhou Hangkong Gongye Guanli Xueyuan Xuebao* (*Journal of Zhengzhou institute of Aeronautical Industry Management*) 125.

Han, X, '2018 nian xingsufa zhong renzui renfa congkuan zhidu (The Guilty Plea Procedure in CPL 2018)' (2019) 1 *Fazhi Yanjiu (Rule of Law Research)* 35.

Hancock, B and Jackson, J, *Standards for Prosecutors: An Analysis of the United Kingdom National Prosecuting Agencies* (Willen-Jan Van Der Wolf, 2006).

Hao, Y and Shi, D, 'Fayuan shiyong feifa zhengju paichu guize shizheng yanjiu: jiyu 587 feng caipan wenshu de fenxi (Empirical Research on the Application of Illegally Obtained Evidence: Analysis of 587 Judgments)' (2017) 1 *Guizhuo Minzu Daxue Xuebao* (*Guizhou People's University Review*) 136.

Hao, Y, 'Jianchaquan zhiyi (Questioning the Power of the Procuratorate)' (1999) 3 *Zhongguo Renmin Daxue Xuebao* (*China Renmin University Review*) 71.

Harris, DA, 'The Interaction and Relationship between Prosecutors and Police Officers in the United States, and How This Affects Police Reform' in E Luna and M Wade (eds), *The Prosecutor in Transnational Perspective* (Oxford University Press, 2012) 56.

He, J, *Wangzhe guilai: xingshi sifa shida wuqu* (*Resurrection: Ten Pitfalls of Criminal Justice*) (Peking University Press, 2014).

He, L, 'Xinxingsufa shijiaoxia zhengren chuting zhidu shilling wenti de jiejue jianyi (Suggestions on the Failure of Witnesses Attending Trial under the CPL 2012) (2013) 6 *Hebei Faxue* (*Hebei Legal Studies*) 186.

He, T, 'Zhencha quzhengzhong qiangzhi xunwen zhengren tanxi (Exploration of Compulsory Witness Interviews during the Investigation)' (2011) 3 *Zhongguo Xingshifa Zazhi* (*China Criminal Law Magazine*) 77.

He, W, 'Yizai suowei jianchaguan jiqi wenti zhe: yu longzongzhi xiansheng shangque (The Surprising Question of Whether the Prosecutor Should Stand Up: A Discussion with Mr Long Zongzhi)' (1997) 2 *Faxue Yanjiu* (*Legal Studies*) 58.

He, X, 'Xunwen changsuo jianshe ruogan wenti yanjiu (Research on Interrogation Venues)' (2015) 25 *Tielu Jingcha Xueyuan Xuebao* (*Journal of Railway Police College*) 22.

He, Y, *Duanlie yu yuanxu. Renmin fayuan jianshan (1978 2005)* (*Construction of the People's Court: 1978–2005*) (China Social Science Press, 2008).

Hodgson, JS, 'Hierarchy, Bureaucracy, and Ideology in French Criminal Justice: Some Empirical Observations' (2002) 29 (2) *Journal of Law and Society* 227.

Hodgson, JS, *French Criminal Justice: A Comparative Account of the Investigation and Prosecution of Crime in France* (Hart Publishing, 2005).

Hou, S and Keith, R, 'The Defence Lawyer in the Scales of Chinese Criminal Justice' (2011) 20(70) *Journal of Contemporary China* 379.

Howard, BS, 'Comparative and Non-comparative Forensic Linguistic Analysis Techniques: Methodologies for Negotiating the Interface of Linguistics and Evidential Jurisprudence in the American Judiciary' (2006) 83 *University of Detroit Mercy Law Review* 285.

Hsia, T and Zeldin, WI, 'Recent Legal Developments in the People's Republic of China' (1987) 28 *Harvard International Law Journal* 249.

Hu Y, 'Zhengren chuting zuozhengnan jiqi jiejue silu (The Difficulties and Solution of Witnesses Come to Court to Testify)' (2006) 28 *Huanqiu Falv Pinglun* (*Global Law Review*) 557.

Hu, L, 'Juanzong yisong zhuyi: dui lixiang de tuoxie haishi dui xianshi de zunzhong: 2012 nian xingshi susongfa queli juanzhong yisong de zhengdangxing (Transferring Files: Compromising the Ideal or Respecting the Reality: The Legitimacy of Establishing Case File Transference System in CPL 2012) (2013) 43 *Xibei Daxue Xuebao* (*Journal of Northwest University*) 84.

Hu, W and Tian, K, 'Jiancha jiguan tiqi xingzheng gongyi susong shidian qingkuan yanjiu (Research on the Public Interest Litigation Pilot Work Instituted by the Procuratorate)' (2017) 2 *Xingzheng Faxue Yanjiu (Administrative Law Studies)* 19.

Hu, X, 'Woguo jiancha jiguan zhiquan de jiantao yu chonggou (Rethink and Reconstruct the Power of the Procuratorate in China)' (2001) 10 *Legal Research and Exploration* 43.

Hu, Y, 'Xingshi cuoan jiuji jizhi yanjiu: Zhongguo ban wuguzhe jihua tanwei (The Mechanism of Redressing Miscarriages of Justice in China: Exploring the Chinese Version of Innocent Project)' (2016) 24 *Chengdu Keji Daxue Xuebao* (*Journal of Chengdu University of Technology*) 28.

Huang, Q, 'The Research on the Quality of the Cases Prosecuted by Taizhou Procuracy' (2007) 5 *Zhejiang Procuracy* 87.

Huang, J, 'Xingshi hejie de zhengcexing junxing dao fazhihua yunxing: yi dangshiren hejie de qingshang anjian wei yangben de fenxi (From the Policy Operation to Legal Operation of the Criminal Reconciliation: Analysis of the Parties' Reconciliation of Minor Injuries)' (2013) 3 *Zhongguo Faxue* (*China Law Studies*) 163.

Huang, S, 'The Psychological Reason of Wrongful Convictions' (2014) 3 *Legal Studies* 26.

Huang, X, 'Nongcun liushou ertong fanzui wenti yanjiu (Research on Crimes Committed by "Left-behind Children") (2008) 12 *Fazhi yu Shehui* (*Legal System and Society*) 286.

Huff, R and Killias, M, *Wrongful Conviction: International Perspectives on Miscarriages of Justice* (Temple University Press, 2008).

Hull, MS, 'The File: Agency, Authority, and Autography in an Islamabad Bureaucracy' (2003) 23 *Law and Communication* 287.

Inbau, F et al, *Criminal Interrogation and Confessions*, 3rd edn (Williams and Wilkins, 1986).

Ip, EC, 'The Supreme People's Court and the Political Economy of Judicial Empowerment in Contemporary China' (2011) 24 *Columbia Journal of Asian Law* 367.

Ji, W, 'Chengxu bijiaolun (Comparative Proceduralism)' (1993) 1 *Bijiaofa Yanjiu* (*Comparative Law*) 1.

Ji, W, *Falv chengxu de yiyi: dui zhongguo faxhi jianshe de lingyizhong sikao* (*The Meaning of Legal Procedure: Alternative Thoughts on Chinese Legal Construction*) (China Legal Publication, 2004).

Jinting, D, 'The National Supervisory Commission: A New Anti-corruption Model in China' (2018) 52 *International Journal of Law, Crime and Justice* 58.

Johnson, DT, *The Japanese Way of Justice: Prosecuting Crime in Japan* (Oxford University Press, 2002).

Johnson, EA, 'Criminal Justice, Coercion and Consent in "Totalitarian Society": The Case of National Socialist Germany' (2011) 51 *British Journal of Criminology* 599.

Karstedt, S, 'Trusting Authorities: Legitimacy, Trust and Collaboration in Non-Democratic Regimes' in J Tankebe and A Liebling (eds), *Legitimacy and Criminal Justice: An International Exploration* (Oxford University Press, 2013).

Kassin, SM, 'On the Psychology of Confessions: Does Innocence Put Innocents at Risk' (2005) 60 *American Psychologist* 215.

Kassin, SM. et al, 'Police-induced Confession: Risk Factors and Recommendation' (2010) 34 *Law and Human Behavior* 3.

Kawachi, I et al, 'Crime: Social Disorganisation and Relative Deprivation' (1999) 48 *Social Science and Medicine* 719.

Kennedy, BP et al, 'Social Capital, Income Inequality, and Firearm Violent Crime' (1998) 47 *Social Science & Medicine* 7.

Kerstholt, J and Jackson, J, 'Judicial Decision Making: Order of Evidence Presentation and Availability of Background Information' (1998) 12 *Applied Cognitive Psychology* 445.

Kun, H, 'Lun Renzui renfa congkuan zhidua zai zhencha jieduan de shiyong (On the Application of The System of Leniency for Pleading Guilty and Accepting Punishment at the Investigation Stage)' (2019) 4 *Fazhi yu Shehui* (*Legal System and Society*) 33.

Lan, R, 'Killing the Lawyer as the Last Resort: The Li Zhuang Case and its Effects on Criminal Defence in China' in M McConville and E Pils (eds), *Comparative Perspective Criminal Justice in China* (Edward Edgar, 2013).

Langbein, JH, 'The Historical Origins of the Privilege against Self-Incrimination at Common Law' (1994) 92 *Michigan Law Review* 1047.

Langbein, JH, *Torture and the Law of Proof: Europe and England in the Ancient Regime* (University of Chicago Press, 1976).

Latour, B, *The Making of Law: An Ethnography of the Conseil D'Etat* (Polity, 2010).

Lau, U and Staack, T, *Legal Practice in the Formative Stages of the Chinese Empire: An Annotated Translation of the Exemplary Qin Criminal Cases from the Yuelu Academy Collection* (Brill, 2016) 298.

Lea, J and Young, J, 'Relative Deprivation' in E McLaughlin, J Muncie and G Hughes (eds), *Criminological Perspectives: Essential Readings* (Sage Publications, 2003) 147.

Lei, C and Nesossi, E, 'China's Pre-trial Detention Centres: Challenges and Opportunities for Reform' in E Nesossi et al (eds), *Legal Reforms and Deprivation of Liberty in Contemporary China* (Routledge, 2016) 101.

Leng, S and Chiu, H, *Criminal Justice in Post-Mao China: Analysis and Documents* (SUNY Press, 1985).

Leo, RA and Ofshe, RJ, 'The Social Psychology of Police Interrogation: The Theory and Classification of True and False Confessions' (1997) 16 *Studies in Law, Politics and Society* 9.

Leonard, RA, et al, 'Forensic Linguistics: Applying the Science of Linguistics to Issues of the Law' (2017) 45 *Hofstra Law Review* 881.

Li, B, 'Xingshi sucai chengxu de sifa zaizao (Judicial Re-invention of the Expedite Procedure)' (2016) 5 *Zhongguo Xingshifa Zazhi* (*China Criminal Law Magazine*) 33.

Li, C and Xing, Y, 'Woguo soucha zhidu de yunxing xianzhuang, wenti ji wanshan (The Status Quo, Problem and Perfection of the Operation of Search in China)' (2014) 2 *Jiangxi Shehui Kexue* (*Jiangxi Social Science*) 158.

Li, C, 'Lun futiaojian buqisu yu zhuoding buqisu de guanxi (On the Relationship between Conditional Non-prosecution and Discretionary Non-prosecution)' (2014) 4 *Faxue Luntan* (*Legal Forum*) 115.

Li, C, 'Xingshi yishen caipan zhiliang baozheng tixi lungang (The Systematic Outline of the Quality of the First Instance Criminal Trials)' (2009) 1 *Zhengfa Xuekan* (*Journal of Political Science and Law*) 56.

Li, E, 'Prisonization or Socialisation? Social Factors Associated with Chinese Administrative Offences' (2010) 27 *UCLA Pacific Basin Law Journal* 213.
Li, E, 'The Li Zhuang Case: Examining the Challenges Facing Criminal Defense Lawyers in China' (2010) 24:1 *Columbia Journal of Asian Law* 129.
Li, H, 'Maixiang jianchaweiyuanhui: quanli jiandu zhongguo moshi de fazhihua zhuanxin (Heading Towards the National Supervisory Commission: The Change of Paradigm of Power Supervision in the Chinese Model in Rule of Law) (2017) 3 *Faxue Pinglun* (*Law Review*) 150.
Li, K and Zhang, F, 'Xingshi susong jiandu gongzuo jizhi yanjiu (The Research on the Mechanism of Procuratorate)' in Mu Ping and Zhen Zhen (eds), *Jiancha gongzuo jizhi yu shiwu wenti yanjiu* (*Research on the Work Mechanism of Procuratorate and Practical Issues*) (China Law Press, 2008) 9.
Li, M, 'Qianxi woguo xixingsufa zhengren zuozheng zhidu de jingbu yu chizhi (On the Improvement and Stagnation of Encouraging Witnesses to Attend the Trial)' (2015) 21 *Xinxibu* (*New West*) 84.
Li, X, 'Yuanjia cuoan de chengyin fenxi ji fangfan: Chongti tupeiwu an (The Analysis and Prevention of the Causes of Miscarriages of Justice)' (2014) 10 *Hubei Jingguan Xueyuan Xuebao* (*Journal of Hubei Police College*) 25.
Li, X, *Xingshisusong gouzaolun (The Structure of the Criminal Procedure)* (The China University of Political Science and Law Press, 1992) 238.
Li, Y, 'Renzui renfa congkuan zhidu xia de youxiao falv bangzhu wenti yanjiu (Research on Effective Defence in the Context of Leniency for A Guilty Plea)' (2019) 2 *Xibu Faxue Pinglun* (*Western China Law Review*) 30.
Li, Y, 'Xianchang zhiren bilu de zhengju shuxing ji shengcha panduan (The Nature and Examination of Crime Scene Identification)' (2017) 9 *Chuanbo yu Banquan* (*Broadcast and Copyright*) 180.
Li, Y, 'Xingshi cuoan jiuzhengnan wenti yanjiu: jiyu 34 qi xingshi cuoan jiuzheng lichen de sikao (Research on the Difficulty in Correcting Wrongful Convictions: Based on 34 Corrected Miscarriages of Justice)' (2015) 30 *Shanghai Zhengfa Xueyuan Xuebao* (*Journal of Shanghai University of Political Science and Law*) 19.
Li, Y, 'Xingshi jianyi chengxue de xinxiuzheng jiqi shiyong tanxi (The Revision of the Simplified Criminal Trial and its Application)' (2012) 9 *Zhongguo Jianchaguan* (*The Chinese Procurators*) 33.
Li, Y, 'Zhiban lvshi zhidu de shizheng kaocha yu gaige zhanwang (Empirical Research and Reform Prospect of the Duty Lawyer Scheme)' (2019) 3 *Xinzheng yu Fa* (*Administration and Law*) 90.
Lian, Y, 'Xingzheng zhifa yu xingshi sifa xianjie zhong zhengju zhuanhua yanjiu (Research on the Admissibility of Criminal Evidence Obtained in the Course of the Administrative Process Which Was Later Used in Criminal Proceedings)' (2017) 4 *Tansuo yu Zhengming* (*Exploration and Free Views*) 97.
Lian, Y, 'Xinxingshi susongfa xia dui zhiban lvshi zhidu de tanxi (Exploring the Duty Lawyer Scheme under the New Criminal Procedure Law)' (2019) 3 *Fazhi bolan* (*Legal Exhibition*) 194.
Liao, D and Bai, Y, 'Xingshi anjian sucai chengxu shidian yunxing xianzhuang shizheng fenxi: yi T shi bajia shidian fayuan wei yanjiu yangben (Empirical Analysis of the Operation of the Criminal Expedite Procedure: Based on the Sample of 8 Pilot Courts in T City)' (2015) 12 *Falv Shiyong* (*Legal Application*) 23.
Liao, Y and Li, S, 'Woguo minshi heyi zhidu zhi yunxing xianzhuang: yi yige qianfada diqu jiceng fayuan de minshi shenpan wei kaocha duixiang (The Status Quo of the Civil Collegiate Benches: Based on the Study of a Local District Court in a Less Developed Area in Mid China)' (2007) 3 *Shehui Kexue* (*Social Science*) 85.
Lin, D, 'High Justice versus Low Justice: The Legacy of Confucian and Legalist Notion of Justice' in F Sapio et al (eds), *Justice: The China Experience* (Cambridge University Press, 2017).
Lin, L, 'Zhengcha chengxu lvshi zaichangquan bianxi (Defence Lawyers' Right of Access to Police Interrogations)' (2004) 12 *Falv Shiyong* (*Legal Application*) 33.
Lippke, RL, *The Ethics of Plea Bargaining* (Oxford University Press, 2011).
Liu J, 'Jianjing yitihua moshi zai jiedu (Reinterpretation of the Integration of the Investigation and the Prosecution)' (2013) 6 *Zhongguo Faxue* (*China Law Studies*) 147.

Liu, B and Duan, Y, 'Xingshi zaisheng chengxu cuoan jiuzuo gongneng zhi chongsu: yi shenpan jieduan cuoan he jiuzheng wei shijiao (Reshaping the Correcting Function of Wrongful Convictions in Criminal Justice: Based on the Perspective of Identifying and Correcting Wrongful Convictions)' (2014) 6 *Zhongguo Xingshifa Zazhi* (*China Criminal Law Magazine*) 91.

Liu, B, 'Lun chenmoquan linian: jianlun dui woguo xingshisusongfa xiugai de qishi (On Right to Silence: Revelation to the Revision of Criminal Procedure Law in China)' (2013) 12 *Fazhi yu Shehui* (*Legal System and Society*) 66.

Liu, C, 'Dangqian nongcun liushou ertong fanzui wenti yanjiu (Research on Current Crimes Committed by "Left-Behind Children")' (2014) 6 *Fazhi yu Shehui* (*Legal System and Society*) 285.

Liu, F, *Zhencha Chengxu Shizheng Yanjiu* (*Empirical Research on Investigations*) (China Procuratorate Press, 2007).

Liu, J, *Zhengju shencha guize yu fenxi fangfa: yuanli, guifan, shili* (*Criminal Evidence Examination and Analysis Rules: Norms, Regulations and Examples*) (China Law Press, 2018).

Liu, S al, *Susong zhengju guize yanjiu* (*A Study on Evidence in Litigations*) (China Legal Press, 2000) 307.

Liu, S and Halliday, T, 'Dancing Handcuffed in the Minefield: Survival Strategies of Defence Lawyers in China's Criminal Justice System' (2008) *May SSRN Electronic Journal 34*, www.ssrn.com/abstract=1269536.

Liu, S and Halliday, T, *Criminal Defence in China: The Politics of Lawyers at Work* (Cambridge University Press, 2016).

Liu, S and Halliday, TC, 'Political Liberalism and Political Embeddedness: Understanding Politics in the Work of Chinese Criminal Defence Lawyers' (2011) 45 *Law and Society Review* 831.

Liu, W, 'Renzui renfa de "321" jietishi congkuan niangxin jizhi (The Sliding Scale Sentencing Mechanism of 3-2-1 in Guilty Plea Cases)' (2018) 12 *Hubei Shehui Kexue* (*Huibei Social Science*) 147.

Liu, X, 'Jiancha jiguan futiaojian buqisu cailiangquan yunyong zhi tantao (The Exploration of the Operation of the Conditional Non-prosecution Discretions)' (2014) 6 *Zhongguo Faxue* (*China Law Studies*) 205.

Liu, X, 'Liudong renkou fanzui wenti shizheng fenxi: yi tianjinshi weili (Empirical Study of the Crime on Floating Population: A Case of Tianjin) (2010) 5 *Chengshi Wenti* (*City Problems*) 75.

Liu, Y, 'Shehui fencing zhong de bianyuan qunti jiqi liuminghua wenti (Social Stratification, the Marginalised Group and Being Vagrant)' (2000) 3 *Fazhi yu Shehui* (*Legal System and Society*) 18.

Liu, Z, 'Investigation of the Wrongful Conviction of 11/28 Yibin Sichuan Murder Case' (2005) 9 Fenghuang Zhoukan (*Phoenix Weekly*) 27.

Loeber, DA, 'The Soviet Procuracy and the Rights of the Individual against the State' (1958) 1 *Journal of the International Commission of Jurists* 59.

Loftus, EF and Hoffman, HG, 'Misinformation and Memory: The Creation of New Memories' (1989) 118 *Journal of Experimental Psychology* 100.

Loftus, EF, *Eyewitness Testimony* (Harvard University Press, 1979).

Long, Z, '"Queding weuyi" – woguo xingshi susong de zhenming biaozhun ("Absolute Certainty": The Standard of Proof in Chinese Criminal Justice)' (2001) 11 *Faxue* (*Studies of Law*) 29.

Long, Z, 'Jiancha tizhi gaige zhong de shiwu fanzui diaocha zhidu wanshan (Improving the National Supervisory Reform in Professional Crime Investigation)' (2018) 1 *Zhengzhi yu Falv* (*Politics and Law*) 1.

Long, Z, 'Jianchaguan gaibugai qili: dui tingsheng yishi de yizhong sikao (Should the Prosecutor Stand Up? Some Thoughts about the Court Rituals)' (1997) 3 *Faxue* (*Studies of Law*) 45.

Long, Z, 'Lun jianchaquan de xingzhi yu jiancha jiguan de gaige (The Nature of the Power of the Procuratorate and the Legal Reform)' (1999) 10 *Faxue* (*Studies of Law*) 2.

Long, Z, 'Xingshi yinzheng zhengmin xintan (Exploration of the Corroboration Rule)' (2017) 2 *Faxue Yanjiu* (*Legal Studies*) 149.

Long, Z, *Xingshi Tingshen Zhidu Yanjiu* (*The Research on the Trial of Criminal Process*) (China University of Political Science and Law Press, 1998) 51.

Lu, S and Liu, Y, 'Jixia kaohe, guojia peichang yu xingshi cuoan: yi jianchajiguan wei shijiao (Appraisal System, State Compensation and Miscarriages of Justice: From the Perspective of the Procuratorate)' (2016) 7 *Fazhi yu Shehui* (*Legal System and Society*) 30.

Lu, X and Xu, R, 'Renzui renfa congkuan zhiyuxia zhiban lvshi zhidu de wanshan (The Perfection of the Duty Lawyer Scheme in the Context of Guilty Plea and Sentence Mitigation System)' (2019) 36 *Zhengfa Xuekan (Journal of Political Science and Law)* 92.

Luo, W, 'Yinzheng yu zuijia jieshi tuili: Xingshi zhengming moshi de duoyuan fazhan (Corroboration and IBE: The Pluralistic Development of Criminal Proof)' (2017) 5 *Faxuejia (Jurist)* 117.

Lustgarten, L, 'The Future of Stop and Search' (2002) 8 *Crim LR* 603.

Lyu, P, 'Xingshi lian chengxu de dulixing zhiyi (Enquiry on the Independence of the Case Filing Process in the Criminal Procedure)' (2002) 3 *Zhongguo Faxue (China Law Studies)* 142.

Ma, J and Zhang, L, 'Xunwen Lunying lunxiang yu feifa zhengju paichu: yige shizheng de kaocha (Video-Recording and Exclusion of Illegally Obtained Evidence: An Empirical Research)' (2016) 7 *Xinan Minzu Daxue Xuebao (Southwest People University Review)* 87.

Ma, J, 'Feifa xunwen yu jiankongshi xunwen jizhi: yi gongan jiguan zhengcha xunwen wei zhongxin de kaocha (Unlawful Interrogation and Monitored Interrogation Mechanism: On the Basis of Police Interrogation)' (2015) 6 *Faxuejia (Jurist)* 116.

Ma, J, 'Xianchang kanyan jiancha guize chonggou: yi xingshi susongfa xiugai zhi guiding wei qierudian (Reconstruction of Crime Scene Inspection and Examination: From the Perspective of the Revision of Criminal Procedure Law)' (2012) 5 *Zhongguo Renmin Gongan Daxue Xuebao (Journal of Chinese People's Public Security University)* 60.

Ma, L, 'Xingshi xianchang zhiren bilu de zhengju shuxing jiqi guifan (The Nature of Crime Scene Identification and Its Legal Regulation)' (2017) 24 *Renmin Jiancha (The People's Procuratorate)* 49.

Ma, X, 'Xinxingshi susongfa shiye xia lvshi xunwen zaichangquan zhi zaipanduan (Rejudging the Defence Lawyer's Right of Access to Interrogations within the Context of New Criminal Procedure Law) (2014) 32 *Jiamusi Daxue Shehui Kexue Xuebao (Jiamusi University Social Science Review)* 39.

MacCormack, G, *The Spirit of Traditional Chinese Law* (University of Georgia Press, 1996).

Malleson, K, 'Appeals against Conviction and the Principle of Finality' (1994) 21 *Journal of Law & Society* 151.

Manson, J, *Qualitative Researching*, 2nd edn (Sage Publications, 2002).

Mao, Y and Yan, J, 'Xinxingshi susongfa shiyexia zhengren chuting shixiao guancha: yi Z sheng fayuan wei yangben (Observation of Witnesses Giving Testimonies at Trial after the Implementation of CPL 2012: Based on the Sample of the Courts in Z Province)' (2015) 1 *Jiangxi Jingcha Xueyuan Xuebao (Journal of Jiangxi Police Institute)* 107.

Mathias, E, 'The Balance of Power between the Police and the Public Prosecutor' in DM Mireille and J Spencer (eds), *European Criminal Procedures* (Cambridge University Press, 2002) 459.

McConville, M and Bridges, L, *Criminal Justice in Crisis* (Edward Elgar, 1994) 14.

McConville, M and Marsh, L, *Criminal Judges: Legitimacy, Courts and State-induced Guilty Pleas in Britain* (Edward Elgar, 2014).

McConville, M and Pils, E (eds), *Comparative Perspectives on Criminal Justice in China* (Edward Elgar, 2013) 66.

McConville, M et al, *Criminal Justice in China: An Empirical Enquiry* (Edward Elgar, 2011).

McConville, M et al, *Standing Accused* (Clarendon Press, 1994).

McConville, M, 'Comparative Perspectives on Criminal Justice in China' in M McConville and E Pils (eds), *Comparative Perspectives on Criminal Justice in China* (Edward Elgar, 2013) 65.

McConville, M, 'Criminal Justice in China and the West' in McConville M and Pils E (eds), *Comparative Perspectives on Criminal Justice in China* (Edward Elgar, 2013) 50.

McConville, M, Sanders, A and Leng, R, *The Case for the Prosecution* (Routledge, 1991).

McDonald, WF, 'From Plea Negotiation to Coercive Justice: Notes on the Respecification of a Concept' (1979) 13 *Law and Society Review* 385.

Min, S, 'Jianchaquan peizhi de lishi bianqian yu fansi (The Historical Change and Rethink about the Power of the Procuratorate)' (2010) 5 *Guojia Jianchaguan Xueyuan Xuebao (Journal of National Prosecutors College)* 52.

Mo, D, 'Zhiquan zhuyi susong zhong yuduan paichu zhiyi (Reconsideration of Prior Belief in the Inquisitorial System)' (2012) 4 *Zhengzhi yu Falv (Politics and Law)* 150.

Mou, J, 'Jiekai zhengcha xunwen gongneng de miansha: jiyu shizheng jiaodu de fenxi (Unveal the Function of Investigatory Interrogation: An Analysis from An Empirical Perspective)' 1 (2013) *Nanjing Daxue Falv Pinlun* (*Nanjing University Law Review*) 200.

Mou, L, 'Lun feifazhengju paichu guize he yinzheng zhengming moshi de chongtu ji mihe lujing (The Conflict between Exclusionary Rule of Inappropriately Obtained Evidence and Corroboration Rule and Its Solution)' (2017) 29 *Zhongwai Faxue* (*Peking University Law Review*) 1068.

Mou, Y, 'Beyond Legitimate Grounds: External Influences and the Discretionary Power not to Prosecute in the People's Republic of China' in M Caianiello and J Hodgson (eds), *Discretionary Criminal Justice in a Comparative Context* (North Carolina Press, 2015) 121.

Mühlhahn, K, *Criminal Justice in China* (Harvard University Press, 2009).

Mulgan, R, *Holding Power to Account: Accountability in Modern Democracies* (Palgrave, 2003).

Munday, R, *Evidence* (Oxford University Press, 2017).

Murray, C, 'The Underclass' in E McLaughlin, J Muncie and G Hughes (eds), *Criminological Perspectives: Essential Readings* (Sage Publications, 2003) 133.

Na, J, *Wrongful Convictions in China* (Springer, 2016).

Nash, RA and Wade, KA, 'Innocent but Proven Guilty: Eliciting Internalised False Confessions Using Doctored Video Evidence' (2009) 23 *Applied Cognitive Psychology* 624.

Naughton, M, 'The Criminal Cases Review Commission: Innocence versus Safety and the Integrity of the Criminal Justice System' (2012) 58 *Criminal Law Quarterly* 207.

Nesossi, E and Trevaskes, S, *Procedural Justice and the Fair Trial in Contemporary Chinese Criminal Justice* (Brill, 2017) 7.

Nesossi, E, 'Compromising for "Justice"? Criminal Proceedings and the Ethical Quandaries of Chinese Lawyers' in M McConville and E Pils (eds), *Comparative Perspective Criminal Justice in China* (Edward Edgar, 2013) 256.

Nesossi, E, 'The Politics of Torture and Miscarriages of Justice in Contemporary China' (2016) 11 *Journal of Comparative Law* 166.

Niao, Z, 'Woguo sixing anjian zhengmin biaozhun de chongxin xuanze (Re-think about the Standard of Proof in Capital Cases)' (2008) 8 *Rule of Law Research* 28.

Nobles, R and Schiff, D, *Understanding Miscarriages of Justice: Law, the Media and the Inevitability of a Crisis* (Oxford University Press, 2012).

Norton, L et al, 'Burnout and Compassion Fatigue: What Lawyers Need to Know' (2015) 84 *University of Missouri at Kansas City Law Review* 987.

Oda, H, 'The Procuracy and the Regular Courts as Enforcers of the Constitutional Rule of Law: The Experience of East Asian States' (1986) 61 *Tulane Law Review* 1339.

Ogletree, CJ, 'Beyond Justifications: Seeking Motivations to Sustain Public Defenders' (1993) 6 *Harvard Law Review* 1239.

Otey, BS, 'Buffering Burnout: Preparing the Online Generation for the Occupational Hazards of the Legal Profession' (2014) *South California Interdisciplinary Law Journal* 147.

Packer, HL, *The Limits of the Criminal Sanction* (Stanford University Press, 1968).

Paine, T, *Rights of Man, Common Sense and Other Political Writings* (Oxford University Press, 1995).

Pan, C, 'Zhongmei susongfa bijiao shiye zhong de lvshi zaichangquan yanjiu (Comparative Study of the Defence Lawyer's Right of Access to Interrogations between the USA and China)' (2013) 5 *Guangxi Zhengfa Guanli Ganbu Xueyuan Xuebao* (*Journal of Guangxi Administrative Cadre Institute of Politics and Law*) 30.

Pardo, MS and Allen, RJ, 'Judicial Proof and the Best Explanation' (2008) 27 *Law and Philosophy* 223.

Peer, E and Gamliel, E, 'Heuristics and Biases in Judicial Decisions' (2013) 49 *Court Review* 114.

Peerenboom, R, 'Judicial Independence in China: Common Myths and Unfounded Assumptions' in R Peerenboom (ed), *Judicial Independence in China: Lessons for Global Rule of Law Promotion* (Cambridge University Press, 2010).

Peerenboom, R, *China's Long March toward Rule of Law* (Cambridge University Press, 2002).

Pei, C, *Zhengju faxue xinlun (New Studies on Evidence)* (China Law Publishing, 1989).

Peng, H and Zhang, J, 'Renzui renfa congkuan zhidu de hexin jiazhi quxiang bianxi (The Central Value of the System of Leniency for Pleading Guilty and Accepting Punishment)' (2018) 1 *Jingxue yanjiu* (*Police Science Research*) 68.

Pennington, N and Hastie, R, 'A Cognitive Theory of Juror Decision Making: The Story Model' (1991) 13 *Cardozo Law Review* 519.

Pennington, N and Hastie, R, 'Evidence Evaluation in Complex Decision Making' (1986) 51 *Journal of Personality and Social Psychology* 242.

Pennington, N and Hastie, R, 'Explaining the Evidence: Tests of the Story Model for Juror Decision Making' (1992) 62 *Journal of Personality and Social Psychology* 189.

Pennington, N and Hastie, R, 'Explanation-Based Decision Making: The Effects of Memory Structure on Judgement' (1988) 14 *Journal of Experimental Psychology: Learning, Memory and Cognition* 521.

Pennington, N and Hastie, R, 'Juror Decision Making Models: The Generalisation Gap' (1981) 89 *Psychological Bulletin* 246.

Pennington, N and Hastie, R, 'Reasoning in Explanation-Based Decision Making' (1993) 49 *Cognition* 123.

Perillo, JT and Kassin, SM, 'Inside Interrogation: The Lie, the Bluff and False Confessions' (2011) 35 *Law and Human Behaviour* 327.

Persson, S, 'China Talks Juvenile Justice Reform: A Constructivist Case Study' (2014) *Columbia Public Law Research Paper* 14.

Pi, J et al, 'Fanzui xianchang kanyan DNA wuzheng wuran de fangkong (Crime Scene Inspection and Prevention of DNA Contamination)' (2012) 3 *Zhongguo Renmin Gongan Daxue Xuebao* (*Journal of Chinese People's Public Security University*) 21.

Pils, E, '"Disappearing" China's Human Rights Lawyers' in M McConville and E Pils (eds), *Comparative Perspective Criminal Justice in China* (Edward Edgar, 2013).

Ping, Y, 'Glittery Promise vs Dismal Reality: The Role of a Criminal Lawyer in the People's Republic of China after the 1996 Revision of the Criminal Procedure Law' (2002) 35 *Vanderbilt Journal of Transnational Law* 827.

Qian, M, 'Guojia tongyi sifa kaoshi zhidu shishi qinianlai cunzai de wenti yu sikao (Problems on the 7-year Implementation of the National Justice Examination)' (2009) 4 *Fazhi Yanjiu* (*Rule of Law Research*) 98.

Qiang, S and Zhao, X, 'Shuangchong jiegouhua xia de falv jieshi: dui 8 min zhongguo faguan de diaocha (The Legal Explanation of the Dual Structure: An Inquiry on 8 Chinese Judges)' in Liang Zhiping (ed), *Falv Jieshi Wenti* (*Questions on Legal Explanation*) (China Law Press, 2010) 237.

Qu, X and Lyu, Y, 'Cong youxiao dao zhengyi: Lvshi zaichangquan zai woguo de shiyong kongjian (From Effectiveness to Justice: The Scope of Application of Defence Lawyer's Right of Access to Interrogations)' (2017) 6 *Renmin Fazhi* (*People's Rule of Law*) 10.

Qu, X, 'Lun bianhu lvshi zaichangquan de queli (On the Establishment of the Defence Lawyer's Right of Access to Police Interrogations)' (2011) 1 *Zhongguo xingshifa zazhi* (*China Criminal Law Magazine*) 44.

Rabin, M and Joel Schrag, J, 'First Impression Matter: A Model of Confirmatory Bias' (1997) *UC Berkeley Working Paper* No 97.

Rawls, J, *A Theory of Justice* (Harvard University Press, 2009).

RCCJ, *The Royal Commission on Criminal Justice* (HMSO, 1993).

Reich, K, 'Constructivism: Diversity of Approaches and Connections with Pragmatism' in Hickman LA et al (eds), *John Dewey between Pragmatism and Constructivism* (Fordham University Press, 2009).

Richman, DC, 'Accounting for Prosecutors' in M Langer and DA Sklansky (eds), *Prosecutors and Democracy: A Cross-National Study* (Cambridge University Press, 2017).

Rosenzweig, J, 'State, Society and the Justice Debate in Contemporary China' in F Sapio et al (eds), *Justice: The China Experience* (Cambridge University Press, 2017).

Sanders, A et al, *Criminal Justice*, 4th edn (Oxford University Press, 2010).

Sanders, A, 'Constructing the Case for the Prosecution' (1987) 14 *Journal of Law and Society* 229.
Schünemann, B, 'Experimentelle untersuchungen zur Reform der Hauptverhandlung in Strafsachen' in J Kerner et al (eds), *Deutsche Forschungen zur Kriminalitätsentstehung und Kriminalitätskontrolle* (Heymanns, 1983) 1109.
Scoggins, SE, 'Policing Modern China'; (2018) 3 *China Law and Society Review* 79.
Searle, J, *The Construction of Social Reality* (Penguin, 1995).
Seppanen, S, 'Rawls Rejected, Ignored and Radicalised: Debating Procedural Justice in China' in F Sapio et al (eds), *Justice: The China Experience* (Cambridge University Press, 2017).
Shanghai Municipal Lawyers Association Research Department, 'Shanghai Concentrates on Doing a Good Job of Criminal Defence Work in Turmoil-Related Cases' (1990) 427 *Shanghai Lawyer* 15.
Sheng, H, 'Xingshi susongfa zhong zhiban lvshi zhidu eryuan jiazhi fenxi (Binary Analysis of the Duty Lawyer Scheme in the Criminal Procedure Law)' (2019) 31 *Hunan Jingcha Xueyuan Xuebao (Journal of Hunan Police Academy)* 66.
Shi, J and Wu, X, 'Woguo diqu shouru chaju, liudong renkou yu xingshi fanzuilv de shizheng yanjiu (An Empirical Study on China's Regional Income Inequality, Floating Population and Criminal Offence Rate)' (2010) 40 *Zhejiang Daxue Xuebao (Journal of Zhejiang University)* 74.
Shi, L, 'Zhenren chuting zuozheng zhidu yanjiu (The Study of Witnesses' Attending to Courts)' (2002) 10:2 *Guojia Jianchaguan Xueyan Xuebao (Journal of National Prosecutors College)* 60.
Shi, S and Guo, L, 'Lilin de falv jiandu sixiang yu zhongguo jiancha zhidu (Lenin's Supervisory Theory of Law and Chinese Procuratorate)' (2003) 6 *Falv yu Shehui Fazhan* (*Law and Social Development*) 3.
Shytov, A and Duff, P, 'Truth and Procedural Fairness in Chinese Criminal Procedure Law' (2019) 23 *International Journal of Evidence and Proof* 299.
Sida, L and Halliday, TC, 'Political Liberalism and Political Embeddedness: Understanding Politics in the Work of Chinese Criminal Defence Lawyers' (2011) 45(2) *Law and Society Review* 831.
Sida, L and Halliday, TC, *Criminal Defence in China: The Politics of Lawyers at Work* (Cambridge University Press, 2016).
Simon, W, 'The Organisation of Prosecutorial Discretion' in M Langer and DA Sklansky (eds), *Prosecutors and Democracy: A Cross-National Study* (Cambridge University Press, 2017) 176.
Skogan, W, *Contacts between Police and Public: Findings from the 1992 British Crime Survey* (HMSO, 1994).
Skogan, W, *The Police and the Public in England and Wales: A British Crime Survey Report* (HMSO, 1990).
Smith, D, *Police and People in London. Vol. 1. A Survey of Londoners* (Policy Studies Institute, 1983).
Smith, GB, 'The Impact of Socialism on Soviet Legal Institutions and Procedures' (1984) 23 *Columbia Journal of Transnational Law* 315.
Song, J, 'Lun shehui fenhua yu fanzui: jianping shehui jiegou zhuanxing lilun he erzhong fanzui chenyin shuo (Social Stratification and Crime: On Social Restructure Theory and Two Causes of Crime) (2000) 14 *Jiangsu Jingcha Xueyuan Xuebao* (*Review of Jiangsu Police College*) 19.
Song, L, 'Zhiban lvshi zhidu yunxing de fumian xingtai ji duice (The Negativities and Solution to the Operation of the Duty Lawyer Scheme)' (2019) 4 *Fazhi Bolan* (*Legal Exhibition*) 5.
Spronken, T, *An EU-Wide Letter of Rights* (Intersentia, 2010).
Sukumar, D et al, 'Strategic Disclosure of Evidence: Perspectives from Psychology and Law' (2016) 22 *Psychology Public Poicy and Law* 306.
Summers, SJ, *Fair Trials: The European Criminal Procedural Tradition and the European Court of Human Rights* (Hart Publishing, 2007).
Sun, C, 'Renzui renfa congkuan zhidu de jiben neihan (The Basic Connotation of Leniency for a Guilty Plea)' *Fazhi Ribao* (*Law Daily*) (Beijing, 14 August 2019) 3.
Sun, C, 'Wanshan renzui renfa congkuan zhidu de liangge zhongdian (Two Essential Points of the System of Leniency for Pleading Guilty and Accepting Punishment)' (2018) 11 *Renmin Jiancha* (*The People's Procuratorate*) 5.
Sun, IY et al, 'Procedural Justice, Legitimacy, and Public Cooperation with Police: Does Western Wisdom Hold in China?' (2017) 54 *Journal of Research in Crime and Delinquency* 454.

Sun, IY et al, 'Social Capital, Political Participation, and Trust in the Police in Urban China' (2012) 45 *Australian & New Zealand Journal of Criminology* 87.

Sun, Q, 'Renmin jiancha de guanghui lichen: jinian renmin jianchayuan huifu chongjian 30 zhounian (The Glory Journey of the People's Procuratorate: In Memory of the Recovery of the People's Procuratorate for 30 years)' (2008) 11 *Renmin Jiancha* (*The People's Procuratorate*) 5.

Sun, X, 'Faxue jiaoyu de zhidu kunjin yu tupo: guanyu faxue jiaoyu yu sifa kaoshi deng falv zhiye zhidu xiang xianjie de yanjiu baogao (The Dilemma of the Legal Education and How to Break Through: An Report on the Connection of Legal Education and The National Justice Examination System)' (2012) 9 *Faxue* (*Studies of Law*) 108.

Sun, Y, 'Juanzong yisongzhidu gaige zhi fansi (Reconsideration of the Transference of Case Files) (2009) 27 *Zhengfa Luntan* (*Political Science and Law Forum*) 167.

Sun, Y, 'Quanan yisong beijing xia kongfang juzong bilu zai shenpan jieduan de shiyong (The Use of Prosecution Case Dossier at Trial within the Context of Full Transference of Dossiers)' (2016) 6 *Faxue Yanjiu* (*Legal Studies*) 155.

Suresh, M, 'The "Paper Case": Evidence and Narrative of a Terrorism Trial in Delhi' (2019) 53 *Law and Society Review* 173.

Tak, PJP, 'The Dutch Prosecutor: A Prosecuting and Sentencing Officer' in E Luna and M Wade (eds), *The Prosecutor in Transnational Perspective* (Oxford University Press, 2012) 141.

Tan, S and Lai J, 'Xingshi susong zhidu gaige beijing xia zhiban lvshi zhidu de goujian yantaohui zongshu (Symposium of the Construction of the Duty Lawyer System in the Context of Criminal Procedure Law Reform)' (2017) 6 *Zhongguo Sifa* (*China Justice*) 24.

Tan, S and Li, M, 'Nongcun liushou ertong jianhu wenti yu fanzui shizheng yanjiu (Empirical Research of the Custody of "Left-Behind Children" and Crimes in Rural China)' (2010) 3 *Zhongguo Renmin Gongan Daxue Xuebao* (*Journal of Chinese People's Public Security University*) 133.

Tanner, H, *Strike Hard: Anti-crime Campaigns and Chinese Criminal Justice, 1979–1985* (Cornell University East Asia Program, 1999) 31.

Tanner, MS, 'Campaign-Style Policing in China and Its Critics' in B Bakken (ed), *Crime, Punishment and Policing in China* (Rowman and Littlefield Publisher, 2005).

Tao, L, 'The Criminal Law of Communist China' (1966) 52 *Cornell Law Review* 43.

Tapper, C, *Cross and Tapper on Evidence*, 12th edn (Oxford University Press, 2010).

Thaman, SC, *World Plea Bargaining: Consensual Procedures and the Avoidance of the Full Criminal Trial* (Carolina Academic Press 2010).

The People's Procuratorate of Haidian District of Beijing, 'Futiaojian buqisu zhidu shizheng yanjiu (The Empirical Study of the Conditional Non-prosecution Decisions regarding Juvenile Cases)' (2009) 6 *Journal of National Procurators College* 74.

Tian, C, 'Jiceng jiancha jiguan jingfei baozhang wenti tanxi (The Financial Safeguards of the District Procuratorate)' (2012) 8 *Fazhi yu Jingji* (*Law and Economy*) 95.

Tong, Z, 'Dui jiancha weiyuanhui zishen de jiandu zhiyue heyi qianghua (How to Strengthen the Self-Regulation of the National Supervisory Commission)' (2017) *Faxue Pinglun* (*Law Review*) 1.

Trevaskes, S, 'Severe and Swift Justice in China' (2007) 47 *British Journal of Criminology* 23.

Trevaskes, S, *Policing Serious Crime in China: From 'Strike Hard' to 'Kill Fewer'* (Routledge, 2010).

Tudi, M and Niyazi, D, 'Cong Luoji dao shijian: Dui Lvshi zaichangquan ji gongneng de zai renshi (From Logics to Practice: Rethink about the Defence Lawyer's Right of Access to Interrogations)' (2016) 3 *Zhongguo Yilizhou Dangxiao Xuebao* (*Journal of Yili Perfecture Communist Party Insitute*) 74.

Un, M and Tian, G, 'Xunwen zhengren guifanhua zhi tanjiu (Exploration of the Way to Interview Witnesses)' (2007) 22 *Jiangsu Jingchaguan Xueyuan Xuebao* (*Journal of Jiangsu Police Officer College*) 53.

Wagenaar, WA et al, *Anchored Narratives: The Psychology of Criminal Evidence* (St Martin's Press, 1993).

Wagenaar, WA, *Identifying Ivan: A Case Study in Legal Psychology* (Harvard University Press, 1988).

Walker, MA and Jefferson, T, 'Ethnic Minorities in the Criminal Justice System' [1992] *Crim LR* 83.

Wan, Y, 'Jiancha jiguan zhengju guize de xiugai yu wanshan: dui renming jianchayuan xingshi susong guize zhengju zhang xiugai jianyi (Revision and Perfection of the Evidence Rule in Relation to the Procuratorate: Revision Suggestions on the Evidence Chapter of the Criminal Procedure Law in Relation to the Procuratorate)' (2014) 3 *Zhongguo Xingshifa Zazhi* (*China Criminal Law Magazine*) 61.

Wan, Y, 'Jianchaquan ruogan jiben lilun wenti yanjiu (Basic Study on the Power of Procuratorate)' (2008) 26 *Zhengfa Luntan* (*Political Science and Law Forum*) 91.

Wan, Y, 'Lun "buqiangpo zizhengqizui" tiaokun de jieshi yu shiyong: xingshi susongfa jieshi de celv yu jishu (The Interpretation and Application of "No One Shall Be Forced to Provide Evidence against Herself": Strategy and Technique of the Construction of CPL)' (2012) 3 *Faxue Luntan* (*Legal Forum*) 31.

Wan, Y and Shi, Q, 'Jianchayuan jixiao kaohe shizheng yanjiu: yi S shi jianchajiguan wei yangben de fenxi (Empirical Study on the Appraisal System for the Procuratorate: Analysis of the Procuratorate in S City)' (2009) 1 *Dongfang Faxue* (*Oriental Law*) 28.

Wang, B, 'Fayuan neibu kongzhi xingshi caipanquan de fangfa he fansi (The Methods and Reflection of the Control of the Judicial Power within the Court System)' (2013) 1 *Zhongguo Xingshifa Zazhi* (*Chinese Criminal Law Magazine*) 65.

Wang, G, *Zhonghua renmin gongheguo jianchazhidu yanjiu* (*A Study of the Procuratorate in the People's Republic of China)* (China Law Press, 1991) 164.

Wang, H, 'Jiancha zhidu yu xingshi susong fa de xianjie (The Coordination between the Supervisory Commission System and the Criminal Procedure Law)' (2017) 6 *Zhengfa Luntan* (*Political Science and Law Forum*) 84.

Wang, H, 'Yinzheng: Jingyanfaze, zhengju guize yu zhengming moshi (Corroboration: Rule of Experience, Evidence Rule and Model of Proof)' (2018) 3 *Dangdai Faxue* (*Contemporary Law*) 4.

Wang, H, 'Zhongfa bijiao shiyu xia woguo gongsu anjian hejie chengxu zhi zai wanshan (Further Perfection of the Reconciliation of Public Prosecution Cases in a Comparative Context Between China and France)' (2013) 6 *Zhongguo Faxue* (*China Law Studies*) 131.

Wang, J, 'Lun qisu fading zhuyi he qisu pianyi zhuyi de tiaohe (The Reconciliation between the Principle of Legality and the Principle of Opportunity)' (2000) 2 *Beijing Daxue Xuebao* (*Peking University Review*) 90.

Wang, L, 'Xingsufa xiugaihou zhengren chuting zuozhenglv rendi de yuanyin (The Reason Why Witnesses Still Do Not Go to Court after the Revision of CPL)' (2013) 4 *Daqing Shehui Kexue* (*Daqing Social Science*) 116.

Wang, M, 'Dui woguo ezhi xingxun bigong falv jizhi de kaocha yu fansi (Reconsideration of the Legal Mechanism of Curbing Tortures in China)' (2012) 4 *Jiangsuo Jingguan Xueyuan* (*Journal of Jiangsu Police Officer College*) 21.

Wang, Q, 'Xinxingsufa xia guanyu chengmoquan zhidu de sikao (Thoughts about the Right to Silence in CPL 2012)' (2017) 6 *Fazhi Molan* (*Legality Version*) 224.

Wang, S, 'Xingshi susongfa xiugai de ruogan wenti (Certain Issues in Relation to Criminal Procedure Law Reform)' (1994) 5 *Faxue Yanjiu* (*Legal Studies*) 76.

Wang, W, 'Continuing with People's Dictatorship Is Not Short of Reasoning (Jianchi renmin minzhu zhuanzheng bingbu shuli)' (2014) 18 *Hongqi* (*Red Flag*) 14.

Wang, Y and Tu, L, 'Zhiban lvshi tigong youxiao falv bangzhi de fali dingwei yu zhidu goujian (Jurisprudence and Institution Construction of Duty Lawyer Scheme That Can Provide Effective Legal Service)' (2009) 2 *Fazhi Shehui* (*Rule of Law Society*) 40.

Wang, Y, 'Empowering the Police: How the Chinese Communist Party Manages its Coercive Leaders' (2014) 219 *The China Quarterly* 625.

Wang, Y, 'Woguo xingshi juanzong yisong fangshi de kunjin jiqi gaige chulu (The Plight of the Way Case File Transference and its Reform)' (2006) *Shidai Faxue* (*Contemporary Law Science*) 56.

Wang, Y, 'Zhongguo gudai yuanyu fangfan zhidu de fali fenxi (Legal Analysis of the Prevention of Miscarriages of Justice)' (2018) Master's dissertation, Zhejiang Financial University.

Wang, Z, 'Dui jinnianlai liudong renkou fanzui wenti de shizheng fenxi (Empirical Study of Crimes Committed by Migrants in Recent Years)' (2006) 2 *Zhongguo Renmin Gongan Daxue Xuebao* (*Journal of Chinese People's Public Security University*) 44.

Wang, Z, 'Zhengcha xunwen shishi zhuangkuang shizheng yanjiu (Empirical Study of the Implementation of Investigative Interrogation)' (2015) 24 *Wuhan Jingcha Xueyuan Xuebao (Journal of Henan Police College)* 115.

Weatherly, R, *The Discourse of Human Rights in China: Historical and Ideological Perspectives* (Palgrave, 1999).

Weber, M, *Economy and Society: An Outline of Interpretive Sociology*, vol 1 (University of California Press, 1978).

Webster, C and Kingston, S, *Anti-poverty Strategies for the UK: Poverty and Crime Review* (Joseph Rowntree Foundation, 2014) 6.

Wei, W and Beken, TV, 'Police Torture in China and its Causes: A Review of Literature' (2010) 43 *Australian & New Zealand Journal of Criminology* 557.

Weigend, T, 'Is the Criminal Process about Truth? A German Perspective' (2003) 26 *Harvard Journal of Law & Public Policy* 157.

Wen, D, 'Woguo gongsu anjian zhengju yisong zhidu zhi fansi yu chonggou (Reconsideration and Reconstruction of the Evidence Transference by Public Prosecution)' (2003) 4 *Zhongguo Xingshifa Zazhi* (*China Criminal Law Magazine*) 81.

Wikstrom, P and Butterworth, D, *Adolescent Crime. Individual Differences and Lifestyle* (Devon Willan, 2006).

Wilson, HT, *Marx's Critical Dialectical Procedure* (Routledge, 1991).

Wong, KC, 'The Police Legitimacy Crisis and Police Law Reform in China: Part I' (2004) 6 *International Journal of Police Science & Management* 199.

Wong, KC, 'The Police Legitimacy Crisis and Police Law Reform in China: Part II' (2005) 7 *International Journal of Police Science & Management* 1.

Wu, C, 'Xianchang zhiren jiqi lifa guizhi (The Crime Scene Identification and Its Statutory Regulation)' (2011) 1 *Lilun Tansuo* (*Theoretical Exploration*) 128.

Wu, H, 'Zhongguo gudai ruhe fangzhi yuanjia cuoan de fasheng (How Did Ancient China Prevent Miscarriages of Justice)' (2016) 7 *Renmin Luntan* (*The People's Forum*) 136.

Wu, M and Sui, O, 'Xingshi susong zhineng de yihua yu zhili: yi gongjianfa xingshi susong guanlian jixiao kaohe wei zhongxin (The Alienation of Solution of the Function of Criminal Justice: Based on the Correlation of the Appraisal System in Criminal Justice Institutions)' in He, R (ed.), *Gongzheng Sifa yu Xingzhengfa Shishi Wenti Yanjiu (Shang Ce) (Judicial Justice and the Implementation of the Administrative Law (Part 1))* (People's Courts Press, 2014) 348.

Wu, X, 'Lun gongsu cailiangquan de yunxing yu chengxuxing kongzhi (On the Operation and Procedural Control of the Prosecutorial Discretion)' (2016) 1 *Zhongguo Xingshifa Zazhi* (*China Criminal Law Magazine*) 70.

Wu, Y and Sun, IY, 'Citizen Trust in Police: The Case of China' (2009) 12 *Police Quarterly* 170.

Xiang, R, 'Shilun xianchang zhireng yu "bude qiangpo zizhengqizui (On Crime Scene Identification and the Privilege against Self-Incrimination)' (2015) 24 *Guangxi Zhengfa Guanli Ganbu Xueyuan Xuebao* (*Journal of Guangxi Administrative Cadre Institute of Politics and Law*) 95.

Xiao, Y, 'Diyuxing zhiye fanzui qunti zhili tanjiu: yi fujiansheng sanmingshi weili (Research on Local Criminal Communities: An Example of Sanming City, Fujian Province)' (2016) 6 *Yunnan Jingcha Xueyuan Xuebao* (*Journal of Yunnan Police College*) 79.

Xiao, Z, 'Zhiban lvshi zhidu zai renzui renfa congkuan shiyu zhong de wanshan (The Improvement of the Duty Lawyer's Role in Leniency for a Guilty Plea)' (2019) 4 *Fazhi yu Shehui* (*Legal System and Society*) 32.

Xie, P and Ren, W, 'Sulian jiancha zhidu dui woguo de yingxiang (The Influence of the Soviet Procuracy on Our Legal System)' (2010) 7 *Hebei Faxue* (*Hebei Legal Studies*) 195.

Xie, P, 'Lun jianchaquan de xingzhi (The Nature of the Power of Procuratorate)' (2000) 2 *Faxue* (*Studies of Law*) 34.

Xie, X, 'Jiancha jiguan yewu mubiao guanli kaoping dui xingshisusong de yingxiang (Influence on Criminal Justice over the Management of the Procuratorate's Tasks)' (2014) 6 *Anhui Daxue Xuebao* (*Anhui University Journal*) 119.

Xiong, M and Miao, M 'Miscarriages of Justice in Chinese Capital Cases' (2018) 41 *Hastings International and Comparative Law Review* 273.

Xiong, Q, 'Shenpan zhongxin shiye xia de lvshi youxiao bianhu (Effective Defence in the Context of Trial Centred Criminal Justice Reform)' (2017) 6 *Dangdai Faxue* (*Contemporary Law*) 14.

Xu Xianghua Research Team, 'Shenpanweiyuanhui zhidu gaige lujin shizheng yanjiu (Empirical Research on the Perspective of Reform of the Adjudicative Committee)' (2018) 2 *Zhongguo Faxue* (*China Law Studies*) 28.

Xu, G, 'Jianchayuan zuowei "falv jiandu jiguan" de lishi jieshi yu sikao (Historical Explanation and Rethink about the Procuratorate as a Supervisory Institution)' (2013) 10 *Dongyue Luncong* (*Dongyue Review*) 144.

Xu, J (ed), *Criminal Procedure Law (I)* (China Law Press, 1999).

Xu, J and Fang, B, 'Woguo xingshi feifa zhengju paichu guize sifa shijian shizheng yanjiu: yi W shi xingshi shengpan shiwu wei shijiao (Empirical Study of Judicial Practice in the Use of the Exclusionary Rule of Illegally Obtained Evidence) (2016) 24 *Zhengju Kexue* (*Evidence Science*) 682.

Xu, J, 'Legitimation Imperative: The Production of Crime Statistics in Guangzhou, China' (2018) 58 *British Journal of Criminology* 155.

Xu, M, 'Zuijia yilu ruzui de chuzui lujin tanxi (On the Exculpation of Minor Drunk Driving Cases)' (2013) 15 *Wuhan Kejie Daxue Xuebao* (*Journal of Wuhan University of Science & Technology*) 202.

Xu, X, 'Faguan Weishenme Bu Xiangxing Zhenren? Zhenren zai Zhuanxing Zhongguo Sifa Guochengzhong de Zuoyong (Why Judges Do Not Trust Witnesses? The Witnesses' Role in the Transition of Chinese Criminal Justice)' (2006) 18 *Beida Falv Pinglun* (*Peking University Law Journal*) 337.

Yan, H, 'Shenpanweiyuanhui Gongneng de Yihua yu Chongzu (The Alienation and Reconstruction of the Function of the Adjudicative Committee)' (2005) 6 *Xinan Zhengfa Daxue Xuebao* (*Journal of Southwest University of Political Science and Law*) 95.

Yan, X, 'Lishishang yuanjia cuoan shi zenyang liangcheng de (How Did the Miscarriages of Justice Come into Being in Chinese Legal History?)' (2014) 6 *Jiancha Fengyun* (*The Legendary Life of Procuratorates*) 10.

Yang, G and Guo, X, 'Feifazhengju paichu guize shishi kaocha baogao: yi J sheng jianchajiguan wei shijiao (Empirical Report on the Implementation of the Illegally Obtained Evidence: From the Perspective of the Procuratorate in J Province)' (2014) 22 *Zhengju Kexue (Evidence Science)* 5.

Yang, G and Yang, G, 'Feifazhengju paichu guize shishi kaocha baogao: yi J sheng jianchajiguan wei shijiao (Empirical Report on the Implementation of the Illegally Obtained Evidence: From the Perspective of the Procuratorate in J Province) (2014) 22 *Zhengju Kexue* (*Evidence Science*) 5.

Yang, J and Yang, Z, 'Dui "falv zhenshi" zhenming biaozhun de zhiyi (Questioning the Standard of Proof Based on Legal Truth)' (2002) 4 *Faxue Yanjiu* (*Legal Studies*) 8.

Yang, J, 'Yifa xuwen zhenren, renzheng zhizuo bilu (Interviewing Witnesses According to the Law and Making Statements Carefully)' (2001) 2 *Liaoning Jinzhuan Xuebao* (*Journal of Liaoning Police Academy*) 37.

Yang, J, 'Yinzheng zhengming de lixing jiangou: Cong xingshi cuoan zhili lunzheng chufa (Construction of Corroboration Rule: From the Argument of Miscarriages of Justice)' (2016) 6 *Fazhi yu Shehui Fazhan* (*Legal System and Social Development*) 173.

Yang, L, 'Renzui renfa congkuan zhidu lijie yu shiyong (The Interpretation and Application of the System of Leniency for Pleading Guilty and Accepting Punishment)' (2019) 1 *Guojia Jianchaguan Xueyuan Xuebao* (*Journal of National Prosecutors College*) 51.

Yang, S, 'Xingshi xunwen bilu de yupian fenxi fangfa yanjiu (Research Methods of the Content Analysis of Criminal Interrogation Record)' (2013) 3 *Fazhi yu Jingji* (*Law and Economy*) 110.

Yang, W, 'Minan zhengcha zhong de "xianqi poan" yu "xianchang zhiren" (The Deadline of Cracking Criminal Cases and the Crime Scene Identification in Murder Investigations) (2018) 26 *Shanxi Jingcha Xueyuan Xuebao* (*Journal of Shanxi Police College*) 12.

Yang, W, 'Shilun renzuirenfa congkuan anjian de zhengmin biaozhun (An Argument on the Standard of Proof in Relation to Cases Applying Leniency for Pleading Guilty and Accepting Punishment)' (2019) 3 *Changbai Xuekan* (*Changbai Journal*) 73.

Yang, Y, 'Xingshisusongfa xiugai aoxian renquan baozhang: lun bude qiangpo zizheng youzui he feifa zhengju paichu tiaokuan (Human Rights Protection of CPL: The Provision of Illegally Obtained Evidence and the Privilege against Self-Discrimination)' (2012) 5 *Faxue Zazhi* (*Law Magazine*) 19.

Yang, Z, *Sixing anjian de chengxu xianzhi* (*Procedural Constraints on Capital Punishment*) (China People's Public Security University Press, 2008) 157.

Yao, X, 'Lun xingshi hejie anjian sifa gongxinli de fazhi baozhang (On the Legal Safeguard of the Judicial Credibility of Criminal Reconciliation)' (2014) 5 *Zhongguo Xingshi fa Zazhi* (*China Criminal Law Magazine*) 67.

Ye, R and Wu, Q, 'Feifa zhengju paichu guize shiyong wenti shizheng yanjiu: yi S sheng C shi wei yangban (Empirical Research on Exclusionary Rule of Illegally Obtained Evidence: Based on the Sample of S province and C city)' (2015) 6 *Tielu Jingcha Xueyuan Xuebao* (*Journal of Railway Police College*) 78.

Ye, Y, 'Xinxingsufa shishi hou de zhengren chuting zuozheng wenti yanjiu (Research on Witnesses Giving Testimonies after the Implementation of CPL 2012)' (2014) 9 *Shehui Kexuejia* (*Social Scientist*) 111.

Yi, Y, *Zhongguo Xingsu yu Zhongguo Shehui* (*The Chinese Criminal Process of Chinese Society*) (Peking University Press, 2010) 79.

Yu, C, 'Lun woguo lvshi zaichangquan zhidu de goujian (On the Establishment of the Defence Lawyer's Right of Access to Police Interrogations)' (2015) 3 *Zhongguo Jianchaguan* (*The China Procurator*) 36.

Yu, H, 'Fanzui yuanyin de xinweidu – jieceng fenhua (A New Dimension of Crime: Social Stratification)' (2017) 8 *Sheke Zongheng* (*Social Science Review*) 86.

Yuan, C, 'The Financial Safeguards of the Procuracy' (2014) 4 *Falv yu Shehui* (*Law and Society*) 229.

Yuan, L, 'Lun xunwenzhong de lvshi zaichangquan zhidu (On Defence Lawyers' Right of Access to Interrogations)' (2007) 2 *Zhongshang Daxue Xuebao Luncong* (*Sun Yatsen University Forum*) 187.

Zander, M, 'Where the Critics Got It Wrong' (1993) 143 *New Law Journal* 1364.

Zedong, M, *Mao Zedong Wenji* (*The Selection of Mao Zedong's Works*), vol 4 (People's Press, 1991).

Zhang, B and Zhang, H, 'jiancha yewu kaoping yu cuoan zeren zhuijiu jizhi de wanshan (The Appraisal System for the Procuratorate and the Perfection of Mechanisms to Prevent Miscarriages of Justice)' (2014) 4 *Zhongguo Xingshifa Zazhi* (*China Criminal Law Magazine*) 94.

Zhang, J, 'Feifa zhengu paichu guize shishi Beijing xia de tingshen fangong wenti yanjiu: dui 2011 dao 2013 nian 655 qi anjian de shizheng kaocha (Research on Retracting Confessions in the Context of the Implementation of Exclusionary Rules)' (2015) 4 *Jinan Xuebao* (*Jinan Journal*) 108.

Zhang, J, 'Lun Lvshi zaichangquan zai wo guo de zhidu goujian (On the Establishment of the Defence Lawyer's Right of Access to Police Interrogations in China)' (2016) 8 *Lilun Guancha* (*Theoretic Observation*) 94.

Zhang, J, 'Shenpai zhongxin gaige beijing xia feifa zhengju paichu guize de luoshi yu wanshan: jiyu 2013nian lai 486 feng xingshi panjueshu de shizheng kaocha (Implementation and Perfection of Exclusionary Rule of Illegally Obtained Evidence Against the Background of Trial Focused Reform: Empirical Research on 486 Judgments since 2013)' (2016) 5 *Xi'an Dianzi Kejie Daxue Xuebao* (*Journal of Xi'an Electronic and Techonology University*) 40.

Zhang, J, 'Xingshi shengpan shang de yuduan paichu yuanze yanjiu (Research on the Prevention of Prior Belief in Criminal Trials)' (2005) 10 *Susongfa Luncong* (*Procedure Law Review*) 81.

Zhang, L, 'Xingshi jianyi chengxu de gaige yu wanshan: yi woguo Taiwan diqu xiangguan lifa wei cankao (The Reform and Perfection of the Simplified Criminal Trial: In Comparison with Taiwan Legislations)' (2012) 10 *Faxue Zazhi* (*Law Magazine*) 160.

Zhang, S, 'Gongsu huanjie chengxu fenliu jizhi de fansi yu wanshan: yi 2009 zhi 2012 nian D jianchayuan buqisu zhidu yunxing zhuangkuang wei fenxi shijiao (Reconsideration and Perfection of Divisionary Mechanism in the Public Prosecution: Analysis of D Procuratorate's Non-prosecution Operation between 2009 and 2012)' (2013) 8 *Zhongguo Xingshifa Zazhi* (*China Criminal Law Magazine*) 93.

Zhang, X and Xu, L, 'Guanyu wanshan guojia sifa kaoshi de yanjiu yu sikao (Research on the National Justice Examination)' (2011) *Zhongguo Sifa* (*China Justice*) 77.

Zhang, X, 'Qiantan jiancha jiguan renshi guanli zhidu gaige (On Reform of the Personnel Management of the Procuratorate)' (2010) 6 *Fazhi Shikong* (*Legal Space and Time*) 162.

Zhang, Y, 'Xunwen zhengren zhong de budang fangfa jiqi fangzhi (Inappropriate Ways to Interview Witnesses and Its Prevention)' (2006) 4 *Shanxi Jingguan Gaodeng Zhuanke Xuexiao Xuebao* (*Journal of Shanxi Police Academy*) 75.

Zhang, Z, 'Jianchaquan yu falv jiandu (The Power of Procuratorate and its Supervisory Nature)' (2004) 3 *Shanxi Jiancha* (*The Procuratorate of Shanxi*) 76.

Zhang, Z, 'Jianshi yu wanshan: Woguo weichengnianren futiaojian buqisu zhidu ruogan wenti tantao (Review and Perfection: Exploration of the Conditional Non-prosecution System of Juvenile Cases)' (2013) 7 *Zhongguo Xingshifa Zazhi* (*China Criminal Law Magazine*) 84.

Zhang, Z, 'Zhongguo Tese Jiancha Zhidu de Lilun Tansuo – Jianchaquan Jichu Lilun 30nian Yanjiu Pingshu (The Theoretical Exploration of the Procuratorate System with Chinese Feature: A Literature Review over the 30 Years' Procuratorate Theory)' (2009) 16 *Zhongguo Faxue* (*China Law Studies*) 150.

Zhang, Z, *Jianchaquan yanjiu* (*A Study of the Power of the Procuratorate*) (China Procuratorate Publishing 2007).

Zhang, Z, *Xingshi susongfa jiaocheng* (*Criminal Procedure Law Textbook*) (Masses Publishing, 1987) 192.

Zhao, B and Yuan, B, 'Zuijia ruxing zhu wenti xin tantao (Exploration on Issues Concerned with Criminalisation of Drunk Driving)' (2012) 8 *Faxue Zazhi* (*Law Magazine*) 15.

Zhao, H, 'Xingshi sucai shengxu shidian shizheng yanjiu (Empirical Research on Pilots of the Expedite Procedure)' (2016) 2 *Zhongguo Xingshifa Zazhi* (*China Criminal Law Magazine*) 93.

Zhao, L, 'Xinxingsufa shishi hou zhengren chuting zuozheng zhidu zai tantao (Reconsideration of Witnesses Giving Testimonies at Trial after the Implementation of CPL 2012)' (2014) 5 *Fazhi yu Shehui* (*Legal System and Society*) 47.

Zhao, X and Liu, T, 'Lun zhonghua renmin gongheguo jiancha jiandu zhineng de xingcheng yu fazhan (The Shaping and Development of the Procuratorate of the People's Republic of China)' (2006) 3 *Faxuejia* (*Jurist*) 39.

Zheng, Y, 'Jini xishu yu liudong renkou fanzui (Gini Coefficient and Crimes Committed by Floating Populations)' (2004) 17 *Hubei Jingguan Xueyuan Xuebao* (*Journal of Hubei Police College*) 47.

Zheng, Y, 'Xin xingsufa beijingxia zhengcha xunwei shizheng yanjiu: yi gansusheng tianshuishi maizhequ wei zhongdian (Empirical Study of Interrogation against the Background of the New Criminal Procedure Law: Focused on Maizhe District, Tianshui City, Gansu Province)' (2016) 16 *Hebei Gongan Zhiye Daxue Xuebao* (*Journal of Hebei Vocational College of Public Security Police*) 27.

Zhou, F, 'Xingxunbigong de fansi yu duice (Reconsideration on Interrogational Torture and Countermeasures') (2006) 2 *Ganxu Zhengfa Xueyuan Xuebao* (*Gansu Political and Law School Review*) 116.

Zhou, G, 'Xingshi anjian zhenren chuting zuozheng zhidu yanjiu (The Study of Testifying Witnesses' Testimony in Criminal Cases)' (2002) 2 *Zhongguo Xingshifa Zazhi* (*China Criminal Law Magazine*) 14.

Zhou, H, 'Zhongguo xingsh yinzheng lilun pipan (Criticism over the Corroboration Rule)' (2015) 6 *Faxue Yanjiu* (*Legal Studies*) 136.

Zhou, M, 'Renzui renfa congkuan zhidu yu zishou tanbai shiyong lujin tansuo (The Applicable Pathways of the System of Leniency for Pleading Guilty and Voluntarily Surrender Oneself and Confession)' (2019) 2 *Jiangxi Guangbodianshi Daxue Xuebao* (*Jiangxi Broadcast University Journal*) 65.

Zhou, Q, 'Congkuan zhidu shidian gongzuo qingkuang de zhongqi baogao (The Mid-term Report of the Work in Relation to the Pilot Project of Mitigating Sentencing Regime)' *Renmin Fayuanbao* (*The People's Court Post*) (Beijing, 24 December 2017) 1.

Zhou, X, 'Renzui renfa congkuan zhidu lifahua de zhongdian wenti yanjiu (Research on the Central Points of the Legislation of the System of Leniency for Pleading Guilty and Accepting Punishment)' (2018) 6 *Zhongguo Faxue* (*China Law Studies*) 172.

Zhu, K and Siegel, DM, 'Electronic Recording of Custodial Interrogations with Chinese Characteristics: Tool for Transparency or Torture' (2015) 45 *Hong Kong Law Journal* 795.
Zhu, K, 'Bijiao yu shizheng: Lvshi zaichangquan toushi (Comparison and Empiricism: Perspectives on the Defence Lawyer's Right of Access to Police Interrogations)' (2008) 3 *Sichuan Daxue Xuebao (Journal of Sichuan University Review)* 125.
Zhu, K, 'Xingxunbigong zhili yu lvshi xunwei zaichangquan de gongneng dingwei (Regulation of Torture and the Lawyers' Role in Interrogations)' (2011) 11 *Xinan Mingqu Daxue Xuebao (Journal of Southwest University for Nationalities)* 94.
Zhu, T, 'Jixiao kaohe yu xingshi sifa huanjing zhi bian: G sheng X xian jianchayuan, sifaju guilai suosi (Analysis of the Appraisal System and the Criminal Justice Environment: Thoughts on the Visit of the Procuratorate and Justice Bureau in X Town, G Province)' (2007) 2 *Xingshifa Pinglun (Criminal Law Review)* 253.
Zhu, T, 'Xingshi susong zhong de jijian kaohe (The Appraisal System in the Criminal Justice System)' (2009) 1 *Falv he Shehui Kexue (Law and Social Science)* 5.
Zhu, Y and Li, N, 'Xingshi falv yanzhu zhiban lvshi gongzuo zhize tanxi (Exploring the Role of Criminal Law Duty Lawyer Scheme)' (2019) 32 *Shanxisheng Zhengfa Guanli Ganbu Xueyuan Xuebao (Journal of Shanxi Politics and Law Institute for Administrators)* 62.
Zhu, Y and Li, N, 'Xingshi falv yuanzhu zhiban lvshi gongzuo zhize tangxi (Exploration of the Obligations of Duty Lawyers in Criminal Legal Aid Work)' (2019) 32 *Shanxisheng Zhengfa Guanli Ganbu Xueyuan Xuebao (Journal of Shanxi Politics and Law Institute for Administrators)* 62.
Zuo Weimin, 'Yinzheng zhengmin moshi fansi yu chongsu: Jiyu zhongguo xingshi cuoan de fansi (Rethink and Recast of the Corroboration Rule: Rethink about the Miscarriages of Justice)' (2016) 1 *Falv Kexue (Legal Science)* 162.
Zuo, W and Ma, J, 'Xingshi zhengren chutinglv: Yizhong jiyu shizhengyanjiu de lilun chanshu (The Rate of Witnesses' Attendance: An Empirical Analysis)' (2005) 6 *Zhongguo Faxue (China Law Studies)* 164.
Zuo, W and Wu, W, 'Dangdai zhongguo xingsu faxue: yanjiu yangshi de shanbian yu qianzhan (The Transition of Research Model and Chinese Legal Reform: Debate Based on Empirical Study)' (2001)1 *Faxue Pinglun (Law Review)* 62.
Zuo, W et al, *Zhongguo Xingshi Susong Yunxing Jizhi Shizheng Yanjiu er: Yi, Shenqian Chenxu wei Zhongxin (The Empirical Study on the Operational Mechanism of the Chinese Criminal Justice II: The Focus of Pre-trial Stage)* (China Law Press, 2009) 22.
Zuo, W, 'Guibi yu tidai: Soucha yunxing zhidu de shizheng kaocha (Avoidance and Substitute: Empirical Study of the Operation of Searches)' (2007) 3 *Zhongguo Faxue (China Law Studies)* 114.
Zuo, W, 'Shenpanweiyuanhui yunxing zhuangkuang de shizheng yanjiu (Empirical Research on the Operation of the Adjudicative Committee)' (2016) 3 *Faxue Yanjiu (Legal Studies)* 159.
Zuo, W, 'Xingshi zhengren chuting zuozheng chengxu: Shizhengyuanjiu yu lilun chanxi (The Legal Process of Witnesses Appearing at Criminal Courts: Empirical Research and Theoretical Analysis)' (2005) 6(17) *Zhongwai Faxue (Peking University Law Journal)* 641.
Zuo, W, 'Yinzheng zhengming moshi fansi yu chongsu: Jiyu zhongguo xingshi cuoan de fansi (Rethink and Recast of the Corroboration Rule: Rethink about the Miscarriages of Justice)' (2016) 1 *Faxue Yanjiu (Legal Studies)* 162.
Zuo, W, 'Zhongguo xingshi juanzong zhidu yanjiu: yi zhengju juanzong wei hexin (Chinese Criminal Case Dossiers: On the Basis of Evidence Dossiers)' (2007) 6 *Faxue Yanjiu (Legal Studies)* 94.

INDEX

www.ingramcontent.com/pod-product-compliance
Ingram Content Group UK Ltd.
Pitfield, Milton Keynes, MK11 3LW, UK
UKHW020220041026
15470UKWH00012B/865

9 781509 91302